Radiotracer Methodology in Biological Science

PRENTICE-HALL BIOLOGICAL SCIENCE SERIES

William D. McElroy and Carl P. Swanson, *Editors*

BIOCHEMICAL SYSTEMATICS,* by Ralph E. Alston and B. L. Turner
CLASSIC PAPERS IN GENETICS, by James A. Peters
EXPERIMENTAL BIOLOGY, by Richard W. Van Norman
FOUNDATIONS OF EXPERIMENTAL EMBRYOLOGY, by Benjamin H. Willier and Jane M. Oppenheimer
MECHANISMS OF BODY FUNCTIONS, by Dexter M. Easton
MILESTONES IN MICROBIOLOGY, by Thomas D. Brock
PAPERS ON HUMAN GENETICS, by Samuel H. Boyer, IV
POISONOUS PLANTS OF THE UNITED STATES AND CANADA, by John M. Kingsbury
PRINCIPLES OF BIOLOGY, by Neal D. Buffaloe
RADIOTRACER METHODOLOGY IN BIOLOGICAL SCIENCE, by C. H. Wang and David L. Willis
SELECTED BOTANICAL PAPERS, by Irving W. Knobloch
SELECTED PAPERS ON VIROLOGY, by Nicholas Hahon
A SYNTHESIS OF EVOLUTIONARY THEORY, Herbert H. Ross

Concepts of Modern Biology Series

BEHAVIORAL ASPECTS OF ECOLOGY,* by Peter H. Klopfer
MOLECULAR BIOLOGY: GENES AND CHEMICAL CONTROL OF LIVING CELLS. by J. M. Barry

Foundations of Modern Biology Series

ADAPTATION, 2nd ed., by Bruce Wallace and A. M. Srb
ANIMAL BEHAVIOR, 2nd ed., by Vincent Dethier and Eliot Stellar
ANIMAL DIVERSITY, 2nd ed., by Earl D. Hanson
ANIMAL PHYSIOLOGY, 2nd ed., by Knut Schmidt-Neilsen
THE CELL, 2nd ed., by Carl P. Swanson
CELL PHYSIOLOGY AND BIOCHEMISTRY, 2nd ed., by William D. McElroy
CHEMICAL BACKGROUND FOR THE BIOLOGICAL SCIENCES, by Emil H. White
GROWTH AND DEVELOPMENT, 2nd ed., by Maurice Sussman
HEREDITY, 2nd ed., by David M. Bonner and Stanley E. Mills
THE LIFE OF THE GREEN PLANT, 2nd ed., by Arthur W. Galston
MAN IN NATURE, 2nd ed., by Marston Bates
THE PLANT KINGDOM, 2nd ed., by Harold C. Bold

*These titles are also in the Prentice-Hall International Series in Biological Science. Prentice-Hall, Inc.; Prentice-Hall International, United Kingdom and Eire; Prentice-Hall of Canada, Ltd., Canada.

Radiotracer Methodology in Biological Science

C. H. Wang
Professor of Chemistry
Oregon State University

David L. Willis
Assistant Professor of Biology
Oregon State University

Prentice-Hall, Inc.
Englewood Cliffs, New Jersey

Library of Congress Catalog Card Number 65-12879

Printed in The United States of America

C-75220

PRENTICE-HALL INTERNATIONAL, INC., *London*
PRENTICE-HALL OF AUSTRALIA, PTY., LTD., *Sydney*
PRENTICE-HALL OF CANADA, LTD., *Toronto*
PRENTICE-HALL OF INDIA (PRIVATE) LTD., *New Delhi*
PRENTICE-HALL OF JAPAN, INC., *Tokyo*

Preface

The radiotracer method is clearly one of the most powerful tools in scientific research. Despite the number of excellent volumes that have appeared during the past two decades describing radioisotope techniques, it appears that a need still exists for a systematic treatment of this subject which covers the necessary fundamental background as well as up-to-date developments, such as liquid scintillation counting.

As the title implies, this volume is written primarily for students and investigators in the biological sciences. However, the approach and contents will be found equally worthwhile by readers in the physical, medical, and engineering sciences. Specifically, the purpose is to provide general background information in nuclear physics and radiochemistry and to stress the considerations of radiotracer experimental design necessary for the successful application of radioactive isotopes as a research tool. The organization of the text stems both from the authors' research interests and, more importantly, from teaching experience involving students from the various fields of biology.

The logical development of the subject matter is described in detail in the Introduction. The presentation is divided into three major portions. The first division describes the nature and characteristics of radionuclides, radioactivity detection methods, and various practical considerations in the use of radioisotopes as tracers in biological systems. The second division comprises a set of laboratory exercises in the measurement and characterization of radioactivity. In the third division will be found detailed and practical descriptions of six experiments illustrating the employment of various radioactive tracers in several different fields of biology. The authors clearly recognize the impossibility of completely and adequately treating all the facets of radiotracer methodology in a work of this size. In fact, to attempt to do so would destroy its usefulness as an introductory volume. Clearly then, the approach taken and the topics emphasized are subject to the personal views and background experiences of the authors.

Many hands and minds have aided in the preparation of this work. Particularly appreciated are the contributions made by the following colleagues at Oregon State University: Dr. Donald J. Reed, who critically reviewed the entire manuscript; Dr. Thomas H. Norris, who provided much helpful counsel; Mr. Richard A. Adams, who materially contributed to Chapter 13; Mr. John R. Prince, who reviewed Chapter 12. In addition, the accumulated experiences from contacts with numberless students, research associates, and co-workers over the past decade have helped shape the eventual form and content of the present volume.

Dr. Andrew A. Benson, Professor of Biology at the University of California, San Diego campus, thoroughly reviewed the entire manuscript. His detailed evaluation was particularly appreciated in the light of his own long experience in the field of radiotracer methodology. In addition, Dr. Seymour Rothchild of the New England Nuclear Corporation kindly reviewed Chapter 11 on the availability of radioisotope labeled compounds, and, as well, generously permitted the inclusion of the substance of Chapter 13, which is based largely on material to be published in *Advances in Tracer Methodology*, Vol. 2, of which he is the editor. The preparation of Chapter 13 on the design of radiotracer laboratories was aided considerably by Mr. Wyman K. Bear of the architectural firm of Bear, McNeil, Schneider, Bloodworth and Hawes, Portland, Oregon. Packard Instrument Company, ANS, Inc., and Nuclear-Chicago Corporation have been most generous in supplying illustrative material and data concerning liquid scintillation counting used in Chapter 6.

To all of the above, named and nameless, the authors are deeply indebted. Any errors and shortcomings in this volume are in spite of their counsel and aid, certainly not because of it.

The authors also wish to express their gratitude to the United States Atomic Energy Commission, the National Science Foundation, and the National Institutes of Health. These agencies have provided generous support to the authors' research and instructional programs over the years at Oregon State University. It is the personal experience gained from these supported programs that forms much of the basis for the practical portions of this volume.

For secretarial assistance the authors are indebted to Mrs. Jolene Wuest, who typed the entire finished manuscript, and to Miss Joan Norris, who both typed and edited major portions of the manuscript. A most special recognition is due Mrs. Earline Willis, who served variously as secretary, typist, proofreader, and a general source of encouragement to the co-author throughout the long course of manuscript preparation. Finally, without the sympathetic consideration of all the members of both of our families, this work would yet be unfinished.

C. H. Wang
David L. Willis

Corvallis, Oregon

Contents

PART ONE *Principles of Radiotracer Methodology* **1**

CHAPTER ONE *Atoms and Nuclides* **3**

A. ATOMIC STRUCTURE AND ENERGY RELATIONS 3
B. THE NUCLEUS 4
C. NUCLIDES AND ISOTOPES 5
D. STABLE NUCLIDES 6
E. RADIONUCLIDES (RADIOISOTOPES) 7
BIBLIOGRAPHY 16

CHAPTER TWO *The Nature of Radioactive Decay* **18**

A. RADIONUCLIDES AND NUCLEAR STABILITY 18
B. TYPES OF RADIOACTIVE DECAY 20
C. RATE OF RADIOACTIVE DECAY 24
D. THE STANDARD UNIT OF RADIOACTIVITY—THE CURIE 34
E. SPECIFIC ACTIVITY 35
BIBLIOGRAPHY 36

CHAPTER THREE *Characteristics of Ionizing Radiation* **37**

A. ALPHA PARTICLES 37
B. BETA PARTICLES 44
C. GAMMA RAYS 52
D. SUMMARY 64
BIBLIOGRAPHY 64

CHAPTER FOUR *Measurement of Radioactivity: General Considerations and the Methods Based on Gas Ionization* **65**

A. TYPES OF RADIOACTIVITY MEASUREMENTS 65
B. RELATIVE COUNTING 66
C. BASIC PRINCIPLES OF RADIATION DETECTION 66
D. GAS IONIZATION 68
BIBLIOGRAPHY 86

CHAPTER FIVE *Measurement of Radioactivity by the Solid (External-Sample) Scintillation Method* **88**

A. BASIC FACETS OF THE SCINTILLATION PHENOMENON 88
B. SOLID EXTERNAL-SAMPLE SCINTILLATION DETECTORS 89
BIBLIOGRAPHY 102

CHAPTER SIX *Measurement of Radioactivity by the Liquid (Internal-Sample) Scintillation Method* **104**

A. MECHANISM OF LIQUID (INTERNAL-SAMPLE) SCINTILLATION DETECTION 105
B. EVALUATION OF THE LIQUID SCINTILLATION METHOD 108
C. COMPONENTS OF A LIQUID SCINTILLATION COUNTER 112
D. SPECIAL TYPES OF LIQUID SCINTILLATION DETECTORS 123

E. OPERATING CHARACTERISTICS OF LIQUID SCINTILLATION COUNTERS 125
F. SUMMARY 135
BIBLIOGRAPHY 137

CHAPTER SEVEN *Detection of Radioactivity by Autoradiography* **144**

A. THE NATURE OF AUTORADIOGRAPHY 144
B. GENERAL PRINCIPLES OF AUTORADIOGRAPHY 145
C. SPECIFIC AUTORADIOGRAPHIC TECHNIQUES 148
BIBLIOGRAPHY 150

CHAPTER EIGHT *Preparation of Counting Samples* **152**

A. FACTORS AFFECTING CHOICE OF COUNTING SAMPLE FORM 152
B. CONVERSION OF ORIGINAL SAMPLE TO SUITABLE COUNTING FORM 154
C. ASSAY OF SAMPLES IN VARIOUS COUNTING FORMS 158
D. PREPARATION AND ASSAY OF LIQUID SCINTILLATION COUNTING SAMPLES 163
BIBLIOGRAPHY 173

CHAPTER NINE *Analysis of Data in Radioactivity Measurements* **186**

A. STATISTICAL CONSIDERATIONS 187
B. CORRECTION FACTORS IN RADIOTRACER ASSAY 193
C. SUMMARY 206
BIBLIOGRAPHY 206

CHAPTER TEN *Design and Execution of Radiotracer Experiments* **210**

A. UNIQUE ADVANTAGES OF RADIOTRACER EXPERIMENTS 210

B. PRELIMINARY CONSIDERATIONS IN DESIGN OF RADIOTRACER EXPERIMENTS 211
C. BASIC FEATURES OF EXPERIMENTAL DESIGN 217
D. EXECUTION OF RADIOTRACER EXPERIMENTS 223
E. DATA ANALYSIS 223
BIBLIOGRAPHY 227

CHAPTER ELEVEN *Availability of Radioisotope-Labeled Compounds* **229**

A. PRIMARY PRODUCTION OF RADIOISOTOPES 229
B. CONVERSION OF PRIMARY RADIOISOTOPES TO LABELED COMPOUNDS 233
BIBLIOGRAPHY 240

CHAPTER TWELVE *Safe Handling of Radioisotopes* **242**

A. THE STANDARD UNITS OF RADIATION EXPOSURE AND DOSE 243
B. HAZARD FACTORS IN HANDLING RADIOISOTOPES 245
C. RADIATION MONITORING INSTRUMENTATION 248
D. DECONTAMINATION 250
E. DISPOSAL OF RADIOACTIVE WASTES 251
F. RADIOISOTOPE LABORATORY SAFETY RULES 252
BIBLIOGRAPHY 254

CHAPTER THIRTEEN *Design Features of Radiotracer Laboratories* **256**

A. THE NEED FOR SPECIALLY DESIGNED LABORATORIES 256
B. THE PLANNING COMMITTEE 257
C. BASIC DESIGN PREREQUISITES 258
D. SPECIFIC DESIGN FEATURES 258
BIBLIOGRAPHY 265

PART TWO *Basic Experiments in the Measurement of Radioactivity* **267**

EXPERIMENT I *Operation and Characteristics of a Geiger-Mueller Counter* 269

EXPERIMENT II *Operation and Characteristics of a Proportional Counter* 276

EXPERIMENT III *Operation and Characteristics of a Solid (External-Sample) Scintillation Counter* 281

EXPERIMENT IV *Operation and Characteristics of a Liquid (Internal-Sample) Scintillation Counter* 289

EXPERIMENT V *The Nature of Radioactive Decay* 299

EXPERIMENT VI *Interaction of Radiation with Matter* 303

EXPERIMENT VII *Statistical Considerations in the Measurement of Radioactivity* 309

PART THREE *Illustrative Radiotracer Experiments* **311**

EXPERIMENT A *Incorporation of $^{14}CO_2$ into Amino Acids in Yeast* 313

EXPERIMENT B *A Time Course Study of $^{14}CO_2$ Production from Rats Metabolizing Glucose-^{14}C Substrate* 323

EXPERIMENT C *The Effect of X Irradiation on Bone Marrow Activity in Rats as Measured by Iron-59 Incorporation into Erythrocytes* 333

EXPERIMENT D *An Investigation of Sodium Ion Regulation in Crayfish Using Sodium-22* 343

EXPERIMENT E *Determination of Coefficients of Zinc-65 Accumulation in Freshwater Plants* 351

EXPERIMENT F *Determination of the Content of Aspartic Acid in Cheese by Means of the Isotope Dilution Method* 360

General Bibliography **367**

Problems **369**

Index **373**

Introduction

The detonation of the first nuclear weapon on the New Mexico desert in July, 1945, marked the beginning of the nuclear age. Although military development of nuclear weapons continues, since the end of World War II peaceful uses of nuclear energy have advanced at a very rapid pace. These uses include not only the more impressive employment of nuclear reactors for power generation, but the development of an entirely new methodology concerned with the utilization of some of the by-products of nuclear fission reactions—radioisotopes.

The use of radioisotopes in industrial processes and as a research tool can be generally classified into five major categories on the basis of the respective properties of the radioisotopes that are utilized. These categories are: (1) Uses based on the effect of ionizing radiation on matter; (2) Uses based on the effect of matter on ionizing radiation, that is, the absorption of ionizing radiation by matter; (3) Age-dating based on the characteristic radioactive decay of certain natural radioisotopes; (4) Direct energy transformation, such as thermoelectric nuclear batteries for spacecraft; and (5) The use of radioisotopes to trace the fate of stable isotopes in physical or biological processes.

The first attribute of radioisotopes involves providing high energy radiation. The energy of each quantum unit of gamma radiation, for example, far exceeds chemical bond energies and can induce chemical reactions or disrupt structures in biological systems. Thus, gamma irradiation in varying doses is commonly employed at present in polymer manufacture, cancer therapy, and food sterilization. In this type of application, the important consideration is the delivery of a massive dose. The chemical identity of the isotope used is of little importance here, as long as the desirable amount and type of radiation energy is provided.

The second category of radioisotope technology takes advantage of the characteristic interaction of ionizing radiation with matter. Such interaction results in the absorption of a defined amount of the energy associated with nuclear radiation determined by the type of matter and its thickness. The phenomenon has been employed as the basic principle in the devising of various types of industrial thickness gauges. Most such thickness gauges involve the use of small amounts of beta emitters and occasionally some soft gamma emitters.

The basic principle underlying the age-dating method is the defined half-life that is a distinctive characteristic of each radioisotope. Use is made of the presence in the environment of a number of naturally occurring radioisotopes such as uranium-238, potassium-40, carbon-14, hydrogen-3, etc. In the case of carbon-dating, the carbon-14 content of living matter is the same as that of atmospheric carbon dioxide. After the death of any living matter, such as a tree, the ^{14}C in its remains would no longer be able to exchange with atmospheric ^{14}C, and hence the ^{14}C content will continuously decline at a defined rate determined by the half-life of ^{14}C. If one analyzes the amount of ^{14}C in a given weight of ancient timber, for example, one can fairly accurately calculate its age by comparing this determined value with the ^{14}C content in the atmosphere. For the development of this unique method Libby received the Nobel Prize. Age-dating methods have very much benefited the fields of geology and archaeology in recent years.

The heat produced by certain radioisotopic sources (plutonium-238, strontium-90, etc.) may be directly converted to electricity by means of an assembly of thermocouples. Such isotopic power generators require no battery storage system and are quite compact. Thus, they are highly suited for applications where weight-to-power ratios must be kept low. Since 1961, several such devices (designated SNAP) have been successfully employed as the electrical power sources in orbiting satellites. Slightly different units have found use as power sources for unattended, automatic weather stations in the Arctic.

The use of radioisotopes as tracers has provided research workers with a powerful new tool. Not only can the fate of a given compound in either physical or biological processes be readily traced by the use of radioisotope labeled compounds, but the ease and sensitivity of radioactivity assay make possible the detection of an extremely minute amount of a given labeled compound in a sample. The manifying power of a typical radiotracer experiment may be as high as 10^8 fold with respect to the amount that can be detected. The radiotracer method is readily applicable to problems in the biological, chemical, and engineering sciences. In the present text the discussion is primarily limited to the application of radiotracers as a research tool in the biological sciences.

The value of this powerful research tool can be illustrated by the accomplishments of Calvin and Benson at the University of California in the study of photosynthetic mechanisms. The fate of CO_2 in the photosynthetic process has long been a challenging problem and had defied many earlier research endeavors. Using $^{14}CO_2$ as a tracer, these workers were able to elucidate the complete fate of atmospheric CO_2 in plants leading to the formation of sucrose and other carbohydrates.

The use of the radioisotope method as a research tool necessitates a good understanding of certain basic concepts involved in radiotracer experiments. One must recognize the properties of radioisotopes and their radiation. The detection of radioactivity also constitutes a basic facet of radiotracer methodology since proper instruments and procedures have to be selected for a given experiment. This is a particularly difficult task inasmuch as the advances in nuclear instrumentation have been following a very rapid pace in recent years.

Good experimental design is also a prerequisite in insuring the reliability of results in any radiotracer experiment. Acquiring such a background in nuclear physics, radiochemistry, and electronics through formal course work, in addition to gaining the required depth and breadth in his own field, often works a hardship on the biological scientist. Moreover, an adequate background in radiotracer methodology is of paramount importance in the evaluation of the research findings of fellow scientists employing the radiotracer method. The intended purpose of this text, therefore, is to present a summary of the essential and pertinent information for the biological scientist. The content has been chosen on the basis of courses in radiotracer methodology in the biological sciences taught at Oregon State University for many years to senior undergraduates, graduate students, and research workers.

This book is in no way intended as a comprehensive reference or source book in the field. Rather it attempts to set forth only the most basic concepts of radioactivity necessary to the practical use of radiotracers. Nevertheless, it ranges from a coverage of the older techniques, such as the use of the Geiger-Mueller counter for beta assay, up to such current techniques as liquid scintillation counting of tritium labeled compounds. Thus, it is primarily intended as a brief, but up-to-date introduction to the field of radiotracer methodology. It has been developed with a formal course sequence in mind, but should prove equally valuable to the established biological investigator who desires to familiarize himself with this field.

In view of the introductory character of this book, it was deemed especially important to include a rather comprehensive bibliography. The interested reader can thus readily find the additional information concerning theory and technique that he may require, without the text itself taking on an encyclopedic nature. References are grouped by text chapters and further subdivided into major topics. Other general texts concerning radiotracer methodology in general are listed in the appendix. Since references to older techniques are thoroughly covered in these texts, it was felt that the bibliography in the present book should stress the more recently developed and currently used radiotracer methods. To this end, a most comprehensive bibliography of liquid scintillation detection and sample preparation techniques, as well as of tritium labeling methods is included.

The presentation is divided into three major divisions: (1) the text proper, covering primarily the principles, (2) a set of basic experiments concerned with procedures in detecting and characterizing radioactivity, and (3) an additional set of selected experiments illustrating typical radiotracer applications in the biological sciences. The first and largest division lays the foundation of essential information regarding the nature of radioactive isotopes and ionizing radiation. It further describes in detail various means of detecting the radiation from radiotracers. A practical coverage is also included of the preparation of biological samples for radioactivity assay, the sources of error in such assay, radiation safety precautions to be observed, proper design of radiotracer laboratories, and the availability of isotopically labeled compounds.

The most salient feature in this first section is the discussion of proper experimental design in radiotracer research. The authors feel this to be one of the most vital, but commonly overlooked aspects of experimental work with radiotracers. The question, "How much radioisotope shall I use?", is ultimately asked by every worker approaching an experiment involving radiotracers. Guide lines are presented to help answer this question and the related one concerning specific activty. As illustrations, these principles of design are applied in a step-by-step manner in the selected tracer experiments found in the last section of the book.

The second division of this volume is made up of a set of basic experiments. These are designed to familiarize the student with the operation and characteristics of the most commonly used radiation counting assemblies. Particular attention is given to comparing the distinctive features of these counters as a basis for selecting the correct counting assembly for a given detection task. Stress is also placed on deriving meaningful data from the counters by recognition and correction of sources of counting errors. Some of the fundamental characteristics of radiation, such as half-life and absorption by matter, are also considered on an experimental basis.

A carefully chosen group of applied radiotracer experiments forms the last division of the book. These experiments were selected to illustrate a diversity of research applications in various fields of biological science.

They involve such varied functions as ion uptake, red blood cell synthesis, and carbon dioxide incorporation. Furthermore, they utilize a wide range of organisms including mammals, invertebrates, plants, and microorganisms. The experiments were chosen to employ a variety of radioisotopes —^{59}Fe, ^{14}C, ^{65}Zn, ^{22}Na—with a broad span of decay types and energies. Such a span requires, of course, the use of a variety of detectors.

In general, these applied experiments are intended to be on the level of course term projects. As employed in courses at Oregon State University, such projects occupy the last month of the students' laboratory time. Inspection will show that they were adapted from original research efforts. With the class-time factor in mind, the original procedures were simplified and the statistical sampling neglected. Ample citations of the original literature are given with each experiment to allow further pursuit of the problem as an advanced research project at the professor's discretion.

A set of problems selected from practical situations facing the user of radiotracers is appended. It is strongly suggested that the reader take the effort to work through these problems as a part of the study of this text.

It is the authors' sincere hope that this book will serve as a key to open the door to the utilization of radiotracer techniques for many a hopeful or experienced biological scientist. Although brilliantly exploited over the past two decades, the methodology has only begun to shed light into some of the dark corners of our present ignorance.

PART ONE

Principles of Radiotracer Methodology

CHAPTER ONE

Atoms and Nuclides

In order to use radioisotopes advantageously as tracers in the study of biological functions, it is highly important to understand their physical nature. Although detailed knowledge of nuclear physics may not be necessary, it is essential to comprehend at least some of its general concepts. Hence, a brief, simple review of some basic information on atomic and nuclear structure should precede our discussion of radioisotopes. Readers well versed in the physical sciences may not need this review, but many whose formal training is largely in the biological sciences may find it valuable. (See the general references at the end of this chapter for a more detailed discussion of the physical aspects of radioisotopes covered in the first three chapters of this book.)

A. ATOMIC STRUCTURE AND ENERGY RELATIONS

It is well known today that an atom is characteristically composed of two major components, a positively charged nucleus and a surrounding cloud of negatively charged electrons. The electron cloud may include from 1 to over 100 electrons which move in orbits of varying distance from the nucleus. Atoms typically have radii of the order of 1 Å (10^{-8} cm); the dense nuclei have radii of the order of 0.0001 Å (10^{-12} cm), and the radius of an electron is of the same order of magnitude. Such dimensions are well below even the best resolving powers obtainable with the electron microscope. These figures show that the nucleus occupies only a minute fraction of the volume of the atom.

The phenomenon of radioactivity is concerned with changes within the nuclei of atoms, whereas ordinary chemical phenomena involve interactions between the orbital electrons of atoms. Energy changes resulting from orbital electron interaction during a chemical reaction are relatively small. In comparison, the energies involved in nuclear transformations are large indeed. As an example, the complete combustion of 1 gram atom of carbon (graphite) to CO_2 would liberate approximately 94,000 calories; by contrast, it can be calculated that the energy released in the complete radioactive transformation of a gram atom of carbon-14 to nitrogen would amount to well over 3 billion calories!

Energy relations involving radioactivity are most commonly discussed on a per gram basis. Since the calorie is too large an energy unit to be suitable for such usage, another unit—the electron volt (ev)—is employed. The electron volt is equivalent to the kinetic energy an electron would acquire while moving through a potential gradient of 1 volt. This is an exceedingly small energy unit; hence several larger units are more commonly used; namely, the kilo electron volt (kev), the million electron volt (Mev), and the billion electron volt (Bev). The electron volt may also be expressed in the more familiar energy unit of calories; 1 electron volt is equivalent to 3.85×10^{-20} calories.

With reference to these energy units, it can be stated that the energy range of chemical reactions involving orbital electrons is of the magnitude of 10 ev per atom, whereas the kinetic energy of individual gas molecules in ordinary room air is only a few hundredths of an electron volt. On the other hand, nuclear changes associated with radioactivity involve energies on the kev to Mev levels per atom.

B. THE NUCLEUS

Atomic nuclei are presently believed to be composed of two major components: protons and neutrons. The collective term for these is *nucleons*. Protons are positively charged particles, with a mass approximately 1850 times greater than that of an orbital electron. A proton must not be thought of as an immobile particle in the nucleus. Protons have a significant angular momentum of their own within the nuclear energy levels.

Since the atom is known to be neutral with respect to electrical charges, the number of protons must equal the number of orbital electrons in any given atom. This number of nuclear protons is equivalent to the *atomic number* of the element or, symbolically, the Z value. Proton numbers run from 1 for hydrogen, up to 103 for lawrencium, the most recently produced element. The term *element* thus specifies a type of atom having a defined nuclear proton number and hence, the same number of electrons. For example, atomic nuclei with 6 protons and various numbers of neutrons are called *carbon atoms*; if the proton number is 53, the element is known as *iodine*.

Neutrons are uncharged nucleons with masses approximating those of protons. The sum of the numbers of protons and neutrons in a given nucleus is the *mass number*, or the A value. Since the number of neutrons in a given nucleus is not related to the atomic number, it does not affect the chemical properties of the atom. Thus, for a given element the number of neutrons may vary within limits. Carbon atoms, for example, all have six protons and six electrons, but their neutron number may vary from four through nine. All six species are essentially similar in chemical behavior, but obviously the nuclei differ drastically in composition and in mass.

The term *isotopes* (from the Greek, "same place") means atoms that contain the same number of protons but varying numbers of neutrons and occupy the same place in the periodic table. In other words, they are atoms of the same atomic number (Z value), but differing mass numbers (A value). The number of known isotopes for each element varies quite widely. It ranges from hydrogen with three isotopes to polonium with twenty-seven. In general, the lighter elements tend to have fewer isotopes than those of higher atomic numbers.

C. NUCLIDES AND ISOTOPES

Obviously, the specification of a certain element should include its exact nuclear composition. This concept is embodied in the term *nuclide*. There are today approximately 1400 known nuclides, that is, specific nuclear species. As a biological analogy, it can be said that the relation between element and nuclide corresponds roughly to the relation between the classification levels of genus and species, respectively.

Symbolically, a specific nuclear species is represented by a subscript number for the atomic number and a superscript number representing the mass number, followed by the alphabetical symbol for the element. An example is ${}^{14}_{6}C$, which is seen to be an isotope of the element carbon with a mass number of 14. Since the symbol for the element denotes the atomic number, it is common to describe the species simply as ${}^{14}C$.

The International Union of Pure and Applied Chemistry (9) in 1960 approved the preceding form of designating specific nuclides. This system of nomenclature is employed in the present volume although it has not yet come into widespread use in the United States. On the contrary, it has long been common practice in this country to use the alphabetical symbol for the element, *followed* by a superscript number representing the A value, that is, C^{14}. That system of nomenclature still is followed in the commercial radiochemical literature, many current textbooks, and a majority of the journals. Nevertheless, there appears to be a trend toward gradual, although grudging acceptance of the newly approved international system. Note, too, that the international nomenclature approves the alternative form in which the name of the element is spelled out, followed by a hyphen and the mass number of the nuclide in question, that is, carbon-14.

It should be emphasized that it is not true that any number of neutrons could be associated with the fixed number of protons in a nucleus to produce an indefinite number of isotopes of an element with the same chemical properties. Only a relatively few combinations are stable enough to persist in nature. These are known as *stable isotopes.* Certain other combinations are possible, but for reasons to be seen later, they are unstable and do not persist indefinitely. Other conceivably possible combinations of neutrons and protons are essentially so unstable as to be nonexistent. Even if produced artificially, they apparently disintegrate in too short an interval to be detectable. Table 1-1 illustrates some stable, unstable, and nonexistent combinations for several elements.

TABLE 1-1

Neutron-proton combinations for hydrogen and carbon

Element	Atomic Number (number of protons)	Neutron Number	Mass Number (number of nucleons)	Nuclide Stability
Hydrogen	1	0	1	Stable
(Deuterium)	1	1	2	Stable
(Tritium)	1	2	3	Unstable
	1	3	4	Nonexistent
Carbon	6	3	9	Nonexistent
	6	4	10	Unstable
	6	5	11	Unstable
	6	6	12	Stable
	6	7	13	Stable
	6	8	14	Unstable
	6	9	15	Unstable
	6	10	16	Unstable
	6	11	17	Nonexistent

D. STABLE NUCLIDES

The number of stable nuclides varies widely from element to element. The element uranium, for example, has no stable nuclear species. Others, such as sodium, have only one stable nuclide. From this point the range extends up to a maximum of ten stable isotopes for tin. The total number of stable nuclides for all the elements lumped together is approximately 260. The natural elements found in the earth's crust or atmosphere are actually composed of mixtures of the stable isotopes of each element. For any given element, the relative abundance of stable isotopes is remarkably constant, regardless of the geographic locality from which samples come. The one exception to this rule is the element lead, whose isotopic composition varies according to its origin, as will be seen later.

The chief reason that the atomic weight of a given element often varies widely from a theoretical whole number is that the element it represents is a mixture of several isotopes (nuclides) of varying mass number. Consequently, the atomic weight of that element is merely a representation of the relative abundance and the mass number (A value) of the individual isotopes. Chlorine, for example, has an atomic weight of 35.457. One can see how this is derived by noting that two stable isotopes of chlorine exist in nature. The one, chlorine-35 makes up 75.53 per cent of the element, while the other, chlorine-37, makes up only 24.47 per cent.

Table 1-2 shows the relative abundance of naturally occurring stable isotopes for several of the biologically important elements. In a number of cases, one stable isotope is much more abundant than the others and is considered the "normal" nuclide for that element. Some examples are ^{1}H, ^{12}C, ^{14}N, ^{16}O, ^{40}Ca, and ^{32}S, each of which accounts for more than 95 per cent of the isotopic abundance of its respective element.

At present, we do not fully understand all the reasons for the stability of certain combinations of neutrons and protons and the instability of others. It is apparent, however, that nuclear stability in general is related to the ratio of neutrons to protons, which is in turn related to the binding within the nuclei. The forces tending to nuclear stability are greatest in those nuclides where the nuclear particles are paired. This principle can be readily deduced from the following observations: (1) The greatest number of stable nuclides, about 164, are those which contain even numbers of both protons and neutrons in the nuclei. (2) Fewer stable nuclides are found when either the number of protons or the number of neutrons is odd—about 105. (3) Only four stable nuclides have an odd number of both protons and neutrons. This situation is restricted to elements with a mass number less than 14, which are rather exceptional cases.

E. RADIONUCLIDES (RADIOISOTOPES)

It will be recalled that, although certain neutron-proton combinations in a given nucleus are possible, these nuclides may not be stable. Because of this basic instability, they will sooner or later undergo nuclear changes. These changes usually result in an adjustment of the neutron-to-proton

TABLE 1-2
Relative natural abundance of the stable isotopes of several elements of biological importance [data from Goldman (1962)]

Element	Nuclide	% Natural Abundance
Hydrogen	^{1}H	99.985
	^{2}H	0.015
Carbon	^{12}C	98.89
	^{13}C	1.11
Nitrogen	^{14}N	99.63
	^{15}N	0.37
Oxygen	^{16}O	99.759
	^{17}O	0.037
	^{18}O	0.204
Sodium	^{23}Na	100
Magnesium	^{24}Mg	78.70
	^{25}Mg	10.13
	^{26}Mg	11.17
Phosphorus	^{31}P	100
Sulfur	^{32}S	95.0
	^{33}S	0.76
	^{34}S	4.22
	^{36}S	0.014
Chlorine	^{35}Cl	75.53
	^{37}Cl	24.47
Potassium	^{39}K	93.10
	^{41}K	6.88
Calcium	^{40}Ca	96.97
	^{42}Ca	0.64
	^{43}Ca	0.145
	^{44}Ca	2.06
	^{46}Ca	0.0033
	^{48}Ca	0.18
Iron	^{54}Fe	5.82
	^{56}Fe	91.66
	^{57}Fe	2.19
	^{58}Fe	0.33

ratio so that the nucleus reaches a position of greater stability. Such changes in the nucleus are explored in greater detail in Chapter 2.

The nuclear changes described involve spontaneous disintegration of one or more of the nucleons. Such disintegration results in the emission of particles and/or electromagnetic radiation from the nucleus. (This electromagnetic radiation is in the characteristic form of discrete energy quanta known as *gamma rays*, or *photons*, which are much like X rays, but considerably shorter in wavelength.) This type of event is known as *radioactivity*, and nuclides possessing it are termed *radioactive nuclides* or isotopes. The term is frequently contracted to *radioisotopes*. The number of these radioisotopes known today exceeds 1100 and, thus, far exceeds the number of known stable nuclides. The vast majority of radioisotopes are artificially produced. Only a small minority occur naturally.

1. Naturally Occurring Radioisotopes

At the time of the earth's creation, probably many radioisotopes were formed which do not occur naturally today. These nuclides were so unstable that they have long since decayed to stable forms. Those originally formed radioisotopes which still appear today are nuclides that either decay very slowly or are members of *decay series*; that is, unstable nuclides which decay to other unstable nuclides, reaching stability only after a dozen or more decay steps. Such nuclides are always of high atomic number.

The three following decay series have member nuclides occurring in the earth's crust: the uranium-radium series, in which ^{238}U decays through some 14 intermediates to stable ^{206}Pb; the actinium series, in which ^{235}U decays through a series of 11 intermediate nuclides to stable ^{207}Pb; and the thorium series in which ^{232}Th decays through a series of 10 intermediates to stable ^{208}Pb. One may note in passing that the stable end nuclide of each of these natural decay chains is an isotope of lead, but a different isotope in each case. This is the explanation of the previous observation that the isotopic composition of naturally occurring lead varies with the locality from which samples are taken. Thus, lead in a deposit derived largely from decay of the actinium series will differ in percentage composition of isotopes from a sample derived largely from decay of the thorium series.

Of the several originally formed natural radioisotopes of lower atomic number, only one is biologically significant—^{40}K. Owing to the general solubility of potassium compounds, this nuclide is quite widely distributed in both the earth's crust and bodies of water. Even more significant, potassium is a common constituent of living tissue; hence a small, but measurable amount of ^{40}K is present in all living tissue. An average 160-lb man, for example, contains about 0.031g of ^{40}K in his body, or 0.012 per cent of all the potassium present. These factors make ^{40}K a significant contributor to the "background" radiation to which all living things are constantly exposed.

Other radioisotopes decay too rapidly to have remained since the time of the creation of matter. A few, however, are being continually produced in the earth's upper atmosphere owing to cosmic ray bombardment of atmospheric atoms. In the case of these nuclides, the rate of decay has reached an equilibrium with the rate of formation, so that their abundance is relatively constant in nature.

Tritium (^3H) is one of the nuclides being produced in this way. When the nuclei of ^{14}N atoms are struck by neutrons, the resultant unstable atom may break up into tritium and ^{12}C. Such bombarding neutrons are derived from cosmic ray interaction with other atoms in the upper atmosphere. Alternatively, an unstable ^{14}N-plus-neutron combination may eject a proton and become a ^{14}C atom. Thus, either ^3H or ^{14}C can be produced as a result of cosmic ray interaction with ^{14}N. The ^3H so formed combines readily with oxygen atoms in the vicinity and slowly mixes with the molecular water on the surface of the earth. Likewise, the ^{14}C apparently combines with available oxygen atoms to form radioactive $^{14}CO_2$. Both these radioactive molecules are readily incorporated into living organisms. Thus, during the life of an organism there is a defined concentration of carbon-14 in its tissue. The decrease in this concentration following death makes possible radiocarbon, or ^{14}C dating, as previously described (12).

2. Artificially Produced Radioisotopes

The first artificial production of radioisotopes was not achieved until 1934, when Curie and Joliot transformed ^{27}Al to ^{30}P. In the intervening three decades, hundreds of artificial radionuclides have been formed. This has amounted essentially to the transmutation of elements—the long-sought goal of the medieval alchemists.

The basic method for inducing nuclear transformations commonly involves the bombardment of stable nuclei with various particles, either charged or uncharged. This bombardment brings about temporary imbalance in the target nuclei, usually resulting in the ejection of nuclear particles or the emission of electromagnetic radiation, and the resultant formation of a new nuclear species. Physicists have investigated many such nuclear reactions. The most important reaction types in the production of radioactive nuclides involve the use of various charged particles or neutrons.

a. By particle accelerators. If charged particles are actually to enter and interact with the target nucleus, they must have sufficient kinetic energy. Particles lacking the requisite energy would be merely repelled or deflected from the nucleus. A variety of particle-accelerating devices have been developed to impart sufficient energy to the various bombarding particles. In general these devices produce stepwise acceleration of the charged particles by means of a pulsing electrostatic or magnetic field. Acclerators of many different designs are in use. In linear accelerators, the particles move in a straight path, whereas they follow a circular path in such machines as the cyclotron, betatron, or synchrotron. Such devices can accelerate particles up to the Mev and Bev level.

Many types of charged particles, such as electrons, protons, deuterons (deuterium nuclei—one proton and one neutron), or alpha particles (helium nuclei—two protons and two neutrons), have been used for bombardment experiments. A typical reaction is that in which ^{24}Mg is exposed to a beam of accelerated deuterons and the target nucleus responds by ejecting an alpha particle and being transformed to ^{22}Na. Such a reaction would be shown symbolically as $^{24}\text{Mg}\ (d,\ \alpha)\ ^{22}\text{Na}$. The original nuclide is shown first, then in parenthesis, first the bombarding particle, followed by the ejected particle, and finally the resultant nuclide. Some other similar typical reactions follow: $^{10}\text{B}(d, n)^{11}\text{C}$; $^{26}\text{Mg}(\alpha, 2p)^{28}\text{Mg}$; $^{31}\text{P}(\alpha, n)^{34}\text{Cl}$.

Of all the charged particles just listed the deuteron is the most useful in bringing about transmutation. The greatest advantage of deuteron bombardment is the rather loose combination of a proton and a neutron in the deuteron; hence it may become partially polarized when approaching a nuclear force field. The proton may be repulsed, while the neutron slips into the nucleus to interact. Thus, the neutron may be captured by the nucleus without the entire deuteron entering the nucleus. This occurs at energy levels far lower (only a few Mev) than required for capture of the entire deuteron. In other words, deuteron bombardment affords a relatively easy process of adding neutrons to the nucleus. This phenomenon is known as the *Oppenheimer-Phillips process* after its two discoverers. (Note that the uncharged neutrons have a much greater efficiency for interacting with nuclei than the charged particles.)

b. *By nuclear reactors.* Nuclear transformations can also be brought about by direct neutron bombardment. A massive source of neutrons for inducing nuclear transformations is found in the atomic pile, or nuclear reactor. Since World War II, nuclear reactors have become the primary producers of radioisotopes commonly used for biological purposes. Thus, reactors at the Oak Ridge National Laboratory in Tennessee supply a major portion of the radioisotopes currently being produced.

In brief, nuclear reactors are devices to control and sustain nuclear *fission* reactions. In the fission process, nuclei of ^{235}U, ^{239}Pu, or certain other heavy nuclides spontaneously divide into two smaller nuclei of roughly equal size following the capture of a neutron. Fission of a heavy nucleus is accompanied by the simultaneous emission of several neutrons (an average of 2.5–3.0) with a spectrum of energies. A very great quantity of thermal energy (averaging 177 Mev per fission) is also released. The following equation indicates a typical fission reaction:

$$^{235}_{92}\text{U} + n \rightarrow {}^{95}_{42}\text{Mo} + {}^{139}_{57}\text{La} + 2n + 208 \text{ Mev thermal energy}$$

The thermal energy release is important in reactors used for nuclear power or propulsion, but it is the neutron emission that is of value in radioisotope production.

In order to achieve a self-sustaining, or *chain reaction* in a mass of fissionable material, it is necessary to conserve the neutrons emitted at each fission in such a manner that at least one of them induces a successive fission in another nucleus. Such neutron-induced fission is highly energy dependent. The neutrons emitted by fissioning nuclei have kinetic energies ranging roughly from 10 kev to over 10 Mev and are termed *fast neutrons.* Unfortunately, fast neutrons are not readily captured by fissionable nuclei; hence they are quite ineffective in inducing fission. In order that these fast neutrons may be absorbed by other fissionable nuclei they must be slowed to thermal energies by a series of elastic collisions. *Thermal neutrons*, as they are called, have velocities of approximately 2200 meters/sec at room temperature or kinetic energies of about 0.025 ev—equivalent to the energy of atmospheric gas molecules. Moderating substances, such as graphite, water (or heavy water), or beryllium, are incorporated into nuclear reactor cores in order to slow the fast neutrons to thermal energies without necessarily capturing them.

There are many kinds of nuclear reactors, but it is beyond the scope of this book to consider in detail these variations. The essential components of all reactors are the fissionable material, a moderating substance, some mechanism for controlling the rate of fission, shielding material around the reactor core to protect operating personnel, and some means of removing the heat produced in the reactor core. In reactors used for radioisotope production, channels into the core must be provided for inserting and removing materials to be irradiated.

A specific example of reactor design may be seen in the illustration of the Oak Ridge National Laboratory's Graphite Reactor (Figure 1-1). In

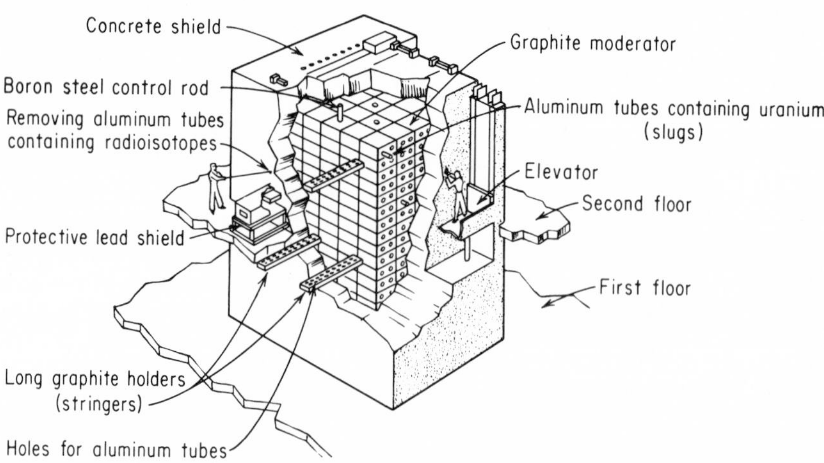

Figure 1-1. Cutaway view of the Oak Ridge National Laboratory graphite reactor.

this design, graphite is used as the moderator; normal uranium serves as the fissionable material; movable boron-surfaced rods are employed to control the chain reaction; and the core is cooled by the circulation of air through the fuel channels. The reactor core is a cube measuring 24 ft on an edge and is surrounded by a 7-ft concrete shield. Within the core, a maximum flux of 8×10^{11} thermal neutrons/cm^2/sec is obtained. This reactor was first put into service in 1943 as part of the wartime nuclear weapons program, but was subsequently operated as the primary production source of radioisotopes in this country until its recent retirement.

If a sample material, such as ^{31}P, for example, is placed within the reactor, it will be exposed to a massive flux of thermal neutrons. Those nuclei which capture a thermal neutron will be converted to radioactive ^{32}P by the following reaction: $^{31}P\ (n, \gamma)\ ^{32}P$. Thus, the typical result of thermal neutron absorption is the emission of gamma radiation from the excited nucleus, and the resultant nuclide is the next higher isotope of the sample material. Other similar thermal neutron reactions of importance are $^{44}Ca\ (n, \gamma)\ ^{45}Ca$; $^{64}Zn\ (n, \gamma)\ ^{65}Zn$; $^{59}Co\ (n, \gamma)\ ^{60}Co$.

In a few exceptional cases involving light nuclei, bombardment with thermal neutrons results in the emission of one or more nucleons rather than gamma photons. Hence, the product nucleus is of a different element than the initial nucleus. Fortuitously, the products of such reactions are some of the most important radionuclides for tracer purposes. The best examples of such thermal neutron reactions are $^{6}Li\ (n, \alpha)\ ^{3}H$; $^{14}N\ (n, p)\ ^{14}C$; $^{35}Cl\ (n, p)\ ^{35}S$.

The neutron flux in a reactor also consists of many neutrons of higher than thermal energies (epithermal). The capture of such neutrons by a sample nucleus greatly increases the energy of the nucleus. Such capture is most commonly followed by the emission of one or more nucleons. Some important examples of fast neutron reactions of this type are $^{32}S\ (n,p)\ ^{32}P$; $^{58}Ni\ (n, p)\ ^{58}Co$; $^{40}Ca\ (n, \alpha)\ ^{37}Ar$; $^{12}C\ (n, 2n)\ ^{11}C$.

The likelihood of neutron capture by a nucleus is generally expressed as the neutron-capture cross section of the nucleus. It is stated in units of $10^{-24}\ cm^2$, called *barns* (from the expression "hitting the broad side of a barn"). Neutron-capture cross sections differ widely from nuclide to nuclide. In addition, cross-section values for any given nuclide vary according to the energy of the impinging neutrons. In general, since neutrons are uncharged particles, the longer they remain in the region of a nucleus, i.e., the less their energy, the greater the chance of interaction.

For any given sample material in a nuclear reactor, many competing nuclear reactions may be occurring simultaneously as a result of interaction with neutrons of various energies. Thus, it is necessary to select a starting material carefully so as to minimize production of undesirable radionuclides and to maximize output of the desired radioisotope product. Further, the starting compound must be sufficiently stable under the thermal and gamma radiation conditions existing in the reactor core. For example, NH_4NO_3 in solution was originally employed in the production of ^{14}C, but because of its excessive rate of decomposition, it was soon discarded and replaced by the more stable Be_3N_2 in solid form.

Besides the neutron-produced isotopes from nuclear reactors, many fission products themselves are useful radioisotopes. Chief among these of importance in biological research is ^{131}I. Commonly used isotopes of strontium, cesium, and barium are also derived from fission sources.

The source of starting material presents another production problem which is very important to the user of radioisotopes. If, for example, ^{32}P is produced by the following reaction: $^{31}P\ (n,\ \gamma)\ ^{32}P$, it will be inseparably mixed with the unreacted stable ^{31}P. The *specific activity*, that is, the amount of radioactivity per unit weight of the element, is unavoidably low and its use as a radiotracer is limited. If on the other hand, the following route was used; $^{32}S\ (n,\ p)\ ^{32}P$, the product ^{32}P could be readily separated by chemical means from the unreacted ^{32}S, so that almost all the phosphorus in the sample would be the radioactive ^{32}P. Such a sample would be known as *carrier-free*, that is, free of any stable isotope of the same element. Unfortunately, for some nuclides, a carrier-free state is impossible owing to the limited choice of starting materials available.

In some cases a high specific activity can be obtained from a $(n,\ \gamma)$ reaction by utilizing the Szilard-Chalmers process. In this process, emission of the gamma photon imparts a recoil momentum to the product nucleus sufficient to break chemical bonds. Thus the radioactive atoms produced are in a different chemical form from the starting material, and are readily separated from it (see Experiment V).

More recently neutron irradiation has been used in *neutron activation analysis*. Here, the purpose is not to produce radioisotopes in bulk for subsequent separation and employment as tracers. Instead, a sample of unknown composition to be analyzed is bombarded with neutrons from a reactor or other source. After irradiation, the radioactive nuclides now present are identified by their disintegration characteristics and assayed quantitatively. This information is then used as a basis for determining the elements originally present in the sample.

Activation analysis is far more sensitive than the more commonly used spectrographic and chemical methods of analysis. Neutron-activation techniques are even capable of detecting as little as 10^{-13} g of some elements under optimal conditions. In addition, activation analyses can be carried out with a great diversity of sample type. As an example, the cause of Napoleon's death has been linked with arsenic poisoning by V. P. Guinn, who used neutron activation of a sample of hair. Unknown biological compounds separated on paper chromatograms have been identified and estimated by neutron activation analysis of the strips in a new technique devised by A. A. Benson. A method for detecting gunpowder residues on the hands of individuals suspected of having fired weapons has been developed by R. R. Ruch using activation analysis. Further discussion of this analytical method is beyond the scope of this volume. For additional information, see the bibliography at the end of the chapter (7, 13–15, 23).

Conventional large-scale radioisotope production reactors often do not conveniently lend themselves to specialized research applications, such as the small-scale production of short-lived radioisotopes or neutron activation analysis. Hence a number of special-type reactors have been developed for research use and these have proved very helpful in providing the high neutron flux needed in activation analysis. Some, such as the widely used TRIGA reactor (produced by General Atomic Division of General Dynamics Corp.), can produce peak thermal neutron fluxes in excess of 10^{16} neutrons/cm^2/sec in brief pulses of approximately 10 milliseconds.

c. *By other neutron sources.* In addition to the fission reaction, neutrons may also be produced by various nuclear bombardment processes. *Alpha-beryllium sources* of neutrons are often found in laboratories today. They consist of an alpha-emitting substance, such as radium, plutonium, or polonium, intimately mixed with the light element beryllium. This source is surrounded by shielding and/or moderating material (commonly water or paraffin). The alpha radiation induces the excited Be nucleus to eject neutrons—an (α, n) reaction. The flux of thermal neutrons so generated is low compared to that from nuclear reactors, usually less than 10^5 neutrons/cm^2/sec. This flux is generally inadequate for sensitive activation analysis. Neutron sources of this type are, however, frequently useful for educational purposes and their cost is quite low. Historically, radium-beryllium sources served as the original means of producing neutrons in the laboratory.

In recent years several types of *neutron generators* have become commercially available. They represent a compromise, in terms of cost and neutron flux available, between nuclear reactors and radioactive neutron sources. In general, they depend, for the production of neutrons, on the interaction of accelerated charged particles with specific target materials of low atomic weight. These generators are of two basic kinds: those creating neutrons by positive-ion bombardment—(p, n) or (d, n) reactions—and those using electron bombardment—(γ, n) reactions. Deuterium (^{2}H) or tritium (^{3}H) are the target materials of choice. Thermal neutron fluxes of 10^8–10^9 neutrons/cm^2/sec are readily obtained when a moderating substance is used. Even greater fluxes of fast neutrons may be realized. Neutron generators have the advantages of being portable or semiportable; they require a minimum of building modification for installation and are relatively simple to operate. Their versatility in allowing a much wider range of sample materials to be irradiated than do nuclear reactors is also to be considered. For these reasons, neutron generators have found wide usage in both activation analysis studies and specialized production of radioisotopes.

BIBLIOGRAPHY

1. Evans, Robley D. 1955. The atomic nucleus. McGraw-Hill Book Company, New York, 972 p.
2. Friedlander, Gerhart, and Joseph W. Kennedy. 1955. Nuclear and radiochemistry. John Wiley & Sons Inc., New York. 468 p.
3. Gamma emitters by half-life and energy. 1960. Nucleonics 18 (11): 196–197.
4. Glasstone, Samuel. 1958. Sourcebook on atomic energy. 2nd ed. Van Nostrand, Princeton. 641 p.
5. Goldman, David T. 1962. Chart of the nuclides. General Electric, Schenectady, N. Y. 1 sheet.
6. Goldman, David T. 1963. Nuclides and isotopes. 6th ed. rev. General Electric, Schenectady, N.Y. 7 p.
7. Guinn, Vincent P. 1961. Instrumental neutron activation for rapid, economical analysis. Nucleonics 19 (8): 81–84.
8. Hallden, Naomi A. 1955. Beta emitters by energy and half-life. Nucleonics 13(6): 78–79.
9. International Union of Pure and Applied Chemistry. 1960. 1957 Report of the Commission on the Nomenclature of Inorganic Chemistry. Definitive Rules for Nomenclature of Inorganic Chemistry. American Version with comments. Am. Chem. Soc. 82:5523–5544.
10. Kinsman, Simon (ed.). 1960. Radiological health handbook. Rev. ed. U. S. Public Health Service, Division of Radiological Health, Washington. 469 p.
11. Lapp, Ralph E., and Howard L. Andrews. 1963. Nuclear radiation physics. 3d ed. Prentice-Hall, Inc., Englewood Cliffs, N. J. 413 p.
12. Libby, Willard F. 1955. Radiocarbon dating. 2nd ed. Univ. Chicago Press, Chicago. 175 p.
13. Neutron activation analysis. 1963. Atomics 16(4):15–19.
14. Neutron sources for activation analysis. 1963. Atomics 16(4):20–25.
15. Meinke, W. Wayne, and Ronald W. Shideler. 1962. Activation analysis: New generators and techniques make it routine. Nucleonics 20(3):60–65.
16. Oldenburg, Otto. 1961. Introduction to atomic and nuclear physics. 3rd ed. McGraw-Hill Book Company, New York. 380 p.
17. Semat, Henry. 1962. Introduction to atomic and nuclear physics. 4th ed. Holt, Rinehart, and Winston Inc., New York. 628 p.
18. Slack, L., and K. Way. 1959. Radiations from radioactive atoms in frequent use. U.S. Atomic Energy Commission, Washington. 75p.

19. Smith, Gilbert W., and Donald R. Farmelo. 1958. Radionuclides arranged by gamma-ray energy. Nucleonics 16(2):80–81.

20. Stehn, John F. Table of radioactive nuclides. 1960. Nucleonics 18(11):186–195.

21. Strominger, D., J. M. Hollander, and G. T. Seaborg. 1958. Table of isotopes. Rev. Mod. Physics 30:585–904.

22. Sullivan, William H. Trilinear chart of nuclides. 1957–1962. U.S. Atomic Energy Commission, Washington. 9 p.

23. Tittle, C. W. Quantitative and qualitative analysis through neutron activation. 1961. Nuclear-Chicago Tech. Bull. No. 10. Des Plaines, Ill. 6 p.

CHAPTER TWO

The Nature of Radioactive Decay

A. RADIONUCLIDES AND NUCLEAR STABILITY

It has been seen that radioactive nuclides undergo spontaneous nuclear changes leading to a more stable condition. A condition of stability has been shown to be related to the neutron-to-proton ratio in the nuclei. For each element there is a specific neutron-to-proton ratio which makes for the greatest stability. In the elements of lowest atomic weight, this ratio approximates one neutron to one proton, but as one moves up the scale to elements of higher atomic weight, the ratio approaches 1.5 neutrons to one proton for maximum stability. In Figure 2-1 nuclides of lower atomic weight have been plotted on a neutron-proton diagram. The striking feature of this plot is the tendency for all stable nuclides to group within a narrow band. The solid line drawn through this band represents the *line of stability*.

The position of an unstable nuclide with regard to this line of stability generally determines the type of radioactive decay it will show in attempting to reach greater stability. Unstable nuclides to the right of the line of stability in Figure 2-1 have a higher ratio of neutrons-to-protons. Their decay pattern, therefore, represents an attempt to decrease the neutron content and/or increase the proton content. On the other hand, radioactive nuclides to the left of the line of stability have a higher ratio of protons-to-neutrons. Their decay pattern then is an attempt to reduce proton content and/or increase neutron content. Thus, the types of decay to be described are directly related to the foregoing problem of nuclear instability.

Certain other radioactive decay characteristics are influenced by the relative distance of specific nuclides from the line of stability. In general, for a given element the half-lives (see p. 27) of its radioactive isotopes are inversely related to their distance from the line of stability. The energy associated with the particles or photons emitted during decay by these isotopes also normally bears a direct relationship to the distance of the specific nuclide from the line of stability. Table 2-1 illustrates these relations in the case of carbon and of sodium.

TABLE 2-1

The relation of half-life and beta particle energy to stability for isotopes of carbon and sodium

Nuclide	Half-life	Maximum Particle Energy
^{10}C	19 sec	2.1 Mev (β^+)
^{11}C	20.5 min	0.96 Mev (β^+)
^{12}C	Stable	...
^{13}C	Stable	...
^{14}C	5568 yr	0.158 Mev (β^-)
^{15}C	2.3 sec	9.8 Mev (β^-)
^{16}C	0.74 sec	Energy undetermined (β^-)
^{20}Na	0.3 sec	> 3.5 Mev (β^+)
^{21}Na	23 sec	2.5 Mev (β^+)
^{22}Na	2.6 yr	0.54 Mev (β^+)
^{23}Na	Stable	...
^{24}Na	15 hr	1.39 Mev (β^-)
^{25}Na	60 sec	4.0 Mev (β^-)

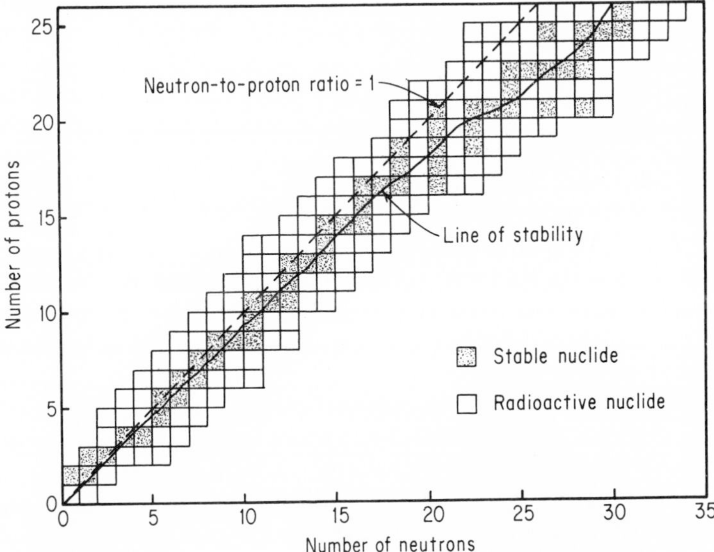

Figure 2-1. Relation of nuclear composition to the line of stability.

B. TYPES OF RADIOACTIVE DECAY

A so-called decay scheme is a convenient means of concisely summarizing information concerning a specific type of radioactive decay. It is a conventionalized plot of energy against atomic number, although no scale is used. The symbol, mass number, and half-life of the nuclide appear on the uppermost horizontal line. Decay leading to emission of a negative particle is indicated by a diagonal arrow to the lower right; decay involving positive particle emission, or orbital electron capture is shown by a similar arrow to the lower left. These arrows terminate on lower horizontal lines representing the lowered energy levels of the daughter nuclei. If a daughter nucleus is in an excited state, the consequent gamma ray emission is denoted by undulating vertical arrows (no change in atomic number) leading to the ground energy state of the nucleus. Notation of the maximum kinetic energy in Mev of emitted particles and the energy in Mev of gamma radiation is made near the respective arrows. Where nuclei may follow more than one decay path, the percentage occurrence of each path is indicated. Typical decay schemes are shown for the various decay types in the following sections.

1. Decay by Negative Beta (Negatron) Emission

Under certain conditions, nuclides with excess neutrons may reach stability by the conversion of a neutron to a proton culminating in the ejection of a negative beta particle (electron). Note that this electron originates in the nucleus and is not to be confused with the orbital electrons. Such a nuclear change results in a loss of one neutron and a gain of one proton, thus shifting the nuclide toward the line of stability. This type of decay can be superficially summarized as follows:

$$n \longrightarrow p^{+} + \beta^{-}$$

(but see p. 47 for a precise presentation of beta decay). Note that negatron emission results in an increase of one unit of atomic number (Z), but no change in mass number (A) for the nucleus involved. Any excess energy in the nucleus following beta emission is given off as one or more gamma rays, or photons.

Decay schemes of varying complexity involving negatron emission are shown in Figures 2-2, 2-3, and 2-4. Close observation of the decay schemes for ^{60}Co and ^{131}I will disclose that, although two or more decay paths may be followed, the total disintegration energy to the stable ground state is essentially a constant value for each respective nuclide. For ^{60}Co this value is 2.81 Mev; for ^{131}I it is approximately 0.972 Mev. This total disintegration energy to reach the ground state of the daughter nuclide is known as the Q value.

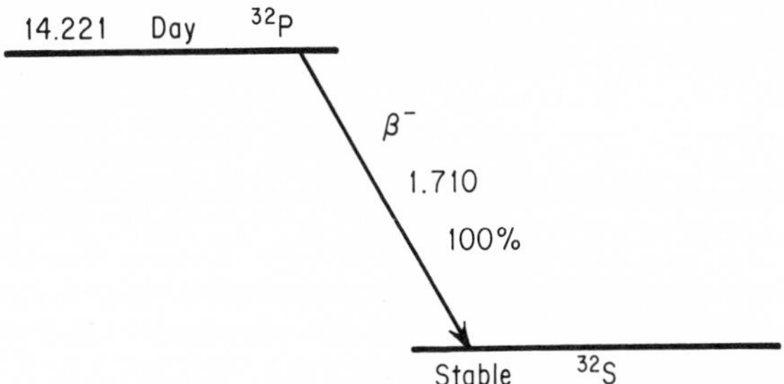

Figure 2-2. Decay scheme of ^{32}P.

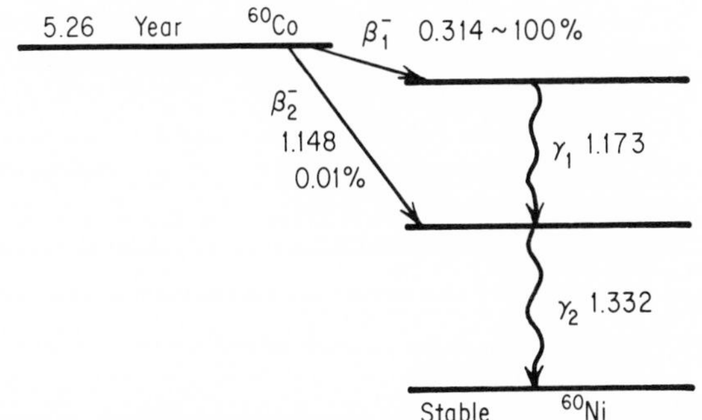

Figure 2-3. Decay scheme of ^{60}Co.

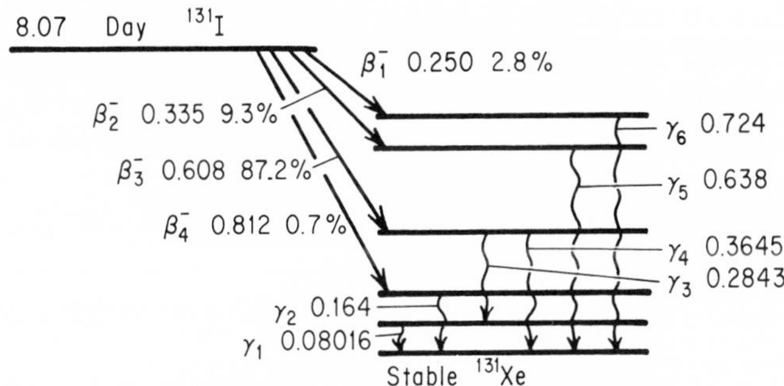

Figure 2-4. Decay scheme of ^{131}I.

2. Decay by Positive Beta (Positron) Emission

Where the number of protons in a nucleus is in excess, positron emission may occur to reach stability. Positrons are positively charged beta particles. In this type of transformation, a nuclear proton is converted to a neutron accompanied by the ejection of a high-speed positron from the nucleus. This type of decay may be generally indicated as follows:

$$p^+ \longrightarrow n + \beta^+$$

(but note the more refined concept of beta decay presented on p. 47). Positron decay results in no change in mass number (A), but the nucleus involved decreases one unit in atomic number (Z). Again, any excess energy in the nucleus following positron ejection is emitted as gamma radiation. The decay scheme of ^{13}N, shown in Figure 2-5, illustrates simple positron decay.

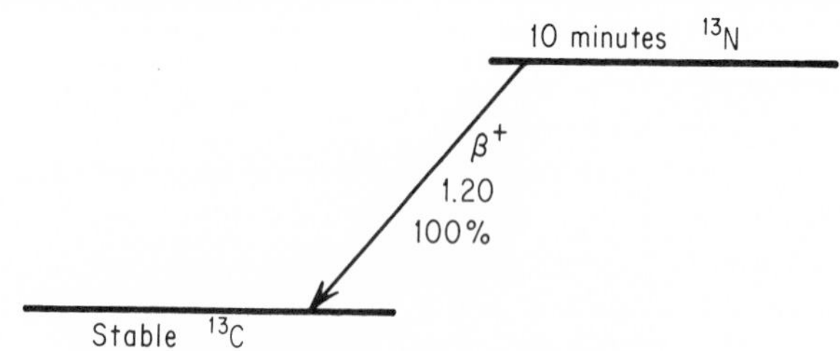

Figure 2-5. Decay scheme of ^{13}N.

3. Decay by Electron Capture

The process of electron capture represents another means of reducing the number of protons in the nucleus. Thus, it has essentially the same result as positron emission. In this type of radioactive decay one of the inner orbital electrons is attracted into the nucleus, where it combines with a nuclear proton to form a neutron. The result is again the loss of one proton and the gain of one neutron per nucleus. No particle emission occurs from the nucleus in this case. X rays, however, are emitted as a consequence of rearrangement of the orbital electron energy levels. This process is also known as *K-capture*, in that the orbital electron captured by the nucleus is normally in the innermost orbit, or K shell. A summary of this decay scheme would be $e^- + p^+ \longrightarrow n$. An isotope of biological interest, ^{55}Fe, follows this mode of decay, as shown in Figure 2-6. For

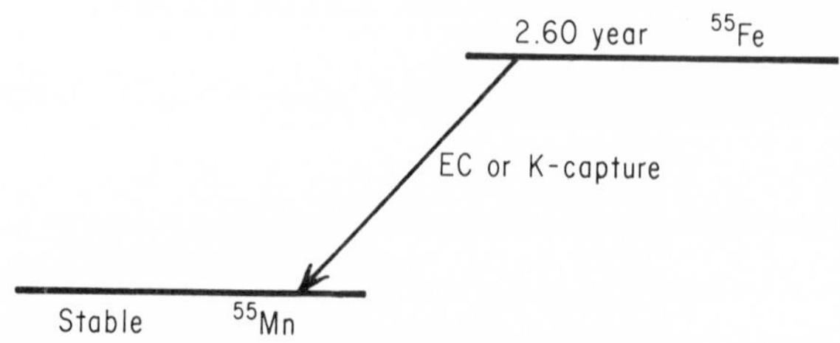

Figure 2-6. Decay scheme of ^{55}Fe.

this radionuclide, the only detectable radiation is the X ray emitted as a result of orbital electron rearrangement.

Frequently an unstable nuclide decays alternately by electron capture or positron emission. ^{22}Na displays this pattern as indicated in Figure 2-7. Note that electron capture, like positron emission, results in no change in mass number (A), but a decrease of one unit of atomic number (Z) for the nucleus involved.

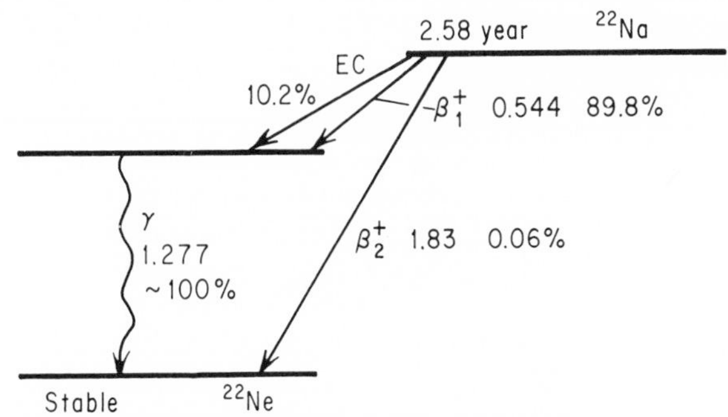

Figure 2-7. Decay scheme of ^{22}Na.

4. Internal Conversion

In modes of decay where gamma rays are normally emitted from the nucleus, an alternative possibility exists. The excited nucleus may interact directly with an inner orbital electron, with the result that all the excitation energy is transferred to the electron. Thereupon, the electron is ejected from the atom. This event is known as *internal conversion* and the emitted electrons are known as *conversion electrons*. Internal conversion is more probable for nuclides of higher atomic number and lower gamma energy. In contrast to the energy spectrum characteristics of negatron and positron emission (see Chapter 3), conversion electrons are homoenergetic.

5. Isomeric Transition

Some nuclides decay by gamma ray emission alone. Of course, this type of decay, like internal conversion, does not change the number of neutrons and protons in the nucleus; hence, the atomic number and atomic mass of the isotope remain the same. Decay of this type is primarily a delayed means of disposing of excess energy in an excited nucleus. Nuclides of this type are known as *metastable*. This mode of decay is termed *isomeric transition.*

6. Decay by Alpha Particle Emission

Among the elements of higher atomic weight only, another means of decay occurs. This is the emission of alpha particles. An alpha particle represents a naked helium nucleus, that is, a tightly bound unit of two neutrons and two protons. As will be seen, emission of an alpha particle results in a considerable lightening of the nucleus, specifically a decrease of two units of atomic number (Z) and four units of atomic mass (A). Alpha emitters are not commonly used in radioactive tracer work, but do have some biological importance. This type of decay is typical of the natural radioactive decay series previously mentioned. Figure 2-8 shows an example of this decay category.

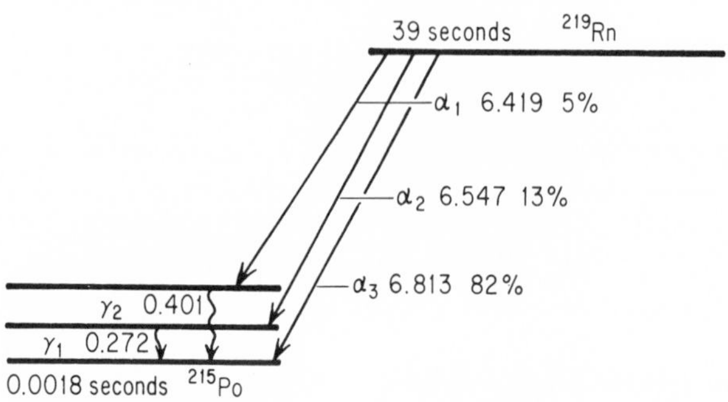

Figure 2-8. Decay scheme of ^{219}Rn.

C. RATE OF RADIOACTIVE DECAY

The number of atoms in a radioactive sample that disintegrate during a given time interval decreases exponentially with time. This rate is independent of pressure, temperature, the mass action law, or any other rate-limiting factors that commonly affect chemical and physical changes. Thus, this decay rate serves as a most useful means of identifying a given nuclide. As seen in Table 2-1, this decay rate is related to the degree of instability of the specific nuclide. Since radioactive decay represents the transformation of an unstable to a stable nuclide, it is an irreversible event for each atom.

The unstable atoms of a given radionuclide do not all decay simultaneously. Instead, the decay of a given atom is an entirely random event. Consequently, studies of radioactive decay events require the use of statistical methods. Thus, one may observe a large number of radioactive atoms and predict with fair assurance that after a given length of time a definite fraction of them will have disintegrated.

1. The Decay Constant

The given fraction of atoms disintegrating in a specific unit of time is the *decay constant*. The actual number of radioactive atoms decaying in a certain time period is not constant, but is dependent on the number of unstable atoms originally present in the sample. This relation may be expressed as follows:

$$\frac{\text{No. atoms decaying}}{\text{in unit time}} \quad \alpha \quad \begin{array}{l}\text{No. atoms originally}\\ \text{present}\end{array} \tag{2-1}$$

Note that the foregoing statement shows only a proportion. By introducing the decay constant, it is possible to convert this expression into an equation, as follows:

$$-\frac{\text{No. atoms decaying}}{\text{in unit time}} = \begin{array}{l}\text{Decay}\\ \text{constant}\end{array} \times \begin{array}{l}\text{No. atoms}\\ \text{originally}\\ \text{present}\end{array} \tag{2-2}$$

A minus sign must be introduced because the decay leads to a diminishing of the number of atoms in the sample. Reworking this decay equation to solve for the decay constant results in

$$\text{Decay constant} = -\frac{\text{No. atoms decaying/in unit time}}{\text{No. atoms originally present}} \tag{2-3}$$

In order to convert the preceding word equations to mathematical statements using symbols, let N represent the number of atoms of a radioisotope present at a given time. Then dN represents the number of atoms which disintegrate in the given time interval dt. The Greek letter λ will represent the decay constant. Using these symbols, the three preceding statements will read as follows:

$$-\frac{dN}{dt}\ \alpha N \tag{2-4}$$

$$-\frac{dN}{dt} = \lambda N \tag{2-5}$$

$$\lambda = \frac{-dN/dt}{N} \quad \text{or} \quad \frac{-dN/N}{dt} \tag{2-6}$$

To calculate the value of the decay constant according to Equation 2-6, it is necessary to determine the number of radioactive atoms in a sample at time zero and the absolute number of disintegrations occurring during time t. Such determinations are exceedingly difficult to make with precision for most nuclides. But the observed activity of a radioactive sample, that is, the actual number of disintegrations per unit time detected by a radiation counter, is proportional to the absolute disintegration rate and the number of radioactive atoms in the sample.

Thus, in actual practice, decay constants can be calculated on the basis of periodic determinations of the decreasing observed activity of a radioactive nuclide (under identical conditions of detection). A plot of such observed activities against time reveals the exponential nature of radioactive decay. As seen in Figure 2-9, such a curve flattens out and approaches zero. If the same plot is made on a semilogarithmic scale (Figure 2-10), the decay curve becomes a straight line, with a slope equal to the value of $-(\lambda/2.303)$. Krohn (5) cites practical methods for estimating exponential decay based on a minimum number of observations. Table 2-2 lists, for several commonly used radionuclides, decay constants that have been thus derived.

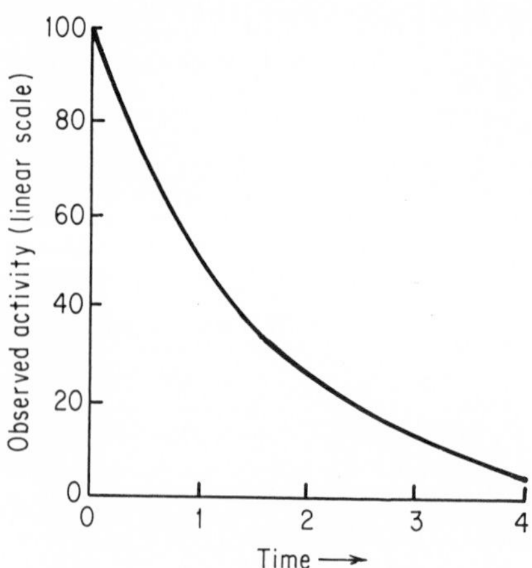

Figure 2-9. Linear decay curve.

In a radiotracer experiment, the reduction of radioactivity due to radioactive decay must be taken into consideration before analysis of the results. This is particularly true with fast decaying radioisotopes. The extent of decay may be determined directly from a graph devised for a given radioisotope, such as that shown in Figure 2-10. In lieu of such a graph, the extent of decay can be readily calculated by applying the law of radioactive decay. To this end, Equation 2-6 is commonly modified to a more convenient form. Let the number of radioactive atoms be N and let N_0 represent the number of radioactive atoms present in the sample at time zero. Integrating the rearranged Equation 2-6, $dN/N = -\lambda dt$, through the limit $N_0 \rightarrow N$ yields

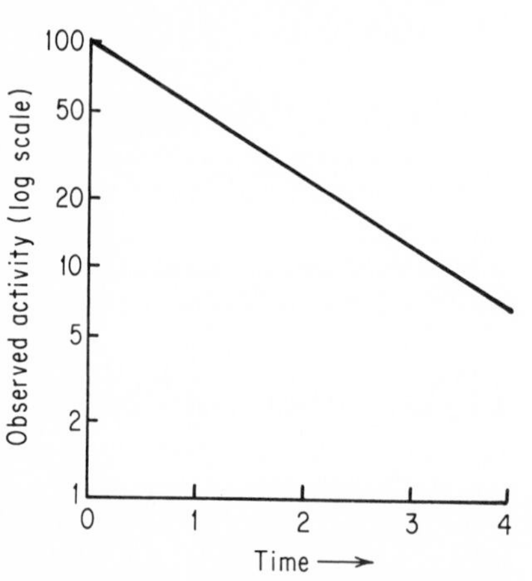

Figure 2-10. Semi-logarithmic decay curve.

(2-7) $\log_n (N/N_0) = -\lambda t$

or, more commonly,

(2-8) $N = N_0 e^{-\lambda t}$

TABLE 2-2

Decay constants for selected radioisotopes

Nuclide	*Decay Constant* (λ)
^{32}P	0.04873/day
^{35}S	0.00794/day
^{45}Ca	0.00422/day
^{55}Fe	0.00493/week
^{59}Fe	0.01530/day
^{60}Co	0.01098/month
^{65}Zn	0.01985/week
^{131}I	0.00358/hr

For practical applications, Equation 2-7 is usually converted to a form using logarithms to the base 10, as follows:

$$(2\text{-}9) \qquad 2.203 \log_{10} \frac{N}{N_0} = -\lambda t, \quad \text{or} \quad \log_{10} N = \log_{10} N_0 - 0.4343\,\lambda t$$

As an example of estimating the extent of decay, let it be assumed that ^{131}I is being employed in a short experiment and that it is essential to know the fraction of activity remaining after a 24-hr period. The N_0 value may be regarded as unity. From Table 2-2, the decay constant of ^{131}I is 0.00358/hr. The calculations would then appear as follows:

$$\log N = \log 1 - (0.4343 \times 0.00358/\text{hr} \times 24\text{ hr})$$

$$\log N = 0 - 0.03732 \quad \text{or} \quad 9.96268 - 10$$

$$N = 0.9177$$

Thus, after 24 hr, the ^{131}I would have decayed to 91.77 per cent of its original activity.

If an investigator expects to make extensive use of a specific radioisotope, it is often convenient to construct a decay correction table for that isotope. Such tables, (easily prepared from the known decay constant for the nuclide) allow rapid, yet accurate determination of the fraction of original activity remaining in a sample after a given interval of time. Tables 2-3 and 2-4 illustrate such compilations for ^{32}P and ^{131}I, respectively.

2. Half-life

The *half-life* ($t_{1/2}$), is another way to express the decay constant. The half-life of a radionuclide is the time required for its activity to decrease by one-half. Thus, after one half-life, 50 per cent of the initial activity remains. After two half-lives, only 25 per cent of the initial activity re-

TABLE 2-3

Decay correction table for phosphorus-32

Hours	0	3	6	9	12	15	18	21
Days								
0	1.0000	.9939	.9879	.9819	.9759	.9700	.9641	.9582
1	.9524	.9466	.9409	.9352	.9295	.9238	.9182	.9127
2	.9071	.9016	.8961	.8907	.8852	.8799	.8746	.8692
3	.8639	.8587	.8534	.8483	.8431	.8380	.8329	.8279
4	.8228	.8178	.8129	.8079	.8030	.7981	.7933	.7885
5	.7837	.7789	.7742	.7695	.7648	.7602	.7556	.7510
6	.7464	.7419	.7374	.7329	.7284	.7240	.7196	.7152
7	.7109	.7066	.7023	.6980	.6938	.6896	.6854	.6812
8	.6771	.6729	.6689	.6648	.6608	.6567	.6528	.6488
9	.6448	.6409	.6370	.6332	.6293	.6255	.6217	.6179
10	.6124	.6104	.6067	.6030	.5994	.5957	.5921	.5885
11	.5849	.5814	.5779	.5743	.5709	.5674	.5640	.5605
12	.5571	.5537	.5504	.5470	.5437	.5404	.5371	.5338
13	.5306	.5274	.5242	.5210	.5178	.5147	.5116	.5085
14	.5054	.5023	.4992	.4962	.4932	.4902	.4872	.4843
15	.4813	.4783	.4755	.4726	.4697	.4668	.4640	.4612
16	.4584	.4556	.4529	.4502	.4474	.4447	.4420	.4393
17	.4366	.4339	.4313	.4287	.4261	.4235	.4209	.4183
18	.4158	.4133	.4108	.4083	.4058	.4033	.4009	.3985
19	.3960	.3936	.3913	.3889	.3865	.3841	.3818	.3795
20	.3772	.3749	.3726	.3703	.3681	.3659	.3637	.3615
21	.3593	.3571	.3549	.3527	.3506	.3485	.3464	.3443
22	.3422	.3401	.3380	.3359	.3339	.3319	.3299	.3279

mains, after three half-lives, only 12.5 per cent is yet present, and so forth. Figure 2-11 shows this relation graphically.

The half-life for a given nuclide can be derived from Equation 2-7 when the value of the decay constant is known. In accordance with acceptance of the term half-life, when $N/N_0 = \frac{1}{2}$, then $t = t_{1/2}$. Substituting these values into Equation 2-9 gives:

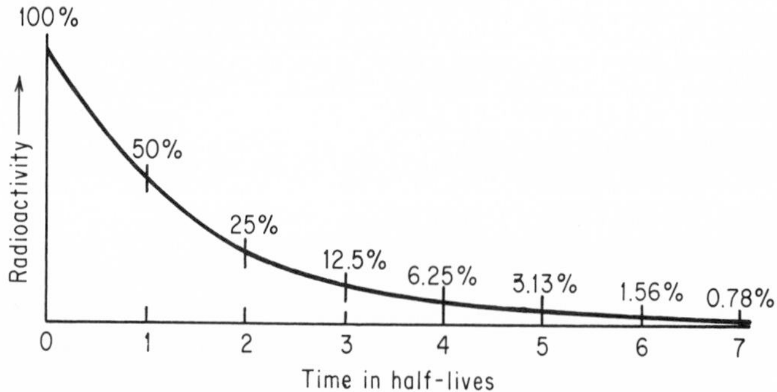

Figure 2-11. Relation between half-life and radioactivity.

TABLE 2-4

Decay correction table for iodine-131

Days \ Hours	0	2	4	6	8	10	12	14	16	18	20	22
0	1.0000	.9929	.9858	.9788	.9718	.9649	.9580	.9512	.9444	.9377	.9310	.9244
1	.9178	.9112	.9047	.8983	.8919	.8856	.8792	.8730	.8668	.8606	.8545	.8484
2	.8423	.8363	.8304	.8244	.8186	.8128	.8070	.8012	.7955	.7898	.7842	.7786
3	.7731	.7676	.7621	.7567	.7513	.7459	.7406	.7353	.7301	.7249	.7197	.7146
4	.7095	.7045	.6995	.6945	.6895	.6846	.6797	.6749	.6701	.6653	.6606	.6559
5	.6512	.6466	.6419	.6374	.6328	.6283	.6238	.6194	.6150	.6106	.6063	.6019
6	.5977	.5934	.5892	.5850	.5808	.5767	.5726	.5685	.5644	.5604	.5564	.5525
7	.5485	.5446	.5407	.5369	.5331	.5293	.5255	.5217	.5180	.5143	.5106	.5070
8	.5034	.4998	.4963	.4927	.4892	.4857	.4823	.4789	.4754	.4721	.4687	.4654
9	.4620	.4587	.4555	.4522	.4490	.4458	.4426	.4395	.4364	.4332	.4302	.4271
10	.4240	.4210	.4180	.4151	.4121	.4092	.4063	.4034	.4005	.3976	.3948	.3920
11	.3892	.3864	.3837	.3809	.3782	.3755	.3728	.3702	.3676	.3649	.3623	.3598
12	.3572	.3546	.3521	.3496	.3471	.3446	.3422	.3398	.3373	.3349	.3325	.3302
13	.3278	.3255	.3232	.3209	.3186	.3163	.3141	.3118	.3096	.3074	.3052	.3030
14	.3009	.2987	.2966	.2945	.2924	.2903	.2882	.2862	.2842	.2821	.2801	.2781
15	.2761	.2742	.2722	.2703	.2683	.2664	.2645	.2627	.2608	.2589	.2571	.2553
16	.2534	.2516	.2498	.2481	.2463	.2445	.2428	.2411	.2394	.2376	.2360	.2343
17	.2326	.2309	.2293	.2277	.2261	.2245	.2228	.2212	.2196	.2181	.2165	.2150
18	.2135	.2120	.2105	.2090	.2075	.2060	.2045	.2030	.2116	.2002	.1987	.1973
19	.1959	.1945	.1931	.1918	.1904	.1890	.1877	.1864	.1851	.1837	.1824	.1811
20	.1798	.1785	.1772	.1760	.1747	.1735	.1723	.1711	.1699	.1686	.1674	.1662
21	.1650	.1638	.1626	.1615	.1603	.1692	.1581	.1570	.1559	.1548	.1537	.1526
22	.1515	.1504	.1493	.1482	.1471	.1461	.1451	.1441	.1430	.1420	.1410	.1400

(2-10) $$2.303 \log_{10} \tfrac{1}{2} = -\lambda t_{1/2} \quad \text{or} \quad 2.303 \log_{10} 2 = \lambda t_{1/2}$$

hence,

(2-11) $$t_{1/2} = 0.693/\lambda$$

Note here that the value thus calculated for $t_{1/2}$ will be in the same units as λ. However, Equation 2-11 is only valid when one expresses λ in units that are much smaller than those in which $t_{1/2}$ is to eventually be expressed. Thus, if $t_{1/2}$ is of the order of hours, λ must be expressed in minutes or seconds. This is because the decay equation was derived by integration of a series of infinitesimal time intervals.

The half-life for different nuclides ranges from under 10^{-6} sec to 10^{10} years. This value has been ascertained for all the commonly used radionuclides. When an unknown radioactive isotope is encountered, a determination of its half-life is normally the first step in its identification. This can be done by preparing a semilog plot of a series of activity observations made over a period of time. A short-lived nuclide may be

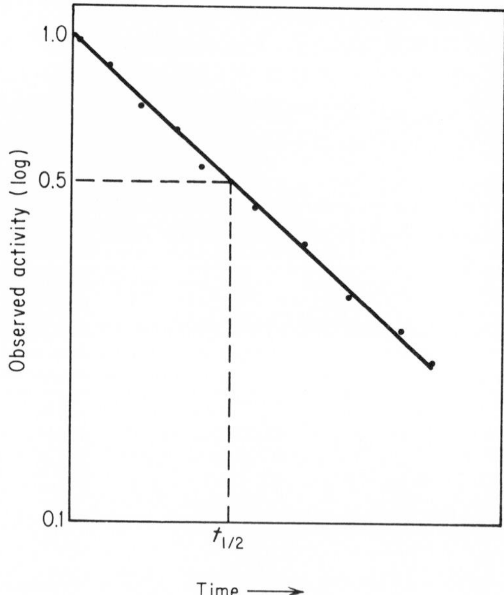

Figure 2-12. Direct graphic determination of half-life.

observed as it decays through a complete half-life, and the time interval observed directly (Figure 2-12).

It is difficult to measure the half-life of a very long-lived radionuclide. Here, variation in disintegration rate may not be noticeable within a reasonable length of time. In this case, the decay constant must be calculated from the absolute decay rate according to Equation 2-6. The absolute number of atoms of the radioisotope present (N) in a given sample can be calculated according to

$$N = \frac{6.02 \times 10^{23}\text{ (Avogadro's no.)}}{\text{At. wt. radioisotope}} \times \text{weight of the radioisotope} \tag{2-12}$$

The weight of the radioisotope in the given sample can be determined once the isotopic composition of the sample is ascertained by such means as mass spectrometry. When the decay constant is known, the half-life can then be readily calculated (Equation 2-11). It is obvious, however, that the degree of accuracy of the calculated half-life is limited by the accuracy associated with the decay constant determination. Estabrook (2) lists factors allowing single-step conversion of $t_{1/2}$ to λ in any desired time unit.

Precise determinations of half-life values are difficult tasks, as evidenced by the variation in published data from time to time. The technical problems involved in such determinations are described by

Anders (1) for the short-lived nuclide ^{32}P, and by Mann (6) in the case of the long-lived radio element ^{14}C. The values indicated in Table 2-4 are average values as given by Slack and Way (8). Geiger (3) gives an extensive table of slow-neutron capture radioisotopes arranged by half-life.

Several important practical considerations arise from the foregoing discussion of radioactive decay. In the first place, it has already been mentioned that corrections for decay must be made when radionuclides with short half-lives are being used in tracer studies extending over a period of time.

TABLE 2-5

Half-life values for some selected radioisotopes

Nuclide	$t_{1/2}$	Nuclide	$t_{1/2}$
^{42}K	12.42 ± 0.03 hr	^{35}S	87.2 ± 0.1 day
^{24}Na	14.97 ± 0.02 hr	^{45}Ca	164 ± 4 days
^{90}Y	64.03 ± 0.05 hr	^{65}Zn	244.4 ± 0.5 day
^{198}Au	2.696 ± 0.002 day	^{22}Na	2.58 ± 0.03 yr
^{131}I	8.066 ± 0.02 day	^{60}Co	5.26 ± 0.01 yr
^{32}P	14.221 ± 0.015 day	^{3}H	12.262 ± 0.004 yr
^{86}Rb	18.66 ± 0.02 day	^{90}Sr	28.0 ± 0.3 yr
^{51}Cr	27.8 ± 0.1 day	^{14}C	5568 ± 30 yr
^{59}Fe	45.3 ± 0.2 day	^{36}Cl	3.03 ± 0.03 × 10^5 yr

The rate of radioactive decay is also a factor in evaluating the biological effect of a given radioisotope. If one experimentally administers a high level of radioactivity to an organism, a certain amount of radiation damage to tissues may be anticipated, depending on the rate of elimination of the nuclide from the organism (biological half-life). This biological effect tends to be minimized where the isotope used decays rapidly. Thus, with all other factors equal, an organism could more readily tolerate a large dose of a short-lived radioisotope than an equivalent dose of a longer-lived nuclide of the same element. Where a choice of radioisotopes of the element in question exists, as in the case of sodium (^{22}Na or ^{24}Na), this may become an important factor in designing the experiment.

The third consideration involving rate of decay deals with the problem of disposal of radionuclide wastes at the end of an experiment. This will be considered in a later chapter in greater detail. It will readily be seen, however, that, particularly in the case of isotopes with long half-lives, disposal can be a problem. Where the half-life is a matter of a few days or weeks, and only small tracer amounts of isotope are involved, it is possible to store the wastes in a restricted area for a time equal to about 10 half-lives. The rate of decay is such that at the end of this period the amount of activity will be reduced by a factor of 1000, and the wastes may often be disposed of through public channels (see pp. 251–252).

3. Composite Decay

Where two or more radioisotopes with different half-lives are present in a sample, a composite decay rate will be observed. The decay curve drawn on a semilogarithmic plot will, in this situation, not be a straight line. The decay curves of each of the isotopes present may be resolved by graphic means, if their half-lives differ sufficiently, and not more than three radioactive components are present. In the graphic example shown in Figure 2-13, line *C* represents the observed activity. Only the activity

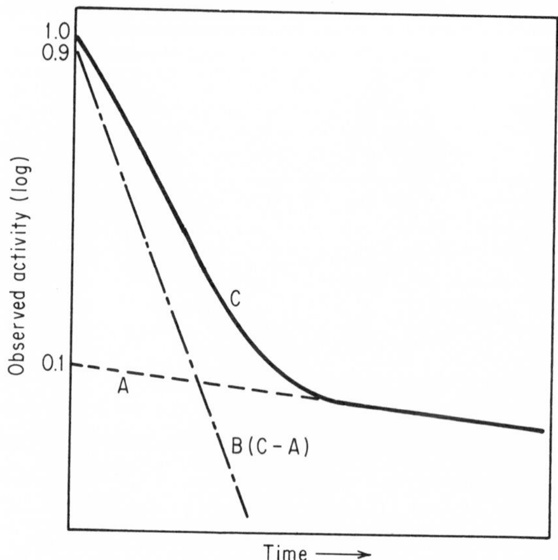

Figure 2-13. Graphic resolution of a composite decay curve.

of the longer-lived component *A* is observed after the shorter-lived component *B* has become exhausted through decay. Extrapolation of this linear portion of the curve back to zero time gives the decay curve for component *A*. The curve for component *B* is drawn by subtracting out point by point the activity values of component *A* from the composite curve.

If the half-lives of the two components in such samples are not sufficiently different to allow graphic resolution, the differential detection method may be applicable. If the radiation characteristics of the isotopes in the mixture are suitably distinct, it may be possible to measure the activity of one component without interference from the radiation emitted by the other component. A case in point would be where one nuclide was a pure beta emitter, while the other emitted both beta and gamma rays. Perkel (7) describes several methods for resolving various types of complex decay curves.

Other types of composite decay occur, but are not normally encountered in biological applications of radiotracers. Perhaps the only such situation met with any frequency concerns "parent" radionuclides that decay into "daughter" nuclides that are also radioactive. In this case it is the combined activity of the parent and daughter nuclides that will be observed. Two of the more common examples of parent-daughter mixtures that the biologist may encounter are ^{90}Sr (parent)—^{90}Y (daughter) and ^{137}Cs (parent)—^{137}Ba (daughter). Kirby (4) describes methods of resolving such parent-daughter mixtures mathematically.

4. Average Life

Although the half-life of a given radionuclide composed of large numbers of atoms is a defined value, the actual moment of disintegration for a particular atom can be anywhere from the very beginning of the isotope's life to infinity. The average life of a population can, however, be calculated. The average life (T_A) is naturally related to the decay constant and is, in fact, the reciprocal of the decay constant:

$$T_A = \frac{1}{\lambda} \tag{2-13}$$

or this can also be expressed as

$$T_A = 1.443\, t_{1/2} \tag{2-14}$$

The concept of average life is useful in the calculation of the total number of particles emitted during a defined decay period. This number is essential in determining total radiation dose delivered by a radioisotope sample, as in medical research and therapy. Table 2-6 lists the average life values for several commonly utilized nuclides.

TABLE 2-6

Average life values for some selected radioisotopes

Nuclide	T_A (days)	Nuclide	T_A (years)
^{131}I	11.64	^{22}Na	3.72
^{59}Fe	65.4	^{3}H	17.694
^{35}S	125.8	^{90}Sr	40.4
^{45}Ca	237	^{14}C	8 035

D. THE STANDARD UNIT OF RADIOACTIVITY—THE CURIE

In the early years of this century, radium was chosen as the standard for comparison of amounts of radioactivity. Although radium-226 is a rare element, it can be highly purified and has a long half-life ($\sim$1600 years). As a standard for radioactivity, the long half-life is a most important factor, in that only very slight changes in radioactivity will be detected in standard preparations over long periods.

The *curie* was originally defined as the number of disintegrations occurring in 1 gram of pure radium per second. This value has been measured experimentally many times. It may also be calculated by use of the decay equation. If one uses the earlier half-life value for radium of 1600 years, and substitutes it into Equation 2-11,

$$\text{(2-15)} \qquad 1600 \text{ years} = \frac{0.693}{\lambda}$$

Solving for λ, one finds

$$\text{(2-16)} \qquad \lambda = \frac{0.693}{1600 \text{ years}} = \frac{0.693}{5.046 \times 10^{10} \text{ sec}} = 1.38 \times 10^{-11}/\text{sec}$$

Since the atomic weight of radium is 226, and in accordance with Avogadro's number there are 6.02×10^{23} atoms in 1 g atom, it can be readily calculated that 1 g of radium contains approximately 2.66×10^{21} atoms. Employing the relationship expressed in Equation 2-5, the decay rate of 1 g of radium would be equal to the product of the decay constant times the number of atoms in 1 g, or

(2-17) dn/dt, (that is, disintegrations occuring in 1 g radium/sec) $= (1.38 \times 10^{-11})(2.66 \times 10^{21}) = 3.70 \times 10^{10}$ disintegrations per second (dps)

Such a calculation of the value of the curie clearly depends on the experimentally determined half-life of radium-226, which is subject to subsequent refinement. (In fact, the half-life was later determined to be 1622 years.) Thus, the definition of the curie in terms of the decay rate of a specific nuclide provided a changing standard. In order to avoid this difficulty, the term *curie* was defined arbitrarily in 1950 by the Joint Commission of the International Union of Pure and Applied Chemistry and the Union of Pure and Applied Physics as 3.700×10^{10} dps.

Since the curie is a relatively large unit, several subdivisions of it are in common use. These are the *millicurie* (mc), which is equal to 1/1000 of a curie, or 3.700×10^{7} dps, and the *microcurie* (μc), which is 1/1,000,000 of a curie, or 3.700×10^{4} dps, or 2.220×10^{6} disintegrations per minute (dpm).

Note that the curie unit refers to the number of disintegrations actually occurring in a sample, rather than to the disintegrations detected by a radiation counter, which are usually only a fraction of the total disintegrations occurring. The difficulties of actually detecting the absolute number of disintegrations occurring in a sample will be pointed out in a later chapter.

It should also be emphasized that the curie is based on the rate of nuclear disintegration, not the rate of emission of beta particles, gamma rays, or other radiation. To calculate such emission rates requires reference to the decay scheme of the nuclide. For example, gold-198 usually emits a beta particle and one gamma ray for each nuclear disintegration, whereas cobalt-60 commonly emits a beta particle and two gamma rays of different energies in cascades per nuclear disintegration. Thus, for the same curie level of these two isotopes, the ^{60}Co would emit twice the number of gamma photons as the ^{198}Au. This problem is further complicated where a nuclide has alternate paths of decay. Consideration of this factor is important in connection with the calculation of disintegration rate from the counting rate as measured by a detecting instrument, and in radiation dose calculations.

E. SPECIFIC ACTIVITY

Unless a radionuclide is in a carrier-free state, it is mixed homogeneously with a certain amount of the stable nuclides of the same element. It is therefore desirable to have a simple expression to show the relative abundance of the radioisotope and the stable isotopes. This can readily be accomplished by the use of the concept of *specific activity*, which refers to the amount of radioactivity per given weight or other similar units of the sample. Specific activity is usually expressed in terms of the disintegration rate (dps or dpm), or counting rate (counts/min, cpm, or counts/sec, cps), or curies (or mc, μc) of the specific radionuclide per unit mass of the element. It can also be expressed as the amount of radioactivity per given volume or any other expression of quantity.

Obviously, when comparing the radioactivity of several samples, it is much more meaningful to employ the concept of specific activity. For example, suppose one has a sample of L-alanine-^{14}C having a specific activity of 1000 dpm/mM of compound, but does not know where the ^{14}C labeling is located. Upon degradation of the compound, one manages to recover the carboxyl carbon atoms as CO_2 by means of a ninhydrin decarboxylation reaction in 50 per cent yield. The total radioactivity observed in the CO_2 so recovered is 500 dpm. This figure does not permit one to draw any conclusions. If, however, one expresses the results in terms of specific activity and finds that the CO_2 has a specific activity of 1000 dpm/mM, the latter figure immediately permits one to draw the conclusion that the L-alanine sample contains its ^{14}C activity exclusively in the carboxyl carbon atom.

It should be further realized that confusion may exist in comparing specific activity data. For example, in the foregoing case, the specific activity of the L-alanine-^{14}C sample can also be expressed as 333 dpm/mM of carbon atoms, inasmuch as L-alanine has three carbon atoms. For the indicated purpose, however, it is obvious that it will be desirable to examine the L-alanine-^{14}C sample in units of dpm/mM/compound.

In the design of radiotracer experiments (see Chapter 10) it is essential to calculate the specific activity of the tracer required. Use of a very low specific activity may result in counting samples with too low an activity level to be detected. In general, it is advisable to utilize a fairly high specific activity initially to allow for the dilution factor inherent in most biological radiotracer experiments. Unfortunately, for a given nuclide it is generally true that the higher the specific activity of the sample material, the greater the expense of producing it. This unpleasant economic relationship is illustrated in Table 2-7, based on current prices from the Oak Ridge National Laboratory (see Chapter 11). Experimental design must usually include consideration of this economic factor.

TABLE 2-7

Price and specific activity of calcium-45

Specific Activity	*Price per mc* (dollars)
>15 mc/g Ca	6.50
>500 mc/g Ca	12.00
≅ 10,000 mc/g Ca	45.00

BIBLIOGRAPHY

1. Anders, Oswald U., and W. Wayne Meinke. 1957. P^{32} half-life determination. Nucleonics 15(12):68, 70.
2. Estabrook, Grace M. 1960. Factors for converting decay constants. Nucleonics 18(11):209.
3. Geiger, R. C., and R. C. Plumb. 1956. Slow-neutron capture radioisotopes arranged by half-life. Nucleonics 14(2):30–31.
4. Kirby, H. W. 1952. Determination of tracers in the presence of their radioactive daughters. Anal. Chem. 24:1678–1679.
5. Krohn, Lawrence H. 1953. Estimating exponential decay. Nucleonics 11(2):67–68.
6. Mann, W. B., W. F. Marlow, and E. E. Hughes. 1961. The half-life of carbon-14. Intern. J. Appl. Radiation Isotopes 11:57–67.
7. Perkel, D. H. Resolving complex decay curves. 1957. Nucleonics 15(6):103–106.
8. Slack, L., and K. Way. 1959. Radiations from radioactive atoms in frequent use. U.S. Atomic Energy Commission, Washington. 75 p.

CHAPTER THREE

Characteristics of Ionizing Radiation

As has been described, nuclear radiation occurs as a result of spontaneous disintegrations of atomic nuclei. These nuclear changes can give rise to several types of radiation, which have already been indicated: (1) alpha particles; (2) negative beta particles, or negatrons; (3) positive beta particles, or positrons; (4) X rays resulting from electron capture; (5) gamma rays, either from isomeric transition or, more commonly, as excess energy following particle emission; (6) internal conversion electrons, resulting from gamma ray interaction with orbital electrons.

The types of radiation most commonly encountered when radioisotopes are used as tracers are alpha particles, beta particles (either positive or negative), and gamma rays. These nuclear emissions differ radically in their physical characteristics, and hence, in the manner in which they interact with matter. Alpha radiation is made up of rather massive particles (helium nuclei) with a doubly positive charge that move at a relatively slow velocity (only a small fraction of the speed of light). By contrast, beta radiation consists of singly charged particles of extremely small mass, which are emitted with velocities approaching the speed of light. Gamma rays are electromagnetic radiation (photons); they are uncharged and travel at the speed of light. The characteristics of these three types of radiation will be discussed in more detail in this chapter.

A. ALPHA PARTICLES

1. Energy

Alpha-emitting isotopes are not commonly used as tracers in biological investigations largely because most alpha-emitting nuclides are elements of high atomic number (Z above 82), which are not normally metabolically significant in living plants and animals. Their presence in the environment, however, constitutes a considerable biological hazard and the biologist studies them primarily from this standpoint.

The alpha particle has previously been described as a helium nucleus composed of two neutrons and two protons—a rather massive particle. Owing to this large mass and the doubly positive charge, the alpha particle exerts a considerable electrostatic attraction on the outer orbital electrons of the atoms near which it passes. In addition, alpha particles tend to follow very straight paths. Normally, they are deflected only by a rare direct collision with a nucleus.

Alpha particles are emitted from radionuclides with considerable kinetic energy. The range of energy from natural alpha-emitting sources lies between about 4 to 8 Mev. Probably the most significant feature of alpha particle energy is that it is discrete; that is, all the alpha particles emitted by a specific nuclide will emerge at one or a few defined energy levels. As examples, ^{221}Ra emits all its alpha particles at an energy of 6.71 Mev, whereas ^{230}U emits alpha particles with energy levels of 5.89 Mev, 5.82 Mev, and 5.66 Mev. Such discrete energy levels of alpha emission serve as a means of identifying specific nuclides.

2. Half-life and Energy Relationships

It was noted quite early that the half-life of a specific nuclide generally seemed inversely related to the alpha particle energy of that nuclide. The current concept of the mechanism of alpha particle emission provides an explanation of this relationship. According to this concept, the dense concentration of positively charged protons in the nucleus of an atom of high atomic weight produces an extremely strong potential barrier immediately around the nucleus. This potential barrier acts to repel charged particles approaching the nucleus. Moreover, the barrier serves to entrap the nucleons within it in an "energy well," preventing their escape in the form of an alpha particle. The term *barrier* is used only in a figurative sense to represent a repulsive force field.

Figure 3-1 is a graphic representation of a cross section through this barrier and the nuclear energy well. The stippled area denotes excess energy in the nucleus which may be imparted to an alpha particle when the nucleus undergoes alpha decay. Such an event will reduce the energy level of the nucleus to a more stable level. Since this excess energy in the nucleus is much lower than the energy of the potential barrier, an alpha particle, as such, cannot escape from the nucleus. According to the principles of quantum mechanics, however, a finite probability exists that the alpha particle may "tunnel" through the barrier in the form of a wave

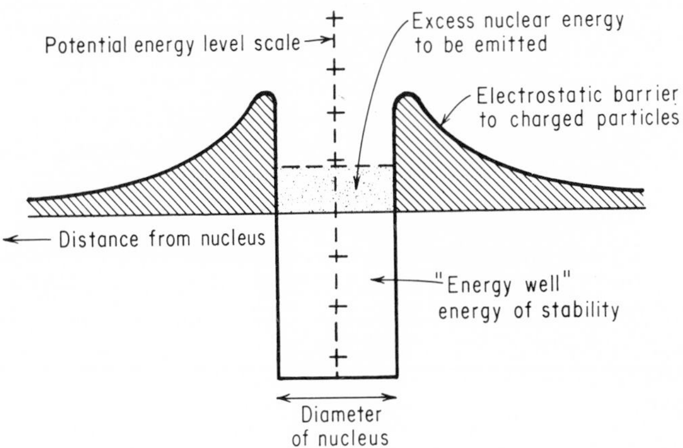

Figure 3-1. Diagram of the nuclear potential barrier and "energy well" concept.

and emerge as a particle which is then actively repelled. The probability of such an occurrence is inversely related to the magnitude of the potential barrier to be penetrated, as depicted in Figure 3-1. Therefore, the higher the excess energy level within the "energy well," the less the potential barrier to be penetrated and, thus, the greater the probability of alpha particle escape, that is, a shorter half-life. On the other hand, where the alpha energy is relatively low, the probability of escape is small, and the half-life is longer. This same general concept, with modifications, is also involved in beta and gamma radiation from the nucleus.

3. Interaction with Matter

The strong electrostatic field surrounding a doubly charged alpha particle exerts a considerable attraction for the orbital electrons of the atoms near its path. In many cases, electrons in the outermost orbits may be stripped completely away from their atoms. In other cases, electrons in inner orbits may be drawn out to orbits farther from their nuclei. Such interactions with orbital electrons dissipate the kinetic energy of the alpha particle.

a. Excitation. The term *excitation* is used to describe interaction whereby orbital electrons take up energy from the passing alpha particle, but are not removed completely from their atoms. Afterward, the excited electrons fall back into their former orbits and emit their excess energy as photons in the visible or near visible range. Detection of such light flashes, as will be seen in Chapter 5, is the basis of scintillation counting. The amount of energy transferred by the excitation process is usually small.

b. *Ionization.* When an alpha particle strips an orbital electron from an interacting atom, the loss of the negatively charged electron leaves the atom as a positively charged ion. The electron and the positive atom together are known as an *ion pair*, and the process is known as *ionization.* The formation of each ion pair in a gas requires on the average about 34 ev of the alpha particle's kinetic energy. Stated another way, a 6.8 Mev alpha particle will produce about 2×10^5 ion pairs in air before its energy is completely dissipated. Consequently, ionization constitutes by far the most important process in the transfer of energy from the alpha particle to the interacting matter. The effect of ionization can be visualized in a cloud chamber, where each ion produced serves as a nucleus for the formation of a fog droplet in a supersaturated atmosphere. An alpha track in a cloud chamber appears as a straight, dense fog track, made up of thousands of droplets per centimeter.

c. *Specific ionization.* To describe the intensity of ionization, the term *specific ionization* is generally used. *Specific ionization* is the number of ion pairs formed per unit length (centimeter) of the alpha particle's path (or that of any other ionizing particle) in air at standard pressure. Figure 3-2 shows the variation in specific ionization for alpha particles

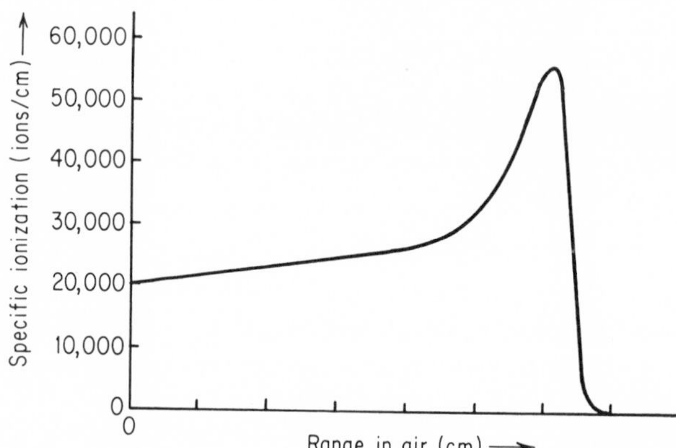

Figure 3-2. Typical specific ionization curve for alpha particles in air.

over the extent of their range in the air. Obviously, the specific ionization of a beam of alpha particles increases sharply toward the end of their range. This occurs because, as a result of many collisions with gas molecules, the alpha particles have lost much kinetic energy and their velocity has decreased. Owing to this reduced velocity, they remain in the vicinity of the molecules along their path for a longer period of time and, thus, have a much greater probability of interacting with these molecules. After the magnitude of specific ionization reaches a peak, it declines sharply to zero. At this point, the alpha particles have expended their kinetic energy, picked up two electrons, and become neutral helium-4 atoms.

4. Range

a. *Determination.* Because of the discrete energy of alpha emission, alpha particles from a given radioactive source will travel through a clearly defined range in air. Alpha range can be experimentally determined by measuring the intensity of alpha radiation at increasing distances from an alpha emitter. Figure 3-3 represents a plot of such data.

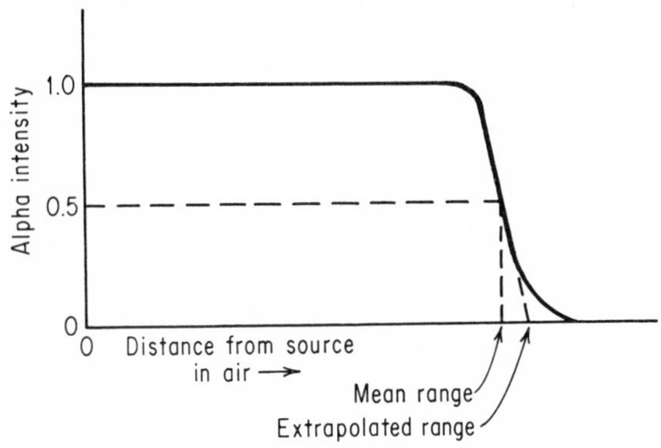

Figure 3-3. Typical range curve for alpha particles in air.

It will be seen that the number of alpha particles detected remains constant for a certain distance from the emitting source and then declines sharply to zero.

A certain amount of straggling of the alpha particles produces the tail on the range curve in Figure 3-3. This makes absolute determination of the true range difficult; consequently, the expression *mean range* has often been used. The mean range is the distance from the source at which the initial alpha radiation intensity is reduced to one-half. The mean ranges of alpha particles from common alpha emitters have been accurately determined, and they are generally of the magnitude of a few centimeters in air.

b. *Range-energy relations.* The range of alpha particles is, of course, directly related to the kinetic energy with which they are emitted. Unfortunately, this is not a simple relationship. The use of Equation 3-1 allows the calculation of an approximate range for alpha particles having energies from 4 to 7 Mev.

(3-1) $$R = kE^{3/2}$$

In this equation R = mean range in air in millimeters, E = alpha energy in Mev, and k = a constant of 3.09. As an example, the mean range in air of 7.0 Mev alpha radiation could be calculated as follows:

$$R = 3.09 \times \sqrt[2]{7.0^3} = 3.09 \times 18.5 = 57.1 \text{ mm} \quad \text{or} \quad 5.7 \text{ cm}$$

The range-energy relationship in air for alpha particles with initial kinetic energies between 0.2 and 10 Mev is shown in Figure 3-4.

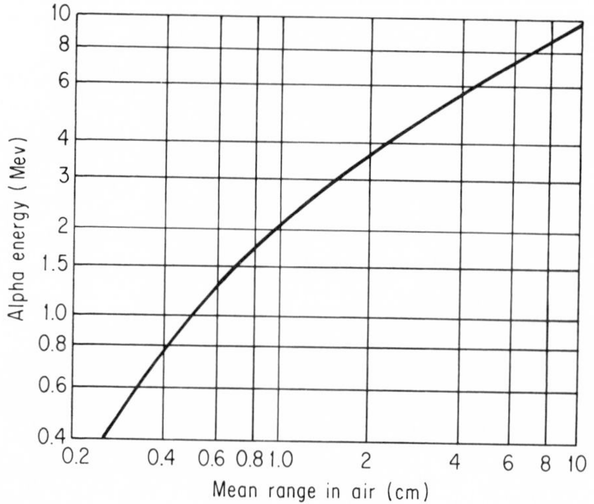

Figure 3-4. Range-energy curve for alpha particles in standard air.

c. *Absorption by other materials.* Alpha range in materials other than gases will necessarily be very much shorter owing to the greater density of liquids and solids. In fact, these ranges are so short they are normally stated in microns. Approximate calculated ranges for alpha particles of seven Mev in several selected absorbers are listed in Table 3-1.

TABLE 3-1

Linear range of 7 Mev alpha particles in some common absorbers

Air	Water (tissue)	Aluminum	Mica	Copper	Lead
$57{,}000\mu$	74μ	34μ	29μ	14μ	2μ

Although, in Table 3-1, range has been expressed as linear distance, it is clear from the table that density is a most significant factor. In addition, since the minute ranges shown there are difficult to measure in a practical manner, another unit for range is commonly used. This unit is termed *equivalent thickness*. It represents the thickness (in centimeters) of an absorber, which is equivalent to 1 cm of air in the absorption of alpha radiation, multiplied by the density of the material (in g/cm^3). The resulting unit is in mass per unit area (g/cm^2), and is more easily determined experimentally. The unit thus obtained is most often multiplied by 1000 to give units of mg/cm^2. The approximate equivalent thicknesses for 7 Mev alpha radiation listed in Table 3-2 should be compared with the previous list of linear ranges for the same materials.

TABLE 3-2

Equivalent thickness in mg/cm^2 for 7 Mev alpha particles of some common absorbers

Air	Mica	Aluminum	Copper	Silver	Gold
1.2	1.4	1.62	2.26	2.86	3.96

5. Practical Considerations

Their very short range in solids makes alpha particles difficult to detect with the usual radiation detection equipment. Because they dissipate their energy in the wall or window of the typical detector, alpha particles do not penetrate to the sensitive volume of the detector. A 7.0 Mev alpha beam, for example, would not penetrate a mica detector tube window 20 microns, or 8 mg/cm^2 thick. As a result, alpha-emitting sources must usually be placed inside the detection chamber.

Alpha radiation poses no great external health hazard, since the outermost horny layers of epidermis are thick enough to absorb almost all external alpha radiation, even from sources deposited directly on the surface of the body. Safe storage of alpha-emitting isotopes is possible because thin glass or metal containers will absorb all the alpha radiation being emitted from sources within them.

When alpha emitters enter the body by ingestion or inhalation the situation is quite different. Alpha particles dissipate their energy in such an exceedingly small volume of tissue that very great local damage can occur. Moreover many natural alpha emitters have long half-lives and some (radium and plutonium) are incorporated into metabolically less active bone tissue, thus increasing the internal hazard. One alpha-emitting nuclide of considerable prominence, ^{239}Pu, is highly toxic from a purely chemical standpoint, in addition to its radiation hazard.

B. BETA PARTICLES

1. General Nature

a. Negatrons and positrons. The term *beta particle* has been used for two different entities, positrons and negatrons. These both represent particles formed by nuclear changes and ejected from the nucleus with velocities approaching the speed of light. They are physically alike in nearly every respect except charge. Positrons carry a positive charge; negatrons are negatively charged, that is, electrons.

Beta particles are only 1/7400 the mass of alpha particles. Because of this very small mass, they are quite easily deflected on passing near other atoms. Their track in a cloud chamber is a very tortuous one indeed, wholly unlike the straight alpha track. In addition, the smaller mass and higher velocity of the beta particle result in a smaller probability of interaction with the orbital electrons of the atoms it passes near. Thus, it has a much greater penetrating power; hence, a much longer range through matter. Where the range in air of alpha particles may be only several centimeters, the range of beta particles from some beta emitters may be as long as several meters.

Since in all respects but origin, the *negatron* is like a normal orbital electron, it will persist after dissipating all its kinetic energy. Usually it ultimately becomes attached to a positive ion as an orbital electron. A *positron*, on the other hand, has only a transient existence. After expending all its kinetic energy, it interacts with an electron and is "annihilated." The mass of both particles is converted to energy in the form of two 0.51 Mev gamma rays which are emitted at angles of 180° to each other ("back-to-back gamma radiation"). Hereafter, following common practice, the term *beta particle* will be used for the negatron.

b. Conversion electrons. A similar, yet distinct type of high-velocity particle is the *internal conversion electron.* Energy from a disintegrating nucleus that would otherwise be emitted as a gamma ray may be quantitatively transferred to an inner orbital electron of the same atom. The orbital electron thus energized is immediately ejected from the atom at high velocity. Since gamma rays are emitted with a discrete energy, internal conversion electrons are ejected with discrete energies from a given nuclide—in contrast to beta particle emission. Thus, the term *beta particle* is restricted to electrons originating in the nucleus. Internal conversion is of only minor importance in the detection of radionuclides commonly used as biological tracers.

2. Energy of Beta Decay

a. Spectral distribution of energy. Perhaps the most striking character of beta radiation is the particle energy. It has been seen that a given nuclide may eject alpha particles at one or a few discrete energy levels. By contrast, in beta decay the particles are emitted over a continuous range of kinetic energy up to a maximum value (E_{max}) characteristic of the nuclide in question. Values for beta E_{max} range from 0.018 Mev for ^{3}H up to 4.81 Mev for ^{38}Cl.

The *magnetic spectrometer* has been used experimentally to determine the beta energy distribution for many nuclides. In this instrument, a collimated beam of beta particles is deflected through 180° by a strong magnetic field. The more energetic particles in the beam swing in a wider arc; the less energetic travel over a shorter arc. As a result, the beam particles of various energies are spread out to form a spectrum, which is detected by exposure of a strip of photographic film (Figure 3-5). Alterna-

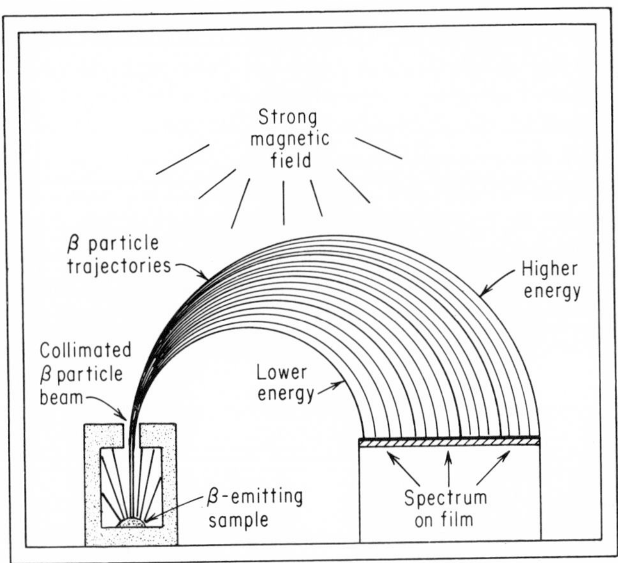

Figure 3-5. Simplified diagram of a magnetic spectrometer.

tively, a beta-sensitive detector may be placed in fixed position, instead of the film, and the magnetic field varied so that successive energy levels of the beta spectrum are detected. The energy of the various beta particles can be calculated from the known strength of the magnetic field and the radius of the arc followed by the particles. Brownell (2) discusses this technique at greater length.

The plot shown in Figure 3-6 of the number of beta particles from phosphorus-32 detected at various energy levels represents a typical beta spectrum. Note that the fraction of beta particles emitted near the *maximum energy* (E_{max}) is very small. A much larger fraction, often the largest, is emitted with the *mean energy* (E_{mean}). The value of E_{mean} is roughly $\frac{1}{3}$

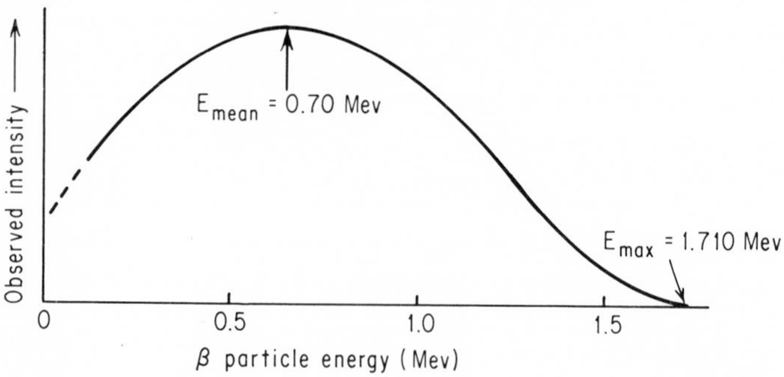

Figure 3-6. Energy distribution curve of beta particles from ^{32}P.

E_{max} for most beta emitters. The range of beta particles quite obviously depends on the value of E_{max}, but in calculating the actual radiation dose from a beta emitter, the E_{mean} value is more suitable.

The energy spectra for several beta emitters commonly used as radiotracers are given in Figure 3-7. Note that the general shape of the curves varies from nuclide to nuclide. The low-energy (soft) emitters have particularly noteworthy spectra. A dashed line at the low-energy portion of each spectrum indicates that this portion is theoretically calculated, since experimental determination is not readily feasible. Marshall (8) presents methods for calculating the shape of beta spectra.

b. *The neutrino and beta decay.* Since discrete energy levels were known to exist within the nucleus (see previous discussion of alpha emission energy), the emission of beta particles over a continuous energy spectrum from the same nuclide was somewhat of an enigma. In 1931, to explain this, Pauli suggested that each event of beta decay actually occurred with a total energy involvement equivalent to the E_{max} of the beta particle in question. He postulated that a hitherto undiscovered particle, the *neutrino*, shares this total energy with the beta particle in varying proportions from disintegration to disintegration. For example, a beta particle emitted from the radionuclide ^{32}P (E_{max} = 1.71 Mev) with an energy of 1 Mev would be accompanied by a neutrino equivalent to 0.71 Mev energy, making a total energy emission of 1.71 Mev.

Pauli indicated that the neutrino had no charge and negligible mass; as a result, its interaction with matter would be virtually nil and its detection a most difficult task. The elusive neutrino long defied detection, but its existence was finally demonstrated by means of an elaborate experimental technique in 1956. The current concept of beta decay can therefore be expressed as follows:

$$\text{Neutron} \longrightarrow \text{proton} + \overbrace{\text{negatron} + \text{neutrino}}^{\text{energy} \,=\, E_{\text{max}}}$$

$$\text{Proton} \longrightarrow \text{neutron} + \overbrace{\text{positron} + \text{neutrino}}^{\text{energy} \,=\, E_{\text{max}}}$$

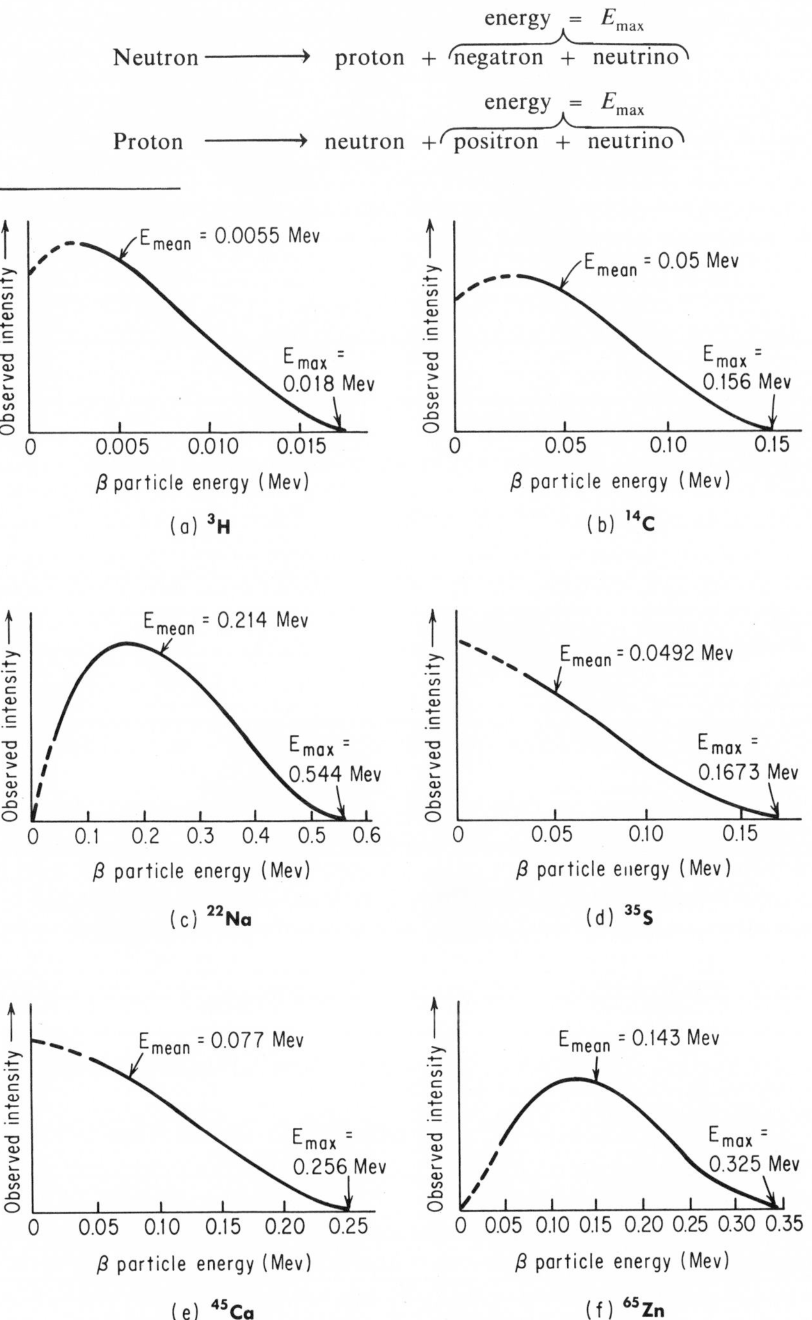

Figure 3-7. Beta energy curves for several beta emitters.

c. The Fermi theory of beta decay. It will be recalled that, for alpha emitters, an inverse relation exists between alpha emission energy and nuclide half-life. In general, such a relation also exists for beta emitters. All beta-emitting nuclides cannot, however, be grouped into a single category in this respect.

In 1934, Enrico Fermi formulated a theory of beta decay which grouped the various emitters in a number of *transition types*, depending on the specific nature of the nuclear change taking place. More than a dozen such types, in each of which the foregoing inverse relationship holds true, have been identified. Comparisons cannot, however, be made between different transition types. For example, ^{32}P and ^{14}C are in the same transition type. The former has a half-life of 14.2 days and an E_{max} of 1.71 Mev, whereas the latter has a half-life of 5568 years and an E_{max} of 0.156 Mev.

Fermi's general equation may be stated as follows:

$$\lambda \text{ (decay constant)} = kE^5_{max} \tag{3-2}$$

The values of the constant k vary with the transition type. Fermi's theory also serves to explain the varying shapes for different beta spectra (see Figure 3-7).

3. Interaction with Matter

a. Modes of interaction. As with alpha radiation, beta particles dissipate their energy largely by ionization and excitation of the atoms with which they interact. A third type of energy loss also occurs. When a high-energy beta particle is decelerated in the coulomb fields of atomic nuclei, electromagnetic radiation with wavelengths equivalent to X rays is emitted. This process is commonly called *Bremsstrahlung* (German for "braking radiation"). This phenomenon occurs principally when high-energy beta radiation interacts with elements of high Z. Bremsstrahlung is of no particular value in detecting beta radiation. On the contrary, it introduces serious problems in studying the absorption of beta particles by matter since the superior penetrating power of X rays will show up as a tail in the absorption curve (see Figure 3-9).

b. Specific ionization. As previously mentioned, the track of a beta particle as seen in a cloud chamber is tortuous, poorly defined, and much longer than that of an alpha particle. In considering an initially unidirectional beam of beta radiation, it is evident that many of the beta particles will be deflected and scattered out of the beam. This will lead to an apparent decrease in intensity of the radiation not due strictly to absorption. The situation is further complicated by the continuous energy spectrum associated with the particles. Consequently, the specific ionization pat-

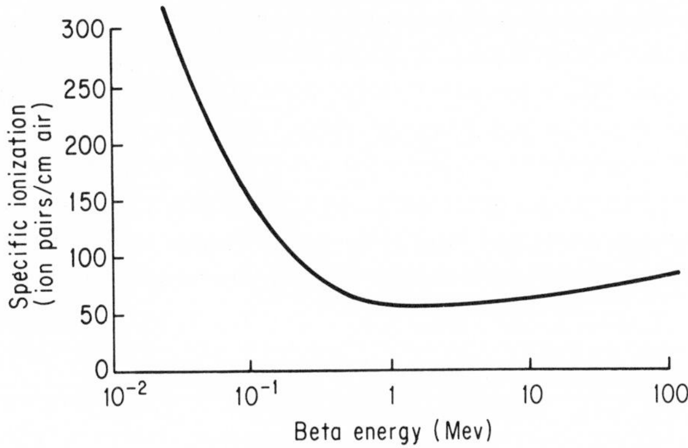

Figure 3-8. Specific ionization curve for beta particles in air.

tern for a beam of beta particles is not directly comparable to that of a beam of homoenergetic alpha particles.

Hence, it should be evident that a specific ionization curve, as shown for alpha radiation (Figure 3-2), cannot be drawn for beta particles. Instead, specific ionization is best expressed as a function of beta particle energy.

Figure 3-8 shows that, with low-energy beta particles, specific ionization decreases sharply as beta energy increases. The maximum specific ionization, 7700 ion pairs per centimeter, occurs with beta particles having energies of 146 ev. Consequently, the preponderance of ionization and, hence, energy loss from a given beta particle occurs toward the end of the beta track when its energy content drops below a few thousand electron volts. With beta particles having higher energy, particularly those having energies above about 2 Mev, relativistic considerations lead to a gradually increasing specific ionization with increasing particle energy.

By comparing Figures 3-2 and 3-8, one sees that specific ionization for alpha particles is many times greater than that for beta particles having the same kinetic energy. This is understandable, since not only do alpha particles carry twice as much charge as beta particles, but in particular, specific ionization is inversely related to particle velocity. Thus, for a given kinetic energy the velocity of a beta particle is much higher than that of an alpha particle.

4. Range

The range of alpha radiation is rather clear-cut, but beta range both in air and in metal absorbers is quite ill defined. Since linear beta range in air is extremely difficult to determine experimentally, range is best expressed in equivalent thickness (in mg/cm^2) of an absorber. Aluminum is the most commonly used absorber for this purpose. It should be emphasized that since the absorption process is a function of the size of the absorbing nuclei, equivalent range for beta radiation in other absorbers of similar Z values (such as air, mica, and so on) varies only slightly from that in aluminum. Figure 3-9 portrays a typical beta absorption curve obtained in range determination. Note the marked contrast to the alpha absorption curve (Figure 3-3), where beam intensity remains constant nearly to the end of the range, then drops rapidly to zero.

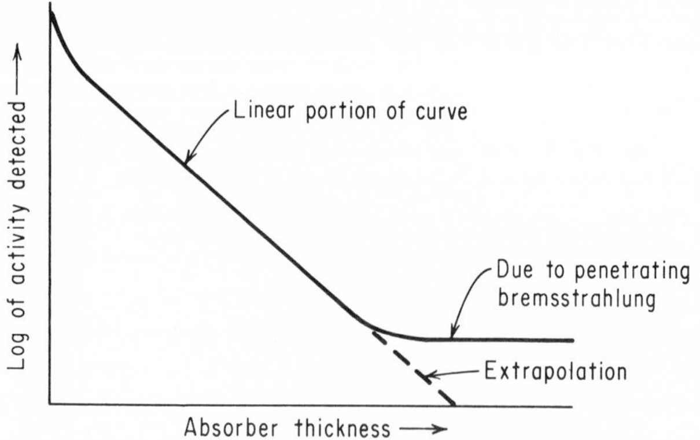

Figure 3-9. Plot of absorption of beta particles in matter.

Several significant items should be noted in Figure 3-9. First, much of the semilog plot is linear, that is, the absorption process is pseudo-exponential in nature, because of the combined effects of a continuous spectrum of energies and particle scattering. It will be seen later that gamma absorption is a truly exponential process. Secondly, the curve flattens out to constant activity owing largely to the production of the very penetrating Bremsstrahlung. Thirdly, although it would seem that extrapolation of the linear portion of the curve would give the true beta range, this is unfortunately not the case.

Accurate experimental determination of the *maximum range* (R_{max}) is important as a basis for calculating E_{max}. Since the E_{max} value is a distinctive characteristic of each nuclide, its determination is most important in identifying the presence of a specific beta emitter in an unknown sample. The Feather analysis is one of the most commonly used methods to derive R_{max} from an absorption curve. This method involves comparison of the absorption curve in aluminum of an unknown beta emitter with that of a beta emitter having a known range. Further discussion of beta range-energy relations will be found in Katz (7), Barreira (1), and Duncan (3).

5. Practical Considerations

a. Detection problems. In the application of radioisotopes as tracers, the identity of the nuclide being used is normally known. Thus, it is not necessary to determine experimentally the R_{max} and E_{max} of the nuclide in question. Instead, the investigator focuses upon the limitations on detection imposed by the characteristic absorption process of beta particles in matter. Since the detection of beta radiation commonly necessitates the particles entering an enclosed detector through a "window," it is important to know and to respect the sizable fraction of the incident beta radiation that will be absorbed by such windows. Transmission curves are available to supply this information for beta particles of various energies and windows of different thicknesses. Curves for beta transmission values of three mica window thicknesses are shown in Figure 3-10. Window

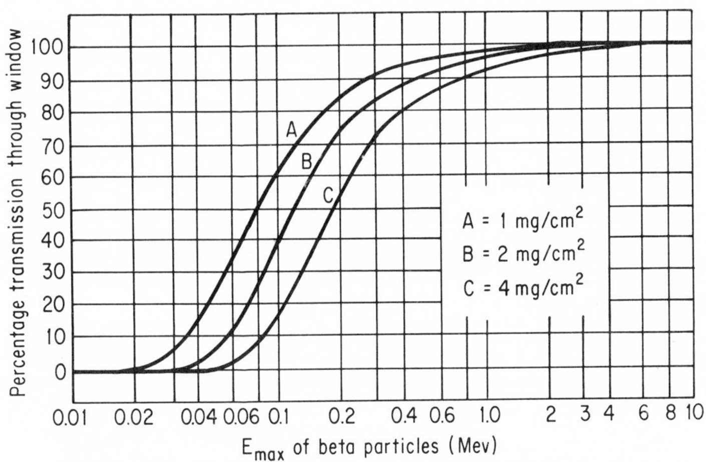

Figure 3-10. Beta transmission curves for three mica window thicknesses.

thickness is stated in equivalent thickness units (mg/cm^2). The effect of increasing window thickness on beta transmission is striking.

Obviously, for a low-energy beta emitter, such as ^{3}H (E_{max} 0.018 Mev), all the beta radiation would be absorbed in even the thinnest window shown in Figure 3-10. Unfortunately, in addition to ^{3}H, several other radioisotopes of biological importance, such as ^{14}C (E_{max} 0.156 Mev), ^{35}S (E_{max} 0.1673 Mev), and ^{45}Ca (E_{max} 0.256 Mev), are also "soft" beta emitters. Much, if not all, the radiation from these isotopes would be absorbed before actually entering the sensitive volume of a gas-filled ionization-type detector. It is often necessary to employ special detecting techniques for these soft emitters. These techniques, which will be further described in later chapters, customarily involve using an ultrathin window detector, placing the radioactive sample inside the detector (windowless type of detector), or mixing the sample in intimate contact with the detecting medium (liquid scintillation method).

The short range of soft beta radiation is used to advantage in autoradiography, where a sensitive film emulsion is employed to record the track of the radioactive particles (see Chapter 7). Such a high resolution is possible by this method that individual beta tracks may be traced.

b. *Biological hazards.* The biological hazards attending the use of beta emitters, as for alpha emitters, differ considerably, depending on whether one considers external or internal hazards. The radiation hazard from an external beta source in a laboratory is not normally significant. Heavy glass or metal containers will absorb most, if not all, beta radiation from enclosed radionuclides. Mere distance from exposed sources is a good safeguard, because of their limited range in air. Even accidental body surface contamination will normally lead to irradiation of only superficial tissues.

Ingested beta emitters, on the contrary, pose a greater hazard. Many of the frequently used beta-emitting nuclides are isotopes of elements commonly found in living tissue, such as C, H, S, and P. As a result, these radionuclides may be readily incorporated into the constituents of the body. If this leads to local deposition or concentration, such as the incorporation of tritium in the DNA of chromosomes, or calcium-45 in the bone, radiation damage may be quite extensive.

C. GAMMA RAYS

1. Nature and Source

a. *Electromagnetic nature.* In contrast to alpha and beta particles, gamma rays are electromagnetic radiation. Gamma radiation, being made up of photons, does not carry electric charge nor significant mass, and consequently, can penetrate matter readily with little interaction. This characteristic accounts for an effective range in matter vastly greater than for alpha or beta particles of comparable energy.

The spectrum of electromagnetic radiation given in Figure 3-11 indicates the relation of gamma radiation to other electromagnetic radiation (light, radio, heat, and so on). Obviously the differences are primarily in frequency, or wavelength, not in essential nature. In fact, there is no clear cut distinction on the electromagnetic spectrum between X radiation and gamma radiation. Their range of wavelengths overlap and they may be regarded as the same, but for origin. Gamma rays, by definition, result

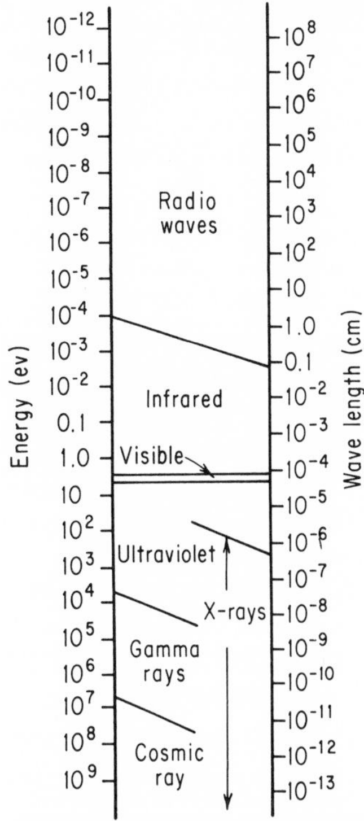

Figure 3-11. The electromagnetic spectrum on a logarithmic energy and frequency scale.

from some transformation in the nucleus of an atom, whereas X rays are emitted as a consequence of excitation involving the orbital electrons of an atom.

Although the wave nature of electromagnetic radiation can be readily recognized and demonstrated, many of the phenomena associated with electromagnetic radiation can be explained only on the basis that these wave motions behave in the manner of discrete particles or quanta of radiation. Each quantum or photon has a defined value of energy and momentum and is consequently corpuscular in nature.

b. *Source of gamma emission.* In chapter 2 it was pointed out that gamma rays are most frequently emitted immediately following alpha or beta particle emission from a nucleus. In the case of certain nuclides, ^{130}I for example, the excess energy of the excited state is carried off by a series, or "cascade" of gamma rays. Such gamma rays are normally emitted within 10^{-12} sec following the particle emission. It therefore appears that the gamma radiation represents the readjustment of energy content in the radionuclide from an excited state to a more stable ground state. With some nuclides the consequent gamma emission is delayed considerably (up to several hours); in that case, the radionuclide is presumably maintained at an "excited state" over a prolonged period. Such delayed gamma radiation is generally known as *isomeric transition.* Nuclear isomers, consequently differ from each other only in the energy content of the nuclei.

Spectrum analysis of gamma rays reveals that they are emitted at defined energy levels. As is the situation in alpha emission, this phenomenon presumably reflects changes in the discrete energy levels existing within the nuclear energy well (see Figure 3-1). Gamma rays from most radioactive nuclides have energies in the range of 10 kev to 3 Mev. A very few range up to 7 Mev. Owing to alternate pathways of decay, many isotopes emit gamma rays of several different energy levels (see Figure 2-4).

c. X rays. X rays from radioactive nuclides are commonly emitted as a result of electron capture and their energies are those characteristic of the energies of the inner orbital electron levels. The energy range is from a few electron volts to about 120 kev, quite in contrast to the gamma energy range. Two common examples are the 8 kev X rays from ^{65}Zn and the 5 kev X rays from ^{51}Cr.

2. Interaction of Gamma Radiation with Matter

Because gamma rays are uncharged and thus carry no appreciable force field with them as they travel through matter, they cannot bring about direct ionization of atoms in their path. But several of their common modes of interaction with matter result in the consequent ejection of electrons. These ejected electrons, moving at high velocity, are capable of causing ionization in the surrounding matter. Thus, gamma radiation brings about ionization, but in an indirect manner.

Gamma rays interact with matter in at least six different ways. Three of these are concerned with nuclear interaction; the other three, with orbital electrons of the interacting atom. The first three modes listed are of only minimal importance in tracer applications of radioisotopes.

a. Nuclear transformation. Very high-energy gamma rays (over 6 Mev) may directly interact with a nucleus, causing excitation of the nucleons. This may result in the ejection of a particle, usually a neutron, and transmutation of the atom to another nuclide (a γ, n reaction). An exceptional situation exists in the case of ^{3}H and ^{9}Be. These nuclides have photodisintegration thresholds of 2.23 and 1.67 Mev, respectively, with respect to gamma energy. Thus, a convenient neutron source can be prepared by the use of ^{9}Be with ^{124}Sb, a gamma emitter having a half-life of 60.9 days. The neutron yield realized from this source can be as high as 3.2×10^{6} neutrons/sec/curie.

b. Mössbauer effect. In certain situations a gamma ray may be absorbed by a nucleus without consequent particle emission. The nucleus remains in this excited state for a brief, but measurable period of time. Subsequent emission of the gamma photon restores the stability of the nucleus. The affected atom has remained the same, without transformation. This type of interaction may be described as *nuclear resonance scattering*.

c. Bragg scattering (diffraction). Low-energy gamma rays may be scattered by a crystal lattice with no loss of energy. The diffraction of X rays has been used effectively in the study of molecular structure; the phenomenon is, however, of little importance in radiotracer methodology.

d. *Photoelectric effect.* If a gamma ray interacts directly with an orbital electron, it may transfer all its energy to the target electron and cease to exist. The electron will be ejected from the atom with kinetic energy equivalent to that of the gamma ray, less the energy needed to overcome the orbital binding force of the electron. Such a photoelectron, like a beta particle except having a discrete energy level, will interact with other atoms in its path, leading to ionization. The effect described is most significant for gamma rays with energies below 0.5 Mev interacting with absorbers of high atomic number.

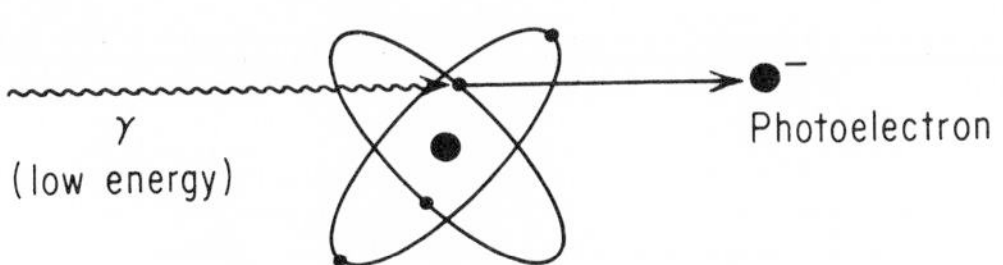

Figure 3-12. Photoelectric effect.

e. *Compton effect.* Gamma rays of medium energy (0.5–1.0 Mev) may undergo elastic collisions with loosely bound orbital electrons. In such events, only a portion of the gamma energy is transferred to the electron, which is ejected. The gamma photon itself is deflected in a new direction with a reduced energy. These recoil electrons may carry away from such an encounter any amount of energy up to a defined maximum. Thus, Compton recoil electrons appear with a wide energy spread although they are derived from a monoenergetic beam of incident gamma radiation. Considerable ionization can naturally be realized as these electrons dissipate their energy upon interaction with matter. Moreover, the attenuated gamma ray may undergo several more such collisions before it finally loses all its energy. The Compton effect is a favored mode of interaction for gamma rays of medium energy interacting with absorbers of medium to low atomic number.

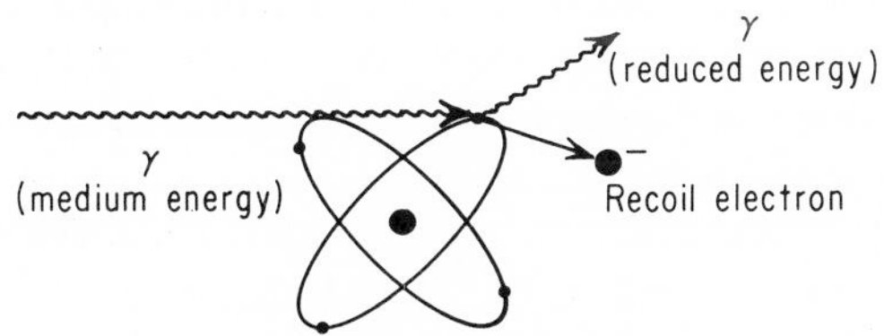

Figure 3-13. Compton effect.

f. *Pair production.* A unique phenomenon may occur when a gamma ray interacts directly with the nuclear force field. In such an event, the photon may cease to exist and have all its energy converted into two particles, a positron and an electron, which are ejected from the site with varying energy. For this to take place, the incident gamma ray must have an energy equal to, or greater than, 1.02 Mev, which is the energy equivalent to the rest mass of one electron and one positron. This occurrence illustrates the interconvertibility of energy and mass. The positron produced quickly undergoes annihilation, with consequent back-to-back gamma emission. On the other hand, the ejected electron may cause ionization of atoms near its path. Pair production increases with increasing atomic number of the absorber and with increasing energy of the incident gamma photon above the absolute minimum level of 1.02 Mev.

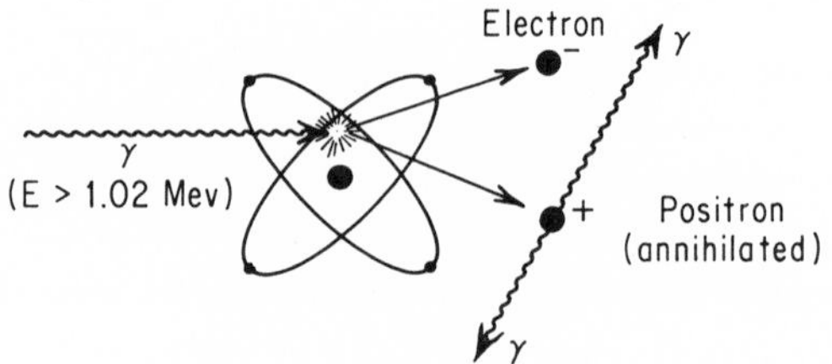

Figure 3-14. Pair production.

In summary, the latter three methods of interaction (photoelectric effect, Compton effect, pair production) are the principal ways in which gamma energy from radionuclides is dissipated. The ionization effects of the secondary electrons produced by gamma absorption provide ready detection of gamma radiation.

3. Absorption relations

a. Linear absorption coefficient. Since the absorption of gamma radiation is exponential in nature, gamma rays have no clear-cut range. This is in contrast to alpha and beta radiation. To examine certain quantitative aspects of gamma absorption, an ideal absorption situation is pictured (Figure 3-15), in which a collimated beam (all parallel rays) of gamma radiation is incident on a thin slab of absorber material.

As the incident gamma beam of intensity I_0 passes through the thin absorber with a thickness x, some of the gamma rays are absorbed, resulting in a decline in gamma intensity equal to ΔI. I_0 minus ΔI then equals the intensity of the emerging gamma beam. It should be clear that the thicker the absorber, the greater will be the absorption. Thus, the fraction of the beam intensity absorbed is proportional to the thickness of the

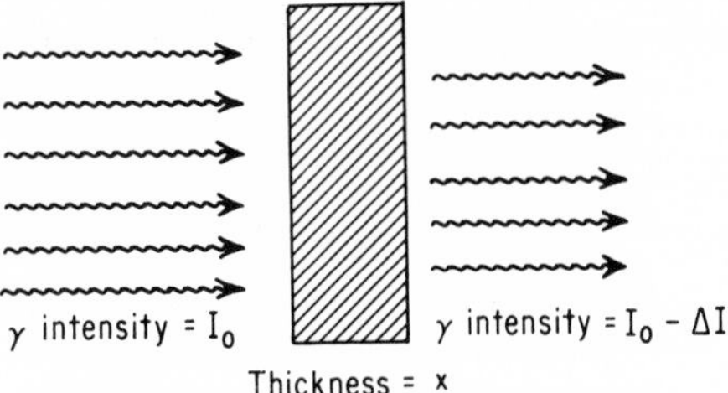

Figure 3-15. Gamma ray absorption.

absorber through which it passes, or:

$$(3\text{-}3) \qquad -\frac{\Delta I}{I_0} \; \alpha \; x$$

The minus sign indicates that a decrease in intensity is occurring.

This expression can be converted to an equation by introducing a constant μ_l, the *linear absorption coefficient*, which represents the fractional decrease in gamma intensity per unit thickness of absorber.

$$(3\text{-}4) \qquad -\frac{\Delta I}{I_0} = \mu \Delta x \quad \text{or} \quad \mu_l = \frac{-(\Delta I/I_0)}{\Delta x}$$

Since absorption is a continuous process through the slab, the process can be best examined by visualizing the absorber's thickness as made up of a great number of infinitesimal thicknesses (dx). This treatment, which is much the same as that used in the examination of radioactive decay, will then allow the integration of Equation 3-4 to give

$$(3\text{-}5) \qquad \log_n \frac{I}{I_0} = -\mu_l x, \quad \text{or} \quad \log_n \frac{I_0}{I} = \mu_l x$$

where I_0 represents the incident gamma beam intensity, and I stands for the intensity that will emerge from an absorber of x thickness. Converting the equation from natural logarithms to common logarithms ($\log_{10}$) gives

$$(3\text{-}6) \qquad \log_{10} \frac{I}{I_0} = -0.434\, \mu_l x, \quad \text{or} \quad \log_{10} \frac{I_0}{I} = 0.434\, \mu_l x$$

The linear absorption coefficient is commonly expressed per centimeter (1/cm). Its value depends on two factors: the energy of the gamma rays involved, and the type of absorber material used. These relationships are seen in the values listed in Table 3-3.

Example. What fraction of a 1.5 Mev gamma beam will pass completely through a 5-cm-thick lead brick? The μ_l for 1.5 Mev gamma rays in lead is 0.590/cm. Let I_o be unity.

$$\log_{10} \frac{1.00}{I} = 0.434 \times 0.590/\text{cm} \times 5 \text{ cm}$$

$$\log_{10} 1.00 - \log_{10} I = 1.28$$

$$\log_{10} I = -1.28$$

$$I = 0.052, \text{ or } \sim 5\% \text{ of the original gamma intensity}$$

b. *Mass absorption coefficient.* As can be seen in Table 3-3, the linear absorption coefficient varies considerably for different absorber materials.

TABLE 3-3

Linear absorption coefficients per centimer for selected absorbers

Incident Gamma Energy (Mev)	H_2O	Al	Fe	Pb
1.0	0.071	0.168	0.44	0.79
1.5	0.057	0.136	0.40	0.590
2.0	0.050	0.117	0.33	0.504

Since the absorption of gamma rays is primarily a function of the mass of the absorber, by taking the density of the absorbing material into account, a more comparable unit can be derived. In considering a volume of absorber that is 1 cm^2 in cross section and x cm long, the volume is numerically equal to the thickness (x). The mass in this volume equals the density (ρ) times the thickness (ρx). It follows that the fractional gamma absorption is proportional to the mass of absorber traversed. Substitution of ρx in place of x in Equation 3-3 gives

$$-\frac{\Delta I}{I_0} \propto \rho x \tag{3-7}$$

This relationship makes it possible to introduce the term *mass absorption coefficient* (μ_m). It is simply the linear absorption coefficient (μ_l) divided by the density of the absorber, or

$$\mu_m = \frac{\mu_l}{\rho}, \quad \text{or} \quad \mu_l = \mu_m \rho \tag{3-8}$$

Equation 3-5 can therefore be modified to give

$$\log_n \frac{I}{I_0} = -\mu_m \rho x, \quad \text{or} \quad \log_n \frac{I_0}{I} = \mu_m \rho x \tag{3-9}$$

and

$$\log_n \frac{I_0}{I} = \mu_m d, \tag{3-10}$$

where d is the mass thickness expressed in the unit g/cm^2. Introducing the term μ_m has the advantage of making the mass absorption coefficient almost independent of the nature of the absorber. As shown in Table 3-4, the mass absorption coefficients are nearly the same for gamma rays of the energies listed in different absorbers. The mass absorption coefficients are commonly expressed in units of cm^2/g, or occasionally as cm^2/mg. An additional advantage of using the mass absorption coefficient is its independence of the chemical or physical state of the absorber. The value for liquid water and water vapor is the same, whereas the μ_l values would differ greatly.

TABLE 3-4

Mass absorption coefficients in cm^2/g

Incident Gamma Energy (Mev)	H_2O	Al	Fe	Pb
1.0	0.071	0.062	0.062	0.070
1.5	0.057	0.050	0.056	0.052
2.0	0.050	0.043	0.046	0.046

Example. What fraction of gamma radiation from a 1 Mev beam would completely pass through 2 cm of lead under ideal conditions? The μ_m value for 1.0 Mev gamma radiation in lead is 0.07 cm^2/g, and the density (ρ) of lead is 11.3 g/cm^3. Let I_0 be unity.

$$\log_{10} \frac{1.00}{I} = -0.434 \times 0.07 \text{ cm}^2/\text{g} \times 11.3 \text{ gm/cm}^3 \times 2.0 \text{ cm}$$

$$\log_{10} 1.00 - \log_{10} I = 0.678$$

$$\log_{10} I = -0.678 = 9.322 - 10$$

$$I = 0.210, \text{ or} \sim 21\% \text{ of the original gamma intensity.}$$

Two other absorption coefficients are occasionally used: the atomic absorption coefficient (μ_a) takes into account the actual number of atoms in the absorbing material and is equivalent to the fraction of energy absorbed per single atom in the absorber. Since low-energy gamma rays interact predominantly with the orbital electrons, the electronic absorption coefficient (μ_e) is occasionally employed. It represents the fraction of intensity absorbed by individual electrons in the absorber.

c. *Half-thickness.* Absorption curves plotted for gamma intensity versus the thickness (or mass) of the absorber appear in Figure 3-16. The exponential nature of the absorption process is clearly indicated by the straight line relationship shown in the semilog plot. This is similar to the

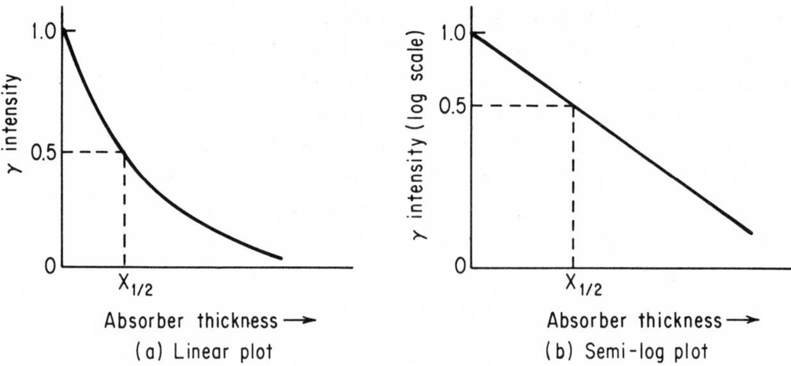

Figure 3-16. Exponential absorption of gamma radiation.

situation with radioactive decay. A concept of half-thickness can be advantageously used to evaluate the extent of absorption. The *half-thickness* ($x_{1/2}$) or "half-value layer," is defined as the thickness of absorber material which will reduce the incident radiation intensity by a factor of two. Half-thickness is a useful expression in calculating the shielding necessary to reduce gamma ray intensity to desired levels.

Half-thickness can be defined as either linear half-thickness ($x_{1/2}$) or mass half-thickness ($d_{1/2}$). For the reasons outlined concerning the mass absorption coefficient, the mass half-thickness is the more useful unit. The mass half-thickness can be derived from Equation 3-9. If the gamma radiation intensity is to be reduced by a factor of two, then, according to Equation 3-10,

$$\text{A. } \log_n \frac{I_0}{I_0/2} = \mu_m d_{1/2}$$

$$\text{(3-11)} \quad \text{B. } \log_n 2 = \mu_m d_{1/2}, \quad \text{or} \quad 2.303 \log_{10} 2 = \mu_m d_{1/2}$$

$$\text{C. } d_{1/2} = \frac{0.693}{\mu_m}$$

This shows that the value of the mass half-thickness can be directly calculated from the mass absorption coefficient. However, as in the case of half-life calculations (see page 29), μ_m must be expressed in very small units relative to $d_{1/2}$.

In gamma-ray shielding problems, the use of the mass half-thickness allows rapid calculation of the approximate shielding necessary to reduce personnel exposure to gamma radiation. If one half-thickness will reduce gamma intensity to one-half its original value, then two half-thicknesses will reduce it to one-fourth, and so on. The number of half-thicknesses (N) of absorber required to reduce gamma intensity by the factor of X would be equivalent to a total absorber thickness of D. The value of N can be readily derived from Equation 3-11B. First, by substitution,

(3-12) $$\log_n X = \mu_m D$$

Introducing the value of μ_m from Equation 3-11C gives

(3-13) $$\log_n X = \frac{0.693}{d_{1/2}} D$$

but since $N = D/d_{1/2}$, this can be reduced to

(3-14) $$\log_n X = 0.693\, N$$

Converting to common logarithms and solving for N yields

(3-15) $$N = 3.33 \log_{10} X$$

This equation therefore provides ready means for the calculation of shielding requirements. Thus, when it is desired to reduce a given gamma intensity to one-eighth of its magnitude,

$$N = 3.33 \log_{10} 8 = 3.0 \text{ half-thicknesses required}$$

d. ***Dependence on gamma energy and absorber density.*** The exponential nature of gamma absorption is evident from Figure 3-16B. The absorption equations (3-5 and 3-9) can also be expressed in an exponential form similar to that used for radioactive decay (Equation 2-8):

(3-16) $$I = I_0 e^{-\mu_l x} \quad \text{(linear absorption)}$$

(3-17) $$I = I_0 e^{-\mu_m d} \quad \text{(mass absorption)}$$

The symbol e used in these equations stands for the value 2.718, the base of the natural logarithms.

It is quite remarkable that gamma absorption should be exponential, since it is actually the result of six distinctly different processes. Of these six interaction processes, only three (photoelectric effect, Compton effect, and pair production) are normally significant at the gamma energies associated with most radionuclides used in radiotracer applications. Each of these processes is highly dependent on the gamma energy involved and the nature of the absorber used. This energy dependence is clearly seen in Figure 3-17, which indicates the plot of μ_m values against gamma energy for the three significant gamma interaction processes.

Note that the photoelectric effect is most pronounced at lower energies, the Compton effect is the predominant interaction type at intermediate energies, and pair production becomes an increasingly important factor above the minimum energy of 1.02 Mev. Only at energies over 10 Mev (not shown in the figure) would nuclear transformations occur significantly.

The dependence of gamma absorption on the density of the absorber can be seen in a plot of mass half-thickness against incident gamma energy in various absorbers (Figure 3-18). Note that for water, aluminum,

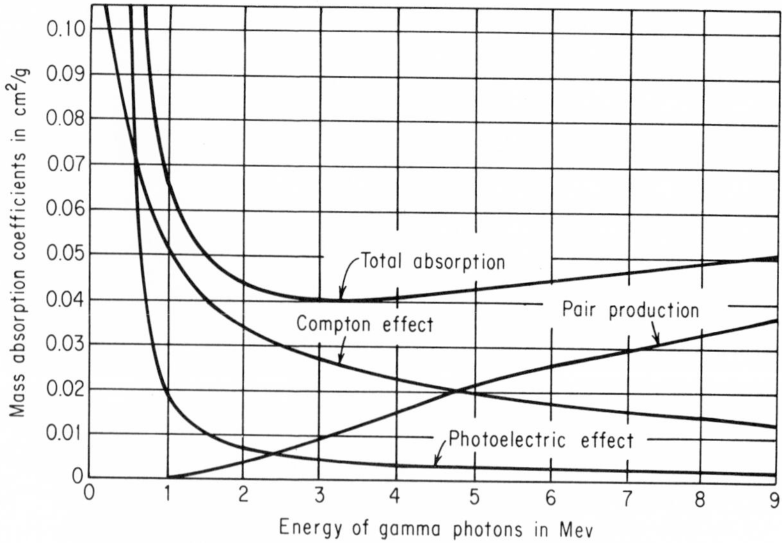

Figure 3-17. Mass absorption coefficients for gamma rays in lead.

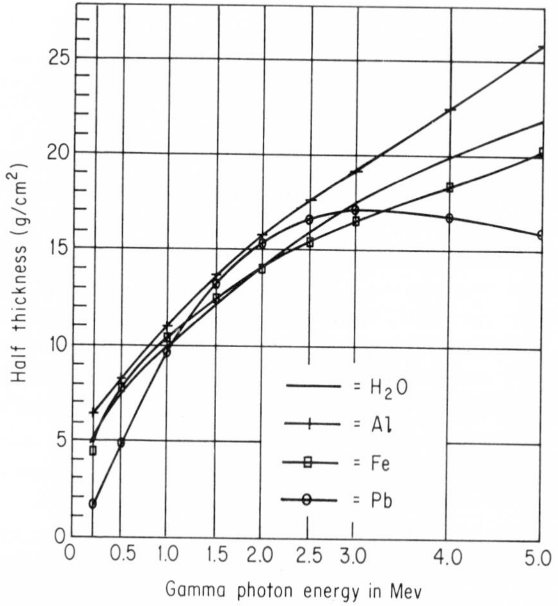

Figure 3-18. Relation between $d_{1/2}$ and gamma energy in various absorbers.

and iron, the $d_{1/2}$ increases steadily with gamma energy. For lead, however, $d_{1/2}$ increases up to 3 Mev, then begins to decrease, indicating that gamma absorption in lead is least efficient at about 3 Mev. This peculiarity is explained by remembering that pair production, which becomes increasingly more operative as a means of gamma absorption with increasing energies, is far more pronounced in absorbers of high atomic weight. Up to 3 Mev, the photoelectric and Compton effects are declining in effectiveness as absorption mechanisms. At this point, however, the effectiveness of pair production offsets the decline of the other two effects and reverses the trend of the curve.

For a more extensive discussion of gamma absorption processes see Fano's two excellent articles (4, 5). Tittle (9) presents a briefer treatment of gamma absorption calculations; Green (6) has prepared a useful nomogram for such determinations.

The general features of gamma absorption also apply to X-ray absorption. The major difference is that X rays are not emitted from radionuclides with sufficient energy to cause pair production. Because the X-ray energies are generally low, diffraction is a more significant phenomenon. This latter characteristic is utilized in the study of crystalline structure. The diffraction pattern produced when a beam of soft X rays strikes a crystal face permits a very exact determination of the spacing of atoms within the crystal.

4. Practical Considerations

The presence of even moderate quantities of gamma-emitting nuclides in a laboratory poses a problem because of the highly penetrating nature of gamma radiation. The isotopic material must commonly be stored in a shielded container of lead or other dense material. If the radiation level is sufficiently high, manipulation of the gamma-emitting material may require shielding and/or remote control apparatus of a simple type. The external hazard from gamma-emitting radionuclides is quite in contrast to that from alpha and beta emitters. The entire volume of body tissue can be irradiated from an external gamma source. When taken internally, gamma emitters can produce essentially whole body radiation effects, regardless of the localization of the material. The presence of gamma-emitting nuclides in the laboratory likewise tends to increase the normal background radiation level, which prolongs the necessary counting time for a desired accuracy in radioactivity assays (see Chapter 9).

In detecting gamma rays, interaction is such that the gas-filled chambers used to detect alpha and beta radiation are most inefficient. It is desirable to use detectors of great density for maximum absorption. Sodium iodide crystals are most generally employed for this purpose.

The excitation energy from absorbed gamma quanta in such a crystal is emitted as minute flashes of visible light (photons). These scintillations may be converted to an electron flow, which can be amplified and measured (see Chapter 5).

D. SUMMARY

It will be recalled that alpha and beta particles cause primary ionization as they interact with matter. On the other hand, gamma radiation produces only a primary excitation, with ionization only a secondary effect. Alpha and beta radiation are charged particles, whereas gamma radiation is electromagnetic in nature. The range of alpha particles is quite discrete, that of beta particles is not as well defined; gamma radiation has no clearly delimited range, but is continuously absorbed on an exponential basis.

BIBLIOGRAPHY

1. Barreira, F., and M. Laranjeira. 1957. A graphical absolute method for range determination of β-particles. Intern. J. Appl. Radiation Isotopes 2:145–148.
2. Brownell, Gordon L. 1952. Interaction of phosphorus-32 beta rays with matter. Nucleonics 10(6):30–35.
3. Duncan, J. F., and F. G. Thomas. 1957. Three beta-absorption methods—how do they compare? Nucleonics 15(10):82–85.
4. Fano, U. 1953*a*. Gamma-ray attenuation. Part I. Basic processes. Nucleonics 11(8):8–12.
5. Fano, U. 1953*b*. Gamma-ray attenuation. Part II. Analysis of penetration. Nucleonics 11(9):55–61.
6. Green, Marvin H. 1959. Absorption of mono-energetic X- and γ-rays. Nucleonics 17(10):77.
7. Katz, L., and A. S. Penfold. 1952. Range-energy relations for electrons and the determination of beta-ray end-point energies by absorption. Rev. Mod. Phys. 24(1):28–44.
8. Marshall, John H. 1955. How to figure shapes of beta-ray spectra. Nucleonics 13(8):34–38.
9. Tittle, C. W. 1960. How to compute absorption and backscattering of gamma rays. Nuclear-Chicago Tech. Bull. No. 9. Des Plaines, Ill. 4 p.

CHAPTER FOUR

Measurement of Radioactivity: General Considerations and the Methods Based on Gas Ionization

A. TYPES OF RADIOACTIVITY MEASUREMENTS

Radioactivity may be detected and measured on several different bases. In *absolute counting*, every disintegration occurring in the sample is accounted for; hence, the results are expressed in disintegrations per minute (dpm). On the other hand, radioactivity may be measured on the *relative counting* basis, where only a given fraction of the true disintegration rate of the sample is detected. A specific proportionality can be maintained between this relative counting rate and the absolute counting rate in a series of samples by utilizing identical counting conditions. In this way, repeated relative counts will be comparable to one another. The results of relative counting are usually stated as counts per minute (cpm).

The foregoing description of the measurement of radioactivity is not to be confused with the measurement of *radiation dose*. Absolute and relative counting pertain to detecting and measuring events; dosimetry is concerned with measuring the energy dissipation and absorption in a defined system. The radiation dose depends heavily on the energy and type of the incident radiation and the nature of the absorbing material; hence, precise determinations are much more difficult to make. Radiation dose values are commonly given in roentgen or rad units (see Chapter 12).

The purposes and applications of these three types of measurement are quite different. Radiation dosimetry, being concerned with the absorption of radiation energy, is important chiefly to radiation biologists and health physicists. (Further discussion of this aspect will be found in Chapter 12.) Absolute counting, where the true radioactive disintegration rate is measured, is an extremely tedious and time-consuming method. It is employed in precise studies of such nuclear phenomena as the determination of long half-lives and in the preparation of radioactive standard sources for instrument calibration and is therefore used largely by physicists, nuclear engineers, and radiochemists. Thus, it is not discussed further in this book. Since relative counting is the most important and simplest type of radioactivity assay where radiotracer studies are involved, it is the only method considered in this and the following chapters.

B. RELATIVE COUNTING

For relative count rate determinations to be truly comparable from one sample to another, one must give careful attention to the preparation of the radioactive samples. The mounting of the sample in relation to the detector (the "geometry") must also be clearly delimited in order to obtain reproducible results. Counting data are meaningful only when both these factors are considered and precisely defined.

Sample preparation involves converting the biological sample (tissue, blood, urine, and so on) containing a radioisotope label to a form suitable for radioactivity assay. Most frequently this includes a process converting organic materials to an inorganic compound to reduce sample bulk. Further changes in the physical or chemical form of the sample may subsequently be required. Especially in the case of solid samples, the choice of the planchet to hold the sample may have a significant effect on the counting results. (A more detailed discussion of sample preparation techniques will be deferred to Chapter 8.)

Other factors in relative counting that must be carefully considered are the amount of coincidence loss in the counting system, scattering of radiation, and absorption of radiation before it enters the detector. (These are discussed in Chapter 9.) For counting results to be comparable and reproducible, these factors must be kept constant. It is assumed, in the following discussion of detectors, that the sample has been properly prepared and mounted in a defined geometry.

C. BASIC PRINCIPLES OF RADIATION DETECTION

In the previous chapter, we saw that alpha, beta, and gamma radiation can interact with matter in a variety of ways. Of these types of interaction, the most commonly utilized in detecting radiation are those which ionize gas atoms, cause orbital electron excitation in solids or liquids, or induce specific chemical reactions in sensitive emulsions. The detectors themselves will be described in detail after a brief survey of the mechanisms involved.

1. Gas Ionization

Several detector types take advantage of the ionizing effect of radiation on gases. The ion pairs so produced can be separately collected. When a potential gradient is applied between the two electrodes in a gas-filled ion chamber, the positively charged molecules move to the cathode and the negative ions (electrons) move swiftly to the anode, thereby creating a measurable pulse. Such pulses can be readily measured by the associated devices as individual events or integrated current.

2. Scintillation

a. *In a solid fluor.* A portion of the energy of ionizing radiation can be transferred to fluor molecules (that is, compounds that can give rise to fluorescence) in a crystalline solid. The absorbed energy causes excitation of orbital electrons in the fluor. De-excitation gives rise to the emission of the absorbed energy as electromagnetic radiation in the visible or near ultraviolet region (scintillations). It is possible to observe these weak scintillations visually under certain circumstances, but visual observation is not normally a feasible detection method. Instead, a photomultiplier tube in close proximity to the solid fluor is employed. In the photomultiplier, the photons are converted to photoelectrons, and these are greatly amplified by secondary electron emission through a series of electrodes (dynodes) to a sizable electrical pulse. Thus, the original excitation energy is transformed into a measurable pulse. (This means of detection is further described in Chapter 5.)

b. *In a liquid fluor.* This detection mechanism is quite similar in principle to the preceding one. Here, however, the radioactive sample and the fluor are the solute in a liquid medium, usually a nonpolar solvent. The energy of nuclear radiation first excites the solvent molecules. This excitation energy eventually appears as photons emitted from the fluor following an intermediate transfer stage. These photons are detected by means of a photomultiplier arrangement. (Further discussion of the detection method will be found in Chapter 6.)

3. Autoradiography

This mechanism is a photochemical process. A sample containing radioactivity is placed in close contact with a photographic emulsion on film. Ionizing radiation from the sample interacts with the silver halide grains in the emulsion to bring about a photochemical reaction. Subsequent development of the film produces an image and hence permits a semiquantitative estimation of the radiotracer in the sample. Historically, this is the way in which radioactivity was first detected (by Becquerel in 1896). Unlike detectors of the gas ionization or scintillation types, which require relatively complex electronic components, autoradiography can be carried out without specialized apparatus and is adequate for crude detection. (Chapter 7 includes a more detailed discussion of autoradiography.)

D. GAS IONIZATION

As an energetic charged particle passes through a gas, its electrostatic field will dislodge orbital electrons from atoms sufficiently close to its path. In each case, the negatively charged electron dislodged and the more massive positive ion comprising the remainder of the atom form an *ion pair*. The minimum energy (in electron volts) required for such ion pair formation in a given gas is called the *ionization potential*. This value differs markedly for different gases and is dependent on the type and energy of the charged particle. A more meaningful value is the average energy lost by the particle in producing one ion pair (see Table 4-1).

In a defined volume of gas, the amount of ionization that will occur as a result of the passage of an alpha particle, a beta particle, or a gamma photon of the same energy differs strikingly. The alpha particle will create intense ionization (about 10^4–10^5 ion pairs/cm), whereas the beta particle will produce a rather diffuse ionization (about 10^2–10^3 ion pairs/cm), and

TABLE 4-1

Average energy lost by 5 Mev alpha particles in producing one ion pair in some common gases

Gas	*Average Energy Lost* (ev)
Argon	26.2
Methane	29.2
Oxygen	32.3
Ethyl alcohol	32.6
Air	35.2
Nitrogen	36.4
Hydrogen	36.6
Neon	36.8
Helium	44.4

the gamma ray will give rise to little ionization (about 1–10 ion pairs/cm) and that only by secondary mechanisms. Accordingly, it can be seen that alpha and beta particles produce sufficiently intense specific ionization for detection, but gamma rays are poorly detected at best by this means.

1. Without Gas Amplification

a. Ionization chambers in general. A chamber for ion collection may consist of a cylindrical closed metal container filled with air, or some other gas and fitted with a central collecting electrode, as illustrated in Figure 4-1. The chamber wall is connected to the negative pole of a po-

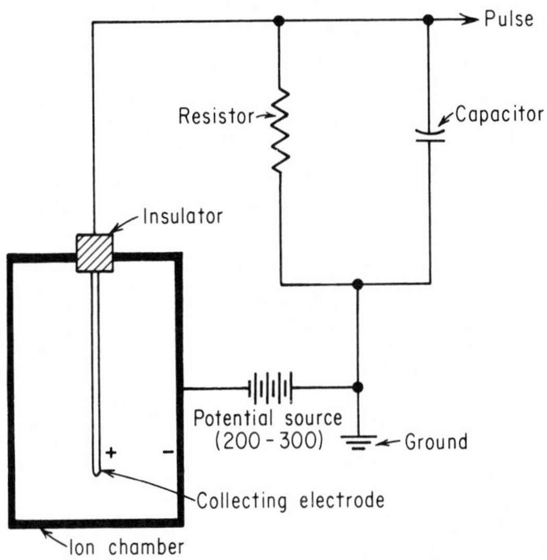

Figure 4-1. A simple ionization chamber circuit (integrating type), (source given in volts).

tential source, making it the cathode; the collecting electrode is connected through a resistor to the positive side of the power supply, so that it serves as the anode. The collecting electrode is carefully insulated from the chamber wall. A capacitor is included in the circuit in such a way that it will be charged by a current originating at the collecting electrode.

Now, if a 3.5 Mev alpha particle traverses the chamber, intense ionization will occur along its short path. Since about 35 ev are expended on the average in forming an ion pair in air, the 3.5 Mev alpha particle could form approximately 1×10^5 such ion pairs before dissipating all its energy. Owing to the potential impressed on the chamber electrodes, these ions migrate rapidly to the respective electrodes. The lighter electrons move more quickly to the central collecting anode and produce a rapid build-up of charge there. The magnitude of this charge can be calculated as follows:

$$\text{One } e^- \text{ charge} = 1.6 \times 10^{-19} \text{ coulomb} \tag{4-1}$$

$$1 \times 10^5 e^- \times 1.6 \times 10^{-19} \text{ coulomb}/e^- =$$

$$1.6 \times 10^{-14} \text{ coulomb}$$

The collected charge flows through the external circuit as a surge, or pulse. If a 20 $\mu\mu$f capacitor is being used, the potential of the pulse is found as follows:

$$\frac{\text{charge in coulombs}}{\text{capacitor size in farads}} = \text{pulse size in volts} \tag{4-2}$$

$$\frac{1.6 \times 10^{-14} \text{ coulomb}}{2.0 \times 10^{-11} \text{ farad}} = 8 \times 10^{-4} \text{ volt,} \quad \text{or} \quad 0.0008 \text{ volt}$$

The precise measurement of such minute pulses constitutes a basic difficulty in using the simple ionization chamber for detecting ionizing radiation.

If, instead, a beta-emitting source is brought near the ionization chamber, a much smaller degree of ionization will occur along beta tracks in the chamber. It is not possible to calculate the actual number of ion pairs that will be formed for an individual beta particle and the consequent charge collected, since beta particles are emitted over a continuous energy spectrum. The mean kinetic energy associated with beta particles is generally much lower than with alpha particles and the ionization power of the particles (singly charged electrons) is inherently low. As a result, the size of pulse produced by an individual beta particle will be smaller by a hundred- or a thousand-fold than that produced by an alpha particle. Gamma rays produce only secondary ionization and have such very low specific ionization that the pulse produced in an ion chamber, before their escape, is very small indeed.

Up to this point, it has merely been stated that a potential is applied across the electrodes of the ionization chamber. We now examine the relationship between the potential in the ionization chamber and the amount of charge collected on the anode. If no potential is applied, a negligible charge will be collected, although ionization does occur in the chamber. Recombination of the ions will take place rapidly in the wake of the ionizing particle. At only a few volts potential, some ions will be collected, but most will still recombine before reaching the electrodes. Continued increase in potential gradient will result in an increasingly larger fraction of the ions being collected, until eventually all ions are collected and almost no recombination occurs. From this point an increase of chamber potential over perhaps several hundred volts gives essentially no increase in charge collected. Under these conditions a *saturation current* is realized at the collecting electrode. Ionization chambers are usually operated toward the middle of the saturation current region, so that any fluctuation in the supplied potential will not affect the ion current. (Figure 4-2 shows this relationship.) One advantage of the

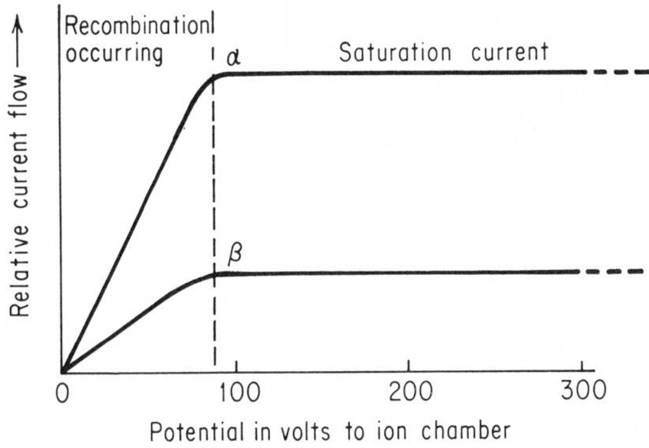

Figure 4-2. The relationship of ionization current to ion chamber potential.

simple ionization chamber, then, is that a highly stable chamber potential supply is not required.

Until this point, we have discussed only a single surge of current produced by a solitary ionizing particle. Of course, a radioactive sample will be emitting particles continuously into an ion chamber, so that volleys of pulses will be initiated in the external circuit. These pulses may be recorded in two different manners. The individual pulses may be tallied to give a record of the number of ionizing particles entering the chamber (a *differentiating* circuit). Because of the pulse size involved, such a method is generally feasible only for alpha particles and has the disadvantage of requiring an elaborate pulse amplifier. Consequently, some type of *integrating* circuit is most commonly employed with a simple ionization chamber. In this way, the total current flow over a given time interval is measured, rather than the discrete pulses. This total ion current is proportional to the degree of ionization occurring in the chamber during the time interval. Two major types of integrating instruments, electroscopes and electrometers, are currently in common use. We now describe in detail an example of each type used for radiotracer assay.

b. *Lauritsen electroscopes.* The Lauritsen electroscope is merely a highly refined version of the classic gold-leaf electroscope. In this instrument the total ionization is integrated over a defined period of time. The details of this type of electroscope are seen in Figure 4-3. Within the ionization chamber, an insulated L-shaped wire supports a delicate gold-plated quartz fiber. A microscope tube is so mounted that the end of the quartz fiber is in focus against a transparent scale. The quartz fiber and supporting wire assembly are charged by an external battery through a charging terminal. When charged, the end of the flexible quartz fiber is repelled by the supporting wire. As a source of ionizing radiation is brought near and ionization occurs within the chamber, the ions are collected on the quartz fiber assembly. This reduces its charge and the quartz fiber moves back toward the supporting wire. This motion can be observed against the scale. The rate of this movement is directly proportional to the amount of ionization occurring in the ionization chamber during the observation period.

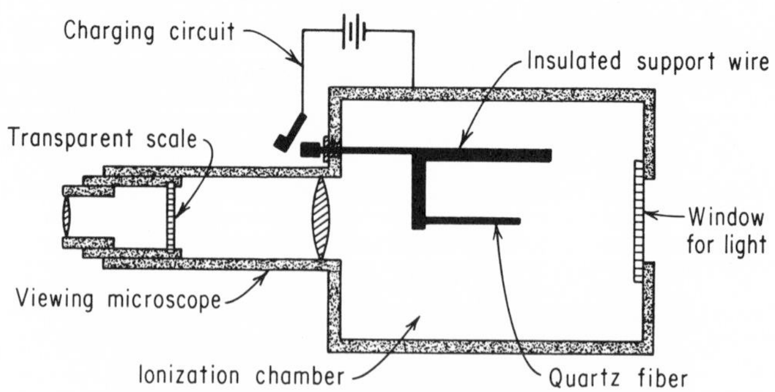

Figure 4-3. Diagram of a Lauritsen electroscope.

Electroscopes are not in common use for radiotracer assay because of the length of time required for each determination. This type of instrument, however, can measure respectable levels of activity without being overwhelmed (in contrast to the common Geiger-Mueller counter) and can be constructed in a readily portable form. Since the electroscope measures total ionization occurring per unit time, it is useful for determinations of radiation dose. The familiar pocket dosimeter, worn by personnel in radiation hazard areas, is essentially a miniaturized version of the electroscope just described.

c. *Ion chamber—electrometers.* The second major type of integrating instrument, the electrometer, amplifies and measures the current from the ionization chamber. Several methods of achieving the degree of amplification required are available. Those which employ vacuum-tube circuits to amplify d-c pulses are frequently used in portable, battery-operated monitoring devices. These, however, lack the degree of precision needed for radiotracer assay in the laboratory, largely because of the inherent instability of d-c amplifiers when used with such extremely small currents.

The *vibrating-reed electrometer*, also known as a dynamic capacitor electrometer, circumvents the problem of amplifying small d-c currents. In this instrument, one plate of the dynamic capacitor is mechanically driven so that it vibrates at a frequency of several hundred cycles per second. The direct current from the ionization chamber flows into this continuously varying capacitor, and accordingly, an alternating current is produced. This alternating current may now be amplified by a stable a-c amplifier, and then rectified.

The magnitude of the amplified ion current from the ionization chamber may be determined by one of two methods. First, the current may be passed through a calibrated resistor, and the equilibrium voltage across the resistor measured. Secondly, the ion current may be allowed to charge a calibrated capacitor, and the rate of charge across the known capacitor measured. In general, the first method of measurement (*potential-drop*) is used with large ion currents; the second (*rate-of-charge*) is used where highest sensitivity is desired. In either method some calibration is necessary to equate the magnitude of the current observed with the amount of radioactivity being assayed.

The vibrating-reed electrometer system has several noteworthy features. It allows highly precise measurements to be made over a wider range of sample activities ($5 \times 10^{-5} \cdots 10^{3}\ \mu c$) than any other type of detector. This system is sufficiently versatile to accommodate solid, liquid, or gaseous samples. A common practice is to fill the ion chamber with gaseous samples. In practice, these gaseous samples have been almost entirely limited to ^{14}C- or ^{3}H-labeled compounds, since biological samples containing them can usually be readily transformed into a gaseous state. The counting efficiency for stationary gas samples of such low-energy beta-emitting isotopes approaches 100 per cent with a 1-liter ion chamber. It is also possible to measure the radioactivity associated with flowing gas samples. Note that the detection efficiency declines sharply with smaller sizes of ion chambers. Here the counting efficiency is heavily dependent on both flow rate and ion chamber volume and is usually somewhat lower than for stationary samples. With liquid or solid samples, it is necessary to cover the samples with an open-end ion chamber, so that the ionization of the chamber atmosphere by the liquid or solid radioactive samples can be measured.

A common use of the electrometer system is to measure $^{14}CO_2$ in the respiratory flow of air from an organism metabolizing a ^{14}C-labeled compound. (Experiment B, Part Three, illustrates this type of application; for further discussion, see the references accompanying that experiment.) Brownell and Lockhart (13) have reviewed methods of $^{14}CO_2$ measurement by means of the electrometer; Springwell (17) has described ion current measurements of aqueous solutions containing ^{14}C. Tolbert (18) gives the most thorough and practical coverage of electrometer assay of radioactive gases.

In summary, simple ionization chamber instruments are quite stable and normally require only minimal associated electronic circuitry. Their relatively low voltage requirements make them well suited for use as battery-operated, portable radiation detectors. As such, they are more frequently used for radiation health purposes than for accurate radiotracer analyses. In general, they are not employed as differentiating pulse detectors, but to measure the integrated rate, or total amount of ionization occurring.

2. With Gas Amplification

It has been previously pointed out that the basic problem with the simple ionization chamber is the exceedingly small pulse produced in it by an individual ionizing particle. A high degree of external amplification is required in order to measure these individual pulses. Such amplification is difficult because of the noises and instabilities associated with electronic circuitry. A simple type of amplification within the ion chamber itself would be more desirable, so that the output pulse would already be of measurable size. Fortunately, this is possible.

a. The nature of gas amplification. In a simple ionization chamber operating at the potential of the saturation current, essentially all the ions produced by an incident ionizing particle are collected. This is due to the effect of the potential gradient between the chamber electrodes which accelerates the ions and allows them to be collected at the electrodes before substantial ion recombination can occur. If the potential in the chamber is increased beyond that required to produce saturation current, the negative ions (electrons) will be accelerated toward the anode at a rather high velocity. This will result in the ionization of gas atoms in the chamber, much the same as the ionization caused by the primary beta particles. The secondary ions so formed are accelerated by the prevailing potential gradient, thus producing still more ionization. Thus, from a few primary ion pairs, a geometrical increase results in a veritable torrent of ions moving toward the chamber electrodes. The process described is known as *gas amplification*; the flood of ions produced is termed the *Townsend avalanche* in honor of the discoverer of this phenomenon. As a result of gas amplification, a very large number of electrons are collected at the anode within a microsecond or less from a single beta particle in the chamber. A strong pulse is thereby formed and fed into the external circuit, which can be directly measured after only a low magnitude of amplification.

As the potential gradient between the electrodes of the ionization chamber is further increased, the number of electrons, mostly secondary, reaching the anode rises sharply for a given original ionization event from either an alpha or beta particle. Eventually, a potential will be reached at which the chamber undergoes continuous discharge and is no longer usable as a detector. Figure 4-4 shows that there are three distinct po-

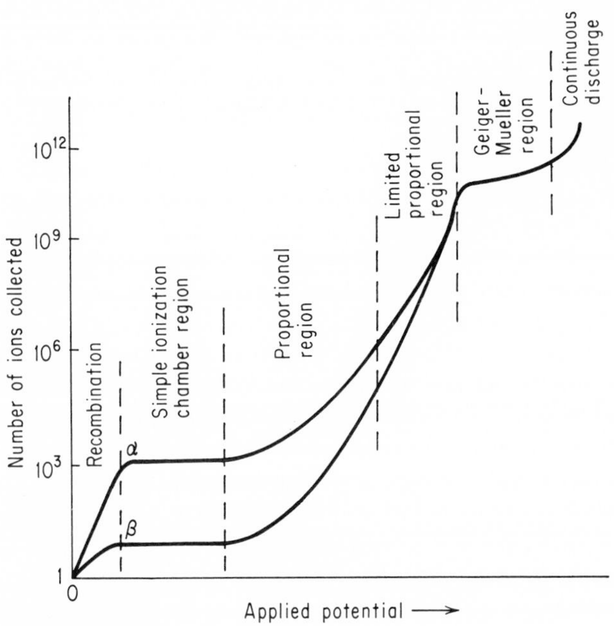

Figure 4-4. Relation of pulse size to potential gradient in an ionization chamber.

tential regions between the saturation current and continuous discharge, namely, the proportional region, the limited proportional region, and the Geiger-Mueller region. One should not deduce from the graph that a given ionization chamber can be readily operated in any of these regions by a mere change of potential gradient. Normally, chambers are designed to be operated in a particular region under specific conditions of internal pressure and potential. Moreover, the potential gradient needed to define each region is dependent on many factors, including the filling gas, chamber size, and so on.

b. *The proportional region.* This region is so named because of the proportionality observed between the charge collected and the extent of the initial ionization. In detectors operating in the *proportional region*, the number of ions forming an output pulse is very much greater than, yet proportional to, the number formed by the initial ionization. Gas amplification factors ("A" values) of the order of 10^3–10^4 are commonly obtained. The amplification factor is primarily dependent on the composition of the chamber filling gas and the potential gradient. At a given potential, the "A" value is the same for all ionizing events. Consequently, if an alpha particle traversing the ionization chamber causes 10^5 primary ion pairs, with an amplification factor of 10^3, a charge equivalent to 10^8 electrons would be collected at the anode. An incident beta particle, on the other hand, producing only 10^3 ion pairs, would, after amplification by the factor of 10^3, result in a collected charge equivalent to only 10^6 electrons.

As in the case of simple ionization chambers, then, it is possible in the proportional region to differentiate between alpha and beta particles on the basis of pulse size. This is one advantage of operating a detector in this region. Because the amplification factor in the proportional region is so heavily dependent on the applied potential, it is necessary to employ highly stable high voltage supplies.

The avalanche of electrons in proportional detectors is collected on only a portion of the anode wire, usually the tip. Furthermore, only a small fraction of the gas volume of the ionization chamber is involved in the formation of ions. These characteristics make for a very short *dead time*, that is, the interval during which ion pairs from a previous ionization event are being collected and the chamber is rendered unresponsive to a new ionizing particle. Ionization chambers operating in the proportional region are thus inactivated for only 5–50 μsec following each ionization event.

c. *The limited proportional region.* The next potential region is similar to the proportional region in operating characteristics, with one important exception: the extent of gas amplification possible has an upper limit set by the size of the detector chamber, the form of the collecting electrode, and the number of gas atoms present. As this limit is approached, ionization extends essentially throughout the entire chamber involving nearly all the available gas atoms, and electrons are collected along the entire length of anode wire. At potentials above this limit there is insufficient "ion space" in the chamber to accommodate all the ion pairs which theoretically could be formed. At first, this limits the amplification possible only for highly ionizing radiation, such as alpha particles.

Let it be assumed, for example, that the total number of ion pairs that a given chamber can accommodate is limited to 10^{10} ion pairs, and an "A" value of 10^7 is obtained at the potential being used. An incident alpha particle that created 10^5 primary ion pairs could be amplified by a factor of only 10^5, to a maximum of 10^{10} (instead of 10^{12}) ion pairs. Under the same conditions, a low E_{max} beta particle initiating only 10^2 primary ion pairs would be amplified to a collected charge of 10^9 electrons. Accordingly, in these circumstances, the proportionality between primary ionization and collected charge is limited, and the distinction between alpha and beta particles is minimized. This will be observed by the convergence of the curves for alpha and beta radiation in Figure 4-4. For this reason the limited proportional region is not normally used for purposes of detection.

d. *The Geiger-Mueller region.* At still higher potential gradients, the "A" value may reach 10^8. Now even a weak beta particle or gamma ray is able to initiate sufficient ion pair formation to completely fill the available "ion space" in the chamber. Consequently, the size of the charge collected on the anode is no longer dependent on the number of primary ions produced; hence, it is no longer possible to distinguish between the various types of radiation. This potential level is called the *Geiger-Mueller region*, after the German physicists who first investigated it. Ionization chambers operated in this potential region are commonly called Geiger-Mueller (G-M) detectors. Since maximal gas amplification is realized in this region, the size of the output pulse from the detector will remain the same over a considerable voltage range until continuous discharge occurs. This fact makes it possible to use a less expensive high-voltage supply than that required for proportional detectors.

Dead time: Employing a very high amplification factor in the Geiger region is not without problems. One of these is the longer dead time of the chamber. Following the passage of an ionizing particle through a detector, an electron avalanche occurs along the entire anode wire. This gives rise to a cylindrical space charge of positive ions with respect to the anode. The number of such positive ions per pulse will be one or more orders of magnitude greater than in chambers operated in the proportional region. To be discharged, this mass of positive ions must migrate to the cathode wall. Being much more massive than the electrons, these ions move at a considerably slower velocity in the electrical field. During this migration, the chamber is unresponsive to any new ionizing particles passing through it. Thus, the dead time of a detector operated in the Geiger region is from 100–200 μsec or more. The importance of this characteristic in radioactivity determinations is considered in Chapter 9.

Quenching: Another important problem is the perpetuated chamber ionization resulting from complications associated with the discharge of positive ions at the cathode wall of a detector. As a positive ion approaches the cathode, it attracts an electron from the wall and becomes a neutral atom. The newly acquired electron, however, tends to reside at an orbit having a higher energy state in comparison with that of the electron originally ejected during ionization. The newly acquired electron will soon fall to the ground state orbital in the atom, and the surplus energy so resulting is released in the form of electromagnetic radiation. The magnitude of the energy involvement is generally in the region of ultraviolet or soft X radiation. Such radiations are basically similar to gamma radiation and are capable of creating ionization events via the intermediary formation of secondary electrons. Thus, a new avalanche of ion pairs will be formed and self-perpetuating ionization will prevail in the chamber, rendering the detector unresponsive to incoming ionizing particles.

Hence, we need a means of terminating, or "*quenching*" the perpeutal ionization in the detector. Earlier methods to this end were in the nature of an *external quench*, which relied on the momentary reduction of the potential gradient across the detecting chamber. This was accomplished by either a suitable external resistance or an external electronic circuit which lowered the potential across the electrodes for a sufficiently long period to allow all positive ion discharge and secondary photoelectron production to cease. The entire process was rather slow, however, and accentuated the dead time of this type of detector.

More recently, certain gaseous compounds have been introduced into the commonly used inert gas atmosphere of G-M detectors to serve as quenching agents. This process is generally known as *internal quenching*, or self-quenching. Two different types of quenching gases are in common use: polyatomic organic compounds and halogen gases.

Choosing as an example ethyl alcohol vapor (one of the commonest organic compounds used), the chain of events in quenching action may be followed: As they move toward the cathode wall, positive ions of the inert filling gas (usually argon, helium, or neon) collide with alcohol molecules. Since the quenching gas has a lower ionization potential than the inert gas, for example, argon, the net result is that the positive argon ions are discharged into neutral argon atoms, while the alcohol molecules are ionized. The positive alcohol ions then migrate to the cathode wall, pick up electrons, and become neutral ethyl alcohol molecules. But instead of releasing their surplus excitation energy as electromagnetic radiation, leading to a perpetuated pulse in the tube, the alcohol molecules irreversibly dissociate chemically into degradation products. This is an effective quenching mechanism, but has the obvious disadvantage that, since a quenching gas molecule is destroyed after each discharge event, the life of the detector is finite. The useful life of such an organic-quenched tube is about 10^8–10^{10} pulses.

In halogen-quenched tubes, on the other hand, the dissociated molecules of the quenching gas readily recombine. In this way, quenching occurs without irreversible loss of the quenching gas. Theoretically at least, the useful life of such a G-M detector is infinite. Bromine or chlorine is commonly employed for this purpose. Unlike the uniform quenching action in organic-filled detectors, the halogen-quenched G-M tubes may show considerable variation in quenching efficiency for various portions of the chamber volume. This limits their use to applications not requiring a high degree of precision, such as radiation monitoring.

3. Proportional Detectors

a. Construction. The operation and characteristics of a complete proportional counting assembly are discussed in Experiment II, Part Two. Only the detector itself will be considered here. Detectors made to operate in the proportional region have taken many forms. The commercially produced detectors used in radiotracer assay are commonly either of the cylindrical end-window type (much like the G-M detector shown in Figure 4-7*A*) or the hemispherical windowed or windowless variety (Figure 4-5*B*). A variety of specialized proportional detectors has been developed, of which the Bernstein-Ballentine internal gas counter (Figure 4-5*A*) is a good example.

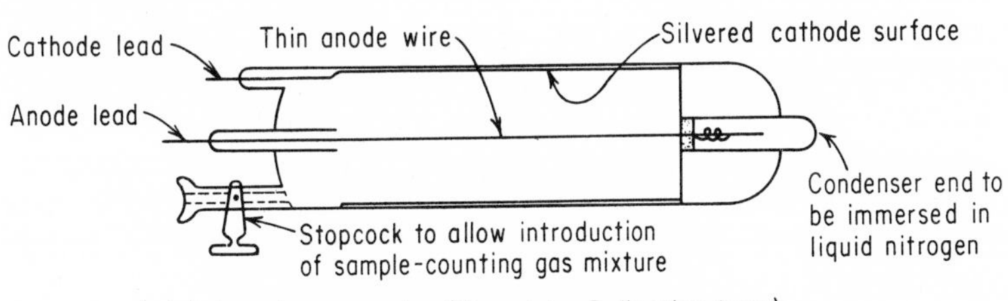

(a) Internal gas counter (Bernstein-Ballentine type)

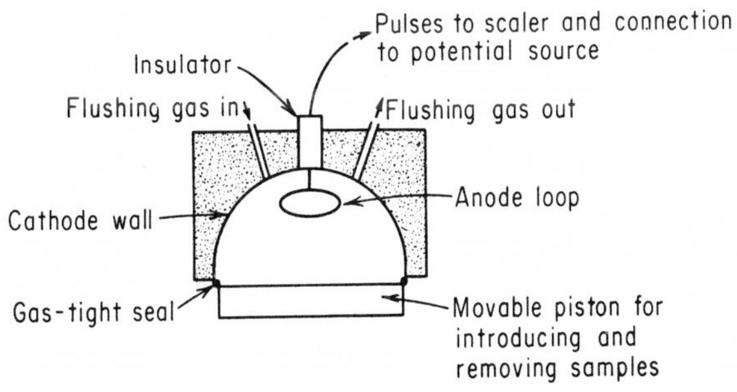

(b) Windowless hemispherical detector (also used as G-M detector)

Figure 4-5. Common forms of proportional detectors.

A distinctive characteristic of the proportional detector is the very fine wire used for the anode. This is essential in order to produce a steep potential gradient immediately around the anode for maximal gas amplification. By contrast, the collecting electrode of the simple ionization chamber often consists of a thick rod. The cylindrical form of a proportional detector (Figure 4-7*A*) utilizes a straight wire anode, whereas in the hemispherical detector (Figure 4-5*B*) the anode wire is shaped into a loop for optimal performance (19).

Since one advantage of operating a detector in the proportional region is the ability to distinguish alpha particles either alone or in the presence of beta radiation, it is necessary that weakly penetrating alpha particles be permitted to reach the sensitive volume of the detector. With the cylindrical variety of detector a very thin window of split mica or mylar plastic covers one end of the tube. This can be so thin (down to 150 $\mu g/cm^2$) that the absorption of alpha particles by the window is not too extensive. An even more efficient arrangement is found with the hemispherical detector, where the radioactive sample can be introduced directly into the detector chamber. Such windowless detectors are widely used for alpha and weak beta particle counting.

With either ultrathin end-window or windowless detectors a certain amount of air leaks into the counting chamber. Both the oxygen and nitrogen of the air reduce the detection efficiency. Detectors of this variety, therefore, must be purged with an appropriate counting gas before counting is started and continually flushed at a lower flow rate during the counting operation. For this reason, such chambers are often called *gas flow detectors*. The operating potential of the chamber is determined to a large extent by the gases using for the foregoing purpose. Argon, methane, or a 90 per cent argon–10 per cent methane mixture known as P-10 gas are commonly used counting gases.

A unique feature of the proportional detector is that a radioactive gaseous sample can actually be incorporated in the detector filling-gas mixture. A detector operated in this manner is known as an *internal gas counter*. The detector designed by Bernstein and Ballentine (12) shown in Figure 4-5*A* utilizes a $^{14}CO_2$-methane counting gas mixture. The gas mixture is introduced into the detector through the stopcock from a vacuum line manifold. In other internal gas counters, carbon dioxide alone is used as the filling gas.

A proportional detector must be connected to accessory equipment, such as a high voltage supply, amplifier, and scaler, so that the pulses produced may be properly registered. The functions of these components are discussed in Experiment II, Part Two.

b. *Operating characteristics.* When the count rate of a sample emitting both alpha and beta particles is determined over the voltage range of a proportional detector and the data are plotted, the results are as seen in Figure 4-6. This curve should be carefully distinguished from the plot illustrated in Figure 4-4, which shows the variation of charge collected for a *single* ionizing particle. The *characteristic curve* for a proportional detector exhibits two plateaus. The plateau at the lower potentials represents alpha radiation alone because, at this potential range, only the alpha particles, with their much greater specific ionization, produce pulses large enough to be detected by the associated circuitry. Not only may the alpha particles thus be counted apart from accompanying beta radiation at this potential, but the background radiation counting rate (primarily cosmic rays and gamma rays) is extremely low—of the order of a few counts per hour.

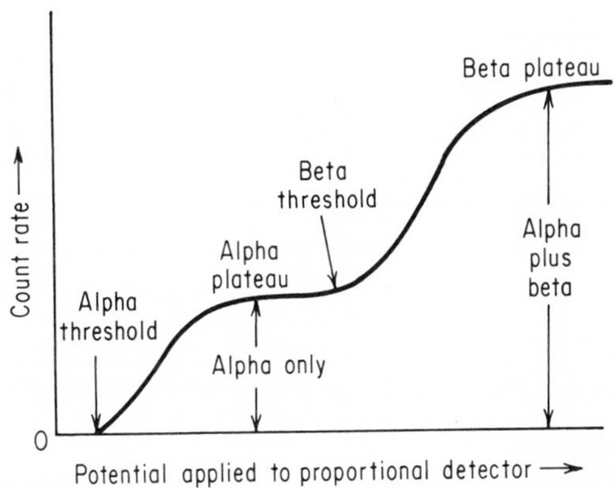

Figure 4-6. Characteristic curve for a proportional detector.

As the potential gradient is increased, the amplification factor becomes greater. Eventually, the primary ions produced by the most energetic beta particles are amplified sufficiently to produce pulses large enough to be recorded. This point represents the *beta threshold*. Further increase in potential gradient allows even the pulses from the weaker beta particles to be registered. The *beta plateau* has now been reached. The count rate here actually represents alpha plus beta radiation. The efficiency of the proportional detector for gamma radiation is so low that it is seldom used for gamma counting.

4. Geiger-Mueller Detectors

a. *Construction.* The operation and characteristics of complete Geiger-Mueller counting assemblies are described in Experiment I, Part Two. Only the G-M detector itself will be discussed here. This detector

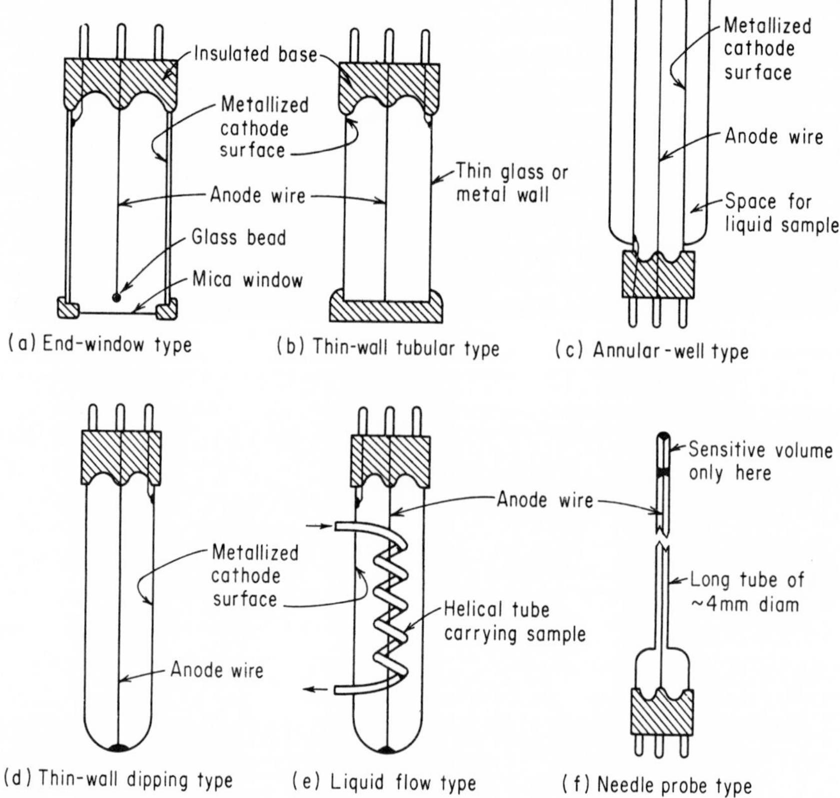

Figure 4-7. Various forms of G-M detectors.

is the most widely used of all types of radiation detectors. In general construction, it does not differ significantly from the proportional detectors previously discussed. A G-M tube conventionally takes the form of a cylindrical cathode about 1–1.5 in. in diameter by 4–8 in. in length. A fine central wire is suspended from insulation at one or both ends of the tube to act as the collecting anode. The cylindrical cathode may be of metal or of glass with an applied metallic film. Sensitivity to gamma rays may be increased by using a bismuth coating on the inside of the cylinder as a cathode.

The G-M detector tube is filled with a gas mixture, usually at a reduced pressure. A readily ionizable, inert gas (argon, helium, neon) makes up the bulk of the gas filling; only a small amount of organic or halogen gas is introduced as the quenching agent. Windowless G-M flow detectors, mostly hemispherical in shape, are similar to the corresponding proportional detectors in construction. They also must be flushed continuously with a special gas mixture made up of about 99 per cent helium and 1 per cent butane, or isobutane.

A broad range of different G-M tube varieties is commercially available (19). Figure 4-7 illustrates some of these. The end-window type (a) is the most widely used for radiotracer assay. A variety of end-window materials are used. By employing a window of split mica 1–2 mg/cm^2 in thickness, it is possible to obtain the transmission of approximately two-thirds to three-fourths of even the weak beta particles from ^{14}C into the sensitive volume of the detector (see Figure 3-10). Tubes with thicker windows would be utilized primarily for assay of more energetic beta emitters. Ultrathin windows (less than 150 $\mu g/cm^2$) of mylar plastic will transmit even alpha particles, but such tubes must be operated as flow detectors to counteract the inward diffusion of air. With the windowless flow chamber (see Figure 4-5b), the maximum detection efficiency is obtained, but this detector type allows the possibility of contamination of the interior of the chamber by radioactive dust or adsorbed vapors.

G-M tubes designed primarily for monitoring (*b*) are commonly constructed with thin glass (about 30 mg/cm^2) or metal cylindrical walls. This restricts their use to detection of more energetic beta particles or gamma rays. Such tubes are commonly mounted in probes equipped with adjustable metal "beta shields," which optionally allow gamma rays to be detected to the exclusion of beta radiation.

Tube types *c*, *d*, and *e* were developed for use with radioactive solutions. In the case of type *c*, the solution is poured into the annular space around the tube; type *d* is actually dipped into a radioactive solution in a separate container. The design of type *e* was developed for use with a flow of radioactive liquid. Their necessarily thick, glass walls render these tubes rather inefficient for beta detection. Since they are gas filled, gamma rays are not readily detected by them either. In addition, there is the constant problem of radioactive contamination adhering to the outside of the tube. Hence, these three tube types are no longer in common use. Hidalgo, et al. (14), have described a simplified liquid-sample G-M detector which is of value for a specific purpose.

The needle probe detector (*f*) is an example of a highly specialized G-M tube, which illustrates the versatility of design possible with this type of detector. Such tubes have a minute sensitive volume located at the tip of the long, thin probe. They are thus useful in precisely locating radioactive implants or concentrations of radioisotopes in patients.

Lead shielding around the detector proper is commonly used to reduce the background radiation count rate. In some circumstances even this reduced background radiation level cannot be tolerated because of the very low specific activity of the counting sample. This is particularly the case in ^{14}C age-dating measurements. Here, specially designed *low background counters* may prove necessary. These typically consist of an "umbrella" of guard G-M detectors surrounding the sample detector. Anticoincidence circuitry is employed so that external background radiation, mainly high-energy particles, passing through both the guard detectors and the sample detector is not registered. Only pulses originating in the sample detector alone are registered. Thus, background count rates of only a few counts per hour are obtainable.

The G-M tube must be connected to some accessory components, such as a ratemeter or scaler, so that its output pulses may be registered. An external high-voltage supply is also required. Descriptions of these components and details of the operation of the entire counting assembly are given in Experiment I, Part Two.

b. *Operating characteristics.* A plot of the count rate from a fixed radioactive source with increasing potential applied to the G-M tube is shown in Figure 4-8. Do not confuse this with the plot illustrated in

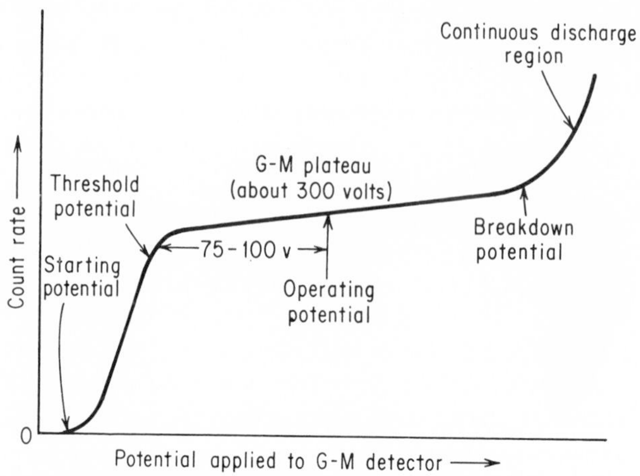

Figure 4-8. Characteristic curve for a G-M detector.

Figure 4-4, which shows the size of the pulse collected for a *single* ionizing particle at different detector potentials. The characteristic curve first shows a sharp rise in counting rate (*starting potential*), where only the most energetic beta particles cause the tube to go into discharge. At the *threshold potential* this rise levels off onto a plateau of perhaps 300 volts length. The extent and slope of this plateau is a measure of the quality of a G-M tube (16). When the detector is operated within the plateau range, every ionization event occurring in the tube causes a measurable pulse. Eventually, the curve displays a second rise with a higher potential gradient. Here the potential across the detector electrodes is so high that spontaneous discharges can occur in the tube without immediate ionizing radiation. The tube should never be operated in this region or it may be irreparably damaged. The exact potentials in volts on the abscissa of the plot are not stated, because these will vary widely with different tube types and filling-gas combinations. In general, the starting potential of commercially available G-M detectors ranges from 700 volts for halogen quenched tubes to 1200 volts for organic quenched tubes.

G-M tubes are nearly 100 per cent efficient in detecting alpha and beta particles that reach their sensitive volume, but only about 1 per cent efficient in detecting gamma rays. The chief difficulty in the detection of alpha and soft (low-energy) beta radiation involves the extent of absorption occurring in the tube window or wall. Once inside, the high specific ionization of alpha and beta radiation assures the initiation of a discharge. The great penetrating power of gamma rays, which enables them to pass through the walls of a G-M tube readily, unfortunately allows nearly all these photons to traverse the filling gas without causing ionization and thus escape detection.

5. Summary of Gas Ionization Detectors

In review, we compare the advantages and disadvantages of detectors operated in the simple ion chamber, proportional, and Geiger regions. We present specific examples of detectors most commonly employed for radiotracer assay in these three regions.

The *ion chamber* used in conjunction with a vibrating-reed electrometer is best employed for precise measurement of low-energy beta particles. It is highly stable and requires only a low chamber potential. A disadvantage of this instrument is that, to achieve maximum counting efficiency, the sample must be introduced in a gaseous form into the ion chamber. Under these conditions it is also possible to determine rather large total activities (as much as 1 mc in a sample). Since here no gas amplification occurs in the ion chamber, the weak ionization current produced requires a very high gain amplification.

Proportional detectors are commonly operated as thin window or windowless flow counters. In this form, their high alpha and beta detection efficiency is best used to advantage. In addition, alpha and beta radiation can be readily distinguished by means of proportional detectors. Probably their chief advantage is that the very short resolving time inherent in these detectors allows determination of very high count rates without significant coincidence loss. Their principal disadvantage lies in the higher gain amplification required, which necessitates more costly electronic accessory components than for *G-M detectors*.

The most widely used G-M tube for radiotracer assay is the thin end-window variety. With this type, beta particles are readily detected, with, of course, decreased efficiency for low-energy beta radiation. The end-window tube is also generally simpler to operate compared to windowless flow detectors. Owing to higher gas amplification factors in the G-M chamber, its output pulses need only moderate amplification, resulting in less costly accessory electronic components. Perhaps the greatest disadvantage of the G-M detector is its long resolving time, which seriously limits the activity of samples that can be assayed by it. (For a comparison of the relative merits of proportional and G-M detectors see reference 15.)

BIBLIOGRAPHY

Detection in General

1. Bleuler, Ernst, and George J. Goldsmith. 1952. Experimental nucleonics. Holt, Rinehart and Winston, Inc., New York. 393 p.
2. Bruner, H. D., and Jesse D. Perkinson, Jr. 1952. A comparison of iodine-131 counting methods. Nucleonics 10(10):57–61.
3. Christman, David R. 1961. Choosing a method for counting soft betas. Nucleonics 19(5):51–55.
4. Jordan, W. H. Detection of nuclear particles. 1952. Ann. Rev. Nuclear Sci. 1:207–244.
5. Nokes, M. C. 1958. Radioactivity measuring instruments. Philosophical Library, New York. 75 p.
6. Pearson, F. J., and R. R. Osborne. 1960. Practical nucleonics. E. & F. N. Spon, Ltd., London. 208 p.
7. Price, William J. Nuclear radiation detection. 1958. McGraw-Hill Book Company, New York. 382 p.
8. Sharpe, J. Nuclear radiation measurement. 1960. Simmons-Boardman, New York. 71 p.
9. Snell, Arthur H. (ed.). 1962. Nuclear instruments and their uses. Vol. I. John Wiley & Sons, Inc., New York. 494 p.
10. Washtell, C. C. H. 1960. An introduction to radiation counters and detectors. Philosophical Library, New York. 115 p.
11. Wolfgang, Richard, and C. F. Mackay. 1958. New proportional counters for gases and vapors. Nucleonics 16(10):69–73.

Gas Ionization Detection

12. Bernstein, W., and R. Ballentine. 1950. Gas phase counting of low energy beta-emitters. Rev. Sci. Instruments 21:158–162.
13. Brownell, Gordon L., and Helen S. Lockhart. 1952. CO_2 ion-chamber techniques for radiocarbon measurement. Nucleonics 10(2):26–32.

14. Hidalgo, J. V., S. B. Nadler, and R. T. Niesets. 1953. A simplified liquid-sample geiger counter. Nucleonics 11(2):66–67.

15. Proportional vs. Geiger counters. 10 June 1960. Picker Scintillator (Picker X-Ray Corp.) 4:1–4.

16. Reddis, J. S., and Wm. C. Roesch. 1956. Two better ways to determine Geiger-Mueller-tube age. Nucleonics 14(7):30–32.

17. Springell, P. H. 1960. Ionization current measurement of aqueous solutions containing C^{14}. Intern. J. Appl. Radiation Isotopes 9:88–93.

18. Tolbert, B. M. 1956. Ionization chamber assay of radioactive gases. University of California Radiation Laboratory, UCRL-3499. 47p.

19. Van Duuren, K., A. J. M. Jaspers, and J. Hermsen. 1959. G-M counters. Nucleonics 17(6):86–94.

20. Williams, A., and R. I. Sara. 1962. Parameters affecting the resolution of a proportional counter. Intern. J. Appl. Radiation Isotopes 13:229–238.

CHAPTER FIVE

Measurement of Radioactivity by the Solid (External-Sample) Scintillation Method

A. BASIC FACETS OF THE SCINTILLATION PHENOMENON

Historically the scintillation phenomenon was in common use early in this century as a means of detecting alpha particles. Because the method involved the tedious visual observation and recording of faint scintillations, it fell into disuse with the advent of gas ionization detectors. The development during World War II, of suitable photomultiplier tubes, which permitted electronic detection and recording of individual scintillation events, brought a resurgence of interest in the scintillation method. Since that time a very rapid expansion of scintillation detector types and applications has occurred.

In the radiation detectors described in Chapter 4, the detection process involved the collection of ion pairs produced as a result of the interaction of radiation with gas in an enclosed chamber. Scintillation detection, on the contrary, is based on the interaction of radiation with substances known as *fluors* (solid or liquid), or scintillators. (The term *phosphor* has often been used for compounds of this type, but the implied relation between phosphor and phosphorescence may create a misleading impression.) Excitation of the electrons in the fluor leads to the subsequent emission of a flash of light (scintillation). An adjacent photomultiplier tube converts such photons into an electronic pulse whose magnitude is proportional to the energy lost by the incident radiation in the excitation of the fluor. Thus scintillation detection is proportional in nature and, when used with a pulse height analyzer, allows determination of the energy spectrum of the incident radiation. Comprehensive discussions of the scintillation mechanism and its application to radiation detectors are found in the work of Curran (5), Birks (2), and Krebs (11).

It is difficult to arrive at a consistent classification of scintillation detectors. The fluor substances may be grouped into two broad categories: inorganic (ionic) and organic fluors. *Inorganic fluors* are normally used in the form of single, large crystals. *Organic fluors*, by contrast, may be employed as single crystals, as a compact mass of fine crystals, as a copolymer in a solid plastic, or dissolved in an organic solvent (liquid fluor). The scintillation process in organic and inorganic fluors differs somewhat. In organic fluors, scintillation is primarily a molecular phenomenon and is marked by a transfer of excitation energy from molecule to molecule. Scintillation in inorganic fluors, on the other hand, results primarily from the electronic excitation in the solid state and the presence of specific activating "impurities" in the crystalline lattice. Further, photon decay times in crystals are of the order of microseconds, whereas, in plastic fluors and liquid scintillators, they are of the order of millimicroseconds. Thus, crystal fluors are relatively slow.

Scintillation detectors may also be categorized according to the relation of the sample and the fluor. In the case of *external-sample* scintillation detectors, radiation from an external source interacts with a fluor (usually a single crystal or plastic block), which is coupled to a photomultiplier. If the radioactive sample and the fluor are in intimate contact (dissolved in a common solvent, or one suspended in a solution of the other) and placed adjacent to one or more photomultipliers, an *internal-sample* scintillation detector results. This arrangement is most commonly referred to as a *liquid scintillation* detector. In this text, scintillation detectors are somewhat arbitrarily divided into external-sample (employing solid fluors) and internal-sample (usually involving liquid fluors) detectors. The first type is described in the remainder of this chapter; Chapter 6 deals with internal-sample detectors.

B. SOLID EXTERNAL-SAMPLE SCINTILLATION DETECTORS

1. Mechanism of Solid Scintillation Detection

Scintillation detection involves a series of energy conversions from the initial interaction of the radiation with the fluor until an output electronic pulse leaves the photomultiplier. These steps will be discussed in their normal sequence, primarily emphasizing gamma ray detection by ionic crystal fluors. Figure 5-1 will aid the reader in visualizing the various portions of a typical scintillation detector in relation to these energy con-

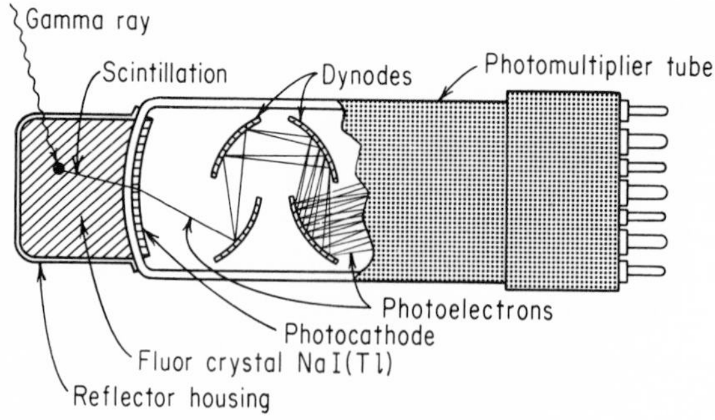

Figure 5-1. Diagram of a typical solid fluor (external sample) scintillation detector.

version steps. Detailed information concerning the various detector components themselves is presented later in the chapter.

a. Energy transfer in the fluor crystal. As a gamma ray traverses a fluor crystal, it may dissipate some of its energy (see Chapter 3). The extent of this energy dissipation is directly related to the density and thickness of the fluor substance. It will be recalled that gamma rays commonly interact with matter by means of three distinct processes: pair production, Compton effect, and the photoelectric process. In each case electrons are ejected, and these in turn can produce excitation or ionization of adjacent portions of the fluor crystal. It is this *secondary excitation* of the fluor that is particularly important here. The total amount of excitation produced in a fluor is directly related to the amount of energy dissipated by a traversing gamma ray.

Excitation of a fluor occurs when one of its orbital electrons is raised to a higher energy level as a result of energy dissipation by a passing charged particle. Immediate de-excitation occurs as the electron returns to its ground state and the excitation energy is emitted as a photon. It is at this point that a difference between the scintillation process in organic and inorganic crystals exists. In organic crystals, the events just described are distinctly *molecular* phenomena; in inorganic crystals, the excitation energy migrates to an *activator center* where de-excitation results in photon emission. Thus, ionic fluors normally require the presence of some activation substance for maximum light production efficiency, whereas organic fluors do not. In fact, organic fluors must be scrupulously purified.

Fluor substances are selected on the basis of emitting a high proportion of excitation energy as visible light (scintillations) with a wavelength near 4100 Å. The number of such photons produced is directly related to the amount of excitation energy resulting from a given gamma ray.

b. ***Energy transfer in the photomultiplier.*** The photons of visible light pass through the transparent fluor substance and out through a clear window to impinge on an adjacent photocathode. The typical photocathode is composed of a thin photosensitive layer (commonly a cesium-antimony alloy) on the inner surface of the end of the photomultiplier tube. Here impinging photons, particularly those having wavelengths between 3000 and 6000 Å are absorbed, with a consequent emission of photoelectrons. The number of photoelectrons ejected is less than, but directly related to, the number of incident photons. Such a burst of photoelectrons resulting from a single gamma ray interaction is still far too weak to be directly registered.

Amplification occurs by means of a series of electrodes, called *dynodes*, spaced along the length of the photomultiplier tube. Each dynode is maintained at a higher potential (usually about 100–200 volts higher) than the preceding one. By means of this arrangement, photoelectrons ejected from the photocathode are accelerated toward the first dynode. Striking the dynode surface, they bring about the secondary emission of a larger number of electrons. This new burst of electrons is attracted by the potential gradient to the second dynode in the series, where a still larger number of electrons is dislodged. This electron multiplying process continues at each dynode until at last the collecting anode is struck by 10^5–10^6 electrons for each original photoelectron ejected from the photocathode. Thus, the magnitude of the output pulse from the photomultiplier is directly related to the quantity of energy dissipated by the incident gamma photon in the fluor.

c. ***Proportionality of energy conversion.*** In order to present a quantitative example of the energy conversions involved in scintillation detection, we trace the results of the interaction of a single 1.17 Mev gamma ray from ^{60}Co with a thallium-activated sodium iodide crystal [NaI (Tl)]:

(1) If 20 per cent of the energy of the gamma ray is transferred to a fluor crystal, and if it is assumed that each excitation event requires an average of 10 ev, then approximately 23,400 excitations could result from this gamma photon.

(2) Assuming that only 5 per cent of the excitation events result in the production of photons of visible light which are seen by the adjacent photocathode, this would mean that about 1170 photons would reach the photocathode.

(3) This number of photons striking a photocathode with a conversion efficiency of 10 per cent would eject approximately 117 photoelectrons.

(4) The successive dynodes of a photomultiplier operated at an over-all gain of 10^6 could then amplify this quantity of photoelectrons so that 1.17×10^8 electrons would be collected at the photomultiplier anode, or a charge of approximately 2×10^{-11} coulomb.

(5) This charge could then be transformed by a preamplifier circuit with a capacitance of 30 $\mu\mu$f into an output pulse of about 0.6 volt. A pulse of this size would be capable of directly triggering the detecting circuitry of a scaler.

Cobalt-60 emits two gamma rays per disintegration. The other gamma ray has an energy of 1.33 Mev. Following the preceding calculations, this 1.33 Mev gamma would result in an output pulse of about 0.7 volt from the detector. It should be appreciated that such energy calculations are based on several variables and are only very crude approximations of true values. These calculations are important because they indicate that the size of the photomultiplier output pulse is directly proportional to the amount of energy dissipated in the fluor by the incident gamma photon. This relationship makes possible the determination of gamma ray energy when a pulse height analyzer is used with the detector, of which more will be said later.

d. *Other advantages.* In addition to the possibility of determining gamma ray energies, we may point out three other advantages of this type of detector: first, because the photons produced in the fluor have *decay times* of microseconds, very high counting rates can be recorded by scintillation counters with no coincidence loss. Secondly, in the example cited, ^{60}Co, the 0.314 Mev *beta particles* also emitted would not be detected appreciably, because the NaI (Tl) crystal is enclosed in an aluminum container, which absorbs most of the beta radiation. In addition, this fluor is not an efficient detector for external beta sources owing to excessive scattering. Thus, solid fluors offer an exclusive means of detecting gamma rays. Thirdly, the higher *densities* of solid fluors, as compared to gases or liquids, result in greater gamma ray stopping power and consequent increased detection efficiency.

e. *Photomultiplier thermal noise.* Unfortunately, scintillation detection is not without complications. The high potential applied between the photocathode and the dynodes in the photomultiplier also gives rise to thermionic emission. A certain number of photoelectrons will thus be emitted, even when no light falls on the photocathode. These produce small-sized pulses known as *thermal noise*, or *dark current.* Since the magnitude of thermal noise is dependent on the potential applied to the photomultiplier, this factor becomes important in determining the optimal operating potential of a scintillation detector (Experiment III).

Thermal noise may be minimized in several ways. Certain new photomultipliers have been designed with considerably reduced thermal noise levels. A simple pulse height discriminator circuit will bar the detection of the weaker noise pulses, while the larger gamma pulses are counted. In cases where the sample pulses do not greatly exceed the size of the noise pulses, other means must be employed. This is the problem in low-energy beta detection using liquid fluors, as will be discussed later. Suffice it to say that cooling the photomultipliers (10) and/or using coincidence circuitry all but eliminates the problem of thermal noise.

f. ***Gamma ray spectrometry.*** In determining the energy levels of gamma rays from a given nuclide (gamma spectrum), it would be highly desirable to have each incident gamma ray dissipate all its energy in the fluor by photoelectric absorption. In this case a *line spectrum*, as shown in Figure 5-2*A*, would be obtained. Partial energy dissipation by Compton interaction also occurs. Since any fraction of the gamma ray energy can be thus dissipated, a *continuous spectrum* (the "Compton smear") is

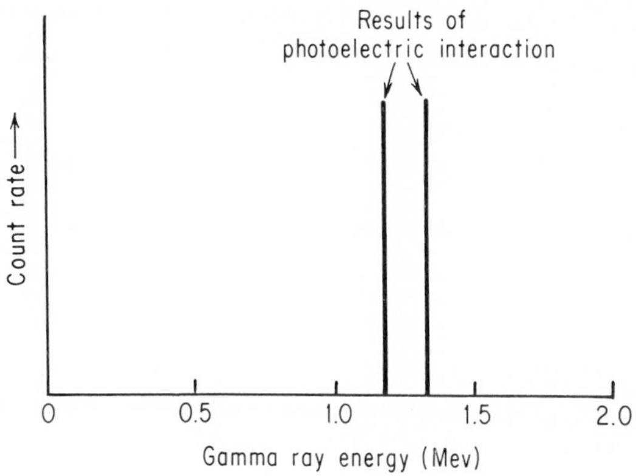

(a) Theoretical line spectrum for Co^{60}

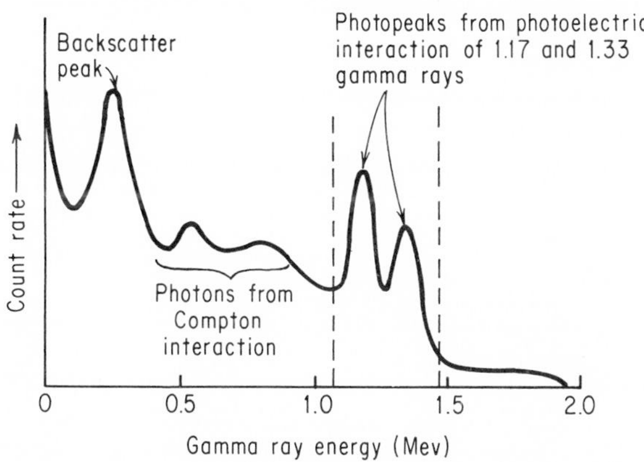

(b) Actual continuous spectrum for Co^{60}

Figure 5-2. Theoretical and actual gamma ray spectra for ^{60}Co.

produced. Interaction by pair production also complicates the spectrum, as well as a number of other factors. Figure 5-2*B* shows a typical gamma-ray spectrum for ^{60}Co. The precise interpretation of such gamma spectra is often quite difficult.

For simple gamma pulse counting (*integral counting*), these various modes of gamma interaction are of little consequence. In integral counting, only a single discriminator ("low gate") is employed. This is set to reject all pulses below a selected pulse height threshold in order to prevent undesirable noise pulses from being recorded (Figure 5-3*A*). Consequently, in this counting mode, all pulses above this discriminator level are counted whatever the type of gamma ray interaction that occasioned

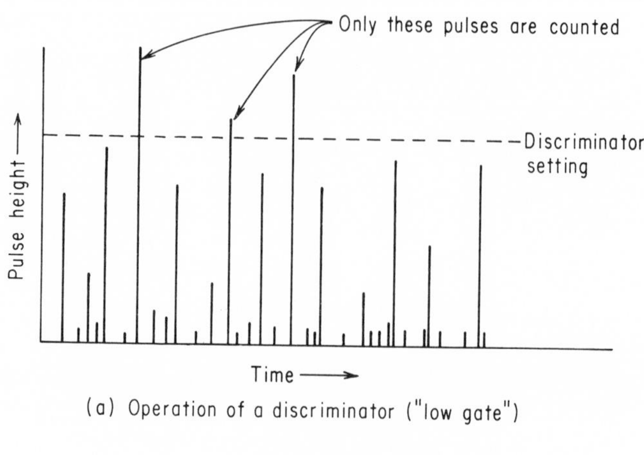

(a) Operation of a discriminator ("low gate")

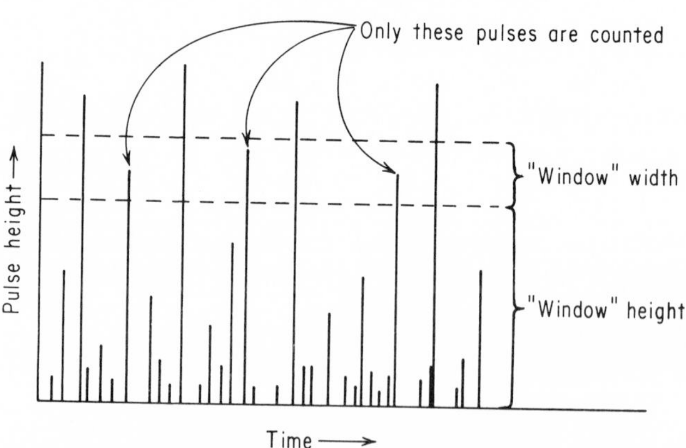

(b) Operation of a pulse height analyzer

Figure 5-3. Pulse height selection by means of single discriminators and pulse height analyzers.

them. In integral gamma pulse counting, however, a rather high background count rate is normally encountered.

The incorporation of a differential discriminator (pulse height analyzer) into the counting system makes possible *differential counting*. A pulse height analyzer consists basically of two discriminators which pass on to the recording device only those pulses whose heights lie between their settings, or in the "window" (channel). Figure 5-3*B* illustrates this counting mode. In most counting assemblies, these discriminators are continuously and independently variable, so that both window width and positioning on the pulse height scale may be adjusted at will. It is therefore possible to set the discriminators to "straddle" the photopeak(s) of a gamma-emitting sample (as shown by the dotted lines on Figure 5-2*B*). Of course, a much lower counting rate from the sample is now observed than from integral counting of the entire spectrum of pulses. The background counting rate in this small portion of the spectrum is, however, decreased proportionately to a much greater extent. Thus, the highest counting efficiency (maximum sample-to-background ratio) is achieved by such differential counting in the vicinity of the photopeak of a gamma-emitting radionuclide.

Differential gamma ray spectrometry finds application primarily in three different types of experimental work. Most obviously, it is the counting mode of choice where gamma-emitting samples with very low levels of radioactivity must be assayed. In experiments where two or more gamma-emitting radiotracers are in use simultaneously, gamma ray spectrometry allows them to be differentiated if their photopeak energies differ sufficiently. Since the gamma energy (photopeak position) is a distinguishing mark of a gamma-emitter, differential spectrometry is invaluable in identifying unknown radionuclides in a sample. [Crouthamel (4) has compiled an extensive set of typical gamma-ray spectra for a wide variety of radionuclides.] All three of these aspects are found in environmental radioactivity studies, where the distribution of fallout or reactor-produced radionuclides through the biosphere is traced (see Experiment E). For such purposes, *multichannel analyzers*, capable of differentiating and recording pulses in several hundred channels simultaneously, are commonly utilized. A more detailed discussion of gamma spectrometry is beyond the scope of this book. For further information, see the concise booklet published by the Baird-Atomic Company (1) or Crouthamel's (4) excellent book.

2. Components of Solid Scintillation Detectors

a. Detector housing. The entire scintillation detector is housed in a light-tight, thin metal cylinder. This gives mechanical protection to all components, as well as preventing stray light from reaching the photocathode while it is in operation. Protection against the effect of exterior magnetic fluxes on the photomultiplier is afforded by a Mu-metal shield. Where directional sensitivity is desired, a lead collimator may be fitted over the scintillation crystal. Incident radiation must pass through the light-tight enclosure around the fluor to interact and be detected. In the case of gamma rays, the thin aluminum "can" (about 0.03 in. thick) presents no absorption problem. For crystal fluors used to detect alpha or beta particles, however, ultrathin entrance windows of aluminum foil or aluminized Mylar film must be employed.

b. *Fluor crystals.* Scintillation crystals are commonly, but erroneously, referred to as *phosphors*. These crystals are used for radiation detection because they show very short-lived fluorescence following energy absorption and are thus technically *fluors*. If they were true phosphors, producing long-lasting phosphorescence, they would be quite unsuitable for this purpose.

As has been previously mentioned, the commonly used fluors can be divided into two categories: inorganic (ionic) crystals and organic crystals. The fluorescent property of the inorganic crystals is lost when the crystals are dissolved, but the organic fluors may be used either in crystalline form or dissolved. When dissolved in various organic solvents, they form *liquid fluors*, which will be further discussed in the next chapter. Organic fluors such as anthracene or *p*-terphenyl have also been used to impregnate polystyrene or polyvinyltoluene. In this form they are called *plastic fluors* and have the advantage of being formed or machined into a wide variety of shapes and sizes (3, 9). Plastic fluors give poor energy resolution and, thus, are not useful in spectrometry. Table 5-1 lists the properties of some common crystalline fluors. In addition, two reviews by Swank (16, 17) provide more detailed information on fluor characteristics.

Since the photoelectric absorption coefficient varies approximately as

TABLE 5-1

Properties of some common fluors

Fluor	Wavelength of Maximum Light Emission (Å)	Half-time of Photon Decay* (μsec)	Relative Light Production Efficiency	Density (g/cc)	Primary Detection Use
ZnS (Ag)	4500	0.007	2.00	4.1	α
NaI (Tl)	4100	0.0002	2.00	3.67	γ
Anthracene	4400	0.022	1.00	1.24	β
Trans-stilbene	4100	0.006	0.73	1.16	β
p-terphenyl	3900	0.004	0.55	1.18	β

*Duration of light pulse down to one-half of maximum intensity.

the fifth power of the atomic number of the absorber, the dense alkali halide fluors are an obvious choice for gamma detection and spectrometry. Large halide crystals (up to 9 in. in diameter and 9 in. in thickness) exhibiting high transparency are routinely produced. Addition of over 0.1 per cent of thallium iodide greatly improves (activates) the light production efficiency of these crystals. Thallium activated sodium iodide crystals [NaI (Tl)] are the most universally used in spite of their hygroscopic nature, but KI (Tl) and CsI (Tl) fluors are also usable. For additional information on the response characteristics and variety of crystal shapes and sizes for NaI (Tl) fluors, see the booklet by the Harshaw Chemical Company (8), one of the leading commercial producers.

When thin radioactive samples are placed against a crystal fluor for assay, a maximum of 50 per cent of the radiation is emitted in the direction of the detector ($2\,\pi$ geometry). In an effort to increase detection efficiency, fluors have been prepared with a "well" drilled into the crystal. Assay samples may then be placed essentially within the crystal, so that a much greater proportion of the radiation emitted may be detected. Such a *well crystal* is particularly suited for direct assay of liquid samples (7, 13, and Experiments C and D, Part Three), homogenized tissue, or ashed specimens (Experiment E, Part Three). NaI (Tl) crystals with well sizes capable of accommodating fluid samples up to 25 ml are commonly available. Plastic fluors can be fabricated with very much larger well sizes.

Organic fluors in the form of single crystals are less commonly employed in radiotracer assay. Because of their low densities, they are considerably less efficient for detecting gamma rays than the alkali halide crystals. Although they are intrinsically quite efficient for beta detection, the G-M detector is as efficient, and considerably cheaper. The organic crystal detectors, however, do have the advantage of an energy-dependent response, and so find limited use in beta-ray spectrometry. Liebson (12) has investigated their temperature dependence.

c. ***Photocoupling.*** In order to direct the maximum number of photons from the scintillation crystal to the photocathode, certain optical features must be included in the detector. The side of the crystal housing facing the photocathode is formed by an optical window of clear glass or quartz. All other surfaces of the crystal are covered with a light-reflecting layer, commonly Al_2O_3 or aluminum foil. Good optical contact between the crystal and the photomultiplier tube is obtained by means of a transparent viscous medium, such as Dow-Corning "200" silicone fluid. In applications where it is desirable to have the scintillation crystal in probe form to reach less accessible positions, a "light pipe" of lucite or quartz is used to connect it with the photomultiplier tube.

d. ***Photomultiplier tubes.*** A photomultiplier tube consists of a photosensitive cathode, a series of dynodes maintained at increasingly positive potentials to the cathode, and an electron-collecting anode, all sealed in a glass envelope. Both the photocathode and the dynodes have sensitive surfaces which are capable of emitting electrons when struck by incident photons or electrons. It is this property of secondary emission that allows electron multiplication to occur through the dynode series, as has been previously described. [Photomultiplier tubes for scintillation detection are presently available from several manufacturers, such as Radio Corporation of American (RCA), DuMont, CBS Labs, and EMI Electronics, Ltd. (EMI).] The review by Sharpe and Thomson (14) describes construction and operating features of all commonly used photomultiplier tubes.

A variety of *photocathode* materials has been used in the past, but antimony-cesium or silver-magnesium alloys are currently the most widely employed (15), both because of these alloys' relatively high light sensitivity (40–60 μa/lumen) and quantum efficiency (10–20 per cent), that is, the ratio of photoelectrons ejected to incident photons, and because their spectral sensitivity matches the emission spectra of the most commonly used fluors. Figure 5-4 graphically illustrates this latter relationship in the case of NaI (Tl) and anthracene fluors. Although photocathodes over

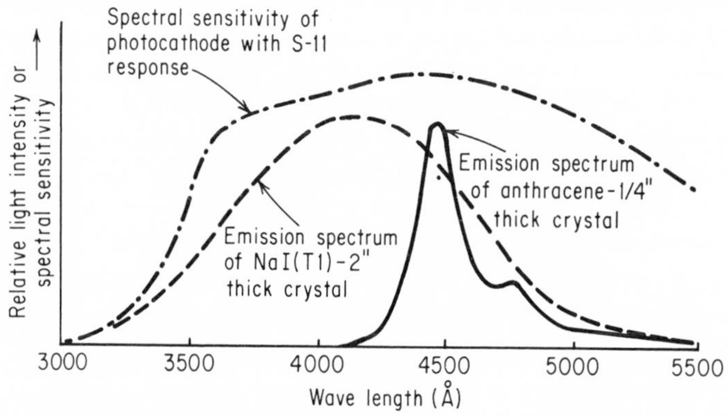

Figure 5-4. Comparison of emission spectra of NaI(Tl) and anthracene with the spectral sensitivity of an Sb-Cs alloy photocathode with S-11 response.

4 in. in diameter are available, the larger sizes commonly lack uniformity of sensitivity over their surface. When large-sized crystals or fluor solutions are employed, a number of small photomultipliers can be arranged to detect the scintillations.

Two principal types of construction are used for the *dynode series* in photomultipliers. Tubes of American manufacture commonly contain curved dynodes arranged so that an electrostatic field focuses the electron burst from one dynode to another. This is diagrammatically shown in Figure 5-1. Many of the EMI tubes use flat dynodes arranged like a series of venetian blinds. In either case, the total amplification depends on the number of dynode stages and the potential applied between successive stages. From 6 to 14 dynodes may be included and the potential applied in approximately equal steps of 100–150 volts. Thus, an over-all potential gradient of up to nearly 3000 volts may be required, depending on the specific photomultiplier used. The stability of the high-voltage supply is essential in view of the direct relation between total amplification and dynode potential. A change of 0.01 volt, or less, in high-voltage output per 1-volt change in the line voltage is desirable. Although gains of $2\text{–}3 \times 10^6$ are most common, with higher voltages and larger numbers of dynodes, over-all gains of $10^7\text{–}10^8$ are possible.

e. *Preamplifier.* This component is not strictly a part of the detector, but is usually attached directly to the foregoing components, often in the same housing. Its function is amplifying the small output pulses from the photomultiplier sufficiently so that they will not be lost in traversing the cable to the scaler.

Other components are needed to form a complete scintillation counting assembly. These include a high voltage supply, scaling unit, mechanical register, and timer, all of which may be combined into one unit, a scaler. If spectrometry is to be done, a linear amplifier and pulse height analyzer will also be required. (These components and their functions are described in Experiment III, Part Two.)

3. Operating Characteristics of Solid Scintillation Detectors

The determination of the optimal operating conditions for scintillation counters involves two parameters: the potential applied to the photomultiplier and the gain of the preamplifier or amplifier. In contrast, such determination for G-M counters involves only the potential applied across the G-M detector electrodes.

a. *Effect of photomultiplier potential.* At a fixed gain setting, a series of activity determinations made at successively higher photomultiplier potentials will yield data which may be plotted as seen for the solid line curve in Figure 5-5. This curve shows the rapid rise in counting rate at lower potentials, the nearly flat *plateau* region of essentially constant counting rate with increasing potential, and finally the second region of rising count rate that superficially appears to resemble the characteristic G-M plateau curve (Figure 4-8). Actually, the two curves are completely unrelated. The plateau on the scintillation counter curve represents potentials at which the detection efficiency of photons produced in the fluor has reached a maximum. Almost all the photons produced in the fluor are

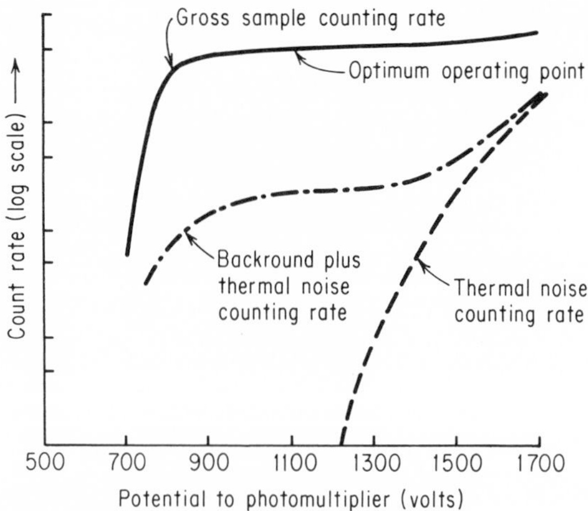

Figure 5-5. Effect of photomultiplier potential on counting rate for a NaI(T1) scintillation counter.

being detected. Engstrom and Weaver (6) have thoroughly discussed the significance of the scintillation plateau.

The counting rate from total background radiation and that due to thermal noise in the photomultiplier alone are also seen in Figure 5-5. Obviously, the rapidly rising thermal noise level at the higher voltages is primarily responsible for the increase in total counting rate of the "background" at the end of the plateau. This being the case, it is best to operate the scintillation detector at the lowest possible potential on the plateau. The optimal operating potential is chosen on statistical grounds as that potential where the ratio of the square of the sample count rate to the total background count rate (both from radiation and thermal noise) is at maximum (S^2/B = max). Since the plateau curves for different gamma-emitting nuclides vary somewhat, the optimal operating potential must be determined individually for each isotope used.

b. *Effect of amplifier gain.* The effect of different amplifier gain settings on the scintillation counter plateau curve is seen in Figure 5-6. It will be found, in general, that increased amplifier gain results in shortened plateau length, increased counting rate, and decreased plateau slope. Since the effects on counting rate of photomultiplier potential and preamplifier gain are somewhat similar, but thermal noise is directly related to photomultiplier potential, it is advisable to operate a scintillation counter at the lowest possible potential and to increase the preamplifier gain as required to compensate.

c. *Gamma energy dependence of detection efficiency.* The gamma detection efficiency of a NaI (T1) scintillation counter is strongly dependent

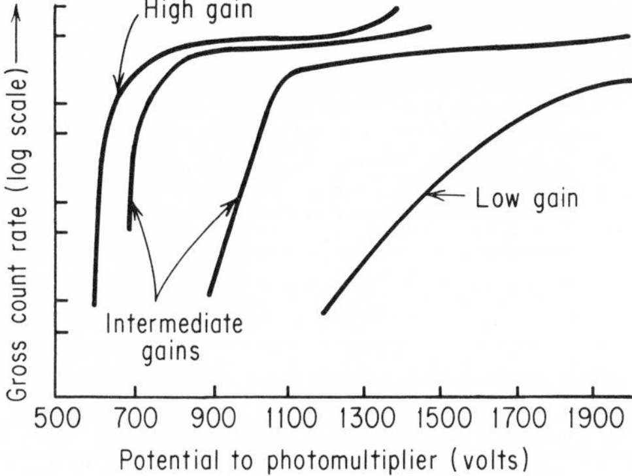

Figure 5-6. Effect of amplifier gain on counting rate for a NaI(Tl) scintillation counter.

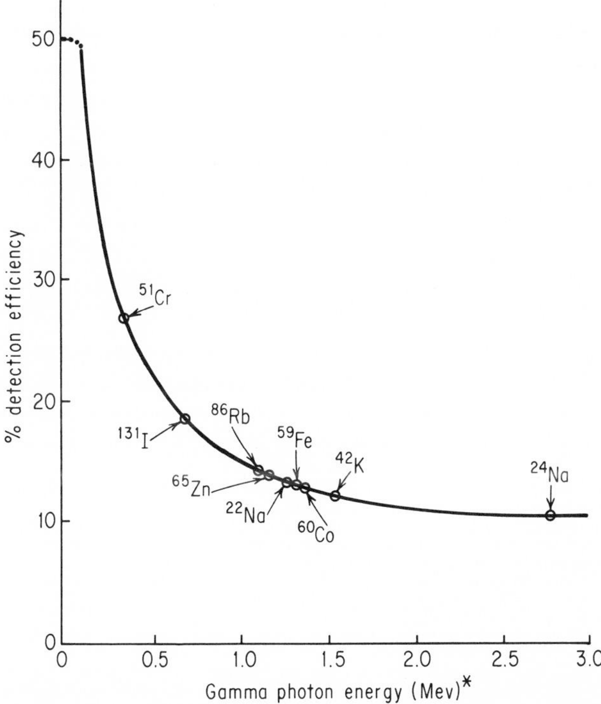

Figure 5-7. Calculated gamma detection efficiency as a function of gamma energy for a 1″ × 1″ NaI(Tl) crystal with sources directly on crystal.

on the energy of the incident gamma rays. This relationship is seen in Figure 5-7. Note that in actual practice a decrease in detection efficiency occurs for very low-energy gamma emitters owing to absorption in the aluminum casing around the crystal.) Such variation in detection efficiency for different isotopes must be considered in experimental design (see Chapter 10). This energy dependence is explained by considering the nature of the competing effect of the three gamma interaction processes (see Chapter 3). It should be clear that use of larger scintillation crystals would improve the detection efficiency at higher gamma energies, since there would be an increased probability of interaction as the gamma rays traversed the crystal. Of course, use of larger crystals also results in increased background counting rate. The background counting rate can be reduced by the use of a spectrometer, although at the cost of reduced counting efficiency for the sample activity.

BIBLIOGRAPHY

1. Baird-Atomic, Inc. Cambridge, 1960. Scintillation spectrometry. Mass. 63 p.
2. Birks, John B. 1953. Scintillation counters. McGraw-Hill Book Company. New York. 148 p.
3. Buck, Warren L., and Robert K. Swank. 1953. Preparation and performance of efficient plastic scintillators. Nucleonics 11(11):48–52.
4. Crouthamel, C. E. (ed.). 1960. Applied gamma-ray spectrometry. Pergamon Press, New York. 443 p.
5. Curran, S. C. 1953. Luminescence and the scintillation counter. Academic Press. New York. 219 p.
6. Engstrom, Ralph W., and J. L. Weaver. 1959. Are plateaus significant in scintillation counting? Nucleonics 17(2):70–74.
7. Haigh, C. P. 1954. Gamma-ray scintillation counter for weak radioactive solutions. Nucleonics 12(1):34–39.
8. Harshaw Chemical Company. 1960. Harshaw scintillation phosphors. rev. ed. Cleveland, 44 p.
9. Hine, Gerald J., and John A. Cardarelli. 1960. Conical plastic scintillators show total gamma absorption. Nucleonics 18(9):92–100.
10. Hinard, Frank E. 1957. Temperature dependence of photomultiplier gain. Nucleonics 15(4):92–97.
11. Krebs, A. T. 1955. Early history of the scintillation counter. Science 122:17–18.
12. Liebson, S. H. 1952. Temperature effects in organic fluors. Nucleonics 10(7):41–45.
13. MacIntyre, William J., and James H. Christie. 1957. A well scintillation counter for improved volume efficiency. J. Lab. Clin. Med. 50:653–656.
14. Sharpe, J., and E. E. Thomson. 1958. Photomultiplier tubes and scintillation counters. *In* Proc. Second UN Intern. Conf. Peaceful Uses Atomic Energy, Geneva, 1958. Nuclear physics and instrumentation. 10:311–324.

15. Sommer, A. H. 1955. New photoemissive cathodes of high sensitivity. Rev. Sci. Instruments 26:725–726.

16. Swank, Robert K. 1954*a*. Recent advances in theory of scintillation phosphors. Nucleonics 12(3):14–19.

17. Swank, Robert K. 1954*b*. Characteristics of scintillators. Ann. Rev. Nuclear Sci. 4:111–140.

18. Verheijke, M. L. 1962. Calculated Efficiencies of a 3 × 3 in. NaI(Tl) well-type scintillation crystal. Intern. J. Appl. Radiation Isotopes. 13: 583–585.

CHAPTER SIX

Measurement of Radioactivity by the Liquid (Internal-Sample) Scintillation Method

Liquid scintillation counting owes its origin to the independent discovery by Reynolds (88) and Kallman (59) in 1950 that certain organic solutions fluoresce noticeably when bombarded with high-energy radiation. This fluorescence can then be readily converted to a burst of photoelectrons in a photomultiplier and measured as an electronic pulse, as in the case of solid fluor detectors. Liquid fluors, however, offer a significant advantage over solid fluors. The radioactive sample and the fluor are mixed intimately in a homogeneous medium (internal-sample), either dissolved or suspended in a suitable solvent. With this system, the sample-to-detector relation is equivalent to 4π detection geometry. Moreover, the detection sensitivity is such that low-energy beta emitters can be assayed with quite respectable efficiency. This latter application has been most widely exploited and is emphasized in this chapter.

The use of liquid scintillation counters has become considerably more popular in radiotracer laboratories in recent years. This is primarily because of the improved reliability of the complete counting assemblies that are commercially available. Their relatively high cost has been a factor impeding their wider use. This expense is due largely to the far greater complexity of the electronic circuitry involved in the liquid scintillation counting assembly, as compared to those used with other detector types.

Another reason for the hesitancy of many investigators in using the liquid scintillation detection method is the inadequacy of the literature on the subject. Several symposia have dealt largely or entirely with liquid scintillation detection and their published proceedings form the core of the readily available literature (11, 27, 94, 120). To the present time, only one monograph on the subject has been produced (97). Articles on the methodology itself are scattered through a wide variety of journals and are not uniform in terminology. There are a number of brief reviews of the detection method (5, 10, 57, 84, 95) and more thorough coverage by Davidson and Feigelson (28), Hayes (48–49), and most recently, Rapkin (127) is to be recommended. Various instrument manufacturers, notably Packard Instrument Company and Nuclear-Chicago Corporation (72), include brief descriptions of the methodology in their instrument manuals. They also provide a series of technical bulletins covering various phases of liquid scintillation detection (23, 26, 51). Because of this situation, this chapter and the portion of Chapter 8 devoted to the preparation of samples for liquid scintillation detection have as their major purpose to provide a fundamental, though brief, survey of liquid scintillation methodology and a comprehensive list of references to its literature.

A. MECHANISM OF LIQUID (INTERNAL-SAMPLE) SCINTILLATION DETECTION

The over-all sequence in liquid scintillation detection might appear superficially to be identical with that described for external-sample scintillation detection in Chapter 5. Fluor molecules are directly or indirectly excited by ionizing radiation resulting in the emission of photons. These in turn interact with the photocathode of a photomultiplier to yield photoelectrons from the photocathode surface. The photoelectrons pass through a dynode series, which results in the production of a greatly amplified electron pulse at the photomultiplier anode. A basic difference between the two detection sequences does exist. It lies in the mechanism of energy transfer from radiation to fluor. This mechanism will be briefly elaborated in this chapter. [For a more detailed discussion of the mechanism of energy transfer in fluor solutions, see the papers by Birks (27, p. 12–36), Furst and Kallman (11, p. 3–22, 28–29, 52–54), Hayes (45), Reynolds (89), and Swank and Buck (106).]

1. Energy Transfer Steps in the Fluor Solution

In liquid scintillation detection a small amount of the fluor substance (the solute) is typically dissolved in a much larger quantity of an organic solvent to form the fluor solution. The radioisotope sample may be either dissolved or suspended in this solution. Owing to the low concentration of fluor in the solvent (usually less than 1 per cent), the energy of the beta radiation is not directly transferred to the fluor molecules to any extent.

The energy of the nuclear radiation is primarily transferred to the more abundant solvent molecules, which are usually of an aromatic hydrocarbon, such as toluene. As a result, the solvent molecules may be ionized, dissociated, or excited. It is the latter effect, primarily with π electrons of the solvent molecules, which contributes most to the ultimate production of detectable photons. Only a very small fraction of interactions result in excitation. The excitation energy of the solvent can either be emitted as photons (in the ultraviolet region) or transferred to molecules of the primary solute (a fluor, such as *p*-terphenyl). The excited fluor molecules return to the ground state by emitting photons with a wavelength in the visible or near ultraviolet region. In the case of *p*-terphenyl in toluene, the wavelength of the fluorescence peak is near 3500 Å.

The emission peak of the primary solute may not match the most sensitive range of the photocathode which is used to detect the photons. Hence, the presence of a secondary solute (also a fluor) may be beneficial. This substance serves to absorb energy from the primary solute and re-emit it as light of a longer wavelength. For this reason, the term *wave shifter* is often applied to the secondary solute. POPOP [1, 4-bis-2-(5-phenyloxazolyl)-benzene] is a commonly used wave shifter. The wavelength of the fluorescence peak of POPOP is at about 4200 Å. The use of a secondary solute often results in greatly improved detection efficiency. Figure 6-1 graphically illustrates this relation between fluorescence peaks of primary and secondary solutes and photocathode spectral sensitivity.

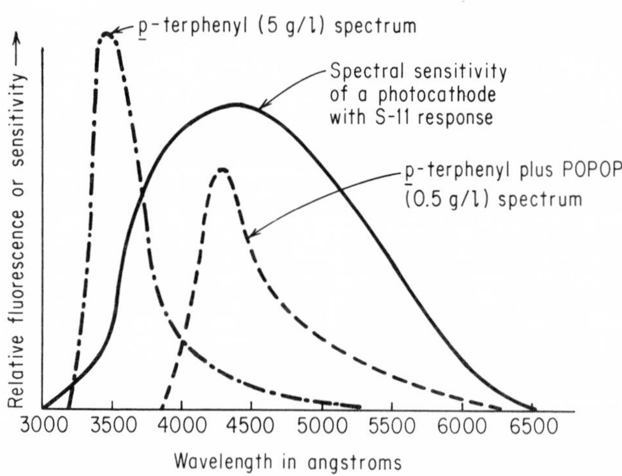

Figure 6-1. Fluorescence spectra of primary and secondary solutes (in toluene solvent) and photocathode sensitivity.

2. Comparative Examples of Energy Transfer Efficiency for Very Soft Beta Particles

It is even more difficult to make a generalized estimation of the efficiency in the energy conversion processes in liquid scintillation detection than in external-sample scintillation. The variable composition of the radioactive sample and the diversity of fluor solutions which may be employed can affect the efficiency of the energy transfer processes and hence render any such quantitative statements meaningless. As an example of the energy transfer process, however, idealized calculations for the detection of a single beta particle from ^{14}C with mean emission energy (0.050 Mev) in a toluene-*p*-terphenyl-POPOP solution are presented.

(1) Owing to the short range of such a weak beta particle, almost all its kinetic energy would be dissipated in the fluor solution. According to Hayes and Ott (49, p. 9), the fluor solution just specified will yield about 7 photons per kev of beta particle energy dissipated. The 50 kev beta particle under consideration would then yield approximately 350 photons.

(2) A fraction of these fluorescence photons do not reach the adjacent photocathode surface. Instead they are lost by absorption in the solution, the counting vial, or the reflector, or by scattering at the air-glass interfaces. Assuming that such loss approximates 15 per cent, about 300 photons would then impinge on the photocathode.

(3) If the conversion efficiency of the photocathode averages 10 per cent, then about 30 photoelectrons would be produced and be subjected to the multiplication mechanism of the dynode series.

(4) A photomultiplier with an amplification factor of 10^6 would then produce 3×10^7 electrons at the output, which is equivalent to a charge of about 5×10^{-12} coulomb. This charge could then be transformed by a preamplifier circuit with a capacitance of 30 $\mu\mu$f into a pulse of about 150 millivolts. This figure should be contrasted with the value calculated for a 1.17 Mev gamma ray, which was 0.6 volt (see p. 92).

The difficulty of detecting a pulse of this small size, makes it necessary to use an external amplifier of higher gain than required for gamma detection with crystal fluors. It should also be emphasized that the foregoing calculations are based on a ^{14}C beta particle having an energy equivalent to its E_{mean}. The situation is in reality much more serious, since half of the beta particles from a ^{14}C sample would be emitted with lower energies. By comparison, following the calculations just given, a beta particle from ^{3}H emitted at E_{mean} (5.5 kev) would yield an output pulse from the photomultiplier of only about 18 mv. Lukens (74) presents further discussion of these quantitative relationships.

Depending on the photocathode sensitivity and the degree of absorption loss, a certain minimum number of photons will be required to result in the ejection of one photoelectron from the photocathode. Beta particles of such low kinetic energy that they result in the emission of less than that minimum number of photons from the fluor solution will not result in an output pulse. In the circumstances specified in the previous example, this minimum energy level would be over 1600 ev. Thus, a sizable fraction of the beta particles from a tritium-labeled sample would have insufficient energy to be detected by the liquid scintillation process. In addition, many of the pulses derived from tritium beta particles would be of the same energy as thermionic noise pulses of the photomultiplier and indistinguishable from them. Note, however, that even weak beta particles lead to the production of several photons, whereas the thermionic noise from a photomultiplier involves single events. If the electronic circuitry is fast enough, it is possible to distinguish between single events and groups of events, thus lowering the background count rate. Swank (11, p. 23–38) discusses this and other factors that limit sensitivity in liquid scintillation counting.

B. EVALUATION OF THE LIQUID SCINTILLATION METHOD

1. Advantages of Liquid Scintillation Counting

In liquid scintillation detection, as in external-sample scintillation detection, the size of the photomultiplier output pulse is more or less directly related to the magnitude of energy associated with the radiation interacting with the scintillation medium. This relationship allows an approximate analysis of the energy spectrum of beta emitters. An advantage of this proportionality of pulse size to particle energy is the possibility of differentiating between radiation from two different beta-emitting isotopes in the same sample (a *double-labeled sample*). For this to be possible, the maximum beta energies of the two nuclides must differ by a factor of at least four. Samples labeled with both ^{14}C and ^{3}H are most commonly encountered. A treatment of the methods of counter operation in such determinations is beyond the scope of this book. [For further information, see the excellent discussions by Okita, et al. (77) and Hendler (54).]

Another advantage of using fluor solutions for detection instead of inorganic crystalline fluors lies in the very much faster *fluorescence decay times* of the former, usually of the order of a few millimicroseconds (58). Fluorescence in most inorganic crystalline fluors decays relatively slowly. Harrison (43) found up to 8 per cent of the peak fluorescence in a NaI (Tl) crystal persisting at 200 μsec following the initial gamma interaction. By contrast, only 1 per cent of the fluorescence in a toluene-*p*-terphenyl solution remained after 0.3 μsec. This characteristic of scintillator solutions allows their use with "fast" amplifiers, avoiding coincidence loss at even very high counting rates.

The most significant application of liquid scintillation detection is for the assay of *beta-emitting samples*, especially those with low energies. Because of the intimate relation of radioactive sample and fluor solution, nearly all disintegrations within the sample are detected, except in the case of tritium samples. The complicating factors of self-absorption, window absorption, geometry, and backscatter that plague traditional G-M assay of weak beta samples are all but eliminated (see Chapter 9). Hence, the major current application of liquid scintillation detection involves assay of ^{3}H, ^{14}C, ^{35}S, or ^{45}Ca. Under optimal conditions, ^{14}C detection efficiency may reach 90 per cent. Because of the large proportion of very low-energy beta particles it emits, tritium is seldom detected with an efficiency exceeding 40 per cent. Counting efficiencies are affected markedly by the nature of the sample-fluor solution and the mode of counter operations, as will be described later.

Although scintillation solutions have been chiefly used for detecting low-energy beta particles, they have detection efficiencies approaching 100 per cent for *alpha particles*. Unfortunately, nearly all alpha emitters are nuclides of high atomic weight and, as such, are insoluble in the aromatic hydrocarbon solvents used. Thus, unusual sample preparation procedures must be employed, as will be described in Chapter 8. By contrast, medium- to high-energy *gamma rays* are poorly detected by small-volume fluor solutions because of the much lower energy-absorbing capability of liquids as compared to solids. On the other hand, an isotope which emits only weak X rays, such as ^{55}Fe, would be difficult to assay by any other method than liquid scintillation detection. High-energy gamma radiation may, however, be detected with reasonable efficiency by large-volume ("giant") liquid scintillators, such as the whole body counters designed for clinical use.

2. Problems Inherent in Liquid Scintillation Counting

a. *Photomultiplier thermal noise.* In liquid scintillation detection, the pulse size from low-energy beta particles is so small that interference from photomultiplier thermal noise must be minimized. A photocathode in complete darkness may emit on the order of 5000 photoelectrons/cm^2/sec at room temperature. It is clearly desirable to minimize the resulting photomultiplier "dark current." *Cooling* the photomultiplier will reduce this noise level by a factor of nearly two for every 10°C near room temperature. Thus, it is common practice to operate the detector in a freezer at temperatures of 0°–5°C. As a further complication, attention must then be given to the choice of scintillation solutions that will not freeze at such reduced temperatures.

Since most "noise" pulses are of very low energy, the simplest means of preventing a liquid scintillation counter from registering them is to include a discriminator circuit ("low gate") that rejects pulses below a given minimal energy level. Note that such a "low gate" does not actually reduce photomultiplier dark current, as does cooling, but simply prevents it from being counted. This is not completely effective when a very low-energy beta-emitting isotope, such as tritium, is being assayed. Here, a sizable fraction of the pulses resulting from the tritium beta particles are of the same energy level as the photomultiplier noise pulses. Thus, other means must be employed to reject noise pulses selectively.

In another method of minimizing thermal noise counts, two photomultipliers are arranged so that they view the same vial of sample-fluor solution. This pair of photomultipliers (the "analyzer" and the "monitor") is connected through a *coincidence circuit* which is arranged to allow a "count" to be registered only when a pulse arrives simultaneously from each photomultiplier. Thus, a noise signal from only one photomultiplier is not registered, unless by coincidence another noise pulse originates in the other tube within the resolving time of the circuit. Since thermal noises are random events and the circuit resolving time is of the order of 10^{-7} sec, the background due to thermionic emission is reduced from perhaps several hundred thousands counts per minute to only a few counts per minute. A minimal disadvantage of the coincidence arrangement is that it also reduces slightly the detection sensitivity, since a minimum of two photoelectrons (one for each photomultiplier photocathode) is now required to yield a detectable signal. This is particularly important in the detection of tritium, since a sizable number of the beta particles from tritium are too low in energy content to give rise to the ultimate formation of two photoelectrons simultaneously.

Another source of noise associated with the photomultiplier is that derived from the preamplifiers attached immediately to the photomultiplier. The noise level of the preamplifier is, in fact, considerably higher than that derived from thermal noise. Since the noise of the preamplifier is also random in nature, however, it can be eliminated to a large extent by the use of coincidence circuitry. The new 3000 Series liquid scintillation counter manufactured by the Packard Instrument Company operates without the use of photomultiplier preamplifiers, thus removing a major source of background noise and permitting one to detect very low-energy beta particles.

b. *Counting sample preparation.* Another complication of liquid scintillation counting concerns sample preparation. The most efficient scintillation solvents are aromatic hydrocarbons which are not readily miscible with aqueous samples. In addition, many of the common biological compounds are polar in nature and will not dissolve in such nonpolar solvents as toluene. Then a certain amount of "witchcraft" is called for in concocting a suitable scintillation solvent mixture. In general, each new compound to be assayed must be investigated for its behavior in any given solvent system and the proper solvent mixture must be determined by previous experimentation. Nevertheless, once a proper scintillation solvent is found, the preparation of samples for liquid scintillation counting is a relatively simple procedure. Ease of routine sample preparation is, in fact, a significant advantage of liquid scintillation detection. In addition, the sample material may normally be readily recovered from the scintillation solution following the counting operation, if desired (90).

c. Fluorescence quenching. A persistent problem in liquid scintillation detection is the effect known as *quenching*. This phenomenon is not to be confused with quenching in G-M detectors (see Chapter 4). Broadly defined, *quenching* is any reduction of efficiency in the energy transfer process in the scintillation solution. Thus, quenching results in a decreased light output per beta particle and, consequently, the production of a smaller output pulse in the photomultiplier, or even failure to yield a detectable pulse. The net effect of quenching is, therefore, to reduce detection efficiency. Furthermore, since the extent of quenching varies considerably with different sample materials, direct comparison of activity determinations with varied sample types is rendered almost impossible. Thus, a determination of just how much the counting efficiency of every sample has been decreased by quenching must be made (see p. 131–135).

Quenching may occur by any of several mechanisms. The substance being counted (most commonly), or other components of the scintillation solution, may absorb some of the energy associated with the beta particle and degrade it to a form not capable of exciting the fluor (*chemical quenching*). Any nonfluorescent solute molecules, particularly polar compounds, are potentially quenching agents, since they may absorb energy from the excited solvent molecules without emitting photons. On the other hand, quenching may occur simply as a result of dilution of the fluor solution by the counting sample and, hence, a reduction of the probability of scintillation events (*dilution quenching*). Even if energy transfer from solvent to fluor is not reduced, colored sample materials will absorb some of the fluorescence photons before they leave the counting vial (*color quenching*) (29). Herberg's study (55) of this phenomenon is particularly valuable. More recently, Ross and Yerick (93) have investigated the relation between color quenching and the absorption spectrum of the quenching agent. Both chemical and color quenching are associated with the molecular structure of the sample material, whereas dilution quenching is related largely to sample concentration. Certain other effects may also result in photon quenching, such as separation of the fluor solution into two liquid phases, partial freezing of the solution, or fogging of the outside of the sample vial (*optical quenching*).

Certain substances exert a more pronounced quenching action than others. Oxygen, water, halogenated compounds, and polar compounds in general are severe quenchers. It is the variable presence of these agents in most biological samples that accounts for the somewhat empirical selection of proper scintillation solutions. Kerr, et al. (66) and Funt and Hetherington (32) have investigated and tabulated the quenching effects of a large number of organic compounds. Helmick (53) described the quenching effect of benzoic acid. The latter study is important, since labeled benzoic acid is often used as an internal standard in liquid scintillation counters to determine counting efficiency (see p. 131).

The quenching effect of dissolved oxygen in the scintillation solution was first pointed out by Pringle, et al (82). Seliger, et al (101) and Berlman (12) subsequently investigated the mechanism of *oxygen quenching* and found it to result from collision transfer of energy from the solvent to oxygen molecules. Since oxygen is an incidental contaminant and not a part of the sample, various means have been devised to remove it from the fluor solution (114). These have included bubbling argon gas (78), carbon dioxide (83), or nitrogen through the solution, or, in addition, using ultrasonic degassing (24). As a means of stabilizing chemical quenching by ethanol, ultraviolet irradiation has been suggested (73). In general practice, the problem of quenching is solved, not by avoiding or eliminating the quenching agent, but rather by devising a reliable method to estimate the precise extent of quenching.

Despite the drawbacks mentioned, the liquid scintillation method of detection is the most generally effective means for assaying low-energy beta-emitting samples, especially ^{3}H and ^{14}C (11, p. 288–292). Because of the ubiquitous occurrence of the latter two elements in living organisms, this detection method is of paramount importance to the biologist using radiotracers. The relative ease of sample preparation, the versatility of sample form possible, 4π detection geometry, and the commercial availability of reliable counting systems with high-capacity automatic sample changers render this detection method the most useful where large numbers and types of samples must be assayed.

C. COMPONENTS OF A LIQUID SCINTILLATION COUNTER

A typical dual-tube liquid scintillation counting assembly is diagramed in Figure 6-2. It is easy to see that even a simplified liquid scintil-

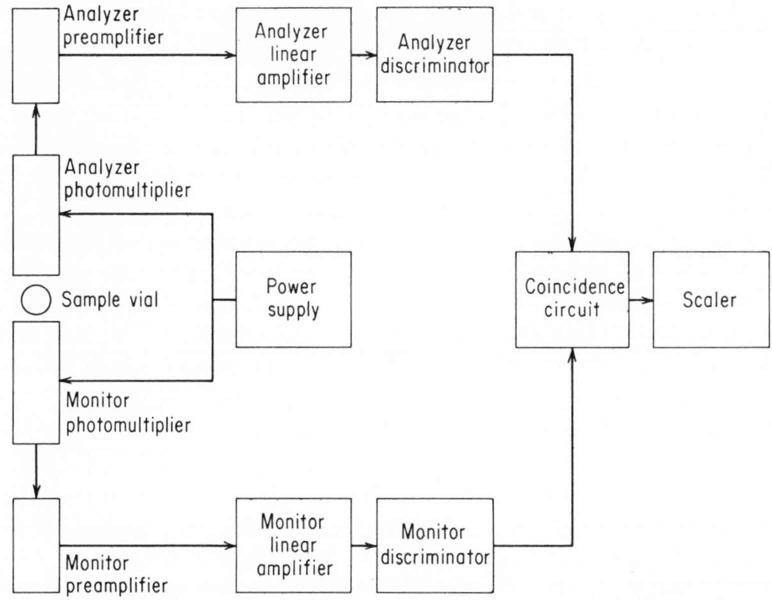

Figure 6-2. Block diagram of a simplified liquid scintillation counting assembly.

lation counter is far more complex than the other counting assemblies previously described (Chapters 4–5). A liquid scintillation counter is divisible into two major units: the detector assembly and the associated electronics. The components of the detector assembly are discussed fully in this chapter, but an extended discussion of the electronic components (11, p. 41–80) is postponed to Experiment IV.

1. The Electronics

In brief, the typical electronics associated with a liquid scintillation counter are indicated on the simplified block diagram in Figure 6-2. Two photomultipliers, provided with a high-voltage power supply, view the sample vial. The pulses from each of the photomultipliers pass successively through separate preamplifiers, linear amplifiers, and discriminator circuits, which must be exceptionally fast, that is have a very short resolving time. In the very simplest form of counter, the discriminators operate solely as "low gates" to reject pulses below a preset height. More elaborate liquid scintillation counters, however, are provided with variable discriminators that allow rejection of pulses both below a given minimum height and above a selected maximum height. Counting assemblies of this type are more accurately termed liquid scintillation *spectrometers*. Pulses pass from the respective discriminators to the coincidence circuitry (p. 110) which permits only legitimate pulses, that is, those derived from scintillation events, to be registered on the scaler. A scaler with a very short resolving time (0.25 μsec) is normally used because of the high counting rates commonly encountered.

A typical arrangement of components in up-to-date, commercially available liquid scintillation counters is given in Figure 6-3 for the counters (models 724 and 725) manufactured by Nuclear-Chicago Corporation, and in Figure 6-4 for the counters (Series 3000 and 4000) manufactured by Packard Instrument Company. Note that in the latter case, by the use of two improved photomultiplier tubes, preamplifiers are not used in the basic circuitry. In addition, contrary to the conventional monitor-analyzer roles (see p. 110) played by the two photomultipliers, respectively (that is, when only the pulse from the analyzer is fed into the detection circuitry), one finds in this case that the pulses derived from both photomultipliers are summed up to give a two-fold increase in size before pulse amplification. Such a situation should facilitate better separation of ^{14}C pulses from ^{3}H pulses when both radioisotopes are present in the counting sample (see p. 129). It is also expected that counting efficiency for either ^{14}C or ^{3}H will be somewhat higher with the background counting rate maintained at a low level.

Both makes of counters can provide reliable performance. Comparative evaluation of commercially available liquid scintillation counters, requires careful examination of the provision of good maintenance service, the stability of counting efficiency with respect to both sample and background under standardized counter settings, and the reliability of the sample-changing mechanism (in the case of a counter equipped with an automatic sample changer). As indicated by the block diagrams, these counters are all equipped with two or three channels and their respective performances are, in general, comparable. The difference in detection efficiency of a few per cent when one counter is compared to another is inconsequential, inasmuch as detection efficiency by the liquid scintillation mechanism is basically much higher than that obtainable with a G-M counter. Moreover, in many cases adequate experimental design often minimizes the need for slightly better detection efficiency in a counter.

More recently, a new liquid scintillation counter has been introduced on the market by ANS, Inc. (Wallingford, Conn.) This counter, designated the ANSitron, offers several unique features in addition to the pulse summation capability recently made available in the liquid scintillation counters just described. The basic circuitry of the ANSitron, which makes extensive use of silicon transistors, is shown in Figure 6-5. Certain of the unique features of this counter deserve more extensive discussion.

It will be noted that the ANSitron circuitry incorporates a *logarithmic*

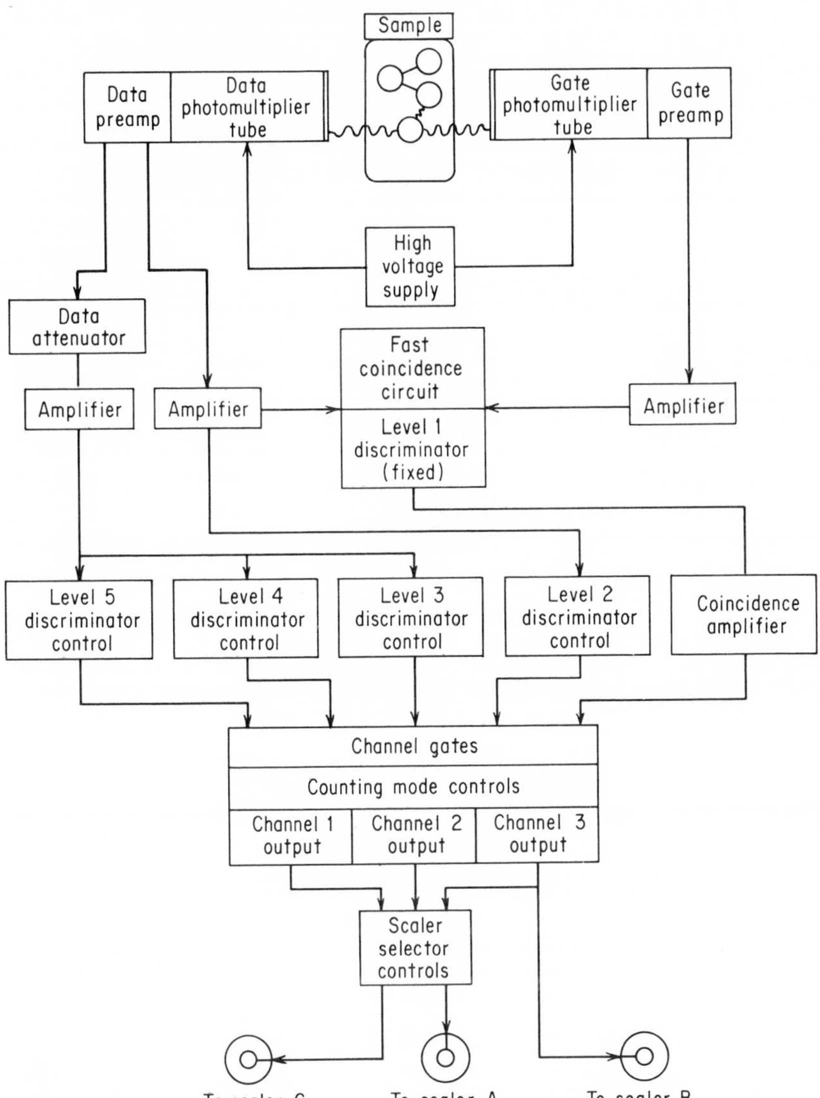

Figure 6-3. Simplified block diagram of a liquid scintillation counter—Nuclear-Chicago Corporation Models 724 and 725.

spectrum converter. This permits one to examine simultaneously the beta spectra of one or more soft beta emitters, such as tritium or ^{14}C, and one or more high-energy beta emitters, such as ^{32}P or ^{36}Cl, without the need for a pulse size attenuator. A set of typical spectra of this type is given in Figure 6-7. It should be emphasized that the pulse spectrum for soft beta emitters, such as tritium, does not actually resemble the true beta spectrum, since it is a record of coincidences and the less energetic beta

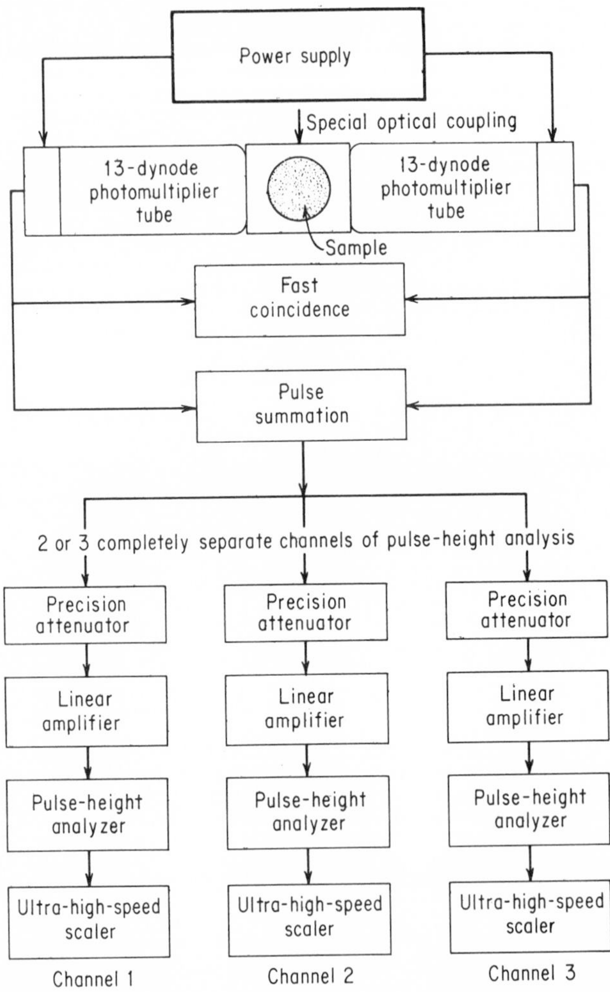

Figure 6-4. Simplified block diagram of a liquid scintillation counter—Packard Instrument Company Series 3000 and 4000.

particles do not always provide sufficient light output to cause pulses in both photomultipliers. Therefore, the ascending slope of the ^{3}H spectrum on the low-energy side, in fact, reflects the statistics of detection of very low-energy events superimposed on the statistics of photomultiplier performance. Essentially all the loss in ^{3}H counting efficiency may be attributed to a combination of these phenomena. It is likely that counting efficiency for the higher-energy tritium beta particles approaches 100 per cent.

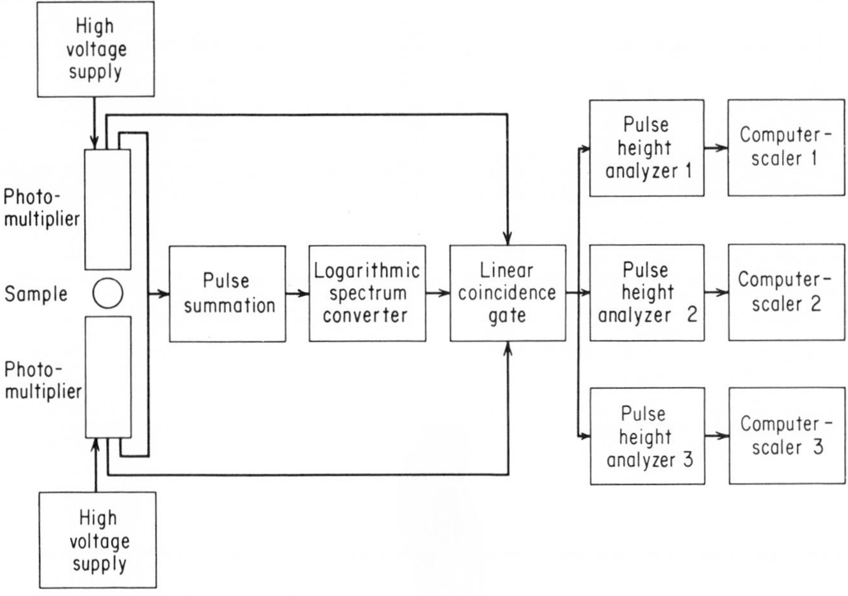

Figure 6-5. Simplified block diagram of a liquid scintillation counter—ANS Corporation ANSitron, Model 1300.

The photograph of the ANSitron control panel (Figure 6-6) reveals the presence of two new features in this counter. First, *ratemeters* are incorporated as an integral part of each counting channel. Because of the sharp fall-off of the logarithmic spectra, use of these ratemeters in conjunction with the upper and lower discriminator potentiometers facilitates selection of appropriate instrument settings. Secondly, it will be seen that a *plug-in discriminator set* (termed a "beta set") is provided for each of the three pulse-analyzing channels. This discriminator set is factory-adjusted to represent the optimal pulse-height window settings for a given radioisotope. Such a device should provide considerable convenience to the users.

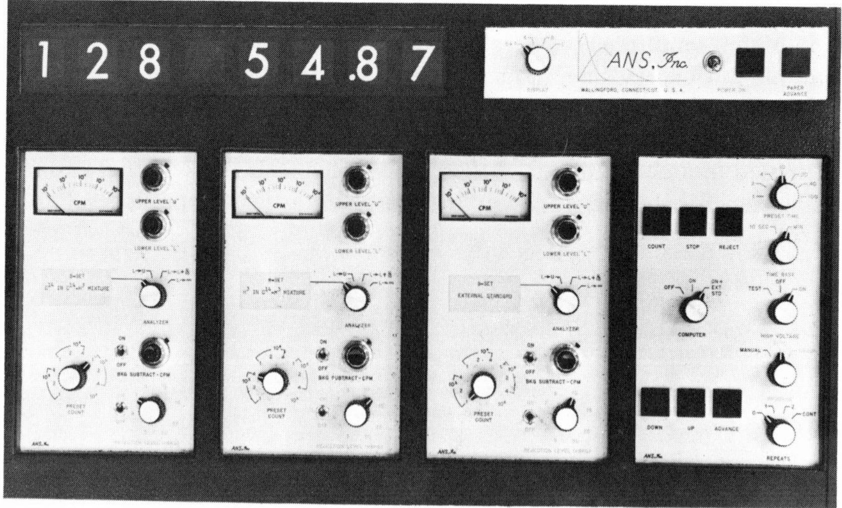

Figure 6-6. Photograph of ANSitron control panel.

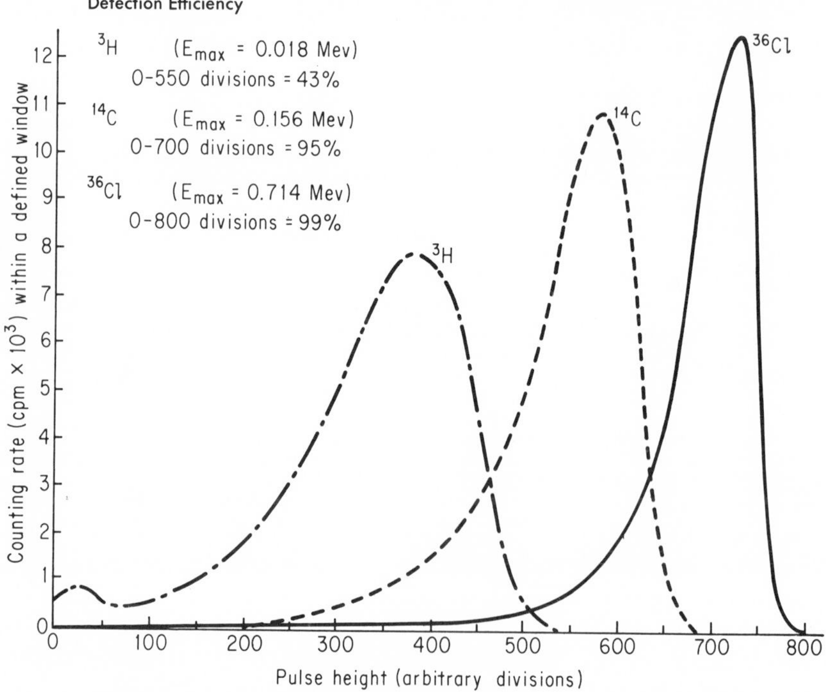

Figure 6-7. Pulse spectra of ^{3}H, ^{14}C and ^{32}P as seen with logarithmic spectrum conversion.

In the ANSitron counter "*live timing*" is used, instead of typical "clock timing," so that the timing device is shut off during the brief interval while a pulse is being electronically processed. This obviates the need for applying coincidence-loss corrections. The use of "live timing" will slightly prolong the counting time for a given sample in comparison to counters equipped with conventional "clock timing" devices. This, however, should not affect too seriously the routine assay of samples with moderate counting rates.

2. The Detector Assembly

With regard to the liquid scintillation detector assembly alone, there are certain basic differences between its components and those of an external-sample scintillation detector as discussed in Chapter 5. These differences center primarily on the composition of the fluor (solution versus crystal). Different optical relations must also be considered, since the photomultiplier is exposed to a succession of fluor solutions, rather than remaining optically coupled to an enclosed crystal fluor.

a. *Optical components.* The photomultiplier (27, p. 198–215) (two with coincidence circuitry), is mounted in a light-tight shield so that it views the sample vial. A mechanical system must be incorporated to prevent light reaching the photocathode when samples are changed. Optical coupling of the sample vial and the surface of the photomultiplier tube is sometimes used and the sample chamber is normally coated with a light-reflecting surface to direct the maximum light to the photocathode. A variety of substances have been used as coating materials, of which titanium dioxide appears to be the most generally effective (7). Benson and Maute (116) have demonstrated an improvement in tritium-counting efficiency by the introduction of a lucite light guide between the sample vial and the photomultiplier.

The *sample holding vial* is normally made of glass. Ordinary glass, however, contains a considerable quantity of the natural radioisotope ^{40}K, which thus contributes significantly to the background count rate. For this reason, it is common practice to employ sample vials made from special low potassium glass. Quartz glass has also been used (1), but its cost is prohibitive except where extremely low backgrounds are essential and few samples are involved. Medium-density polyethylene vials have been suggested (69) as both inexpensive and not contaminated with ^{40}K. Rapkin and Gibbs (86) report an increase in ^{3}H detection efficiency with such vials, but also find them permeable to toluene (the common fluor solvent) and thus of limited usefulness.

b. *Fluor solution components.* The actual preparation of samples will be described in Chapter 8; but the components of the scintillation solution, excluding the sample itself, will be discussed at this point. The bulk of the scintillation solution consists of a primary solvent, with small quantities of primary solute and secondary solute (the wave shifter). Both of the solutes are fluors. Depending on the nature of the sample in question, a secondary solvent may also be employed.

Primary solvents: The primary solvent must absorb energy from the beta particles and transfer it to the fluor. Consequently, an efficient scintillation solvent must have good energy transfer characteristics, as well as a small absorption coefficient for the light emitted by the fluor. Another important attribute of the solvent is that it have a good chemical solvent power for a wide variety of sample materials. Since the majority of biological samples are polar compounds and soluble in water, it is highly desirable that the primary solvent be water-miscible. Unfortunately, few solvents have been found with both these characteristics. Thirdly, the solvent should not freeze at counting temperatures. Otherwise, the operating temperature of the photomultiplier, cooled to reduce thermal noise, may be limited by the freezing point of the solvent in use. The purity of the scintillation solvent used cannot be overemphasized (129–130). Any degree of quenching from contaminants in this component will greatly reduce detection efficiency. Solvent purity is of lesser importance when counting samples in the presence of a considerable water concentration.

The most efficient compounds investigated as scintillation solvents are aromatic hydrocarbons of alkylbenzene structure (xylene, toluene, and so on). Of these, *toluene* is the most widely used. Unfortunately, it suffers from the twin disadvantages of low flash point and poor miscibility with water. A variety of substitutes for toluene have been proposed (76, 117), with either lessened fire hazard or better solvent powers. For one reason or another none have replaced it as yet.

A second group of compounds which are generally less efficient, but very useful for certain sample types, consists of ethers. *Anisole* and 1,4-*dioxane*, with respective energy-transfer efficiencies of 80 per cent and 70 per cent relative to toluene, are commonly employed. Dioxane is especially useful because it is water-miscible. A problem of freezing exists with this solvent, however, as its freezing point is +12°C.

Secondary solvents. Solvent mixtures may be used to make soluble radioactive samples which are not soluble in a good primary solvent, or to increase the energy transfer efficiency of an inferior primary solvent which has desirable solvating properties. As an example, the addition of small amounts of *ethanol* (or methanol) to a toluene primary solvent considerably improves its ability to incorporate aqueous samples, without causing excessive loss of scintillation efficiency. By contrast, where dioxane has been used as a primary solvent because of its miscibility with water, its lower energy transfer efficiency may be improved by the addition of relatively small quantities of *naphthalene*. Furst and Kallman (35) have evaluated the factors that affect energy transfer in such scintillation solvent mixtures.

Secondary solvents of another important class serve as *specific binding agents* for various inorganic substances. These fall into several categories. Metallic ions, for example, may be incorporated into metal-organic complexes which are readily soluble in aromatic hydrocarbons. To date, the best organic complexing agents to be used with liquid scintillator systems are the acidic esters of orthophosphoric acid, that is, dibutyl phosphate, dioctyl phosphate, and the like. Metallic ions may also be converted to salts of 2-ethylhexanoic acid (octoic acid), which are reasonably soluble in aromatic hydrocarbons.

Of particular importance to the biologist are the binding agents for CO_2. Several organic compounds have been employed to trap the gas and convert it to a toluene-soluble carbonate. A methanolic solution of the hydroxide of "Hyamine 10-X" [*p*-(diisobutylcresoxethoxyethyl)-dimethylbenzyl-ammonium chloride] (Rohm & Haas, Inc.) has been the most widely used for this purpose. In addition, at a 1 molar concentration, this reagent is known to be capable of making proteins, tissues, and similar biological specimens soluble. More recently, "Primene 81-R" (Rohm & Haas, Inc.), ethanolamine, and ethylene diamine have been employed because of economy and reduced quenching. Specific scintillation solvent formulations involving these substances are shown in Tables 8-2, 8-3, and 8-4.

Primary solutes: This component of the scintillation solution is the fluor which must efficiently convert excitation energy to light quanta. During recent years, a most extensive search has been conducted, largely by the Biomedical Research Group at the Los Alamos Scientific Laboratory, for compounds with suitable fluor qualities (4, p. 8–9; 13–14, 36–40, 44–46, 67–68, 79–80, 83, 110–111). In 1958, Hayes, et al. (50) listed 483 different compounds that had been investigated.

A common characteristic of the most efficient fluors is that they contain three, and preferably four, aromatic or heterocyclic rings linked together in a linear manner that allows continuous conjugation throughout the molecule (40). In addition to being an efficient light emitter, it is also important that the light emitted by the fluor have a spectrum matched to the photocathode sensitivity. Needless to say, it is desirable that the fluor be economical and soluble in a variety of solvents, particularly at low temperature. In general, for a given solvent, the counting efficiency increases with increasing fluor concentration up to a certain point. Some fluors show the desirable characteristic of reaching a concentration giving constant detection efficiency before exceeding their solubility limit in a given solvent. Obviously, whenever it is possible, the concentration of a fluor should be maintained at a level higher than that required for constant detection efficiency. The relationship between detection efficiency and fluor concentration for PPO in toluene is depicted in Figure 6-8.

The most efficient fluors fall into the classes of oligophenylenes, oxazoles, or oxadiazoles (11, p.101–107). Because of the complexity of standard chemical nomenclature for these classes of compounds, an abbreviated system has been devised to describe them. The letter "P" is used for phenyl, "N" for naphthyl, "B" for biphenyl, "O" for oxazole, and "D" for the oxadiazole group.

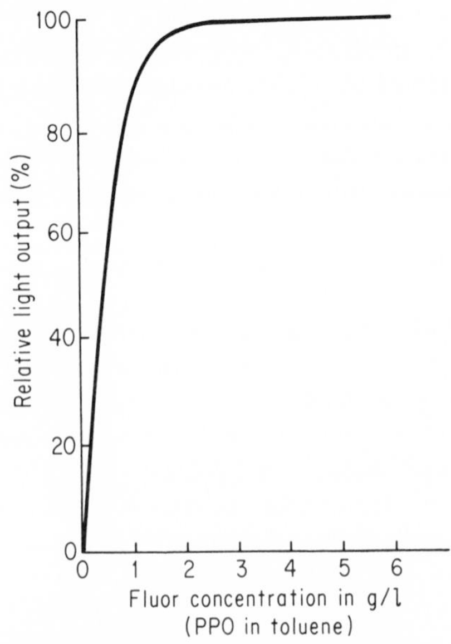

Figure 6-8. Relative light output in relation to primary solute concentration in detection of ^{14}C.

Despite the large number of potential fluors investigated, only three have proved worthy of consideration for practical use. The first substance so employed, *para-terphenyl,* is particularly attractive because of its relatively low cost. For many applications, however, its solubility is too low, particularly at low temperatures. Hence, it has been generally replaced by PPO (2,5-diphenyloxazole). PPO (44), because of its good solubility characteristics at low temperatures, has become the most popular primary solute for counting with cooled coincidence counters despite its high cost. Photons derived from PPO give rise to a relative pulse height 3 per cent greater than *p*-terphenyl. A third compound, PBD (phenylbiphenyloxadiazole), is the most efficient primary solute, giving rise to a relative pulse height 24 per cent greater than *p*-terphenyl. It has the disadvantages of limited solubility and high cost. In such fluor efficiency comparisons, *p*-terphenyl is arbitrarily assigned a relative pulse height value of 1.0. The photons derived from the three previously discussed fluors display emission peaks in the neighborhood of 3460 Å, 3800 Å, and 3700 Å, respectively. This fact implies that it will be advantageous to employ them along with a secondary solute, that is, a wave shifter.

Secondary solutes: This component of a scintillation solution acts as a secondary fluor whose effect is to shift the wavelength of the light emitted by the primary fluor to a region of greater photocathode sensitivity (see Figure 6-1). The secondary solutes are usually too insoluble, too expensive, or have too great a degree of self-quenching to function as primary solutes. They are useful because addition of only minute quantities to the scintillation solution may give impressive increases in counting efficiency. In general, their concentrations in the scintillation solution are only about $\frac{1}{100}$ those of the primary solutes. Hayes, et al (47), have evaluated the merits of a large number of compounds for use as wave shifters.

Several secondary solutes have found common use. POPOP [1,4-bis-2-(5-phenyloxazolyl)-benzene] is by far the most widely employed at present. Dimethyl-POPOP [1,4-bis-2(4-methyl-5-phenyloxazolyl)-benzene] has become available more recently and has the advantages of better solubility and longer wavelength in photon emission peak compared to POPOP. A third compound, α-NPO [2-(α-naphthyl)-5-phenyloxazole], has limited popularity, but is not as desirable as the other two compounds. Relative to PPO, these secondary solutes have pulse heights of 1.45, 1.45, and 1.21, respectively.

D. SPECIAL TYPES OF LIQUID SCINTILLATION DETECTORS

1. Large-Volume External-Sample Detectors

The liquid scintillation detection method is not limited to internal samples, although that is the major emphasis of this chapter. The size restrictions imposed on gas ionization and solid crystal scintillation detectors do not apply to liquid scintillation detectors. Very large volumes of scintillation solution may be used with a number of photomultipliers to produce "giant" detectors (11, p. 246–257; 42). For a variety of reasons, large-volume detectors have been constructed for use with external sources of radiation. Radiation from gamma rays, protons, neutrons, and neutrinos has been detected in this manner.

Of greatest biological interest are the so-called *whole body counters*, which are used to determine total body radioactivity in humans or animals (25). Such measurements give information on both the natural ^{40}K content of the body (87) and the content of internal radioactive material accidentally acquired by an individual (108). The Los Alamos human counter will serve as an example of the immensity of this detector type. It holds 140 gal of scintillation solution (toluene-terphenyl-POPOP) monitored by 108 photomultipliers and is surrounded by 20 tons of lead shielding (2–3, 11, p. 211–219; 27, p. 344–370).

To increase the efficiency of liquid scintillators for *neutron detection*, the solution is best "loaded" with heavy metals. This calls for the use of unusual solvents (21). At various times lead, bismuth, lithium (52), uranium, iron, cadmium, and boron in a variety of chemical forms have been employed, but the latter two appear most desirable. In the case of boron, the reaction $^{10}B\ (n, \alpha)\ ^{7}Li$ occurs, and it is the resultant alpha particle that is detected by the scintillator (18). It was by means of such a cadmium-loaded scintillator that the neutrino (see Chapter 3) was first experimentally detected (91). Using paired detectors, only one of which was sensitive to neutrons, Williams and Hayes (113) developed a scintillation rate meter for differentiating mixed gamma-neutron radiation from a nuclear reactor.

2. Continuous-Flow Scintillation Detectors

An entirely different approach to liquid scintillation type assay has resulted from the work of Steinberg. In 1958, he introduced an efficient method for scintillation counting in a two-phase system, which consisted of a solid, insoluble fluor in intimate contact with an *aqueous solution* containing a radioactive sample. At first, a plastic fluor of Pilot Scintillator B (Pilot Chemicals, Inc.) was used in the form of either fine filaments or beads (103). Aqueous sample solutions were pipetted into counting vials packed with the fluor and counted in the normal manner with quite a respectable efficiency. Later (104–105), Steinberg found that the substitution of blue-violet fluorescence grade anthracene crystals as the fluor gave more reproducible results and higher counting efficiencies. Myers and Brush (124) have used Steinberg's technique to assay with high efficiencies ^{45}Ca, ^{90}Sr, ^{32}P, ^{210}Po and other nuclides.

Although Steinberg's method involved the assay of individual aqueous samples, several investigators have employed his idea to construct continuous-flow detectors. In these detectors, a stream of aqueous or gaseous samples containing radioactive material is passed through a cell loosely packed with fine anthracene crystals. The cell is optically coupled to a pair of photomultipliers, which view the fluorescence of the anthracene crystals resulting from beta interaction (27, p. 222–226). Counter data are displayed by means of a ratemeter and recorder. The primary application of this detection method has been for monitoring *effluents* from gas-liquid chromatographs or amino acid analyzers (125). Schram and Lombaert (99–100), Rapkin and Gibbs (128), and Karmen, et al. (121) have used such a flow counter for ^{14}C and ^{3}H determinations; Scharpenseel and Menke (96) have employed it with ^{35}S-containing effluents, as well. Surprisingly enough, retention of most forms of activity on the surface of the anthracene crystals is minimal, and resolution of a typical column chromatogram is unaltered by passage through the cell. Counting efficiency is heavily dependent on flow rate. Efficiencies of better than 30 per cent for carbon-14 and 1–2.5 per cent for tritium can be realized in routine assays using commercially available detectors. Unfortunately, the monitoring technique cannot be employed whenever organic solvents are used in the chromatography operation, inasmuch as the fluor is readily soluble in organic solvents. Karmen, et al. (64), have more recently employed detectors packed with silicone-coated *p*-terphenyl crystals for such flow monitoring.

Alternatively, Popjak, et al. (126) have described a system in which gaseous chromatographic effluents are trapped directly in a heated fluor solution which is then cooled and continuously circulated between two facing photomultipliers. It is possible to assay ^{14}C and ^{3}H simultaneously with high counting efficiencies by means of this procedure.

A variant type of scintillation flow detector utilizes a cell which is itself the plastic fluor. Schram and Lombaert (98) have described such a detector in which the flowing liquid is passed through a spiral chamber machined in a plastic fluor block. The fluor block was optically coupled to two photomultipliers to complete the detector. Alternatively, the plastic scintillator can be in the form of a tight spiral of tubing, coupled to the photomultipliers. Funt and Heatherington (31) have assayed ^{32}P, ^{22}Na, and ^{14}C solutions with a detector of this type with counting efficiencies of 76 per cent, 51 per cent, and 5.7 per cent, respectively; Kimbel and Willenbrink (70) have assayed ^{14}C and ^{35}S sample flows with a similar arrangement. Boyce, et al. (19), have even monitored tritiated hydrogen gas from a chromatography column in this type of detector. The practical techniques and problems involved in continuous scintillation counting of weak beta emitters in flowing aqueous streams are well discussed in commercial bulletins (26, 85).

E. OPERATING CHARACTERISTICS OF LIQUID SCINTILLATION COUNTERS

Scintillation counting is essentially a proportional counting method, that is, the magnitude of the output signal from the detector is proportional to the energy dissipated by the radiation particle in the scintillation solution. Since beta particles are emitted over a continuous energy spectrum, and in the case of weak betas, nearly all the particle energy is given up to the scintillation solution, a pulse height analyzer is almost universally used with a liquid scintillation detector. This is an electronic component which accepts and passes on for counting only pulses of heights falling between two predetermined discriminator limits (the "window" or "channel"), which can be varied by the operator over an arbitrary voltage scale. Pulse height analysis makes it possible to select the optimal counter settings under different detection circumstances, to determine the extent of quenching in a sample, and simultaneously to count the activity in a sample labeled with two or even three different isotopes (132). Most commercially available counting assemblies have three or four adjustable discriminators allowing two-channel operation (16). A few counters have three channels. Blanchard (15) has described a computer program for the automated analysis of the masses of data provided by such counting systems.

1. Selection of Optimal Counter Settings

a. *Effect of photomultiplier gain and "window" settings.* The size of a detector pulse resulting from a given beta interaction in a scintillation solution is governed by both the energy of the beta particle and the gain of the photomultiplier. This gain is directly related to the potential gradient applied across the dynode chain of the photomultiplier. By increasing this potential, larger pulse sizes will pass to the pulse height analyzer. Thus, photomultiplier voltage is a primary consideration in liquid scintillation counting.

In selecting a proper counter setting, that is, photomultiplier voltage and "window width" of the discriminator, for a given type of counting sample, one must consider two key points. First, it is important to obtain the highest possible counting efficiency of the sample radioactivity and the lowest possible rate of background (the "figure of merit"). This will permit one to count a sample in question at a desirable standard deviation within the shortest possible counting period. Such consideration is obviously very important with samples having a low level of radioactivity. Secondly, the highest possible stability of counting process must be obtained in order to avoid minor changes in counting efficiency due to variations in the nature and the concentration of the quenching agent. This is particularly important when one is faced with a great number of counting samples similar in composition and having a sufficient amount of radioactivity so that background considerations are not too significant. There are several different ways of selecting proper counter settings. Since the concepts underlying these are not entirely the same, they are devised for specific types of counting samples.

b. *Balance point operation.* Under the balance point concept, the optimal counter settings should be such that a so-called balance point is attained. This represents a position where the beta spectrum under consideration is such that, at that specific photomultiplier gain and window width, the efficiency of detection is maximum. The balance point, of course, varies with different radioisotopes and different sample preparations. The balance point setting of the counter can be recognized by examining the beta spectra observed at different photomultiplier gains, that is, different potentials applied at the photomultiplier (see Figure 6-9). As

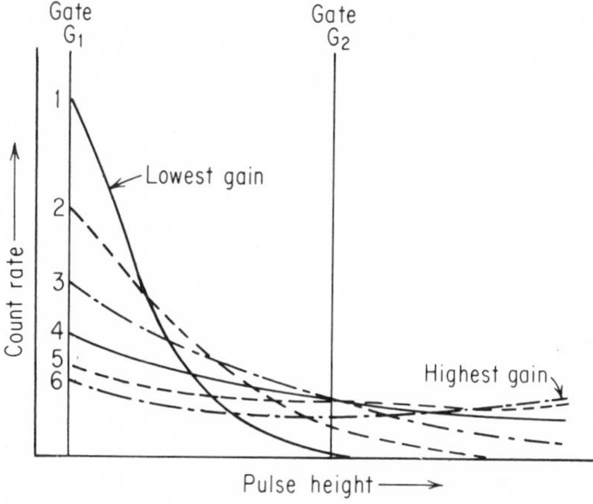

Figure 6-9. Pulse spectra of ^{14}C at different photomultiplier gain settings.

shown in Figure 6-9, the area under each curve represents the integrated counts that can be detected at the specific high voltage setting.

When the high-voltage setting is approximately 800 volts (low gain on the photomultiplier), one finds that all the pulses derived from ^{14}C are confined to the region between "gates" G_1 and G_2. A wider "gate" (discriminator level) than this would not increase detection efficiency but would give rise to higher background counting rates. Consequently, the balance point setting can be readily visualized by setting up gates to cover the major portion of the beta spectrum at given high voltages applied to the photomultiplier.

The balance point, however, is usually ascertained by first determining count rates of the sample and the background for varied window settings at each photomultiplier gain, as shown in Figure 6-10. From these data is then calculated the setting which gives the maximum value to the expression S^2/B, where S equals the net sample count rate and B stands for the background count rate. It should be obvious that the balance point setting should be used when one is counting samples of low activity.

c. *Flat spectrum operation.* The balance point counting procedure is open to considerable error when variation in the concentration of the quenching agent in counting samples occurs. Consequently, the counting efficiency of each counting sample must be determined individually by one of the methods given later. Such determination of the counting efficiency of individual samples when one is handling a large number of similar counting samples becomes an impractical task. It is therefore desirable to modify the counter settings so that one can enjoy some meas-

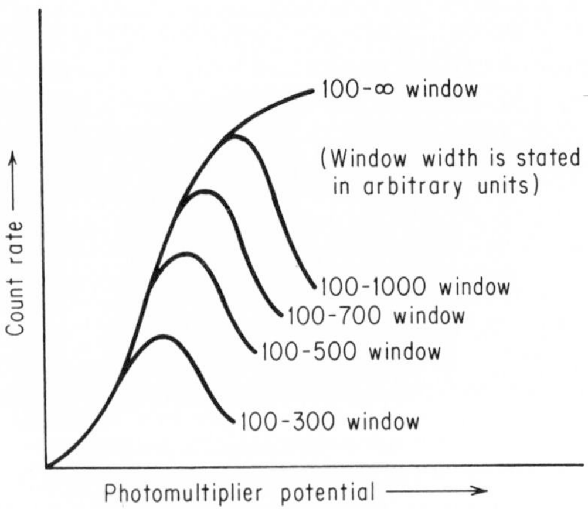

Figure 6-10. Balance point determination—effect of window width on count rate.

ure of immunity from the effects brought on by variations in the concentration of quenching agent in counting samples.

In order to visualize such a different type of counter setting one should first examine the pulse spectra of ^{14}C seen at different photomultiplier gains (Figure 6-9). Note that they are primarily a series of curves having varying slopes. At the higher gain settings the spectra are flat over much of their extent. This flattening of the spectra is to be expected if one considers that, upon increasing the gain factor of the photomultiplier, the pulse size distribution will be spread over a much broader range. Consequently, when one compares the counting rate observed in a given portion of the spectrum (a defined window), one would expect a lower count rate in that window at higher gain. Since the total counts observed from a sample are represented by the area under the curve, the spreading of the upper margin (energy-wise) by increasing the gain will naturally result in a lower counting rate per unit width of the spectrum, particularly in peak areas.

It will be recalled that the effect of quenching is to reduce pulse height, or in other words, to shift the beta spectrum to the left on the figure indicated. This being the case, the effect of quenching on a flat spectrum will be very slight indeed, insofar as bringing about a reduction of counting rate in the window shown (between gates G_1 and G_2). Any loss in count rate from pulses shifted below the level of gate G_1 by quenching will be compensated for by a corresponding shift of higher pulses to below the level of gate G_2.

It is clear from Figure 6-9 that the counting rate in the window between gates G_1 and G_2 is much lower at the higher photomultiplier gain settings than at low gains. Thus, for maximal counting rates in flat spectrum operation it is desirable to use a window setting as wide as possible to cover the major portion of the flat spectrum. True, a wide window of this type will result in a relatively higher counting rate for background radiation in the case of ^{14}C and ^{3}H counting samples. But this fact will not increase the counting time requirements significantly for samples with sufficient amounts of radioactivity, that is, samples with a counting rate of at least several hundred cpm.

The salient advantage of flat spectrum counting of samples is that even moderately severe quenching results in only an insignificant reduction in counting efficiency. This is particularly important when one must count a large number of samples of essentially similar composition. Flat spectrum counting is more fully described by Wang (94, p. 285–289).

d. *Pulse summation.* In its Series 3000 and 4000 liquid scintillation counters (see Figure 6-4) the Packard Instrument Company has introduced the new feature of pulse summation. This innovation involves summing the output pulses from the two photomultipliers viewing the sample. The result is a virtual doubling of pulse heights from sample scintillation events that can create coincident pulses, without any corresponding increase in photomultiplier noise pulses. Thus, an increase in the sample-to-background ratio (figure of merit) occurs—an important consideration in counter performance. The over-all detection efficiency is also slightly improved, since pulse summation results in the pulse heights of some otherwise uncounted coincident pulses being increased above the noise level.

An important consequence of pulse summation is a *better separation of spectral peaks.* Such separation is of considerable importance in experiments employing two beta-emitting isotopes of similar energies concurrently, as for example ^{14}C and ^{3}H. Figure 6-11 shows spectra for ^{14}C and ^{3}H obtained by use of pulse summation. It will readily be seen that by operating the counter with a low gate (discriminator level) at the position indicated on the figure, the great majority of ^{14}C pulses can be counted in the absence of any tritium pulses. By contrast, with counters without the pulse summation feature one would find much greater overlapping of ^{3}H and ^{14}C spectra.

Note that the *shape of pulse spectra* observed with a counter equipped with pulse summation differs considerably from that observed using earlier counters. This effect of pulse summation from two photomultiplier tubes is illustrated by the ^{3}H spectra given in Figure 6-12. Here, the ^{3}H spectra observed with a single photomultiplier (the other photomultiplier was used only as a coincidence monitor) is compared with that observed with two photomultipliers in summation. The net effect of summation is that pulse sizes are considerably increased from a single scintillation

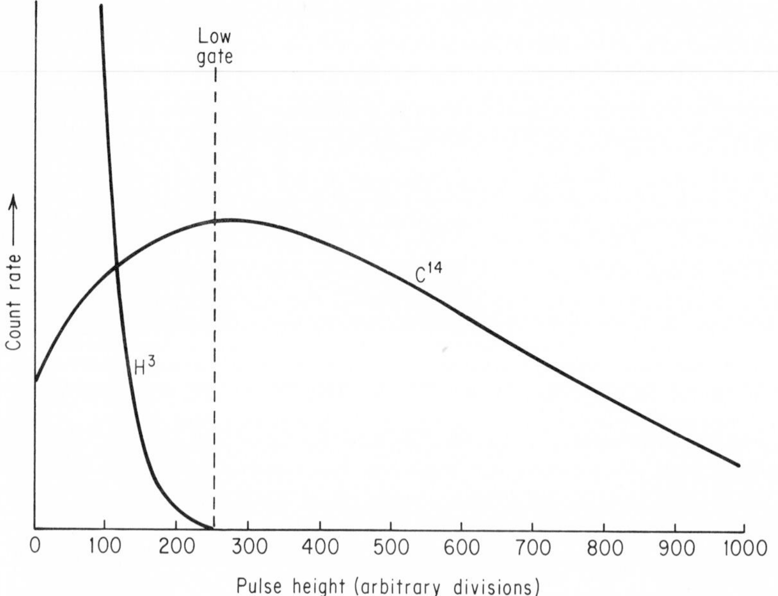

Figure 6-11. Separation of spectra of ^{14}C and ^{3}H by means of pulse summation.

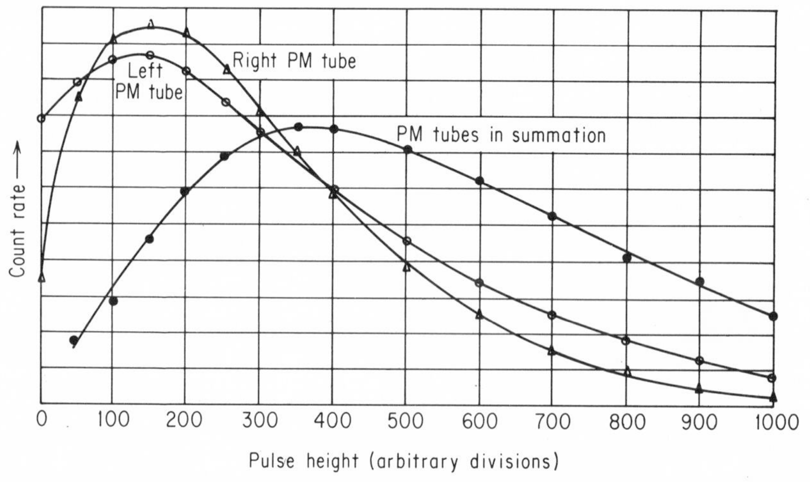

Figure 6-12. Tritium spectra with and without pulse summation.

event, resulting in a general shift of the spectrum toward the right. This allows a more clean-cut separation of small sample pulse heights from noise pulses of the same initial height. It should be pointed out, however, that the rather acute ascending slope of the observed tritium pulse spectrum at the lower pulse height levels represents, in reality, a distortion of the true tritium beta spectrum. This results from the effect of the counter's coincidence circuitry.

2. Determination of Counting Efficiency

The efficiency of a liquid scintillation counter depends on several variable factors. Whisman, et al. (109) have surveyed and evaluated these variables. The effect of temperature on photomultiplier thermal noise has been previously discussed (p. 109). Seliger and Ziegler (102) and Rosenthal and Anger (92) have investigated temperature effects on counting efficiency generally. A study of the relationship between background count rate and efficiency by Domer and Hayes (30) showed a nonlinear relation. To correlate the counting rate to the disintegration rate of a given sample, it is essential to carry out a reliable determination of the counting efficiency.

Quenching has by far the most significant effect on counting efficiency; because of that effect, a determination of counting efficiency for every prepared sample is required. By employing the flat spectrum counting procedure one can, to some extent, ignore the effect of varied quenching. It is, nevertheless, necessary to determine the counting efficiency of each specific group of samples. Several methods for determining counting efficiency have been developed (107).

a. Internal standardization method. The classical method of efficiency determination is known as *internal standardization* or *spiking*. It consists of adding a precisely known amount of the same isotope (an "internal standard") in a nonquenching form to a previously counted sample. The resulting mixture is then re-counted. The counting efficiency of the quenched sample can then be determined as follows:

(6-1) Efficiency (expressed as a fraction of unity) =

$$\frac{\text{Net count rate (in cpm)}_{(\text{int. std.} + \text{sample})} - \text{net count rate (in cpm)}_{(\text{sample})}}{\text{Disintegration rate (in dpm)}_{(\text{int. std.})}}$$

A variety of compounds have been employed as internal standards. Toluene-^{14}C, n-hexadecane-^{14}C, benzoic acid-^{14}C, tritiated toluene, tritiated water, and tritiated n-hexadecane are all commercially available for this purpose. Williams, et al. (112) and Marlow and Medlock (75) have described techniques for preparing the benzoic acid-^{14}C standard. Unfortunately, each standard has its drawback. Accurate pipetting of small amounts of labeled toluene is not a simple task; benzoic acid and water are themselves quenching agents, and consequently, it is necessary to use these compounds at a very low concentration. Moreover, in the case of heterogeneous samples, such as gel preparations (see Chapter 8), it is important to employ an internal standard that can stay in the same phase as the radioactive compound in the counting sample (17).

The internal standardization method suffers from several disadvantages. It is time-consuming in that two counting processes are required for each sample, and the sample vial must be opened between the counts. Furthermore, the accuracy of the determination often depends on accurate measurement of small volumes of liquid containing the compound used as the standard. The precision of the counting process can be jeopardized, since the radioactivity of the sample and standard may differ greatly.

b. *Dilution method.* Another means of determining efficiency involves counting a series of solutions having different concentrations of the same radioactive sample in the fluor solution. This can be accomplished by successive dilution of the sample solution with fluor solution. The specific activity (cpm/unit volume of counting solution (ml)) is plotted against sample concentration and the curve is then extrapolated to zero sample concentration, where theoretically sample quenching is nil. The intersection on the specific activity axis will then represent the activity figure without sample quenching. This method, too, is time-consuming and subject to considerable manipulative error. Peng (27, p. 260–275) has presented an excellent evaluation and comparison of the internal standard and dilution methods of determining counting efficiency.

c. *Pulse height shift method.* When quenching occurs, the average energy of the beta pulse spectrum decreases, and consequently, the entire beta spectrum shifts toward a lower energy level in a typical count rate versus pulse height plot (see Figure 6-13*c*). Baillie (6), in 1960, first suggested a practical means for relating the degree of this pulse height shift to the extent of quenching. Bruno and Christian (20) subsequently refined the technique. Currently the terms *pulse height shift* and *channels ratio* method are used interchangeably in respect to the procedure.

Several practical techniques may be employed; the most common may be briefly outlined as follows: (1) On a dual-channel liquid scintillation spectrometer, the beta spectrum of an unquenched standard sample above the noise level is first ascertained (Figure 6-13*a*). (2) The discriminators are now set to give two pulse windows. Channel 1 covers only the first one-third of the energy spectrum, whereas channel 2 encompasses nearly the whole spectrum (Figure 6-13*b*). Under these conditions a defined ratio will be observed between the net counting rates (that is, sample counting rate minus background counting rate) from the two channels. (3) To the counting sample is then added increasing amounts of a quenching agent and the counting rate observed for each of the concentrations of the quenching agent. In accordance with the quenching phenomena, the net count rate ratio between the two channels for these samples will increase as the concentration of quenching agent in the samples increases (Figure 6-13*c*) and as the counting efficiency decreases. The plot of counting efficiency versus the channels' net count ratio thus provides one with a standard *quench correction curve* (Figure 6-13*d*). It has been reported that such a plot is essentially independent of the nature of the quenching agent. Consequently, from this plot it is possible to ascertain the counting efficiency of a given sample of a specific radioisotope, once the channels' net count ratio is known. Obviously, if one desires to cross-compare radioactivity in a number of samples, one may desire to use this plot to convert all the counting data to a definite counting efficiency, for example,

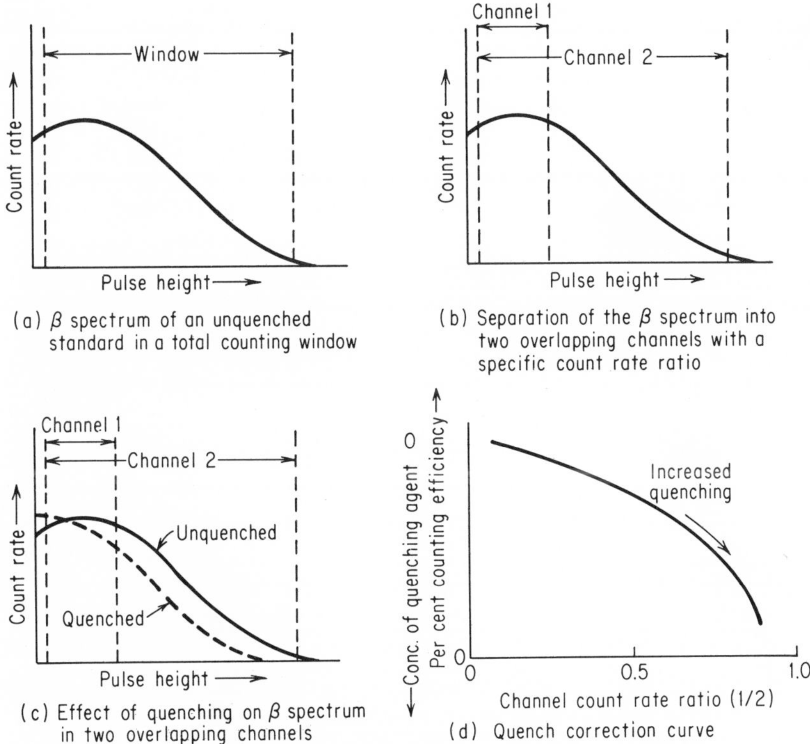

Figure 6-13. Procedure in preparing a quench correction curve by the pulse height shift method.

the counting efficiency without the quencher. (Detailed procedures will be found in Experiment IV.

The advantages of this method are evident (22). A single quench correction curve for either ^{14}C or ^{3}H has been found sufficient to cover many of the common chemical quenching agents, although it will not account for color quenching. Such a curve, however, is strictly valid for only a specified counter and its associated settings such as photomultiplier potential, discriminator settings, and so on. More recently, this method has been applied to dual radioisotope counting by Hendler (54, 119) and Weltman and Talmage (131). Practical suggestions concerning the channels ratio method can be found in commercial material (23).

d. *External standard method.* Recent reports by Fleishman and Glazunov (118) and by Higashimura, et al. (56) have described the use of an external standard, a *gamma emitter*, for determining the counting efficiency associated with a given liquid scintillation counting sample. Use is made of the Compton electrons derived from the interaction of gamma rays with the counting glass vial and the scintillation solution. The energy spectrum of such Compton electrons resembles in shape the beta spectrum of soft beta emitters. It follows that the effect of quenching agents upon energy transfer from the Compton electrons to the fluor, leading eventually to the formation of photoelectrons in the photomultiplier, should be somewhat similar to that on the energy transfer process with beta particles. This fact makes it possible to correlate the counting efficiency of a given beta emitter (such as ^{14}C), as determined by the internal standard method, to the counting rate of a given gamma source. Thus, when ^{137}Cs is used as an external source, a correlation curve for the ^{14}C counting efficiency to the count rate of the ^{137}Cs source is obtained, as shown in Figure 6-14. The nonlinear character of the function probably reflects the difference between the energy spectrum of the Compton electrons and the ^{14}C beta spectrum. Nevertheless, the observed definite correlation makes it possible to use this method to calibrate counting efficiency as affected by chemical quenching, color quenching, or dilution.

The new ANSitron liquid scintillation counter previously described incorporates this external standard method in its routine operation. In this counter, a 5 μc collimated ^{137}Cs point source is stored in a shielded compartment. Upon completion of the counting of a given sample, the observed counting rate, computed to a counts-per-minute basis, is stored in the electronic memory. The cesium source is then brought to a location immediately next to the counting vial, at about half the height of the vial. At this point another 1-min count is taken. From this counting rate, which represents the counting rate for both the external ^{137}Cs source and the sample inside the vial, is subtracted the sample counting rate in the electronic memory, thereby giving the *net* counting rate for the external

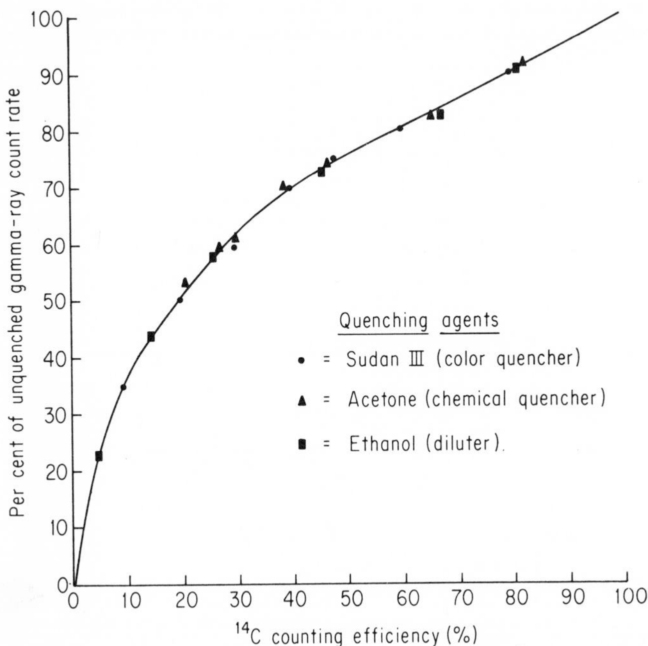

Figure 6-14. Quenching calibration curve for ^{14}C counting efficiency using an external ^{137}Cs standard and three types of quenching agents.

^{137}Cs source. Both the sample counting rate and the net counting rate for the external standard are then printed out automatically. Similar provisions have also been introduced into the Packard Instrument Company's Series 3000, using either ^{137}Cs or ^{226}Ra.

The magnitude of the net counting rate of the external source is naturally affected by the quenching behavior of the liquid counting sample. If a correlation curve has been constructed previously, it is then possible to estimate the counting efficiency of the liquid sample in question from the observed net counting rate of the external source. Even though the external standard method has not been tested extensively with certain types of samples, such as gels, filter paper, and the like, there is no denying that its use will offer some advantages over the internal standard method and possibly the channels ratio method.

F. SUMMARY

Internal-sample scintillation counting has the inherent advantages of high counting efficiency (particularly for low-energy beta emitters),

TABLE 6-1

Summary of Radiation Detector Characteristics

Detector Type	Energy Discrimination	Detection Medium	Reproducibility	Detector Amplification Factor	Relative Electronic Amplification Required	Resolving Time (μsec)	Relative Background	Relative Detection Efficiency α	β	γ	Most Commonly Used Sample Form	Relative Degree of Difficulty in Preparing Sample
Ion chamber with vibrating-reed electrometer	Yes	Gas	Excellent	1	Very high	Not applicable	Low	Good	Good	Poor	Gas	High*
Proportional detector	Yes	Gas	Good	10^2–10^4	High	5–50	Low	Good	Good	Poor	Solid	Medium†
Geiger-Mueller detector	No	Gas	Fair	10^7	Low	100–1000	Medium	Good	Good	Poor	Solid	Medium†
Solid (external-sample) scintillation detector	Yes	Solid	Good	10^6	Low	0.3– > 1	High	Fair	Fair	Very good	Solid or liquid	Medium† or low‡
Liquid (internal-sample) scintillation detector	Yes	Liquid	Fair	10^6	Medium	0.001– < 1	Low	Very good	Very good	Fair	Solution	Low

*Usually involves individual combustion of samples to gaseous form.
†Usually involves preparation of planchet-mounted samples.
‡Where well-type detector used for liquid samples.

spectra analysis, relative ease of sample preparation, and accommodation of relatively large amounts of sample material. Because of its widespread use for assaying samples containing carbon-14 and tritium, it is of special importance to the biologist.

Table 6-1 summarizes pertinent information concerning the characteristics of the detectors discussed thus far: the ion chamber with a vibrating-reed electrometer, the proportional detector, the Geiger-Mueller detector, and both external-sample and internal-sample scintillation detectors. Although the data listed are of necessity general, they are based on the forms of these detectors most commonly used in radiotracer assays.

BIBLIOGRAPHY

1. Agranoff, Bernard W. 1957. Silica vials improve low-level counting. Nucleonics 15(10):106.
2. Anderson, Ernest C., et al. 1955. A whole body gamma counter for human subjects. U.S. Atomic Energy Commission, LA-1717. 43p.
3. Anderson, Ernest C., et al. 1956. The Los Alamos human counter. Nucleonics 14(1):26–29.
4. Arnold, James R. 1955. New liquid scintillation phosphors. Science 122:1139–1140.
5. Audric, B. N., and J. V. P. Long. 1952. Measurement of low energy β-emitters by liquid scintillation counting. Research 5:46–47.
6. Baillie, L. A. 1960. Determination of liquid scintillation counting efficiency by pulse height shift. Intern. J. Appl. Radiation Isotopes 8:1–7.
7. Bannerman, D. E., and R. J. Lanter. 1956. Durable white coating improves liquid scintillation counters. Nucleonics 14(2):60–61.
8. Barnett, Martin D., et al. 1959. Liquid scintillators. VI. 2-aryl- and 2, 7-diaryl-fluorenes. J. Am. Chem. Soc. 81:4583–4586.
9. Barnett, Martin D., et al. 1960. Liquid scintillators. XI. 2-(2-fluorenyl)-5-aryl-substituted oxazoles and 2-(2-fluorenyl)-5-phenyl-1, 3, 4-oxadiazole. J. Am. Chem. Soc. 82: 2282–2285.
10. Belcher, E. H. 1953. Scintillation counters using liquid luminescent media for absolute standardization and radioactive assay. J. Sci. Instruments 30:286–289.
11. Bell, Carlos G., Jr., and F. Newton Hayes (eds.). 1958. Liquid scintillation counting. Proc. Conf. Northwestern University, Evanston, 1957. Pergamon Press, Inc., New York. 292 p.
12. Berlman, Isadore B. 1961. Luminescence in a scintillation solution excited by α and β particles and related studies in quenching. J. Chem. Phys. 34:598–603.
13. Birkeland, Stephen P., et al. 1960. Liquid scintillators. X. Some aryl substituted phenanthrenes and dihydrophenanthrenes, and related *p*-terphenyls and *p*-quaterphenyls. Determination of Kallman parameters. Z. Physik 159:516–523.
14. Birkeland, Stephen P., et al. 1961. Liquid scintillators. IX. Synthesis of some aryl substituted phenanthrenes and dihydrophenanthrenes, and related *p*-terphenyls and *p*-quaterphenyls. J. Org. Chem. 26:2662–2667.

15. Blanchard, F. A. 1963. A computer program for automated testing and reduction of liquid scintillation data. Intern. J. Appl. Radiation Isotopes 14:213–219.

16. Blau, Monte. 1957. Separated channels improve liquid scintillation counting. Nucleonics 15(4):90–91.

17. Bloom, Ben. 1963. Use of internal scintillation standards in heterogeneous counting systems. Anal. Biochem. 6:359–361.

18. Bollinger, Lowell M., and George E. Thomas. 1957. Boron-loaded liquid scintillation neutron detectors. Rev. Sci. Instruments 28:489–496.

19. Boyce, I. S., J. F. Cameron, and K. J. Taylor. 1960. A simple plastic scintillation counter for tritiated hydrogen. Intern. J. Appl. Radiation Isotopes 9:122–123.

20. Bruno, Gerald A., and John E. Christian. 1961. Corrections for quenching associated with liquid scintillation counting. Anal. Chem. 33:650.

21. Buck, Warren L., and Robert K. Swank. 1958. Use of isopropylbiphenyl as solvent in liquid scintillators. Rev. Sci. Instruments 29:252.

22. Bush, Elizabeth T. 1963. General applicability of the channels ratio method of measuring liquid scintillation counting efficiencies. Anal. Chem. 35:1024–1029.

23. Bush, Elizabeth T. 1962. How to determine efficiency automatically in liquid scintillation counting. Nuclear-Chicago Tech. Bull. No. 13. Des Plaines, Ill. 4 p.

24. Chleck, D. J., and C. A. Ziegler. 1957. Ultrasonic degassing of liquid scintillators. Rev. Sci. Instruments 28:466–467.

25. Christian, J. E., W. V. Kessler, and P. L. Ziemer. 1962. A 2π liquid scintillation counter for determining the radioactivity of large samples including man and animals. Intern. J. Appl. Radiation Isotopes 13:557-564.

26. Continuous scintillation counting of weak beta emitters in flowing aqueous streams. 1963. Nuclear-Chicago Tech. Bull. No. 15. Des Plaines, Ill. 4 p.

27. Daub, Guido H., F. Newton Hayes, and Elizabeth Sullivan (eds.). 1961. Proc. Univ. New Mexico Conf. Organic Scintillation Detectors, Albuquerque, 1960. TID-7612. U. S. Government Printing Office, Washington. 417 p.

28. Davidson, Jack D., and Philip Feigelson. 1957. Practical aspects of internal-sample liquid-scintillation counting. Intern. J. Appl. Radiation Isotopes 2:1–18.

29. De Bersaques, J. 1963. Relation between the absorption and the quenching of liquid scintillation samples. Intern. J. Appl. Radiation Isotopes 14:173–174.

30. Domer, Floyd R., and F. Newton Hayes. 1960. Background vs. efficiency in liquid scintillators. Nucleonics 18(1):100.

31. Funt, B. L., and A. Hetherington. 1959. Spiral capillary plastic scintillation flow counter for beta assay. Science 129:1429–1430.

32. Funt, B. L., and A. Hetherington. 1962. The kinetics of quenching in liquid scintillators. Intern. J. Appl. Radiation Isotopes 13:215–221.

33. Furst, Milton, and Hartmut Kallman. 1952. High energy induced fluorescence in organic liquid solutions (Energy transport in liquids). III. Phys. Rev. 85:816–825.

34. Furst, Milton, and Hartmut Kallman. 1954. Energy transfer by means of collision in liquid organic solutions under high energy and ultraviolet excitations. Phys. Rev. 94:503–507.

35. Furst, Milton, and Hartmut Kallman. 1955. Fluorescent behavior of solutions containing more than one solvent. J. Chem. Phys. 23:607–612.

36. Gilman, Henry, et al. 1957. Some derivatives of aza-aromatic heterocycles as liquid scintillator solutes. J. Org. Chem. 22:1169–1171.

37. Gilman, Henry, et al. 1958*a*. Some oxygen-containing heterocycles as liquid scintillation solutes. J. Org. Chem. 23:361–362.

38. Gilman, Henry, et al. 1958*b*. Some N-arylated heterocycles as liquid scintillation solutes. J. Org. Chem. 23:628–629.

39. Gilman, Henry, Eugene A. Weipert, and F. Newton Hayes. 1958*a*. Some polyaryl derivatives of metals and metalloids as liquid scintillator solutes. J. Org. Chem. 23:760–762.

40. Gilman, Henry, Eugene A. Weipert, and F. Newton Hayes. 1958*b*. Some derivatives of biphenyl as liquid scintillator solutes. J. Org. Chem. 23:910–911.

41. Harley, John H., Naomi A. Hallden, and Isabel M. Fisenne. 1962. Beta scintillation counting with thin plastic phosphors. Nucleonics 20(1):59–61.

42. Harrison, F. B. 1952. Large-area liquid scintillation counters. Nucleonics 10(6):40–45.

43. Harrison, F. B. 1954. Slow component in decay of fluors. Nucleonics 12(3):24–25.

44. Hayes, F. N., R. D. Hiebert, and R. L. Schuch. 1952. Low energy counting with a new liquid scintillation solute. Science 116: 140.

45. Hayes, F. Newton. 1953. Liquid solution scintillators. U.S. Atomic Energy Commission, LA-1639. 75 p.

46. Hayes, F. Newton, et al. 1955. Liquid scintillators. I. Pulse height comparison of primary solutes. Nucleonics 13(12):38–41.

47. Hayes, F. Newton, Donald G. Ott, and Vernon N. Kerr. 1956. Liquid scintillators. II. Relative pulse height comparisons of secondary solutes. Nucleonics 14(1):42–45.

48. Hayes, F. Newton. 1956. Liquid scintillators: attributes and applications. Intern. J. Appl. Radiation Isotopes 1:46–56.

49. Hayes, F. Newton, and Donald G. Ott. 1957. The small-volume internal-sample liquid scintillation counter. U.S. Atomic Energy Commission, LA-2095. 37 p.

50. Hayes, F. N., et al. 1958. Survey of organic compounds as primary scintillation solutes. U.S. Atomic Energy Commission, LA-2176. 24 p.

51. Hayes, F. Newton. 1962. Solutes and solvents for liquid scintillation counting. Rev. ed. Packard Instrument Company, Tech. Bull. No. 1. La Grange, Ill. 8 p.

52. Hejwowski, J., and A. Szymanski. 1961. Lithium loaded liquid scintillator. Rev. Sci. Instruments 32:1057–1058.

53. Helmick, Marie. 1960. The quenching effect of benzoic acid in a liquid scintillation system. Atomlight (New England Nuclear Corp.), February, 1960, p. 6–7.

54. Hendler, Richard W. n.d. Dual isotope counting by channels ratio method. Nuclear-Chicago Preliminary Tech. Bull. Des Plaines, Ill.

55. Herberg, R. J. 1960. Backgrounds for liquid scintillation counting of colored solutions. Anal. Chem. 32:1468–1471.

56. Higashimura, T., et al. 1962. External standard method for the determination of the efficiency in liquid scintillation counting. Intern. J. Appl. Radiation Isotopes 13:308–309.

57. Hodgson, T. S., B. E. Gordon, and M. E. Ackerman. 1958. Single-channel counter for carbon-14 and tritium. Nucleonics 16(7):89–94.

58. Jackson, Jasper A., and F. B. Harrison. 1953. A slow component in the decay of the scintillation phosphors. Phys. Rev. 89:322.

59. Kallman, Hartmut. 1950. Scintillation counting with solutions. Phys. Rev. 78:621–622.

60. Kallman, Hartmut, and Milton Furst. 1950*a*. Fluorescence of liquids under gamma bombardment. Nucleonics 7(1):69–71.

61. Kallman, Hartmut, and Milton Furst. 1950*b*. Fluorescence of solutions bombarded with high energy radiation (Energy transport in liquids). Phys. Rev. 79:857–870.

62. Kallman, Hartmut, and Milton Furst. 1951. Fluorescence of solutions bombarded with high energy radiation (Energy transport in liquids) Part II. Phys. Rev. 81:853–864.

63. Karmen, Arthur, Irmgarde McCaffrey, and Bernard Kliman. 1963. Derivative ratio analysis: A new method for measurement of steroids and other compounds with specific functional groups using radioassay by gas-liquid chromatography. Anal. Biochem. 6:31–38.

64. Karmen, Arthur, et al. 1963. Measurement of tritium in the effluent of a gas chromatography column. Anal. Chem. 35:536–542.

65. Karmen, A., and H. R. Tritch. 1960. Radioassay by gas chromatography of compounds labelled with carbon-14. Nature 186:150–151.

66. Kerr, Vernon N., F. Newton Hayes, and Donald G. Ott. 1957. Liquid scintillators. III. The quenching of liquid scintillator solutions by organic compounds. Intern. J. Appl. Radiation Isotopes 1:284–288.

67. Kerr, V. N., et al. 1959*a*. Liquid scintillators. VII. 2,5-diaryl substituted thiazoles as liquid scintillator solutes. J. Org. Chem. 24:1861–1864.

68. Kerr, V. N., et al. 1959*b*. Liquid scintillators. VIII. The effect of the dialkylamino group. J. Org. Chem. 24:1864–1866.

69. Kimbel, K. H., and J. Willenbrink. 1961. An inexpensive disposable sample container for single phototube liquid scintillation counting. Intern. J. Appl. Radiation Isotopes 11:157.

70. Kimbel, K. H., and J. Willenbrink. 1958. Fortlaufende Messung schwacher β-Strahler in Flüssigkeiten mit Szintillatorschlauch. Naturwissenschaften 45:567.

71. Kobayashi, Yutaka. 1961. Liquid scintillation counting and some practical considerations. Tracerlab, Waltham, Mass. 20 p.

72. Liquid scintillation counting. 1962. Nuclear-Chicago Tech. Pub. No. 711580. Des Plaines, Ill. 40 p.

73. Lohmann, W., and W. H. Perkins. 1961. Stabilization of the counting rate by irradiation of the liquid scintillation counting solutions with UV-light. Nuclear Instruments Methods 12:329–334.

74. Lukens, H. R., Jr. 1961. The relationship between fluorescence intensity and counting efficiency with liquid scintillators. Intern. J. Appl. Radiation Isotopes 12:134–140.

75. Marlow, W. F., and R. W. Medlock. 1960. A carbon-14 beta-ray standard, benzoic acid-7-C^{14} in toluene, for liquid scintillation counters. J. Res. Nat. Bur. Standards 64A:143–146.

76. Miranda, H. A., Jr., and H. Schimmel. 1959. New liquid scintillant. Rev. Sci. Instruments 30:1128–1129.

77. Okita, George T., et al. 1957. Assaying compounds containing H^3 and C^{14}. Nucleonics 15(6):111–114.

78. Ott, Donald G., et al. 1955. Argon treatment of liquid scintillators to eliminate oxygen quenching. Nucleonics 13(5):62.

79. Ott, Donald G., et al. 1957. Liquid scintillators. V. Absorption and fluorescence spectra of 2,5-diaryloxazoles and related compounds. J. Am. Chem. Soc. 79:5448–5454.

80. Ott, Donald G., et al. 1960. Liquid scintillators. XII. Absorption and fluorescence spectra of 2,5-diaryl-1,3,4-oxadiazoles. J. Org. Chem. 25:872–873.

81. Popják, G., et al. 1959. Scintillation counter for the measurement of radioactivity of vapors in conjunction with gas-liquid chromatography. J. Lipid Res. 1:29–39.

82. Pringle, R. W., et al. 1953. A new quenching effect in liquid scintillators. Phys. Rev. 92:1582–1583.

83. Protopopov, Kh. V., et al. 1958. New liquid scintillators. Instruments Exp. Tech. 2:200–204. (Translated from Pribory i Tekh. Eksperimenta.)

84. Raben, M. S., and N. Bloembergen. 1951. Determination of radioactivity by solution in a liquid scintillator. Science 114:363–364.

85. Rapkin, Edward. 1963. Liquid scintillation counting with suspended scintillators. (Packard Instrument Company, Tech. Bull. No. 11). La Grange, Ill. 10 p.

86. Rapkin, E., and J. A. Gibbs. 1963. Polyethylene containers for liquid scintillation spectrometry. Intern. J. Appl. Radiation Isotopes 14:71–74.

87. Reines, R., et al. 1953. Determination of total body radioactivity using scintillation detectors. Nature 172:521–523.

88. Reynolds, George T., F. B. Harrison, and G. Salvini. 1950. Liquid scintillation counters. Phys. Rev. 78:488.

89. Reynolds, George T. 1952. Solid and liquid scintillation counters. Nucleonics 10(7):46–53.

90. Rivlin, Richard S., and Hildegard Wilson. 1963. A simple method for separating polar steroids from the liquid scintillation phosphor. Anal. Biochem. 5:267–269.

91. Ronzio, A. R., C. L. Cowan, Jr., and F. Reines. 1958. Liquid scintillators for free neutrino detection. Rev. Sci. Instruments 29:146–147.

92. Rosenthal, Donald J., and Hal O. Anger. 1954. Liquid scintillation counting of tritium and C^{14}-labeled compounds. Rev. Sci. Instruments 25:670–674.

93. Ross, Harley H., and Roger E. Yerick. 1963. Quantitative interpretation of color quenching in liquid scintillator systems. Anal. Chem. 35:794–797.

94. Rothchild, Seymour (ed.). 1963. Advances in tracer methodology, vol. 1. Plenum Press, New York. 332 p.

95. Roucayrol, Jean C., and Erich Oberhausen. 1955. Eine Anordnung zum quantitativen Nachweis von energiearmen β-Strahlern mit fluorezierenden Losungen. Naturwissenschaften 42:411–412.

96. Scharpenseel, H. W., and K. H. Menke. 1961. Radiochromatographie mit schwachen β-Strahlern (^{35}S, ^{14}C, ^{3}H). II. Radiosäulenchromatographie mit Hilfe des Flüssigkeits-Scintillations-Spektrometers. Z. Anal. Chem. 182:1–10.

97. Schram, E. 1963. Organic scintillation detectors. Elsevier, Amsterdam. 212 p.

98. Schram, E., and R. Lombaert. 1957. Determination continue du carbone-14 et du soufre-35 en milieu aqueux par un dispositif a scintillation. Application aux effluents chromatographiques. Anal. Chim. Acta. 17:417–422.

99. Schram, E., and R. Lombaert. 1960. Dosage continu du carbone-14 dans les effluents chromatographiques au moyen de poudres d'anthracene. Arch. Intern. Physiol. Biochim. 68:845–846.

100. Schram, Eric, and Robert Lambaert. 1962. Determination of tritium and carbon-14 in aqueous solution with anthracene powder. Anal. Biochem. 3:68–74.

101. Seliger, H. H., C. A. Ziegler, and I. Jaffe. 1956. Role of oxygen in the quenching of liquid scintillators. Phys. Rev. 101:998–999.

102. Seliger, H. H., and C. A. Ziegler. 1956. Liquid-scintillator temperature effects. Nucleonics 14(4):49.

103. Steinberg, Daniel. 1958. Radioassay of carbon-14 in aqueous solutions using a liquid scintillation spectrometer. Nature 182: 740–741.

104. Steinberg, Daniel. 1959*a*. Radioassay of aqueous solutions mixed with solid crystalline fluors. Nature 183:1253–1254.

105. Steinberg, Daniel. 1959*b*. A new approach to radioassay of aqueous solutions in the liquid scintillation spectrometer. Anal. Biochem. 1:23–39.

106. Swank, Robert K., and Warren L. Buck. 1958. Spectral effects in the comparison of scintillators and photomultipliers. Rev. Sci. Instruments 29:279–284.

107. Tracerlab, Inc. 1961. Quenching in liquid scintillation counting. Waltham, Mass. 7 p.

108. Van Dilla, M. A., R. L. Schuch, and E. C. Anderson. 1954. K-9: A large 4π gamma-ray detector. Nucleonics 12(9):22–27.

109. Whisman, Marvin L., Barton H. Eccleston, and F. E. Armstrong. 1960. Liquid scintillation counting of tritiated organic compounds. Anal. Chem. 32:484–486.

110. Wiley, Richard H., C. Harry Jarboe, Jr., and F. N. Hayes. 1958. Substituted 4, 7-phenanthrolines and benzo (f)-quinolines as scintillation solutes. J. Org. Chem. 23:268–271.

111. Wiley, Richard H., et al. 1958. 1,3,5-triaryl-2-pyrazolines for use as scintillation solutes. J. Org. Chem. 23:732–738.

112. Williams, D. L., et al. 1956. Preparation of C^{14} standard for liquid scintillation counter. Nucleonics 14(1):62–64.

113. Williams, D. L., and F. N. Hayes. 1960. Liquid scintillator radiation rate meters for the measurement of gamma and fast neutron rates in mixed radiation fields. U.S. Atomic Energy Commission, LA-2375. 59 p.

114. Ziegler, C. A., H. H. Seliger, and I. Jaffe. 1956. Three ways to increase efficiency of liquid scintillators. Nucleonics 14(5):84–86.

115. Zutshi, P. K. 1963. Low-level beta counting and absorption measurement with liquid scintillators. Nucleonics 21(9):50–53.

Supplementary References

116. Benson, Royal H., and Robert L. Maute. 1962. Liquid scintillation counting of tritium: Improvements in sensitivity by efficient light collection. Anal. Chem. 34:1122–1124.

117. Faissner, Helmut, et al. 1963. New scintillation liquids. Nucleonics 21:50–55.

118. Fleishman, D. G., and V. V. Glazunov. 1962. An external standard as a means of determining the efficiency and background of a liquid scintillator. Instruments Exp. Tech. (a translation) No. 3:472–474.

119. Hendler, Richard W. 1964. Procedure for simultaneous assay of two β-emitting isotopes with the liquid scintillation counting technique. Anal. Biochem. 7:110–120.

120. International Atomic Energy Agency. 1962. Proc. Symposium Detection Use Tritium Phys. Biol. Sci., Vienna, 1961. vol. 1. 369 p.

121. Karmen, Arthur, Irmgarde McCaffrey, and Robert L. Bowman. 1962. A flow-through method for scintillation counting of carbon-14 and tritium in gas-liquid chromatographic effluents. J. Lipid Res. 3:372–377.

122. Karmen, Arthur, Laura Giuffrida, and Robert L. Bowman. 1962. Radioassay by gas-liquid chromatography of lipids labeled with carbon-14. J. Lipid Res. 3:44–52.

123. Meinertz, Hans, and Vincent P. Dole. 1962. Radioassay of low activity fractions encountered in gas-liquid chromatography of long-chain fatty acids. J. Lipid Res. 3:140–144.

124. Myers, L. S., Jr., and A. H. Brush. 1962. Counting of alpha- and beta-radiation in aqueous solutions by the detergent-anthracene scintillation method. Anal. Chem. 34:342–345.

125. Piez, Karl A. 1962. Continuous scintillation counting of carbon-14 and tritium in effluent of the automatic amino acid analyzer. Anal. Biochem. 4:444–458.

126. Popják, G., A. E. Lowe, and D. Moore. 1962. Scintillation counter for simultaneous assay of H^3 and C^{14} in gas-liquid chromatographic vapors. J. Lipid Res. 3:364–371.

127. Rapkin, E. 1964. Liquid scintillation counting 1957–1963: A review. Intern. J. Appl. Radiation Isotopes 15:69–87.

128. Rapkin, E., and J. A. Gibbs. 1962. A system for continuous measurement of radioactivity in flowing streams. Nature 194:34–36.

129. Tanielian, C., et al. 1964*a*. Influence de la purification du solvant sur le rendement des scintillateurs liquides - I. Intern. J. Appl. Radiation Isotopes 15:11–15.

130. Tanielian, C., et al. 1964*b*. Influence de la purification du solvant sur le rendement des scintillateurs liquides - II. Intern. J. Appl. Radiation Isotopes 15:17–23.

131. Weltman, J. K., and D. W. Talmage. 1963. A method for the simultaneous determination of H^3 and S^{35} in samples with variable quenching. Intern. J. Appl. Radiation Isotopes 14:541–548.

132. Wu, Ray. 1964. Simultaneous studies of phosphate transport and glycolysis by a simple liquid scintillation counting procedure with P^{32}, C^{14}, and H^3 compounds. Anal. Biochem. 7:207–214.

CHAPTER SEVEN

Detection of Radioactivity by Autoradiography

A. THE NATURE OF AUTORADIOGRAPHY

Ionizing radiation acts upon a photographic emulsion to produce a latent image much as visible light does. Light initiates a process in the emulsion which releases electrons leading to a reduction of silver halides to metallic silver, which in turn acts as a catalyst for the further reduction of silver halide in its immediate vicinity during the development process. Ionizing radiation interacts with the emulsion to provide electrons (either primary or secondary) directly, producing the same end effect. In autoradiography (also called *radioautography*), a tissue section or other biological sample containing radioactive material is placed in close contact with a sensitive emulsion. After a given period of exposure, the film is developed and the precise localization of the radioactive matter in the sample may then be determined from the pattern of darkening on the film. This method of radiation detection appeals to the biologist because no electronic equipment is needed. Furthermore, it generally involves use of familiar techniques of microscopy and histology.

Autoradiography is primarily a means of determining the *localization* of radioisotopes in a given tissue section, gross sample, or chromatogram. For example, the sites of ^{45}Ca concentration in growing bone tissue, the relative distribution of ^{32}P through a bean plant, or the localization of thymidine-^{3}H in the DNA of cell nuclei can all be readily demonstrated by this technique. Employment of the technique for precise quantitative measurements of radioactivity in biological samples, however, is attended with considerable difficulty and uncertainty (6, 14). Where gross samples are used, the relative blackening of various areas may be roughly measured with a densitometer. This is the principle behind the film badge dosimeter, as will be described in Chapter 12. Where microscopic sections are to be assayed, the tedious task of counting the individual blackened grains of silver is required (23).

To the biologist, perhaps the chief advantage of autoradiography, particularly with very soft beta emitters, is that it permits a study of function at the level of the individual cell. In addition, a permanent record is produced on film for later examination. Note however, that optimal results with this technique require considerable skill and experience. In short, autoradiography is as much an art as a science.

In this chapter, we present first some general considerations of this detection method and then discuss specific technique briefly. A detailed description of the many and varied techniques in autoradiography is beyond the scope of this book. [For further information see the bibliography at the end of this chapter. Some of these references are comprehensive. Among these, Yagoda (28) and Herz (10) deal more with the fundamental theory of autoradiography; whereas Fitzgerald, et al. (8) and Boyd (2) describe biological applications in detail. Fitzgerald's step-by-step illustrations of technique are particularly instructive. Taylor (25) and Ficq (7) give lengthy discussions of autoradiography at the cellular level. The literature abounds with reports on autoradiographic techniques involving specific tissues and radioisotopes.

B. GENERAL PRINCIPLES OF AUTORADIOGRAPHY

1. Resolution and Radioisotope Characteristics

Since the primary aim in using the autoradiographic technique is to determine localization, it is essential to achieve a high degree of resolution on the autoradiographs. *Resolution* may be defined as the minimum distance between two point sources of activity which still allows them to be distinguished from each other on the developed film. This is a particularly critical factor where intracellular localization is under investigation.

The degree of resolution is affected by a number of factors. The maximum resolution attainable in a given situation is limited by the specific emulsion used. Since radiation is emitted from a point source in all directions, the greater the distance between the radiation source and the emulsion, the more diffuse the film image produced. For optimal resolution use the thinnest feasible sample and emulsion in the closest possible contact.

One of the most significant factors affecting resolution is the character of the radiation being detected. The intensity of film blackening is directly related to the specific ionization of the ionizing particle. Alpha particles produce such intense ionization along their short paths through the emulsion that they are readily distinguished, but unfortunately, alpha-emitting isotopes are of biological interest more for their toxicity than for their usefulness as radiotracers. Beta particles, with their lower specific ionization, traverse longer, more irregular paths through the emulsion and give rise to a somewhat more diffuse image. Gamma rays are seldom involved in autoradiographic studies because of their extremely low specific ionization.

Since the ion density along a particle track is inversely related to the kinetic energy of the beta particle, it follows that low-energy beta emitters will give rise to autoradiographs of high resolution. This relation is seen from the average path length in emulsion of beta particles from the following isotopes: $^{3}H = < 2\mu$, ^{14}C and $^{35}S = < 100\mu$, and $^{32}P = > 3200\mu$. Clearly, tritium should give exceptionally high resolution in autoradiography. Since, in addition, ^{3}H-labeled compounds can usually be prepared at much higher specific activities than the corresponding ^{14}C-labeled compounds (see Chapter 11), there has been a considerable increase in the use of tritium in autoradiography in recent years (1, 15, 21, 22, p. 291–301; 26). By contrast, high-energy betas, as from ^{32}P, produce such diffuse images that highly precise intracellular localization of ^{32}P-labeled compounds is not feasible. This also generally holds true for X and γ rays. The soft X rays resulting from electron capture in such nuclides as ^{55}Fe can, however, be used to produce reasonably good images on specially sensitive emulsions.

2. Film Emulsion and Sensitivity

Film used in autoradiography is made up of three major components. The sensitive agent, usually grains of silver halide, is dispersed through a gelatin medium to form the emulsion. This emulsion is backed by a sheet of cellulose acetate or glass. The size and concentration of the silver halide grains govern both the sensitivity and resolution of the emulsion. Grain size is directly related to emulsion sensitivity, and grain concentration is directly related to the degree of resolution possible. Unfortunately, increased emulsion sensitivity to ionizing radiation of necessity increases sensitivity to background radiation "fogging." The various emulsion types available represent different compromises with regard to these factors.

Autoradiographic emulsions may be generally divided into two groups: those used only for *gross autoradiography* and those suitable for *microscopic applications*. The former group includes the various X-ray sensitive films, of which Eastman Kodak's "No-Screen" film is a typical example. This film has relatively poor resolution and a high background sensitivity. Alternatively, Eastman Kodak's single-coated, blue-sensitive

X-ray film is most often chosen for use with radiochromatograms. The so-called nuclear emulsions are used for microscopic autoradiography. These include emulsions especially sensitized to alpha or beta particles, such as Eastman Kodak's NTA or NTB series. In addition, a wide variety of specialized emulsions are available for specific autoradiographic purposes. Stripping film is one of those in commonest use. It features high resolution, but low sensitivity and is the emulsion of choice for intracellular localization studies. (For further details see descriptions of specific emulsion characteristics available from the various manufacturers who usually supply directions for developing and processing.)

3. Determination of Exposure Time

It should be frankly acknowledged that the determination of exposure time in autoradiography is largely empirical. It is suggested, therefore, in each experiment to prepare a series of duplicate samples and to expose them for varying time intervals. By maintaining careful records of sample characteristics and exposure times for later reference, it is possible to improve one's precision of determination with cumulative experience. It has been estimated that 10^6–10^8 beta particles must strike each square centimeter of X-ray film to produce optimal blackening; detectable blackening may occur as a result of 10^5–10^6 beta interactions per square centimeter. On this basis, a rough estimate of exposure time can be made by measuring the activity of the sample per cm^2 with a thin end-window G-M detector. Assuming that the count rate registered in the detector is approximately equivalent to the rate of particle interaction with the emulsion, the length of time required to accumulate the aforementioned number of beta particle interactions can be crudely estimated.

Other factors affecting exposure time are particle energy, section thickness, and background radiation. Just as background radiation produces a count rate in a G-M counter in the absence of a radioactive sample, so also it produces a general fogging of film emulsions; hence, it is always preferable to use fresh emulsions. Although it may be possible to decrease exposure time by the simple expedient of using higher activity levels, one must take care not to reach specific activities that could cause radiation damage to the tissues under investigation (18).

4. Tissue Preparation and Artifacts

In preparing either gross samples or tissue sections for autoradiography, extreme care must be exercised to avoid treatment that would leach out or move about the radioactive material. Each type of tissue and isotope poses an individual problem. For example, inorganic ^{32}P is easily leached out of many tissues, whereas organically bound ^{32}P is seldom so affected. Where tissue sections are to be prepared, the fixing and dehydrating agents used must be evaluated from this standpoint. For this reason, the freeze-drying technique is highly favored (17). Cosmos (5) has even found that incineration of tissue sections containing ^{45}Ca can be accomplished without displacement of the label. In autoradiographic techniques where tissue sections and emulsions are permanently mounted, the subsequent staining of the tissue may result in a reaction with the emulsion. The common hematoxylin and eosin stain combination, for example, is strongly absorbed by most emulsions.

Artifacts may result from a wide variety of causes and they constitute the chief difficulty in interpreting autoradiographs. Vapors from volatile agents in the sample, mechanical pressure, extraneous light during film processing, dust or debris, fingerprints, and shrinkage or expansion of either sample or film have all been known to result in artifacts on the developed film (27). To recognize and control this problem, it is suggested that parallel samples without radioactivity be processed for comparison.

C. SPECIFIC AUTORADIOGRAPHIC TECHNIQUES

Two basic methods of autoradiography are employed. One involves contact between the emulsion and the sample only during the exposure time, after which the emulsion is removed and developed. This method is most applicable to gross samples. The second method entails permanent contact between emulsion and sample and is used exclusively with thin tissue sections.

1. Temporary Contact Method

The sample under study is placed in contact with the film emulsion (usually with a thin protective sheet intervening to prevent chemical fogging) and held in place by pressure. After the exposure period, the sample is removed and the film developed. This method is most suitable for use with chromatograms of labeled materials (20; see also Experiment A, Part Three), leaf and whole plant tissues, gross bone sections, and tissue sections that have well-defined outlines (to allow subsequent superposition). This method has the advantage that little pretreatment of the sample is required and any subsequent tissue staining cannot affect the film. Generally, poor contact between emulsion and sample results in mediocre resolution ($10–30\mu$), so that this method cannot normally be used for cellular localization studies. It is frequently difficult to superimpose the sample and the developed autoradiograph for comparison.

Furthermore, the required pressure may result in artifacts on the film. The tissue sample often undergoes shrinkage, rendering interpretation of the finished autoradiograph open to some doubt. Since resolution is limited by the nature of the technique, more sensitive emulsions can be utilized for shorter exposure times.

Several unique adaptations of this method have been proposed. Hoecker, et al. (11), have described a technique which involves clamping a flexible coverslip holding a tissue section against the emulsion mounted on a glass slide. After exposure, the coverslip can be bent away from the emulsion to allow development. Later, the section can be superimposed again on the developed autoradiograph without ever having been in contact with the developing solutions. This reduces the occurrence of artifacts. Sudia and Linck (24) suggest the use of individually packaged X-ray film for gross autoradiography of plant tissues. Techniques for preparing serial cross sections of undecalcified bone for autoradiography are described by Marshall, et al. (16). Many other adaptations appear in the literature.

2. Permanent Contact Method

For better resolution and to avoid the problem of realignment, the tissue section may be mounted permanently in contact with the emulsion. After exposure and development of the film, the section may be stained and viewed simultaneously with the autoradiograph, or they may be examined directly by phase contrast microscopy. Three modifications of this method are in common use:

a. *Mounting method.* In the mounting method, the tissue section is floated on water and the emulsion, on a glass slide, brought up underneath it so that the tissue lies on the film. Following the exposure, the film is developed and the tissue stained. This is a relatively simple technique and results in reasonably high resolution (5–7μ). Disadvantages are that the development may be spotty due to nonuniform penetration of the developer through the sample, and that the film images must be viewed through the tissue sections which may be too darkly stained.

b. *Coating method.* To avoid the problems inherent in the mounting method, the tissue section can be mounted directly on a glass slide and the emulsion applied over it. The coating method involves melting the emulsion and pouring it onto the tissue section where it spreads and hardens. A higher resolution is obtained than in the foregoing method. The necessary handling of the emulsion results in a considerable increase in fogging, however, and it is difficult to secure a uniform and reproducible thickness of emulsion on the sample.

c. *Stripping-film method.* The stripping-film method is a less tedious means of applying an emulsion on a tissue section. This involves the use of films that allow the emulsion to be stripped off the base and applied directly onto the tissue section by means of water flotation. Because it gives better resolution than any of the previous methods (1–3μ), the stripping-film technique is commonly the method of choice for determination of intracellular localization. The one disadvantage of the method is the low sensitivity of the film available. Kisieleski, et al. (22, p. 302–308) have investigated the detection efficiency of the stripping-film method for tissue sections containing tritiated thymidine. A number of variations of the method have been developed in recent years (9, 13, 19).

d. *"High-resolution" methods.* More recent techniques allow the application of a monolayer of silver halide crystals on an ultrathin tissue section embedded in methacryalate. Following development of the emulsion, the tissue section is stained with uranyl or lead stains and examined by means of an electron microscope. Resolutions of the order of 0.1μ are obtainable, which are obviously most desirable for studies of intracellular localization. Caro and van Tubergen (3) have clearly described this method and some of its specific applications. In addition, Caro (4) has discussed the problem of resolution using such monolayer preparations with tritium. Some variations of this "high-resolution" method have been termed *molecular autoradiography.* Levinthal and Thomas (12) describe such an application to the autoradiography of separated strands of DNA.

BIBLIOGRAPHY

1. Adamik, Emil R. n.d. Laboratory procedures for tritium autoradiographs. Schwarz Bioresearch, Orangeburg, N. Y. 16 p.

2. Boyd, George A. 1955. Autoradiography in biology and medicine. Academic Press, New York. 399 p.

3. Caro, Lucien G., and Robert P. van Tubergen. 1962*a*. High-resolution autoradiography. I. Methods. J. Cell Biol. 15:173–188.

4. Caro, Lucien G. 1962*b*. High-resolution autoradiography. II. The problem of resolution. J. Cell Biol. 15:189–199.

5. Cosmos, Ethel. 1962. Autoradiography of Ca^{45} in ashed sections of frog skeletal muscle. Anal. Biochem. 3:90–94.

6. Domingues, F. J., A. Sarko, and R. R. Baldwin. 1956. A simplified method for quantitation of autoradiography. Intern. J. Appl. Radiation Isotopes 1:94–101.

7. Ficq, A. Autoradiography. p. 67–90. 1959. *In* J. Brachet[ed], The cell-biochemistry, physiology, morphology, vol. I. Academic Press, New York.

8. Fitzgerald, Patrick J. 1953. Radioautography: theory, technic, and applications. Lab. Invest. 2:181–222.

9. Gomberg, Henry J. 1951. A new high-resolution system of autoradiography. Nucleonics 9(4):28–43.

10. Herz, R. H. 1951. Photographic fundamentals of autoradiography. Nucleonics 9(3):24–39.

11. Hoecker, Frank E., Paul N. Wilkinson, and Jack E. Kellison. 1953. A versatile method of micro-autoradiography. Nucleonics 11(12):60–64.

12. Levinthal, Cyrus, and Charles A. Thomas. 1957. Molecular autoradiography: the β-rays from single virus particles and DNA molecules in nuclear emulsions. Biochim. Biophys. Acta 23:453–465.

13. Lotz, W. E., and P. M. Johnston. 1953. Preparation of microautoradiographs with the use of stripping film. Nucleonics 11(3):54.

14. Mamul, Ya V. 1956. Quantitative autoradiography using a radioactive wedge. Intern. J. Appl. Radiation Isotopes 1:178–183.

15. Markman, Börje. 1963. Autoradiography of tritium chromatograms. J. Chromatog. 11:118–119.

16. Marshall, J. H., V. K. White, and J. Cohen. 1956. Autoradiography of serial cross sections of undecalcified bone. Intern. J. Appl. Radiation Isotopes 1:191–193.

17. Novek, J. 1962. A high-resolution autoradiographic method for water-soluble tracers and tissue constituents. Intern. J. Appl. Radiation Isotopes 13:187–190.

18. Pelc, S. R. 1951. p. 122–137. Radiation dose in tracer experiments involving autoradiography. *In* Ciba Foundation Conf. Isotopes Biochem. Blakiston, Philadelphia.

19. Pelc, S. R. 1956. The stripping-film technique of autoradiography. Intern. J. Appl. Radiation Isotopes 1:172–177.

20. Radiochromatography. n.d. Schwarz Bioresearch, SBR Technical Brochure 64 D 1, Orangeburg, N.Y. 15 p.

21. Robertson, J. S., V. P. Bond, and E. P. Cronkite. 1959. Resolution and image spread in autoradiographs of tritium-labeled cells. Intern. J. Appl. Radiation Isotopes 7:33–37.

22. Rothchild, Seymour (ed.). 1963. Advances in tracer methodology. vol. 1. Plenum Press, New York. 332 p.

23. Stillström, J. 1963. Grain count corrections in autoradiography. Intern. J. Appl. Radiation Isotopes 14:113–118.

24. Sudia, T. W., and A. J. Linck. 1961. Method for autoradiography using individually packaged x-ray film. Intern. J. Appl. Radiation Isotopes 10:55.

25. Taylor, J. Herbert. 1956. p. 545–576. Autoradiography at the cellular level. In G. Oster, [ed], Physical techniques in biological research. vol. 3. Academic Press, New York.

26. Weinstein, Jerry. June, 1958. Radioautography with tritium. Atomlight, New England Nuclear Corp. p. 1–2.

27. Williams, Agnes I. 1951. Method for prevention of leaching and fogging in autoradiographs. Nucleonics 8(6):10–14.

28. Yagoda, Herman. 1949. Radioactive measurements with nuclear emulsions. John Wiley & Sons, Inc., New York. 356 p.

CHAPTER EIGHT

Preparation of Counting Samples

Proper preparation of counting samples is as important in precise radioactivity assay as the counting operation. Samples collected in radiotracer experiments may be in such diverse forms as blood, urine, water, milk, plant or animal tissues, or respiratory gases. In most cases, such varied samples cannot be assayed directly but must be converted to a suitable form for assay. If the counting sample is to be in the form of a solid, it must further be mounted in a uniform and reproducible manner before assay is feasible. This latter feature is of particular importance for alpha-emitting or low-energy beta sources. Where liquid scintillation counting is to be used, the sample material must be suitably incorporated into the fluor medium.

A. FACTORS AFFECTING CHOICE OF COUNTING SAMPLE FORM

The choice of counting sample form depends on several interrelated factors. Of these, the type and energy of radiation emitted by the sample radioisotope is the most determinative. In the case of tissue or liquid (blood, urine, and so on) samples containing low-energy beta activity, the problem of self-absorption leads to decreased counting efficiency and poor reproducibility. This usually necessitates conversion of the sample to a standard and more suitable form. On the other hand, biological samples containing gamma-emitting nuclides can usually be assayed directly with a minimum of pretreatment. The type of *detector* used will normally determine the optimal counting sample form. Furthermore, the assay method employed sets a limit on the detection efficiency and quantity of material that can be included in a single sample—an important consideration where low sample specific activities are encountered. A last factor of importance is that the ease of sample preparation is related to the chemical and physical form of the original biological sample. Table 8-1 summarizes these factors in relation to the preparation of beta-emitting samples for assay by several common detectors.

TABLE 8-1

Sample preparation required for various radiation counter types (for beta-emitting samples)

Original Sample	Geiger-Mueller and Proportional Counters	Ionization Chamber with Vibrating-reed Electrometer	Internal-sample (Liquid) Scintillation Counter
Gas	Sample (1) preferably trapped in suitable solution and converted to solid form, or (2) may be counted directly in gaseous form by introduction into suitable detector chamber with counting gas.	May be introduced directly into detector and assayed without pretreatment.	Must be trapped in suitable solution and treated as liquid sample.
Liquid	Sample (1) preferably converted to solid form for counting, or (2) may be counted directly with suitable detector if particle energy is sufficiently high.	Sample (1) preferably combusted and counted as gas, or (2) solution may be evaporated to solid form and counted with reduced efficiency.	May be dissolved or suspended in a suitable scintillation solvent mixture and assayed directly without pretreatment.
Solid	May be counted directly unless low energy of particles requires pretreatment to concentrate sample.	Sample (1) preferably combusted and counted as gas, but (2) may prepare suitable solid mount and count with considerably decreased efficiency.	(1) Should be dissolved in suitable solvent and treated as liquid sample, or (2) may be counted directly as suspension in a suitable gel mixture.

This chapter outlines the various methods used to convert biological samples into chemical and physical forms more suitable for assay by the common detection methods. Cases where direct assay of the original sample is possible are cited. Finally, we consider the specific procedures necessary to introduce the sample to the detector in either a gaseous, liquid, or solid form.

In the field of liquid scintillation counting there is currently a bewildering array of information on suitable methods of introducing the sample into the fluor medium. Because of this situation and the importance of the assay method, a major portion of this chapter is devoted to the preparation of liquid scintillation counting samples. An extensive bibliography on this topic is given at the end of the chapter to show the present state of the literature in this field. A number of papers survey sample preparation methods for a specific isotope of importance. Those pertaining to liquid scintillation assay will be cited later, but those dealing with preparation of samples for the other detection methods should be noted here. The general preparation of ^{14}C counting samples has been most widely described (3, 11, 16, 19, 20, 40, 43, 51); of these references, the classic work of Calvin, et al., deserves special notice. Somewhat less general consideration has been given to ^{59}Fe (45); ^{131}I (44); ^{35}S (18, 20); ^{3}H (63); and ^{45}Ca (15).

At least some stage of a radiotracer experiment usually requires *pipetting radioactive solutions.* Most frequently this occurs during counting sample preparation. Quite obviously all such pipetting steps must avoid mouth contact with the radioactive material but still allow perfect control of the solution. A variety of commercial suction devices are available for this purpose. Some are suitable for use with micropipettes; others are designed for larger pipettes. Of course, the size of the sample involved will determine the size of pipette to be employed. Some workers prefer to construct their own pipetting controls using a syringe attached by means of a rubber sleeve to the appropriate pipette. Even cotton-plugged pipettes may be suitable for some purposes.

B. CONVERSION OF ORIGINAL SAMPLE TO SUITABLE COUNTING FORM

The pretreatment of biological samples before radioactivity assay is normally concerned with measures to reduce bulk and produce a more uniform material. Depending on the assay method to be used, it may be necessary to convert the sample to a more suitable physical state. It may further be desirable to convert the chemical form of the isotope to one more suitable for both radioactivity measurement and parallel chemical analysis. This is often the case with liquid scintillation samples, where the original sample form is a severe quenching agent, due either to its color or molecular structure. Frequently it is necessary to isolate an active compound from a large volume of sample material (tissue, feces, blood, and so on).

The specific treatment employed for a given sample is dependent on its original form, particle energy, and the desired method of detection. It should be emphasized, however, that the various sample conversion methods are not unique to any given assay method. For example, $^{14}CO_2$ produced by Schöniger flask oxidation can be just as well assayed directly in an ion chamber-electrometer system, or trapped in NaOH, converted to $BaCO_3$ and counted on a planchet using a G-M detector, or yet, trapped in "Hyamine" and assayed by a liquid scintillation counter. A wide variety of standard chemical methods are available for converting biological samples to a more suitable form for assay. Since these are well described in the analytical chemical literature, emphasis is placed here on adaptations specific to radioactive sample conversions.

1. Ashing Methods

When the radionuclide to be assayed is a metallic or mineral component, ashing of the sample is often the most practical method of concentration. This removal of the organic components may be accomplished by either dry or wet ashing. Since the *dry ashing* process produces a friable residue and is often accompanied by volatilization or fusion of the sample with the crucible, wet ashing is generally preferred. Gleit and Holland (21), however, have proposed a useful modification of dry ashing for blood samples. A number of *wet ashing* procedures have been described, but most are variations of the conventional Kjeldahl method. Various combinations of nitric (237), sulfuric, hydrochloric, or perchloric acid and hydrogen peroxide have been successfully employed. Wet ashing is particularly applicable to blood or tissue containing radioiron (108, 158, 185).

Animal tissues may be converted to a homogeneous solution for assay as a liquid by various forms of *pseudo wet ashing*. Several investigators (43, 56, 62) have pointed out the use of formamide to effect such solution. An entire animal or organ is homogenized or cut up with scissors and placed in hot formamide. Complete solution of all but bone results in 1–2 hr.

2. Combustion Methods

Sample material containing the low-energy beta emitters ^{14}C or ^{3}H usually requires complete oxidation. The tritium is recovered as water. The $^{14}CO_2$ produced may be assayed in the gaseous state or trapped in an alkaline solution before conversion to a suitable counting form for other types of activity measurement. Where the samples are to be assayed in a solid form, such treatment is essential to concentrate the isotopic material and reduce sample self-absorption. For assay by the liquid scintillation method, complete oxidation usually has the beneficial effects of improving sample solubility in the solvent and reducing quenching. Jeffay has reviewed succintly the various oxidation techniques for preparation of liquid scintillation samples (152).

a. *Wet combustion.* Several wet combustion methods have been employed, with variations of the *Van Slyke-Folch* being the most common. The apparatus for one previously undescribed modification is illustrated in Figure 8-1. In this procedure the ^{14}C-containing sample is placed in

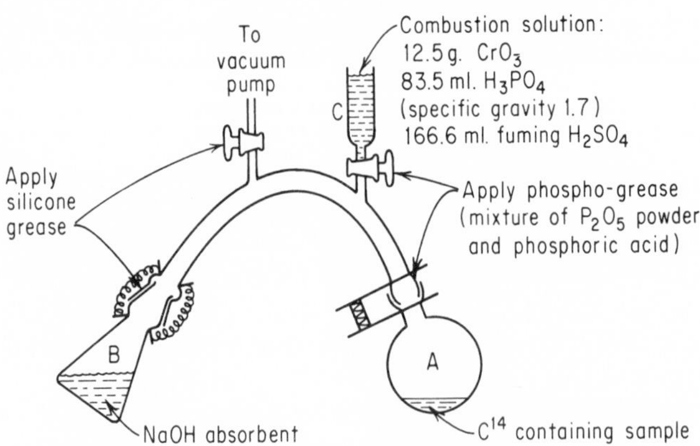

Figure 8-1. A modified Van Slyke-Folch apparatus for wet combustion of ^{14}C-labeled samples.

flask A and the NaOH absorbent solution (carbonate-free variety, such as Acculute, manufactured by Anachemia Chemicals Ltd., Montreal, Canada—Champlain, New York, USA) in flask B. (Note that a saturated NaOH solution is also relatively carbonate-free.) The system is assembled, evacuated, and sealed off. A mixture of fuming sulfuric acid, phosphoric acid, and chromic trioxide (11) is introduced through stopcock C. Flask A is then heated cautiously with a low flame for 10 min to promote the combustion and the $^{14}CO_2$ generated is allowed to come to equilibrium with the absorbent (approximately ½ hr). Subsequent addition of $BaCl_2$–NH_4Cl solution (1 M in strength) to the absorbing solution yields $Ba^{14}CO_3$, which is then collected by filtration or centrifugation for planchet mounting. The production of volatile products, such as aldehydes or chromyl chlorides, and so on, from chlorine-containing compounds sometimes limits the usefulness of this method. Other modifications of it have been made to allow rapid and routine sample preparation (14, 33). The method is not useful for tritium assay.

Persulfate oxidation of carbon compounds is also quite convenient (2, 31, 66). Samples, however, must be soluble in water, which somewhat restricts it application. This method uses a closed Erlenmeyer flask with a center well containing a carbon dioxide absorbent. The aqueous solution of the sample is placed around the well, and sulfuric acid and solid potassium persulfate added. Silver nitrate solution is dropped in to catalyze the reaction and the flask capped immediately. Heating accelerates the oxidation and the CO_2 produced diffuses to the absorbent well. Unfortunately, volatile intermediate products (such as acetaldehyde) may also diffuse into the center well, giving unpredictable results.

Belcher (83) has proposed wet oxidation of tritium-labeled samples using a *nitric-perchloric acid* mixture. The resultant tritiated water is distilled off and the distillate assayed with a liquid scintillation counter.

b. *Dry combustion.* Procedures involving dry combustion in an oxygen atmosphere are of particular value in preparing ^{14}C and tritium samples for liquid scintillation or ion chamber assay. The classical technique of oxidizing the sample by means of an inorganic oxidizing agent (CuO or NiO) in a *combustion furnace* with a flow of oxygen has been adapted by Peets, et al. (183) for liquid scintillation counting. The tritiated water produced is trapped as ice in a trap immersed in dry ice-acetone; the $^{14}CO_2$ is taken up in a suitable alkaline absorbing solution. Recoveries of about 96 per cent were obtained from samples of up to 1.5 g (198, p. 185–191). Others have adapted this combustion train method for preparation of samples for ion chamber (4) and proportional counter assay (28).

In an alternative method of dry oxidation, the sample and oxide catalyst are placed in a Pyrex or Vycor tube, which is then sealed and heated. The *sealed tube* is subsequently broken and the oxidation products removed by vacuum line transfer either to an absorbing solution or directly into an internal sample detector. Wilzbach, et al. (67–69) have employed this method for gas assay in an ion chamber; Buchanan and Corcoran (7) have used it with a proportional detector, and Steel (213) and Jacobson, et al. (148) have adapted it to liquid scintillation assay of tritium. The major disadvantages of this procedure are the small sample size that can be accommodated (less than 25 mg) and the time involved per sample.

The *Schöniger oxygen flask* combustion originally proposed for halogen determinations (55) has been applied by Kallberer and Rutschmann (153) for sample preparation in liquid scintillation counting. In this procedure, the sample material is placed in a cellophane or filter paper bag and dried. The bag is suspended in a platinum basket which is attached to an ignition head. This assembly is placed in a gas-tight flask containing an oxygen atmosphere. When current is applied, the oxidation takes place rapidly (65; 198, p. 185–191). Combustion products, such as ^3H_2O may be frozen out and $^{14}CO_2$ may be trapped in a suitable alkaline absorbent introduced through a side arm. Baxter and Senoner (81) have modified the combustion apparatus to attain 96–100 per cent recovery of ^{14}C activity. MacDonald (37) has reviewed this method and its specific uses for ^{14}C sample preparation; Dobbs has even applied it to ^{35}S-labeled compounds (109) and ^{14}C-labeled halogenic compounds (236). In fact, the method is also suitable for handling samples containing both ^{3}H and ^{14}C.

A major problem of the Schöniger flask technique is the danger of explosion if even traces of organic solvents are present in the flask. Martin and Harrison (171) have attempted to circumvent this problem by designing the top of the flask to act as a safety outlet in case of excessive internal pressure. A modification of this technique achieves ignition by focusing an external infrared beam on the sample wrapped in black paper (178). Because of the simultaneous combustion of the cellophane or paper bag with the sample, specific activity of the sample cannot be determined by this method. Only total sample activity is measurable. Sample size is limited to less than 300 mg according to Kelly, et al. (155). (See Experiment F for an application of this technique.)

The *Parr oxygen bomb* (commonly used in calorimetry) offers the advantage of allowing specific activity determination on larger liquid or tissue samples (42, 168) and has been used on even such volatile compounds as acetone. This metal bomb can be loaded with up to 1 g of lyophilized tissue sample or an equivalent amount of wet tissue. It is then filled with oxygen to 25 atm pressure. Ignition produces rapid combustion and the combustion products are removed through a collecting train. Sheppard and Rodegker (198, p. 192–194; 208) have reported detection of as little as $4 \times 10^{-4} \mu c$ of tritium and $1 \times 10^{-4} \mu c$ of carbon-14 in 3g of fresh tissue.

3. Miscellaneous Methods

With certain samples, the labeled compounds may be chemically extracted without the necessity of ashing or oxidation. Schulze and Long (202) have reported extraction by ultrasonic treatment of the sample directly in the liquid scintillation counting vial. Tritiated water samples may be prepared from biological fluids (plasma, urine) by distillation. Simpson and Greening (59) have investigated the magnitude of isotopic effect on such distillations of tritiated water from urine and found it negligible.

C. ASSAY OF SAMPLES IN VARIOUS COUNTING FORMS

The three physical states of counting samples (gaseous, liquid, solid) can be assayed by a variety of detectors, with, of course, different counting efficiencies. In general, solid counting samples require the most careful attention to mounting in order to insure reproducibility of results. The preparation of counting samples for liquid scintillation assay has been singled out for more extensive discussion because it involves the unique feature of actually introducing the sample into the fluor medium.

1. Assay of Gaseous Counting Samples

Samples to be assayed in a *gaseous form* are usually introduced directly into the detector (ion chamber, G-M detector, or proportional detector) following their preparation from the original biological material (198, p. 167–184). Vacuum transfer technique is involved in this operation. The significant advantage of gas counting is that self-absorption is largely circumvented. Thus, gas counting is largely restricted to the low-energy beta emitters ^{14}C, ^{3}H, and ^{35}S. These nuclides are most commonly assayed in the chemical form of CO_2 or C_2H_2, H_2 or CH_4, and SO_2 or H_2S, respectively. Wilzbach and Sykes (69) have described methods of $^{14}CO_2$ activity determinations in ion chambers; Eidenoff (17) has discussed G-M assay of the same compound. Although counting efficiencies may be reasonably high for soft beta emitters and the precision of the measurement may be greater, compared to other assay methods, the over-all sample preparation is rather tedious and time-consuming. It is necessary to calibrate gas counters with standard gaseous sources of the same nuclide that is being assayed. It is also possible to make continuous measurements of flowing gaseous samples, such as the use of the flow ion chamber for measuring respiratory $^{14}CO_2$ (see Experiment B, Part Three) or the effluent from gas chromatography separations.

2. Assay of Liquid Counting Samples

If a *liquid sample* is to be assayed directly, a minimum of further sample preparation is required. Except for the internal-sample scintillation counting method (described on p. 163–172), liquid sample counting is largely restricted to gamma emitters and high-energy beta emitters. G-M tubes of specialized design are available (see Figure 4-7*C*, *D*, *E*) for the latter sample type. McAuliffe (35) describes typical procedures for G-M counting of ^{32}P solutions.

Because of the low efficiency of ionization-type detectors for gamma photons, a NaI (Tl) scintillation detector is normally employed for gamma ray assay. Scintillation detectors of the well type combine high counting efficiency with simplicity of sample preparation for gamma-emitting biological samples. The homogeneous liquid sample need only be poured into a counting vial and placed in the crystal well. Experiments C and D illustrate such an application for the assay of ^{59}Fe in whole blood and ^{22}Na in water, respectively. For comparison it is essential that standard volumes of sample be used from assay to assay, since detection efficiency is inversely related to counting sample volume and decreases rapidly as the sample volume exceeds the well capacity. Likewise, calibration of such detectors must be done with both the same nuclide and volume as the samples to be assayed. As in the case of gas counters, it is possible to arrange these detectors to make continuous flow measurements on liquid samples, subject to the foregoing limitation on emitter type. Methods for assay of stationary liquid samples in a coiled tubing mounted against the solid fluor have also been described (46, 57).

3. Assay of Solid Counting Samples

Solid counting samples are satisfactory for most radioisotopes and can be more easily handled and stored than the other types. In general, two types of solid counting samples are utilized—those on paper chromatograms and those mounted on planchets. In turn, solid samples of these types may be assayed by ion chamber–electrometer systems, G-M counters, proportional counters, or external-sample scintillation counters. As will be seen later in the chapter, solid samples may also be assayed in a heterogeneous counting system using a liquid scintillation counter.

a. Preparation of planchet mounts. Typically, a solid sample is mounted on a backing material in a deposit of reasonably uniform thickness and area. The more commonly employed backing materials are aluminum, copper, stainless steel, and glass, in the form of flat or cupped *planchets*, or fritted filter plates. These materials vary in their resistance to chemical attack and must be carefully selected with respect to the chemical form of the counting sample. Furthermore, since *backscattering* of beta particles (see Chapter 9) is related to the density of the backing material, it is important to use the same type of material throughout an experiment when comparison of counting data is to be made. Needless to say, the thickness of the planchet should exceed that required for saturation backscattering.

The requirement of preparing counting samples of uniform thickness is most stringent when one is dealing with low-energy beta emitters, since *self-absorption* in solid sources of such nuclides is a significant factor. A number of generally applicable techniques have been developed over the years to produce counting samples of uniform thickness. Those most commonly used will be discussed briefly. [An excellent review of these techniques is found in Nuclear-Chicago Technical Bulletins 7 and 7B (22–23).]

Direct evaporation from solution: Perhaps the simplest means of converting a dissolved sample to a solid counting source is by direct evaporation of the solvent (usually water or alcohol). The sample solution, or an aliquot of it, is pipetted onto a planchet and gently evaporated to dryness under a heat lamp. Accuracy in pipetting is a major factor in this technique. A micro transfer pipette is normally used. Application of the evaporation technique is limited because it is somewhat difficult to secure reproducible sample thicknesses by its use. A number of refinements to improve uniformity of sample deposit have been developed, such as the use of wetting agents on the planchet surface, addition of thin sheets of absorbent material (lens tissue) to the bottom of the cupped planchets, the use of dilute agar solutions (12, 27, 36), and rotation of the mount during evaporation.

Filtration of precipitates: Larger sample amounts than can be easily secured by direct evaporation are obtainable from suspensions of precipitates, such as $Ba^{14}CO_3$. Direct filtration of the suspension, leaving the precipitate as a uniform layer on the filter medium is the simplest procedure. Filter paper or fritted disks are commonly used for this purpose and subsequently serve as the source mount (1, 5, 47). The importance of crystal size for $Ba^{14}CO_3$ has been investigated by Regier (49); Shirley, et al. (58) have compared the effect of oxalate versus carbonate precipitates of ^{45}Ca on reproducibility. When filter paper is used, there is some difficulty in securing reproducible results owing to variable paper texture and damage to the thin sample layer when it is subsequently transferred to a mounting block and dried. With fritted glass (53) or sintered metal disks, this problem is minimized, but their cost is too great to allow holding large numbers of samples for permanent reference. The use of Millipore filters has been suggested by Jervis (29). Bronner and Jernberg (6) have proposed a centrifugal filter assembly for mounting ^{45}Ca and ^{35}S precipitates. A self-absorption correction curve should be made for each type of counting sample containing weak beta emitters. (Details in this regard are given in Chapter 9.)

Settling or centrifugation of slurries: Precipitates that have been separated from excess solvent by centrifugation and decantation may be mounted in slurry form by two different techniques. The precipitate may be resuspended in a volatile solvent and poured into a cup planchet. Slow drying of the slurry with occasional tapping produces a remarkably uniform sample layer. Although this technique gives good reproducibility, it is tedious. Burr and Marcia (8) have used a screw-press to produce a smooth, flat surface with $Ba^{14}CO_3$ mounts. Alternately, the resuspended slurry may be centrifuged again, using an arrangement whereby a removable cupped planchet serves as the false bottom of the centrifuge tube. Such apparatus is commercially available. Following centrifugation, the solvent is decanted and the planchet removed from the tube and dried before counting (26, 32). This is a relatively simple procedure and can be readily used with large numbers of samples. It gives reasonably good reproducibility (see Experiment VI, Section C).

Mounting dry powdered samples: When a sample consists of ash or dried soil, it may be most convenient to weigh it directly into a cup planchet. The particles may be compressed (38) or the planchet tapped to produce a more even distribution. (An example of this method with ^{65}Zn-labeled plant tissues is seen in Experiment E, Part Three.) It is highly desirable to treat such a mounted sample with a binder, such as a solution of collodion, to prevent disturbing or spilling the deposit in handling. In general this method is not applicable to samples containing low-energy beta emitters.

Electroplating: Uniform and thin films of many metals may be prepared by electrodeposition. The sample is usually plated in elemental form which allows a maximal specific activity to be attained. The thin uniform films obtainable have the twin advantages of minimizing self-absorption and insuring reproducibility. Unfortunately, the procedure is quite laborious and time-consuming and is limited to a few metallic ions.

b. ***Radiochromatogram scanning.*** Paper chromatography is so widely used to separate complex mixtures of labeled compounds, that it is not surprising to find that much effort has been expended on developing methods of directly assaying radiochromatograms (24, 70–71). In general, paper chromatograms containing ^{14}C, ^{35}S, or to a lesser extent, ^{3}H lend themselves fairly well to direct assay, despite the problem of self-absorption (see Experiment A). Since the typical paper strip chromatogram may have a series of active spots at varying distances from the point of origin, it is highly desirable to have some means of scanning the length of the strip and recording both the extent of the activity and its location.

Many types of radiochromatogram scanners have been described (13, 30, 34, 41, 48, 50, 54, 60, 238), and several models are commercially available. Basically these consist of a detector (usually a windowless G-M tube), a count ratemeter, a strip chart recorder, and a drive mechanism to move the chromatogram past the collimated detector at a fixed speed. Unfortunately, the counting efficiency of such systems is often poor and the relation between chart recording and chromatogram strip inaccurate. To improve counting efficiency, several commercially available counters use a pair of windowless G-M detectors mounted end-to-end, thus attaining nearly 4π geometry. Alternatively, the strip may be cut into serial sections and these assayed individually. Such a procedure using liquid scintillation counting is described on p. 172. Two-dimensional radiochromatograms pose a most difficult problem, but a few semiautomatic scanners have been developed for this purpose that are of some value (39). Svendsen (61) has suggested a method of eluting the spots onto planchets and counting as solid samples.

The more recently developed procedure of *thin-layer chromatography* (TLC) is finding widespread use in the resolution and analysis of mixtures of radioisotope-labeled compounds. TLC, utilizing a glass plate coated with a uniform thin layer of adsorbent material, generally affords a more clean-cut separation of fractions in considerably less time than either paper or column chromatography. An excellent technical bulletin from the Nuclear-Chicago Corporation (25) describes practical techniques in the use of radioisotopes with TLC.

D. PREPARATION AND ASSAY OF LIQUID SCINTILLATION COUNTING SAMPLES

1. Basic Considerations in the Choice of Scintillation Solutions

a. *Sample solubility.* The unique feature of liquid scintillation counting is that the sample is in intimate contact with the scintillation solution. The components of such solutions have been discussed previously (see Chapter 6). Clearly, the best contact between sample and fluor is achieved when both are dissolved in the same solvent mixture. Unfortunately, simple solution is not always feasible for many biological samples. A variety of alternative methods have been developed to improve *sample solubility* or at least to bring the sample material and the scintillation solutions into defined proximity. Because of these factors and the wide variety of biological samples encountered, suitable scintillation solutions have been prepared on a rather empirical basis. We may cite several general references on the preparation of liquid scintillation counting samples (84, 105, 121, 147, 198), of which the review by Funt and Nuclear-Chicago Technical Bulletin No. 11 are particularly recommended. The Packard Technical Bulletins (106, 125, 146, 192–195) treat specific aspects of sample preparation for liquid scintillation counting in a most thorough manner.

b. *Quenching.* A second technical problem affecting the choice of a suitable scintillation solution is *quenching*. Quenching is commonly caused by the dissolved sample and is a consequence of the sample being polar in nature or colored. *Color quenching* may be avoided by using pretreatment procedures (adsorption or combustion) which decolorize the original biological sample (210). Alternatively, Fales (111) suggests direct addition of ethanolic sodium borohydride solution to the sample in the counting vial to effect decoloration. *Chemical quenching* can often be partially compensated for by addition of naphthalene to the scintillation solution. The extent of quenching should be routinely determined as discussed in Chapter 6.

c. *Homogeneous versus heterogeneous counting systems.* In cases where the sample is, or can be made soluble in the fluor solution, a *homogeneous* counting system may be used. Where this is not possible or solution leads to excessive quenching, the sample and the scintillation solution may still be brought into intimate contact by various means in a *heterogeneous* system. Since the sample types that may be assayed by liquid scintillation counting are so diverse, obviously no single scintillation solution is suitable for all samples. Of course, some fluor solutions do have wider application than others. The remainder of this chapter attempts to point out generally successful means of incorporating various sample types into fluor solutions and to list in tabular form many of the liquid scintillation solutions that have been proposed. These tables are presented as a guide to the choice of a suitable scintillation solution, but not as a substitute either for the discussion in the references cited or for individual experience.

As an added practical point, note that a variety of causes, aside from beta particle interaction, can produce fluorescence of the scintillation solution. Such fluorescence results in spurious pulses. An easily overlooked cause of such induced fluorescence is the light from fluorescent lamps. For this reason, liquid scintillation samples should be prepared in rooms illuminated by incandescent lamps, and the counting samples should be kept in the dark before being assayed.

Equally important is the interference with counting from *chemiluminescence.* As an illustrative example, one can cite the chemiluminescence resulting from the oxidation of an unsaturated compound by molecular oxygen, a reaction readily catalyzed by a base, such as sodium hydroxide or hyamine hydroxide. Note that the emulsifying agents used in the preparation of gel counting samples (see Section 3a of this chapter) are unsaturated in nature. The problems arising from chemiluminescence can often be remedied by allowing the enclosed counting sample to stand for an hour or so before actual counting. By then, the oxygen in the sample will be completely depleted.

2. Homogeneous Counting Systems

a. Direct solution in the scintillation solvent. Where sample solubility in the most efficient scintillation solvents (toluene, xylene, and so forth) is no problem, the most urgent consideration is to choose a fluor solution in which the sample will cause a *minimum quenching* effect. Relatively few biological samples fall into this category, since most are polar compounds and not readily soluble in toluene. Table 8-2 lists scintillation solution "recipes" that are known to contribute little to pulse quenching. The sample recipes marked with an asterisk are those used in carbon-14 dating studies. In this case, maximum detection efficiency is achieved by adding the sample in the same chemical form as the solvent. This usually involves

TABLE 8-2

Composition of minimum-quenched scintillation solutions

Solvent(s)	Primary Fluor	Secondary Fluor (wave shifter)	Anti-quencher	References
Toluene*	PPO, 0.4%–0.6%	POPOP, 0.01%		(117, 134, 136, 154)
Toluene*	*p*-terphenyl, 0.5%	POPOP, 0.05%		(84, p. 101–107)
Methoxybenzene (Anisole)	PPO, 0.3%			(84, p. 88–95)
Methoxybenzene (Anisole)	PPO, 0.7%			(134)
Xylene	PPO, 0.3%			(180)
Xylene	PBD, 1.0%			(84, p. 101–107)
Phenylcyclohexane	*p*-terphenyl, 0.5%			(154)
Phenylcyclohexane	PPO, 0.3%			(134)
Triethylbenzene	PPO, 0.3%			(134)
Triethylbenzene	*p*-terphenyl	POPOP		(103)
1,3-dimethoxybenzene	PPO, 0.3%			(134)
Paraldehyde, 72.3%* Xylene, 4.4%	PPO, 0.4%	POPOP, 0.01%	Naphthalene, 23.3%	(84, p. 261–267; 160, 186)
p-cymene*	*p*-terphenyl, 0.3%			(133, 135, 138, 154)
Hexane-Octane*	*p*-terphenyl, 0.1%			(135, 154)
Toluene, 98% Ethanol, 2% Acetylene*	PPO, 0.3%–0.4%			(84, p. 288–292; 74)
Toluene Ethanol*	PPO, 0.4%	DPHT, 0.002% (diphenylhexatriene)		(73)
Benzene*	*p*-terphenyl, 0.45%			(134, 154)
Benzene*	PPO, 0.3%			(134)
Ethylbenzene*	PPO, 0.3%			(212)
Xylene, 90% Methanol,* 10%	*p*-terphenyl, 0.4%	POPOP, 0.01%		(188, 189)
Trimethyl borate, 47% Xylene, 31%	PPO, 0.3%		Naphthalene, 22%	(122)
Xylene, 83%	PBD, 0.3%		Naphthalene, 7%	(188)
Benzene*	PPO, 0.4%	POPOP, 0.01%		(161)
Benzene-^{3}H, 85% Toluene, 15%	PPO, 0.4%	POPOP, 0.01%		(222)

elaborate chemical or biological syntheses starting with $^{14}CO_2$ (221). The advent of this technique made possible a considerable backward extension of the period of time that could be accurately measured by the ^{14}C-dating method. Several reviews of the procedures involved are available (84, p. 129–134, p. 261–267; 125, 135, 188). More recently, Tamers and Bibron (222) have converted tritiated rain water to benzene for direct incorporation in the scintillation solvent.

b. *Indirect solution in the scintillation solvent.* In general, biological samples are not soluble in toluene, the most efficient scintillation solvent in common use. Thus, it is necessary to take an indirect approach in order to achieve a homogeneous sample-fluor solution (194). One may employ a mixture of solvents that will accommodate small quantities of *aqueous solutions*. Inevitably, this increases quenching and reduces counting efficiency. The mere addition of ethanol to the common toluene solvent results in a mixture that can hold up to 3 per cent of aqueous sample material in solution. Dioxane (112), as a solvent, allows the presence of much larger percentages of water (up to 29 per cent), although it is less efficient in energy transfer than toluene. Dioxane solutions usually require the addition of naphthalene as an antiquenching agent. Dioxane has the additional disadvantage of a relatively high freezing point (+12°C) and often needs the addition of an antifreeze component (163). Table 8-3 lists "recipes" for scintillation solutions with varying degrees of water tolerance. These solutions have particular significance in tritium counting, since it is usually assayed as tritiated water (76, 97, 113, 148). In an attempt to avoid the disadvantage of dioxane as a solvent, Avinur and Nir (75) have used an acid-catalyzed tritium exchange between tritiated water (THO) and toluene. Much improved counting efficiency resulted, but the procedure is quite time-consuming.

The measurement of $^{14}CO_2$ by the liquid scintillation counting method poses the problem of finding a suitable absorption medium. This trapping agent should combine with CO_2 to produce a toluene-soluble salt without introducing additional quenching effect. The first such trapping agent proposed was a methanolic or ethanolic solution of the hydroxide of *Hyamine* 10-X (Rohm and Haas, Inc.) (182). The original technique was later refined by Frederickson and Ono (116). Rapkin has reviewed the uses of this substance in liquid scintillation counting (192). "Hyamine" continues to be the most widely used trapping agent for $^{14}CO_2$ (239). It suffers, however, from the disadvantages of a relatively high cost, derived from the tedious operations involved in converting the commercially available Hyamine chloride to the hydroxide of Hyamine using either silver oxide or Dowex 1-OH resin (84, p. 123–125). Moreover, the use of an alcoholic solution of the hydroxide of Hyamine in a liquid scintillation solution results in significant fluorescence quenching. Fortunately, no additional quenching occurs when, upon absorbing CO_2, the hydroxide of Hyamine is converted to the carbonate form.

Other $^{14}CO_2$ trapping agents have been suggested. *Primene* 81-R (Rohm and Haas, Inc.) is cheaper, may be used directly as supplied, and shows little quenching effect in moderate concentrations (179). Unfortunately, it does not absorb CO_2 as readily as "Hyamine" and requires the use of multiple traps. *Ethanolamine* is relatively inexpensive and shows a tolerable quenching effect (198, p. 113–114). It, however, requires the use of ethylene glycol monomethyl ether (a rather toxic compound) or ethanol to facilitate solubility of the resulting ethanolamine carbonate in toluene.

TABLE 8-3

Scintillation solvent mixtures to make aqueous samples soluble

Solvent(s)	Primary Fluor	Secondary Fluor (wave shifter)	Anti-quencher	Water Tolerance	References
Toluene, 8.5–12.5 ml Ethanol or methanol, 2.5–6 ml	PPO, 0.6%	POPOP, 0.01%		0.15–0.50 ml	(80, 102, 132, 176, 233)
p-dioxane, 76–80%	PPO, 0.7%	POPOP, 0.005%	Naphthalene, 7–12%	20–24%	(96, 123, 227)
Xylene, 5 ml *p*-dioxane, 5 ml Ethanol, 3 ml	PPO, 0.5%	α-NPO, 0.005%	Naphthalene, 6%	1 ml	(156)
p-dioxane, 60% Anisole, 10% 1,2-dimethoxyethane, 10%	PPO, 1.2%	POPOP, 0.005%	Naphthalene, 6% (with ethylene glycerol)	20%, or in place of water, ethylene glycol, 20%	(84, p. 88–95; 148, 183)
p-dioxane, 88% Methanol, 10% Ethylene glycol, 2%	PPO, 0.4%	POPOP, 0.02%	Naphthalene, 6%	10%	(90)
Xylene, 14% *p*-dioxane, 43% Ethylene glycol monoethyl ether, 43%	PPO, 1.0%	POPOP, 0.08%	Naphthalene, 8%	16.1%	(94)
p-dioxane, 83%; Ethylene glycol monoethyl ether, 17%	PPO, 1.0%	POPOP, 0.05%	Naphthalene, 5%	29.2%	(94)
Toluene, 50% Cyclohexene, 50%	PPO, 0.5%	POPOP, 0.01%			(72)
Toluene, 5 ml *p*-dioxane, 5 ml Ethanol, 3 ml	PPO, 0.5%	POPOP, 0.005%	Naphthalene, 10%	6%	(109)
Toluene, 10 ml Ethylene glycol monomethyl ether, 6 ml	PPO, 1.5%	POPOP, 0.005%		0.5 ml	(190)

Ethylene diamine is also usable but, like ethanolamine, can accommodate only limited amounts of CO_2 (up to 1 m mole with 10 ml of an ethanol-ethylenediamine (2:1) solution). *Phenylethylamine* has much greater trapping capacity and less quenching effect than "Hyamine." Rapkin (195) has reviewed in detail the various $^{14}CO_2$ trapping agents proposed. The first portion of Table 8-4 lists several common "recipes" used in solution counting of $^{14}CO_2$.

The method of Gordon, et al. (129), for liquid scintillation assay of $H_2{}^{35}S$ should also be mentioned. Finding "Hyamine" an unsatisfactory trapping agent, they modified the caps of their counting vials to allow direct injection of the gas through a silicone rubber insert into the air

TABLE 8-4

Scintillation solutions to accommodate inorganic ions

Solvent(s)	Primary Fluor	Secondary Fluor (wave shifter)	Binding Agent	Inorganic Ions	References
Toluene, 55% Ethylene glycol monomethyl ether, 39%	PPO, 0.6%		Ethanolamine, 5.5%	CO_2	(150)
Toluene, 93%	PPO, 0.3%		Methanolic primene, 7%	CO_2, sulfate, phosphate, chloride, organic acids	(179, 191)
Toluene, 67%	*p*-terphenyl, 0.3%	POPOP, 0.003%	Methanolic or ethanolic hyamine-OH, 33%	CO_2	(84, p. 123–125; p. 108–114; 142, 182, 223, 224)
Toluene, 67% Ethylene glycol, 3% 2-methoxyethanol, 27%	PPO, 0.6%		Ethylene diamine, 3%	CO_2	(196)
Toluene, 46% Methanol, 27%	PPO, 0.5%	POPOP, 0.01%	2-phenylethylamine, 27%	CO_2	(231)
Toluene, 80%	PPO, 0.6%		2-ethylhexanoic acid, 20%	Hg, Cd, Ca, K	(84, p. 88–95)
Toluene, 70% Methanol, 30%	PPO, 0.3%			KOH, 0.2%, with plasma, urine, and so on	(126)
Toluene, 58.8% N,N-dimethylformamide, 26.5% Glycerol, 5.9% Ethanol, 8.8%	PPO, 0.3%	POPOP, 0.01%		Sulfates	(149)
Phenylcyclohexane	*p*-terphenyl, 0.2%		Methyl isobutyl ketone	Uranium	(78)

(Continued)

Table 8-4 (Continued)

Solvent(s)	Primary Fluor	Secondary Fluor (wave shifter)	Binding Agent	Inorganic Ions	References
Toluene, 90% p-dioxane, 10%	PPO, 0.3%		Methyl isobutyl ketone	Uranium	(146)
Xylene	*p*-terphenyl, 0.4–0.5%	POPOP, 0.01%	Dibutyl phosphate	Pu, Zr, Nb	(144, 165)
Toluene	*p*-terphenyl, 0.5%	POPOP, 0.005%	Dibutyl phosphate	Y, Sr	(115)
Toluene, 78% Isoamyl alcohol, 12%	PPO, 0.545%	POPOP, 0.018%	Orthophenanthroline	Fe	(158, 159)
Toluene	*p*-terphenyl, 0.4%	POPOP, 0.01%	Dioctyl phosphate	Th	(128)
Xylene	*p*-terphenyl, 0.4%	POPOP, 0.01%	Dioctyl phosphate	Pu, Sm, Ni	(145)
Xylene	*p*-terphenyl, 0.4%	POPOP, 0.01%	*p*-toluidine	Ru	(145)
Toluene, 29% Methanol, 29% Phenethylamine, 29%	PPO, 0.5%	POPOP, 0.005%	2-pentene, 6.5% naphthalene, 10% (anti-quencher)	Cl^-, I^-, Br^-	(236)
Xylene	*p*-terphenyl, 0.4%	POPOP, 0.01%	2-ethylhexyl hydrogen 2-ethyl-hexyl Phosphonate	Pu	(145)
Toluene	*p*-terphenyl, 0.04%	POPOP, 0.01%	Octoic acid in Ethanol	Rb, Ca, K, Na, Sm, Pb, Cd, Bi, U	(82, 114, 128, 197, 232)
p-dioxane, 75% 1,2-dimethoxyethane, 12.5% Anisole, 12.5%	PPO, 0.7%	POPOP, 0.005%		Na_2SO_4, $NiCl_2$ in water	(145)
Toluene, 95% Ethanol, 5%	PBD, 0.8%	POPOP, 0.01%		Po, Cs, Ba, Ca in HCl, H_3PO_4 $CoCl_2$, NaI in water	(167, 204, 216)
p-dioxane	PPO, 5%			At in water	(79)
p-dioxane, 95% Naphthalene, 5%	PPO, 0.6%	POPOP, 0.05%		P, Cl, Ca, S in water	(184)
Toluene, 50%	PPO, 0.3%		Tri-*n*-butyl phosphate, 50%	U, Th	(76)
Toluene, 87% Ethanol, 8.7%	PPO, 0.4%	POPOP, 0.01%	*n*-caproic acid, 4.3%	Ni	(127)
p-dioxane, 90% Naphthalene, 10%	PPO, 0.4%	POPOP, 0.005%	Di(2-ethylhexyl)-orthophosphoric acid (HDEHP)	U in water	(91)
Toluene, 44.5% Ethanol, 44.5% Ethylene glycol, 11%	PPO, 0.53%			Ca in nitric acid	(201)
1,2-dimethoxyethane, 91% Naphthalene, 9%	PPO, 0.64%	POPOP, 0.0046%		U in water	(162)

space over a toluene-PPO-POPOP solution. They found very linear counting results with increasing quantities of $H_2{}^{35}S$. It is suggested that this method may have application to other gaseous samples.

In an attempt to overcome the insolubility of most *metallic ions* in the organic scintillation solvents, a variety of specific solubilizing agents have been investigated (110, 146). In general, these act by either forming an organic complex with the ions, or converting them to the salt of an organic acid. To date, the best organic complexing agents to be used with liquid scintillation systems are the acidic esters of orthophosphoric acid, that is, dibutyl phosphate, tributyl phosphate, dioctyl phosphate, and so on. Other organic complexing agents, however, have been used in specific cases to good advantage. Metallic salts of 2-ethylhexanoic acid (octoic acid) are readily soluble in toluene and have high scintillation efficiencies even at quite high concentrations. Table 8-4 lists solvent systems and binding agents useful in incorporating a large variety of inorganic ions into a homogeneous counting system.

Considerable attention has been directed in recent years toward the development of techniques allowing liquid scintillation counting of labeled *whole tissues*, *blood*, and *urine* with minimal sample pretreatment (84, p. 223–229; 92, 143, 237). "Hyamine" in its hydroxide form has been used to make soluble animal tissues (77, 93), bacterial cell debris (131), and blood serum (99, 220). The solubilization process can generally be facilitated by heat (up to 60°C) or sonication. Hyamine in its chloride form and Triton-X-100 (Rohm and Haas, Inc.) have also been suggested for tissues or body fluids (172). The problems of poor solubility and color quenching have plagued such efforts, but decreased counting efficiency can sometimes be tolerated as the price for more simplified sample preparation. The direct liquid scintillation assay of untreated urine samples containing tritium has been attempted (96, 157, 176), but decolorizing and centrifuging are usually necessary. Dioxane is typically used as the solvent in such cases. Such urine assays are of particular importance as a health physics measure for investigators using high levels of certain tritiated compounds.

3. Heterogeneous Counting Systems

Radioactive samples which cannot be dissolved in some suitable solvent system may still be assayed by the liquid scintillation process in a heterogeneous system. The samples may be suspended, either by shaking or in a gel, or they may be dried on filter paper and the paper strips placed in a fluor solution. Rapkin (193) has reviewed these systems in detail. In addition, an aqueous sample may be introduced into a counting vial containing a solid, insoluble fluor (anthracene) as described in Chapter 6.

a. *Gel suspension counting.* Hayes, et al. (137), reported a technique involving the liquid scintillation counting of finely ground sample material that was suspended by agitation immediately before assay. The technique was applied to a wide variety of sample materials but had two disadvantages: it required repeated counting of the same sample and it lacked precision. The technique is not widely used today. The significant point was that the presence of opaque materials, either as dispersed water droplets or fine white solids, did not reduce the counting efficiency significantly as compared to a homogeneous system. Self-absorption appeared to be only a minor problem, except for tritium-labeled samples, when the particulate material was finely ground.

Funt (118) was the first to propose the use of a gelling agent to suspend particulate samples for liquid scintillation counting. He used *aluminum stearate* (5 per cent) as the gelling agent and injected the sample material throughout the already formed gel by means of a fine hypodermic needle. This technique proved particularly suitable for assay of finely ground $Ba^{14}CO_3$ (119). Gel counting is important because samples that would cause severe quenching in solution may be counted in suspension with only minimal quenching. It is essential, however, that the sample material be completely insoluble in the scintillation solvent used, lest variable counting efficiencies from sample to sample result.

A modification of this technique using the gelling agent, *Thixcin* (Baker Castor Oil Co., Inc.), was subsequently introduced by White and Helf (230). They suggested a gel system prepared by adding 25 g of Thixcin to 1 liter of scintillator solution (toluene—0.4 per cent PPO—0.01 per cent POPOP) and blending (84, p. 96–100; 141). The result is a pourable solution which quickly sets to a gel. Approximately 1 gram of suspended material can be supported in 20 ml of gel. This gel system has been used in assaying organic nitrocompounds (140), ground barium carbonate (174), and aqueous solutions of carbon-14 and tritium compounds (206).

More recently, Ott, et al. (181) have used *Cab-O-Sil* M-5 (Godfrey L. Cabot, Inc.), a pure silica of extremely fine particle size, as a gelling agent. It is particularly advantageous since it requires neither blending nor heating, can be used with either toluene or dioxane, and forms an almost transparent gel merely by shaking in the counting vial. Cab-O-Sil gels will support about twice as much sample material as the same weight of Thixcin gel and also give higher counting efficiencies. Gordon and Wolfe (130) have used Cab-O-Sil gels in assaying aqueous solutions (up to 6.5 per cent by volume) with quite respectable counting efficiencies, whereas Snyder and Stephens (211) and Brown and Johnston (234) have used such gels to count ^{14}C- and ^{3}H-labeled scrapings from thin layer chromatograms. Cluley (101) has used a silica gel to hold up to 1 g of $Ba^{14}CO_3$ per

10 ml of gel with reasonable counting efficiency. Cab-O-Sil, however, being finely powdered silica, poses a possible health hazard to its users if proper precaution is not exercised. Cab-O-Sil has also been employed to reduce the extent of adsorption of certain polymer samples to the walls of the counting vials, which would result in decreased counting efficiency (86).

Other gelling agents have also been suggested, such as dissolved polystyrene and methyl methacryalate (Plexiglas). Shakhidzhanyan, et al. (205) have used gels of the latter substance in assaying ^{40}K-containing ash from human organs. Chemiluminescence is often a problem in gel suspension counting when the counting sample is alkaline in nature.

b. *Filter paper counting.* Another effective means of liquid scintillation counting of heterogeneous systems involves direct counting of toluene-insoluble samples on filter paper. This has been applied most successfully to counting *paper chromatogram sections*, but has also been used with pieces of filter paper on which samples have been added and dried in place. Davidson (106) has reviewed the various techniques proposed in this type of system.

A relatively crude technique has been developed in which the filter paper carrying the dried sample is wetted with a scintillator solution and then applied directly to the face of a photomultiplier (120, 199, 203). The paper is rendered relatively transparent by the wetting and can be counted with reasonable, but not very reproducible efficiency.

Wang and Jones (225) first proposed immersing a paper chromatogram section directly in the vial of scintillator solution. They obtained quite respectable counting efficiencies, and the technique allowed the use of automatic sample-changing equipment for handling large numbers of samples. Geiger and Wright (124) have evaluated this technique with regard to the orientation of the paper strips in the counting vial with respect to the photomultipliers. Loftfield and Eigner (164) suggested that the paper strip be formed into a cylinder which completely lines the counting vial to offset the problem of variable orientation. Uniform drying of the paper strip is essential and, as in gel counting, the sample material must be toluene-insoluble. The method of Wang and Jones has been widely used for liquid scintillation counting of paper chromatograms (89, 175; 198, p. 121–126; 218, 227), silica-gel impregnated disks of glass fiber paper (187), ion-exchange paper (209), lens tissue (226), and filter paper disks or strips on which radioisotope samples have been precipitated (85, 170, 235). A recent adaptation of the technique allows the assay of $^{14}CO_2$ trapped on KOH-impregnated filter paper in a Warburg flask (95, 100).

BIBLIOGRAPHY

General Counting Sample Preparation

1. Armstrong, W. D., and Jack Schubert. 1948. Determination of radioactive carbon in solid samples. Anal. Chem. 20:270–271.
2. Baker, Nome, Harold Feinberg, and Robert Hill. 1954. Analytical procedures using a combined combustion-diffusion vessel: simple wet-combustion method suitable for routine carbon-14 analyses. Anal. Chem. 26:1504–1506.
3. Beamer, William H., and George J. Atchison. 1950. Quantitative techniques with carbon-14. Anal. Chem. 22:303–306.
4. Biggs, Max W., David Kritchevsky, and Martha Kirk. 1952. Assay of samples doubly labeled with radioactive hydrogen and carbon. Anal. Chem. 24:223–224.
5. Bloom, Ben. 1956. Filter paper support for mounting and assay of radioactive precipitates. Anal. Chem. 28:1638.
6. Bronner, Felix, and Nils A. Jernberg. 1957. Simple centrifugal filtration assembly for preparation of solid samples for radioassay. Anal. Chem. 29:462.
7. Buchanan, Donald L., and Betty J. Corcoran. 1959. Sealed tube combustions for the determination of carbon-14 and total carbon. Anal. Chem. 31:1635–1638.
8. Burr, William W., and John A. Marcia. 1955. Preparation of pressed samples for counting carbon-14-labeled compounds. Anal. Chem. 27:571.
9. Burr, William W., Jr., and Donald S. Wiggans. 1956. Direct determination of C^{14} and S^{35} in blood. J. Lab. Clin. Med. 48:907–911.
10. Cahn, Arno, and R. M. Lind. 1958. An improved procedure for plating uniform $BaCO_3$ precipitates. Intern. J. Appl. Radiation Isotopes 3:44–45.
11. Calvin, Melvin, et al. Isotopic carbon. 1949. Techniques in its measurement and and chemical manipulation. John Wiley & Sons, Inc., New York. 376 p.
12. Campbell, H., H. A. Glastonbury, and Margaret D. Stevenson. 1958. A direct-plating method for the assay of radioactive isotopes in aqueous and alcoholic samples. Nature 182:1100.
13. Carleton, F. J., and H. R. Roberts. 1961. Determination of the specific activity of tritiated compounds on paper chromatograms using an automatic scanning device. Intern. J. Appl. Radiation Isotopes 10:79–85.
14. Claycomb, Cecil K., Tyra T. Hutchens, and John T. Van Bruggen. 1950. Techniques in the use of C^{14} as a tracer. I. Apparatus and technique for wet combustion of non-volatile samples. Nucleonics 7(3):38–41.
15. Comar, C. L., et al. 1951. Use of calcium-45 in biological studies. Nucleonics 8(3):19–31.
16. Dauben, William G., James C. Reid, and Peter E. Yankwich. 1947. Techniques in the use of carbon-14. Anal. Chem. 19:828–832.
17. Eidinoff, Maxwell Leigh. 1950. Measurement of radiocarbon as carbon dioxide inside Geiger-Müller counters. Anal. Chem. 22:529–534.
18. Eldjarn, L., and O. Nygaard. 1950. Comments on methods in biological work with S^{35}-labeled compounds. Scand. J. Clin. Lab. Inves. 6:160–167.

19. Evans, Ersel A., and J. L. Huston. 1952. Radiocarbon combustion and mounting techniques. Anal. Chem. 24:1482–1483.

20. Garrow, J., and E. A. Piper. 1955. A simple technique for counting milligram samples of protein labeled with ^{14}C or ^{35}S. Biochem. J. 60:527–528.

21. Gleit, C. E., and W. D. Holland. 1962. Retention of radioactive tracers in dry ashing of blood. Intern. J. Appl. Radiation Isotopes 13:307–308.

22. How to prepare radioactive samples for counting on planchets—Part 1. 1961. Nuclear Chicago Tech. Bull. No. 7. Des Plaines, Ill. 4 p.

23. How to prepare radioactive samples for counting on planchets—Part 2. 1961. Nuclear-Chicago Tech. Bull. No. 7B. Des Plaines, Ill. 4 p.

24. How to use radioactivity in paper chromatography. 1959. Nuclear-Chicago Tech. Bull. No. 4. Des Plaines, Ill. 4 p.

25. How to use radioisotopes with thin-layer chromatography. 1963. Nuclear-Chicago Tech. Bull. No. 16. Des Plaines, Ill. 4 p.

26. Hutchens, Tyra T., et al. 1950. Techniques in the use of C^{14} as a tracer. II. Preparation of $BaCO_3$ plates by centrifugation. Nucleonics 7(3):41–44.

27. Isbell, Horace S., Harriet L. Frush, and Ruth A. Peterson. 1959. Tritium-labeled compounds. I. Radioassay of tritium-labeled compounds in "infinitely thick" films with a windowless, gas-flow, proportional counter. J. Res. Nat. Bur. Standards 63A:171–175.

28. Isbell, Horace S., and Joseph D. Moyer. 1959. Tritium-labeled compounds. II. General-purpose apparatus, and procedures for the preparation, analysis and use of tritium oxide and tritium-labeled lithium borohydride. J. Res. Nat. Bur. Standards 63A:177–183.

29. Jervis, R. E. 1959. The use of molecular filter membrane in mounting and assaying of radioactive precipitates. Talanta 2:89–91.

30. Jones, A. Russell. 1952. Instrumental detection of radioactive material on paper chromatograms. Anal. Chem. 24: 1055.

31. Katz, Joseph, Samuel Abraham, and Nome Baker. 1954. Analytical procedures using a combined combustion-diffusion vessel: Improved method for combustion of organic compounds in aqueous solution. Anal. Chem. 26:1503–1504.

32. Larson, Frank C., et al. 1949. Self-absorption of S^{35} radiation in barium sulfate. Anal. Chem. 21:1206–1207.

33. Lindenbaum, Arthur, Jack Schubert, and W. D. Armstrong. 1948. Rapid wet combustion method for carbon determination. Anal. Chem. 20:1120–1121.

34. Ludwig, H., et al. 1960. Automatic direct quantitation of radioactivity on paper chromatograms. Biochim. Biophys. Acta 37:525–527.

35. McAuliffe, Clayton. 1949. Determination of radiophosphorus in plant material by solution counting. Anal. Chem. 21: 1059–1061.

36. McCready, C. C. 1958. A direct-plating method for the precise assay of carbon-14 in small liquid samples. Nature 181:1406.

37. MacDonald, A. M. G. 1961. The oxygen flask method. A review. Analyst 86:3–12.

38. MacKenzie, A. J., and L. A. Dean. 1950. Measurement of P^{32} in plant material by use of briquets. Anal. Chem. 22:489–490.

39. Moses, V., and K. K. Lonberg-Holm. 1963. A semiautomatic device for measuring radioactivity on two-dimensional paper chromatograms. Anal. Biochem. 5:11–27.

40. Moyer, Joseph D., and Horace S. Isbell. 1957. Preparation and analysis of carbon-14-labeled cyanide. Anal. Chem. 29:393–396.

41. Osinski, P. A. 1960. Detection and determination of tritium labeled compounds on paper chromatograms. Intern. J. Appl. Radiation Isotopes 7:306–310.

42. Payne, P. R., and J. Dove. 1954. Assay of tritium-labeled substances: a "combustion bomb" method of preparation of gas for counting. Nature 174:27–28.

43. Pearce, Eli M., et al. 1956. Rapid determination of radiocarbon in animal tissues. Anal. Chem. 28:1762–1765.

44. Perkinson, Jesse D., Jr., and H. D. Bruner. 1952. Preparation of tissues for iodine-131 counting. Nucleonics 10(11):66–67.

45. Peterson, Ralph E. 1952. Separation of radioactive iron from biological materials. Anal. Chem. 24:1850–1852.

46. Pickering, Donald E., Helen L. Reed, and Robert L. Morris. 1960. Detection of calcium-45 in bone solutions. Anal. Chem. 32:1214–1215.

47. Popjack, G. 1950. Preparation of solid samples for assay of ^{14}C. Biochem. J. 46:560–561.

48. Quantitative radiochromatography. 1956, p. 241–548. 2 vols. in 1. ("Selected scientific papers from the Rendiconti of the Instituto Superiore di Sanita," Rome, vol. 1, pts. 2–3. Title taken from preface in Vol. 1, pt 2.) Interscience, New York.

49. Regier, R. B. 1949. Preparation of barium carbonate for assay of radioactive carbon-14. Anal. Chem. 21:1020.

50. Roberts, Henry R., and Frederick J. Carleton. 1956. Determination of specific activity of carbon-14-labeled sugars on paper chromatograms using an automatic scanning device. Anal. Chem. 28:11–16.

51. Roberts, John D., et al. 1948. Measurement of carbon-14. Anal. Chem. 29:904–905.

52. Rockland, Louis B., Jose Lieberman, and Max S. Dunn. 1952. Automatic determination of radioactivity on filter paper chromatograms. Anal. Chem. 24:778–782.

53. Sacks, Jacob. 1949. All-glass filtration apparatus for radioactive tracer experiments. Anal. Chem. 21: 876–877.

54. Salomon, Lothar L. 1960. Sensitive 4π detector for scanning radiochromatograms. Science 131:415–417.

55. Schöniger, W. 1955. Eine mikroanalytische Schnellbestimmung von Halogen in organischen Substanzen. Mikrochim. Acta (1):123–129.

56. Schwebel, A., Horace S. Isbell, and J. V. Karabinos. 1951. A rapid method for the measurement of carbon-14 in formamide solution. Science 113:465–466.

57. Sear, Hubert. 1953. A method for presenting liquid samples to the flat surface of a scintillation crystal. Nucleonics 11(4):52–53.

58. Shirley, Ray L., Riley Deal Owens, and George K. Davis. 1950. Comparison of calcium-45 oxalate and carbonate precipitates for radioactive assays. Anal. Chem. 22:1003–1004.

59. Simpson, J. D., and J. R. Greening. 1960. Preparation of tritiated water samples by distillation. Nature 186:467–468.

60. Soloway, Sidney, Frank J. Rennie, and DeWitt Stetten, Jr. 1952. An automatic scanner for paper radiochromatograms. Nucleonics 10(4):52–53.

61. Svendsen, Reiner. 1959. A method by which radioactive material may be transferred from a paper chromatogram to a planchette. Intern. J. Appl. Radiation Isotopes 5:146–147.

62. Tabern, D. L., and T. N. Lahr. 1954. A simplified method for determining radioisotopes in tissues. Science 119:739–740.

63. Thompson, Roy C. 1954. Biological applications of tritium. Nucleonics 12(9):31–35.

64. Van Erkelens, P. C. 1953. Quantitative paper chromatography of traces of metal with the aid of radioactive hydrogen sulphide. Nature 172:357–358.

65. Von Schuching, Susanne, and Carl W. Karickhoff. 1963. Low-level carbon-14 determination by improved Schöniger combustion and ionization chamber. Anal. Biochem. 5:93–98.

66. Walker, L. A., and R. Lougheed. 1962. A simple method for the assay of carbon-14 in compounds or mixtures. Intern. J. Appl. Radiation Isotopes 13:95–97.

67. Wilzbach, K. E., Louis Kaplan, and W. G. Brown. 1953. The preparation of gas for assay of tritium in organic compounds. U.S. Atomic Energy Commission. ANL-5056. 10 p.

68. Wilzbach, K. E., Louis Kaplan, and W. G. Brown, 1953. The preparation of gas for assay of tritium in organic compounds. Science 118:522–523.

69. Wilzbach, K. E., and W. Y. Sykes. 1954. Determination of isotopic carbon in organic compounds. Science 120:494–496.

70. Winteringham, F. P. W., A. Harrison, and R. G. Bridges. 1952. Radioactive tracer-paper chromatography techniques. The Analyst 77:19–28.

71. Winteringham, F. P. W., A. Harrison, and R. G. Bridges. 1952. Radioactive-tracer techniques in paper chromatography. Nucleonics 10(3):52–57.

Liquid Scintillation Counting Sample Preparation

72. Anbar, M., P. Neta, and A. Heller. 1962. The radioassay of tritium in water in liquid scintillation counters—the isotopic exchange of cyclohexene with water. Intern. J. Appl. Radiation Isotopes 13:310–312.

73. Arnold, James R. 1954. Scintillation counting of natural radiocarbon: I. The counting method. Science 119:155–157.

74. Audric, B. N., and J. V. P. Long. 1954. Use of dissolved acetylene in liquid scintillation counters for the measurement of carbon-14 of low specific activity. Nature 173:992–993.

75. Avinur, P., and A. Nir. 1958. Tritium exchange between toluene and aqueous sulphuric acid. Bull. Res. Council Israel 7A:74–77.

76. Axtmann, R. C., and LeConte Cathey. 1959. Liquid scintillators containing metallic ions. Intern. J. Appl. Radiation Isotopes 4:261.

77. Badman, H. G., and W. O. Brown. 1961. The determination of ^{14}C and ^{32}P in animal tissue and blood fractions by the liquid-scintillation method. Analyst 86:342–347.

78. Basson, J. K., and J. Steyn. 1954. Absolute alpha standardization with liquid scintillators. Proc. Phys. Soc. 67:297–298.

79. Basson, J. K. 1956. Absolute alpha counting of astatine-211. Anal. Chem. 28:1472–1474.

80. Bateman, Jeanne C., et al. 1960. Investigation of distribution and excretion of C^{14} tagged triethylene thiophosphoramide following injection by various routes. Intern. J. Appl. Radiation Isotopes 7:287–298.

81. Baxter, Claude F., and Ilse Senoner. 1963. Liquid scintillation counting of C^{14}-labeled amino acids on paper, using trinitrobenzene-1-sulfonic acid, and an improved combustion apparatus. November, 1963. Atomlight no. 33. New England Nuclear Corp. p. 1–8.

82. Beard, G. B., and W. H. Kelly. 1958. The use of a samarium loaded liquid scintillator for the determination of the half-life of Sm^{147}. Nuclear Phys. 8:207–209.

83. Belcher, E. H. 1960. The assay of tritium in biological material by wet oxidation with perchloric acid followed by liquid scintillation counting. Phys. Med. Biol. 5:49–56.

84. Bell, Carlos G., Jr., and F. Newton Hayes (eds.). 1958. Liquid scintillation counting. Proc. Conf. Northwestern University, Evanston, 1957. Pergamon Press, Inc., New York. 292 p.

85. Blair, Alberta, and Stanton Segal. 1962. Use of filter paper mounting for determination of the specific activity of gluconate-C^{14} by liquid scintillation assay. Anal. Biochem. 3:221–229.

86. Blanchard, F. A., and I. T. Takahashi. 1961. Use of submicron silica to prevent count loss by wall adsorption in liquid scintillation counting. Anal. Chem. 33:975–976.

87. Bloom, Ben. 1962. The simultaneous determination of C^{14} and H^3 in the terminal groups of glucose. Anal. Biochem. 3:85–87.

88. Blüh, Otto, and Fred Terentiuk. 1952. Liquid scintillation beta counter for radioactive solids. Nucleonics 10(9):48–51.

89. Bousquet, William F., and John E. Christian. 1960. Quantitative radioassay of paper chromatograms by liquid scintillation counting. Application to carbon-14-labeled salicylic acid. Anal. Chem. 32:722–723.

90. Bray, George A. 1960. A simple efficient liquid scintillator for counting aqueous solutions in a liquid scintillation counter. Anal. Biochm. 1:279–285.

91. Britt, R. D., Jr. 1961. The radiochemical determination of promethium-147 in fission products. Anal. Chem. 33:602–604.

92. Brown, W. O., and H. G. Badman. 1961. Liquid-scintillation counting of ^{14}C-labeled animal tissues at high efficiency. Biochem. J. 78:571–578.

93. Bruno, Gerald A., and John E. Christian. 1960. Note on suitable solvent systems usable in the liquid scintillation counting of animal tissue. J. Am. Pharm. Assoc. Sci. ed. 49:560–561.

94. Bruno, Gerald A., and John E. Christian. 1961. Determination of carbon-14 in aqueous bicarbonate solutions by liquid scintillation counting techniques: application to biological fluids. Anal. Chem. 33:1216–1218.

95. Buhler, Donald R. 1962. A simple scintillation counting technique for assaying $C^{14}O_2$ in a Warburg flask. Anal. Biochem. 4:413–417.

96. Butler, Frank E. 1961. Determination of tritium in water and urine—liquid scintillation counting and rate-of-drift determination. Anal. Chem. 33:409–414.

97. Cameron, J. F., and I. S. Boyce. 1960. Liquid scintillation counting of tritiated water. Intern. J. Appl. Radiation Isotopes 8:228–229.

98. Carr, T. E. F., and B. J. Parsons. 1962. A method for the assay of calcium-45 by liquid scintillation counting. Intern. J. Appl. Radiation Isotopes 13:57–62.

99. Chen, Philip S., Jr. 1958. Liquid scintillation counting of C^{14} and H^3 in plasma and serum. Proc. Soc. Exp. Biol. Med. 98:546–547.

100. Chiriboga, J., and D. N. Roy. 1962. Rapid method for determination of decarboxylation of compounds labeled with carbon-14. Nature 193:684–685.

101. Cluley, H. J. 1962. Suspension scintillation counting of carbon-14 barium carbonate. Analyst 87:170–177.

102. Cowan, C. L., Jr., et al. 1953. Large liquid scintillation detectors. Phys. Rev. 90:493–494.

103. Cowan, C. L., Jr., et al. 1956. Detection of the free neutrino: a confirmation. Science 124:103–104.

104. Cuppy, Dianna, and Lamar Crevasse. 1963. An assembly for $C^{14}O_2$ collection in metabolic studies for liquid scintillation counting. Anal. Biochem. 5:462–463.

105. Daub, Guido H., F. Newton Hayes, and Elizabeth Sullivan (eds.). 1961. Proc. Univ. N.M. Conf. Organic Scintillation Detectors, Alburquerque, 1960. U.S. Government Printing Office, (TID-7612) Washington. 417 p.

106. Davidson, Eugene A. 1962. Techniques for paper strip counting in a scintillation spectrometer. Rev. ed. Packard Instrument Co. Tech. Bull. No. 4. La Grange, Ill. 8 p.

107. Dern, Raymond J., and Willie Lee Hart. 1961. Studies with doubly labeled iron. I. Simultaneous liquid scintillation counting of isotopes Fe^{55} and Fe^{59} as ferrous perchlorate. J. Lab. Clin. Med. 57:322–330.

108. Dern, Raymond J., and Willie Lee Hart. 1961. Studies with doubly labeled iron. II. Separation of iron from blood samples and preparation of ferrous perchlorate for liquid scintillation counting. J. Lab. Clin. Med. 57:460–467.

109. Dobbs, Horace E. 1963. Oxygen flask method for the assay of tritium-, carbon-14-, and sulfur-35-labeled compounds. Anal. Chem. 35:783–786.

110. Erdtmann, Gerhard, and Günter Herrmann. 1960. Über die Zählung von Radioisotopen metallischer Elemente in flüssigen Szintillatoren. Z. Elektrochem. 64:1092–1098.

111. Fales, Henry M. January, 1963. Discoloration of samples for liquid scintillation counting. Atomlight. New England Nuclear Corp. 25:8.

112. Farmer, Earle C., and Irving A. Berstein. 1952. Determination of specific activities of C^{14}-labeled organic compounds with a water-soluble liquid scintillator. Science 115:460–461.

113. Farmer, Earle C., and Irving A. Berstein. 1953. Determination of specific activities of tritium-labeled compounds with liquid scintillators. Science 117:279–280.

114. Flynn, K. F., and L. E. Glendenin. 1959. Half-life and beta spectrum of Rb^{87}. Phys. Rev. 116:744–748.

115. Foreman, H., and M. B. Roberts. January–June, 1960. p. 61–70. Determination of strontium^{90} in bone. *In* Biological and medical research group (H-4 of the Health

Division, Los Alamos Scientific Laboratory—semiannual report). U.S. Atomic Energy Commission. LAMS-2455.

116. Frederickson, Donald S., and Katsuto Ono. 1958. An improved technique for assay of $C^{14}O_2$ in expired air using the liquid scintillation counter. J. Lab. Clin. Med. 51:147–151.

117. Funt, B. L., et al. 1955. Scintillation techniques for the detection of natural radiocarbon. Nature 175:1042–1043.

118. Funt, B. Lionel. 1956. Scintillating gels. Nucleonics 14(8):83–84.

119. Funt, B. Lionel, and Arlene Hetherington. 1957. Suspension counting of carbon-14 in scintillating gels. Science 125:986–987.

120. Funt, B. Lionel, and Arlene Hetherington. 1960. Scintillation counting of beta activity on filter paper. Science 131:1608–1609.

121. Funt, B. Lionel. 1961. Scintillation counting with organic phosphors. Canad. J. Chem. 39:711–716.

122. Furst, Milton, and Hartmut Kallman. 1955. Enhancement of fluorescence in solutions under high-energy irradiation. Phys. Rev. 97:583–587.

123. Furst, Milton, Hartmut Kallman, and Felix H. Brown. 1955. Increasing fluorescence efficiency of liquid-scintillation solutions. Nucleonics 13(4):58–60.

124. Geiger, John W., and Lemuel D. Wright. 1960. Liquid scintillation counting of radioautograms. Biochem. Biophys. Res. Com. 2:282–283.

125. Gibbs, James A. 1962. Liquid scintillation counting of natural radiocarbon. Rev. ed. Packard Instrument Co. Tech. Bull. No. 8. La Grange, Ill. 14 p.

126. Gjone, Egil, Hugh G. Vance, and David Alan Turner. 1960. Direct liquid scintillation counting of plasma and tissues. Intern. J. Appl. Radiation Isotopes 8:95–97.

127. Gleit, C. E., and J. Dumot. 1961. Liquid scintillation counting of nickel-63. Intern. J. Appl. Radiation Isotopes 12:66.

128. Glendenin, L. E. 1961. Present status of the decay constants. Ann. N.Y. Acad. Sci. 91:166–180.

129. Gordon, B. E., H. R. Lukens, Jr., and W. ten Hove. 1961. Liquid scintillation counting of H_2S^{35} Intern. J. Appl. Radiation Isotopes 12:145–146.

130. Gordon, Charles F., and Arthur L. Wolfe. 1960. Liquid scintillation counting of aqueous samples. Anal. Chem. 32:574.

131. Hash, John H. 1962. Determination of tritium in whole cells and cellular fractions of *Bacillus megaterium* using liquid scintillation techniques. Anal. Biochem. 4:257–267.

132. Hayes, F. N., and R. Gordon Gould. 1953. Liquid scintillation counting of tritium-labeled water and organic compounds. Science 117:480–482.

133. Hayes, F. N., D. L. Williams, and Betty Rogers. 1953. Liquid scintillation counting of natural C^{14}. Phys. Rev. 92:512–513.

134. Hayes, F. N., Betty S. Rogers, and Phyllis C. Sanders. 1955. Importance of solvent in liquid scintillators. Nucleonics 13(1):46–48.

135. Hayes, F. N., Ernest C. Anderson, and James R. Arnold. 1956. p. 188–192. Liquid scintillation counting of natural radiocarbon. *In* Proc. Intern. Conf. Peaceful Uses of Atomic Energy, Geneva, 1955. UN, New York.

136. Hayes, F. Newton, Donald G. Ott, and Vernon N. Kerr. 1956. Liquid scintillators. II. Relative pulse height comparisons of secondary solutes. Nucleonics 14(1):42–45.

137. Hayes, F. Newton, Betty S. Rogers, and Wright H. Langham. 1956. Counting suspensions in liquid scintillators. Nucleonics 14(3):48–51.

138. Hayes, F. N., Elizabeth Hansbury, and V. N. Kerr. 1960. Contemporary carbon-14. The p-cymene method. Anal. Chem. 32:617–620.

139. Helf, Samuel, et al. 1956. Radioassay of tagged sulfate impurity in cellulose nitrate. Anal. Chem. 28:1465–1468.

140. Helf, Samuel, and Cecil White. 1957. Liquid scintillation counting of carbon-14-labeled organic nitrocompounds. Anal. Chem. 29:13–16.

141. Helf, Samuel, C. G. White, and R. N. Shelley. 1960. Radioassay of finely divided solids by suspension in a gel scintillator. Anal. Chem. 32:238–241.

142. Herberg, Richard J. 1958. Phosphorescence in liquid scintillation counting of proteins. Science 128:199–200.

143. Herberg, R. J. 1960. Determination of carbon-14 and tritium in blood and other whole tissues. Anal. Chem. 32:42–46.

144. Horrocks, Donald L., and Martin H. Studier. 1958. Low level plutonium-241 analysis by liquid scintillation techniques. Anal. Chem. 30:1747–1750.

145. Horrocks, Donald L., and Martin H. Studier. 1961. Determination of the absolute disintegration rates of low energy beta emitters in a liquid scintillation spectrometer. Anal. Chem. 33:615–620.

146. Horrocks, Donald L. 1962. Liquid scintillation counting of inorganic radioactive nuclides. Rev. ed. Packard Instrument Co. Tech. Bull. No. 2. La Grange, Ill. 8 p.

147. How to prepare samples for liquid scintillation counting. 1962. Nuclear-Chicago Tech. Bull. No. 11. Des Plaines, Ill. 4 p.

148. Jacobson, H. I., et al. 1960. Determination of tritium in biological material. Arch. Biochem. Biophys. 86:89–93.

149. Jeffay, Henry, Funso O. Olubajo, and William R. Jewell. 1960. Determination of radioactive sulfur in biological materials. Anal. Chem. 32:306–308.

150. Jeffay, Henry, and Julian Alvarez. 1961. Liquid scintillation counting of carbon-14: Use of ethanolamine-ethylene glycol monomethyl ether-toluene. Anal. Chem. 33:612–615.

151. Jeffay, Henry, and Julian Alvarez. 1961. Measurement of C^{14} and S^{35} in a single sample. Anal. Biochem. 2:506–508.

152. Jeffay, Henry. 1962. Oxidation techniques for preparation of liquid scintillation samples. Packard Instrument Co. Tech. Bull. No. 10. La Grange, Ill. 8 p.

153. Kalberer, F., and J. Rutschmann. 1961. Eine Schnellmethode zur Bestimmung von Tritium, Radiokohlenstoff und Radioschwefel in beliebigem organischem Probenmaterial mittels des Flüssigkeits-Scintillations-Zahlers. Helv. Chim. Acta 44:1956–1966.

154. Kallman, Hartmut, and Milton Furst. 1951. Fluorescent liquids for scintillation counters. Nucleonics 8(3):32–39.

155. Kelly, R. G., et al. 1961. Determination of C^{14} and H^3 in biological samples by Schöniger combustion and liquid scintillation techniques. Anal. Biochem. 2:267–273.

156. Kinard, Frank E. 1957. Liquid scintillator for the analysis of tritium in water. Rev. Sci. Instruments 28:293–294.

157. Langham, W. H., et al. 1956. Assay of tritium activity in body fluids with use of a liquid scintillation system. J. Lab. Clin. Med. 47:819–825.

158. Leffingwell, Thomas P., George S. Melville, Jr., and Robert W. Riees. 1958. A semimicrotechnic for iron-59 determinations in biologic systems, using beta counting in a liquid scintillator. U.S. Air Force, School of Aviation Medicine, Randolph AFB, Texas. AF-SAM-58-93. 6 p.

159. Leffingwell, T. P., R. W. Riess, and G. S. Melville, Jr. 1962. Liquid scintillator beta counting of iron-59 in clear and colored systems. Intern. J. Appl. Radiation Isotopes 13:75–86.

160. Legér, Concèle, and Louis Pichat. 1957. Utilisation du paraldéhyde pour incorporer de grandes quantités de carbone marqué dans un scintillateur liquide. Compt Rend. Hebdomadaires Séances Acad. Sci. 244:190–192.

161. Leger, C., and M. A. Tamers. 1963. The counting of naturally occurring radiocarbon in the form of benzene in a liquid scintillation counter. Intern. J. Applied Radiation Isotopes 14:65–70.

162. Levin, Lester. 1962. Liquid scintillation methods for measuring low level radioactivity of aqueous solutions: Determination of enriched uranium in urine. Anal. Chem. 34:1402–1406.

163. Loewus, F. A. 1961. The use of bis-(2-alkoxyethyl) ethers as antifreeze in naphthalene-1,4-dioxane scintillation mixtures. Intern. J. Appl. Radiation Isotopes 12:6–9.

164. Loftfield, Robert Berner, and Elizabeth Ann Eigner. 1960. Scintillation counting of paper chromatograms. Biochem. Biophys. Res. Com. 3:72–76.

165. Ludwick, J. Donald. 1960. Liquid scintillation spectrometry for analysis of zirconium-95-niobium-95 mixtures and coincidence standardization of these isotopes. Anal. Chem. 32:607–610.

166. Ludwick, J. D., and R. W. Perkins. 1961. Liquid scintillation techniques applied to counting phosphorescence emission: Measurement of trace quantities of zinc sulfide. Anal. Chem. 35:1230–1235.

167. Lutwak, Leo. 1959. Estimation of radioactive calcium-45 by liquid scintillation counting. Anal. Chem. 31:340–343.

168. McFarlane, A. S., and K. Murray. 1963. ^{14}C and ^{3}H specific activities by bomb combustion and scintillation counting. Anal. Biochem. 6:284–287.

169. Main, Raymond K., and E. Richard Walwick. 1961. A simplified quantitative assay for tritiated thymidine incorporated into deoxyribonucleic acid. Biochem. Biophys. Res. Com. 4:52–55.

170. Mans, Rusty J., and G. David Novelli. 1961. Measurement of the incorporation of radioactive amino acids into protein by a filter-paper disk method. Arch. Biochem. Biophys. 94:48–53.

171. Martin, L. E., and C. Harrison. 1962. The determination of ^{14}C- and tritium-labeled compounds in biological materials. Biochem. J. 82:18 p.

172. Meade, R. C., and R. A. Stiglitz. 1962. Improved solvent systems for liquid scintillation counting of body fluids and tissues. Intern. J. Appl. Radiation Isotopes 13:11–14.

173. Moss, G. 1961. A simple device for the rapid routine liberation and trapping of $C^{14}O_2$ for scintillation counting. Intern. J. Applied Radiation Isotopes 11:47–48.

174. Nathan, David G., et al. 1958. The counting of barium carbonate in a liquid scintillation spectrometer. J. Lab. Clin. Med. 52:915–917.

175. Nunez, J., and Cl. Jacquemin. 1961. Comptage de radiochromatogrammes par scintillation liquide. J. Chromatog. 5:271–272.

176. Okita, George T., James Spratt, and George V. Leroy. 1956. Liquid-scintillation counting for assay of tritium in urine. Nucleonics 14(3):76–79.

177. Okuyama, Tauneo, and Yutaka Kobayashi. 1961. Determination of diamine oxidase activity by liquid scintillation counting. Arch. Biochem. Biophysics. 95:242–250.

178. Oliverio, Vincent T., Charlene Denham, and Jack B. Davidson. 1962. Oxygen flask combustion in determination of C^{14} and H^3 in biological materials. Anal. Biochem. 4:188–189.

179. Opperman, R. A., et al. 1959. Use of tertiary alkyl primary C_{12}-C_{14} amines for the assay of $C^{14}O_2$ by liquid scintillation counting. Intern. J. Appl. Radiation Isotopes 7:38–42.

180. Ott, Donald G., et al. 1955. Argon treatment of liquid scintillators to eliminate oxygen quenching. Nucleonics 13(5):62.

181. Ott, Donald G., et al. 1959. Cab-O-Sil suspensions for liquid-scintillation counting. Nucleonics 17(9):106–108.

182. Passman, John M., Norman S. Radin, and John A. D. Cooper. 1956. Liquid scintillation technique for measuring carbon-14-dioxide activity. Anal. Chem. 28:484–486.

183. Peets, Edwin A., James R. Florini, and Donald A. Buyske. 1960. Tritium radioactivity determination of biological materials by a rapid dry combustion technique. Anal. Chem. 32:1465–1468.

184. Peng, C. T. 1960. Quenching of fluorescence in liquid scintillation counting of labeled organic compounds. Anal. Chem. 32:1292.

185. Perry, S. W., and G. T. Warner. 1963. A method of sample preparation for the estimation of Fe^{55} in whole blood by the liquid scintillation counting technique. Intern. J. Appl. Radiation Isotopes 14:397–400.

186. Pichat, L., J. Clement, and C. Baret. 1959. Synthèse du paráldehyde au départ de carbonate de baryum en vue du datage d'échantillons archéologiques carbonés par scintillation liquide. Bull. Soc. Chim. France. p. 329–333.

187. Pinter, Karoly G., James G. Hamilton, and O. Neal Miller. 1963. Liquid scintillation counting with glass fiber paper. Anal. Biochem. 5:458–461.

188. Pringle, R. W., W. Turchinetz, and B. L. Funt. 1955. Liquid scintillation techniques for radiocarbon dating. Rev. Sci. Instruments 26:859–865.

189. Pringle, R. W., et al. 1957. Radiocarbon age estimates obtained by an improved liquid scintillation technique. Science 125:69–70.

190. Prockop, Darwin J., and Paul S. Ebert. 1963. A simple method for differential assay of tritium and carbon-14 in water-soluble biological materials. Anal. Biochem. 6:263–271.

191. Radin, Norman S., and Rainer Fried. 1958. Liquid scintillation counting of sulfuric acid and other substances. Anal. Chem. 30:1926–1928.

192. Rapkin, Edward. 1961*a*. Hydroxide of Hyamine 10-X. Rev. ed. Packard Instrument Co. Tech. Bull. No. 3. La Grange, Ill. 8 p.

193. Rapkin, Edward. 1961*b*. Liquid scintillation measurements of radioactivity in heterogeneous systems. Rev. ed. Packard Instrument Co. Tech. Bull. No. 5. La Grange, Ill. 8 p.

194. Rapkin, Edward. 1961*c*. The determination of radioactivity in aqueous solutions. Rev. ed. Packard Instrument Co. Tech. Bull. No. 6. La Grange, Ill. 8 p.

195. Rapkin, Edward. 1962. Measurement of $C^{14}O_2$ by scintillation techniques. Packard Instrument Co. Tech. Bull. No. 7. La Grange, Ill. 8 p.

196. Reed, Donald J. 1963. Unpublished research on use of ethylene diamine in liquid scintillation counting of $C^{14}O_2$. Oregon State University, Dept. Chemistry, Corvallis, Ore.

197. Ronzio, A. R. 1959. Metal loaded scintillator solutions. Intern. J. Appl. Radiation Isotopes. 4:196–200.

198. Rothchild, Seymour (ed.). 1963. Advances in tracer methodology. vol. 1. Plenum Press, New York. 332 p.

199. Roucayrol, Jean-Claude, Erich Oberhauser, and Richard Schussler. 1957. Liquid scintillators in filter paper—a new detector. Nucleonics 15(11):104–108.

200. Ryves, T. B. 1960. Use of a liquid scintillator counter for beta particles. J. Sci. Instruments 37:201–203.

201. Sarnat, Marlene, and Henry Jeffay. 1962. Determination of radioactive calcium by liquid scintillation counting. Anal. Chem. 34:643–646.

202. Schulze, Janos, and F. A. Long. 1962. A method for liquid scintillation counting utilizing ultrasonic extraction. Anal. Biochem. 4:99–102.

203. Seliger, H. H., and B. W. Agranoff. 1959. Solid scintillation counting of hydrogen-3 and carbon-14 in paper chromatograms. Anal. Chem. 31:1607–1608.

204. Seliger, H. H. 1960. Liquid scintillation counting of α-particles and energy resolution of the liquid scintillator for α- and β-particles. Intern. J. Appl. Radiation Isotopes 8:29–34.

205. Shakhidzhanyan, L. G., et al. 1959. Measurement of natural radioactivity in human organs. Trans. Biol. Sci. Sec., Doklady, Akad. Nauk SSSR 125:166–167.

206. Shapira, Jacob, and William H. Perkins. 1960. Liquid scintillation counting of aqueous solutions of carbon-14 and tritium. Science 131:414–415.

207. Shapiro, Irwin, L., and David Kritchevsky. 1963. Radioassay of cholesterol-C^{14} digitonide. Anal. Biochem. 5:88–91.

208. Sheppard, Herbert, and Waldtraut Rodegker. 1962. Determination of H^3 and C^{14} in biological materials using oxygen bomb combustion. Anal. Biochem. 4:246–251.

209. Sherman, John R. 1963. Rapid enzyme assay technique utilizing radioactive substrate, ion-exchange paper, and liquid scintillation counting. Anal. Biochem. 5:548–554.

210. Shneour, E. A., S. Aronoff, and M. R. Kirk. 1962. Liquid scintillation counting of solutions containing carotenoids and chlorophylls. Intern. J. Appl. Radiation Isotopes 13:623–627.

211. Snyder, Fred, and Nelson Stephens. 1962. Quantitative carbon-14 and tritium assay of thin-layer chromatography plates. Anal. Biochem. 4:128–131.

212. Starik, I. E., et al. 1960. Liquid scintillators for radiocarbon dating in archaeology. Intern. J. Appl. Radiation Isotopes 9:193–194.

213. Steel, G. G. 1960. A simple method of estimating the tritium content of biological samples. Intern. J. Appl. Radiation Isotopes 9:94–99.

214. Steele, Robert, William Bernstein, and Clara Bjerknes. 1957. Single phototube liquid scintillation counting of C^{14}. Application to an easily isolated derivative of blood glucose. J. Appl. Physiol. 10:319–326.

215. Steenberg, K., and A. A. Benson. 1956. A scintillation counter for soft-β paper chromatograms. Nucleonics 14(12):40–43.

216. Steyn, J. 1956. Absolute standardization of beta-emitting isotopes with a liquid scintillation counter. Proc. Phys. Soc. 69A:865–867.

217. Stitch, S. R. 1959. Liquid scintillation-counting for (^{14}C) steroids. Biochem. J. 73:287–292.

218. Stitch, S. R., and R. E. Oakey. 1961. The evaluation of radiochromatograms by liquid scintillation counting and photography. Biochem. J. 81:12P–13P.

219. Takahashi, Hajime, Toshie Hattori, and Bunji Maruo. 1961. Liquid scintillation counting of C^{14} paper chromatograms. Anal. Biochem. 2:447–462.

220. Takesue, E. I., et al. 1960. A radiometric assay of tritiated tetracycline in serum and plasma of laboratory animals. Intern. J. Appl. Radiation Isotopes 8:52–59.

221. Tamers, Murray A. 1960. Carbon-14 dating with the liquid scintillation counter: Total synthesis of the benzene solvent. Science 132:668–669.

222. Tamers, M. A., and R. Bibron. 1963. Benzene method measures tritium in rain without isotope enrichment. Nucleonics 21(6):90–94.

223. Toporek, Milton. 1960. Liquid scintillation counting of C^{14} plasma proteins using a standard quenching curve. Intern. J. Appl. Radiation Isotopes 8:229–230.

224. Vaughan, Martha, Daniel Steinberg, and Jane Logan. 1957. Liquid scintillation counting of C^{14}- and H^{3}-labeled amino acids and proteins. Science 126:446–447.

225. Wang, C. H., and D. E. Jones. 1959. Liquid scintillation counting of paper chromatograms. Biochem. Biophys. Res. Com. 1:203–205.

226. Weg, M. W. 1962. Beta-scintillation counting of radioactive tracers insoluble in toluene. Nature 194:180–181.

227. Werbin, Harold, I. L. Chaikoff, and Miles R. Imada. 1959. Rapid sensitive method for determining H^{3}-water in body fluids by liquid scintillation spectrometry. Proc. Soc. Exp. Biol. Med. 103:8–12.

228. Willenbrink, J. 1963. On the quantitative assay of radiochromatograms by liquid scintillation counting. Intern. J. Appl. Radiation Isotopes 14:237–238.

229. Wilson, A. T. 1960. Detection of tritium on paper chromatograms. Biochim. Biophys. Acta 40:522–526.

230. White, C. G., and Samuel Helf. 1956. Suspension counting in scintillating gels. Nucleonics 14(10):46–48.

231. Woeller, Fritz H. 1961. Liquid scintillation counting of $C^{14}O_2$ with phenethylamine. Anal. Biochem. 2:508–511.

232. Wright, P. M., E. P. Steinberg, and L. E. Glendenin. 1961. Half-life of samarium-147. Phys. Rev. 123:205–208.

233. Ziegler, C. A., D. J. Chleck, and J. Brinkerhoff. 1957. Radioassay of low specific activity tritiated water by improved liquid scintillation techniques. Anal. Chem. 29:1774–1776.

Supplementary References

234. Brown, Jerry L., and John M. Johnston. 1962. Radioassay of lipid components separated by thin-layer-chromatography. J. Lipid Res. 3:480–481.

235. Chiriboga, Jorge. 1962. Radiometric analysis of metals using chelates labeled with carbon-14 and liquid scintillation counting procedures. Anal. Chem. 34:1843.

236. Dobbs, Horace E. 1964. Determination of carbon-14 in halogenic compounds by an oxygen flask method. Anal. Chem. 36:687–689.

237. O'Brien, R. D. 1964. Nitric acid digestion of tissues for liquid scintillation counting. Anal. Biochem. 7:251–254.

238. Shipotofsky, S. H. 1964. A simple sensitive geiger counter for scanning chromatograms (A simple radiochromatogram scanner). Anal. Biochem. 7:233–239.

239. Snyder, Fred, and Paul Godfrey. 1961. Collecting $C^{14}O_2$ in a warburg flask for subsequent scintillation counting. J. Lipid Res. 2:195.

240. Steyn, J., and F. J. Haasbroek. 1958. The application of internal liquid scintillation counting to a 4π beta-gamma coincidence method for the absolute standardization of radioactive nuclides. *In* Proc. Second UN Intern. Conf. Peaceful Uses Atomic Energy. vol. 21. Geneva, UN. pp. 95–100.

CHAPTER NINE

Analysis of Data in Radioactivity Measurements

In analyzing the apparent counting data observed in the assay of radioactive samples, two basic considerations are of primary importance. First, how statistically reliable are the data; second, what relation exists between the apparent counting rate of the sample and the actual disintegration rate? It is necessary to subject radioactivity measurement data to statistical analysis, because radioactive decay is a strictly random phenomenon. Needless to say, rigorous statistical treatment is especially essential when low levels of radioactivity are being assayed. A number of general references to the application of statistical methods to radioactivity measurement are given in the chapter bibliography: of these, Jarrett's (12) is the most comprehensive. Herberg's recent papers are particularly important in liquid scintillation counting (7, 8).

Several phenomena prevent all the sample disintegrations from being detected or, on the other hand, lead to the counting of events not related to sample disintegrations. Correction factors for these interferences must be applied to the apparent counting data if one wants to cross-compare measurement data of samples obtained under different circumstances. Many of these factors can be standardized from assay to assay, thus avoiding the necessity of making corrections, but the principle underlying this standardization must be understood.

Radiotracer experiments are, of course, subject to the typical errors of all chemical operations: weighing, volume measurements, the chemical (and radiochemical) purity of reagents used, and general competence of laboratory technique. Such errors are not considered at length in this chapter, but they cannot be ignored in practice.

A. STATISTICAL CONSIDERATIONS

1. Error Probability

As has been discussed in Chapter 2, radioactive decay is a random phenomenon. This can be readily demonstrated by making repeated measurements of the activity of a long-lived nuclide, each for the same duration of time (see Experiment VII). The results will not be identical, but rather varied over a range of values with a clustering near the center of the range. If a sufficiently large number of such measurements are made and the data plotted, a curve such as that shown in Figure 9-1 will result. This is the familiar *normal distribution curve*, which for most radio-

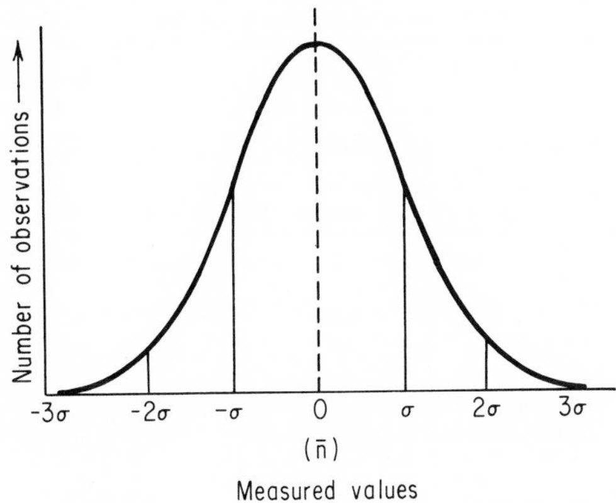

Figure 9-1. A normal distribution curve.

activity measurements is a close approximation of the Poisson distribution curve.

Because of this situation, one obviously cannot know the "true" value of the result of a given counting operation. From the Poisson distribution equation, it can, however, be shown that a mean value ($\bar{n}$) of a given counting is the best estimate of the "true" value when large numbers of determinations are involved. The accuracy of any individual measurement (n) is gauged by the magnitude of its deviation (Δ) from the mean value, or

$$\Delta = n - \bar{n} \tag{9-1}$$

On the plot in Figure 9-1, the vertical dashed line through the apex of the curve represents the $\bar{n}$ value and is arbitrarily labeled zero.

Note that the distribution of positive and negative deviations from the mean value of any given magnitude are of equal occurrence and that the occurrence of small deviations is more probable than that of large ones. The probability of any deviation ("error") being as large or larger than a given value may be calculated. The basic "error" unit used is the standard deviation (σ). For practical purposes, the *standard deviation* can be defined as the square root of the mean value, or $\sigma = \sqrt{\bar{n}}$. Only 31.7 per cent of the values on a normal curve are as large or larger than $\pm 1\sigma$. All other error units are expressed in terms of the standard deviation. Table 9-1 lists the names and values of the common measures of error probability.

TABLE 9-1

Measures of error probability

Name of Error	Deviation / Standard Deviation (Δ/σ)	Probability of an Error Exceeding Such a Deviation
Probable error	0.6745	0.5000
Standard error (deviation), one sigma	1.0000	0.3173
90% error	1.6449	0.1000
95% error	1.9600	0.0500
Two sigma	2.0000	0.0455
99% error	2.5758	0.0100
Three sigma	3.0000	0.0027

The foregoing discussion dealt with repeated measurements on the same sample, but in radiotracer assay it is common to make only one or two activity determinations per sample. In such cases there is no $\bar{n}$ value from which σ may be calculated. Because of the nature of the Poisson distribution, however, the standard deviation (σ) of a single determination of magnitude n may be taken as $\sqrt{n}$, that is, the square root of the total number of counts collected. A related unit, the *relative standard deviation* (or relative σ) is defined as $\sqrt{n} \times 100/n$, or $100/\sqrt{n}$. Thus, the larger the value of n (number of counts collected), the smaller the relative standard deviation. To realize a given relative standard deviation for a given counting operation it is necessary to continue counting only until sufficient counts are collected.

Radiotracer measurements are usually made to have an accuracy equivalent to 1 per cent standard deviation. In order to achieve this specification, it is necessary to collect 10,000 counts from the radioactive sample in question, since when $100/\sqrt{n} = 1$ per cent, $n = 10{,}000$. This is irrespective of the length of time required to collect this number of counts. From this single assay one could then state that there is a 68.3 per cent probability that the true total count was 10,000 ± 100 counts, or (from Table 9-1) a 95 per cent probability that the total count was 10,000 ± 196 counts.

2. Contribution of Background Error

The 10,000 counts collected from the foregoing sample represent a combination of two factors, namely, sample activity and background. The standard deviation of this measurement is therefore actually a combination of the errors of each separate factor. When the ratio of gross sample counting rate (counts per unit time) to background counting rate is high (over ten-fold), the standard deviation of the net sample radioactivity can be calculated simply by taking the square root of the gross counting result. As the ratio becomes smaller, however, the contribution of the background error to the error of the gross sample counts becomes increasingly significant. Furthermore, it is unlikely that the same counting duration will be used for both the sample and the background determination. It is necessary under these circumstances to consider the standard deviations of the counting rates of the sample and the background separately, before the standard deviation of the net sample counting rate can be defined. This is true since the net sample counting rate is derived from the difference of two independent counting operations, that is, gross sample counts (sample plus background) and background.

The standard deviation of the net sample counting rate (σ_s) is equal to the square root of the sum of the squares of the standard deviations of the gross sample count rate (σ_g) and the background count rate (σ_b), or

$$\sigma_s = \sqrt{\sigma_g^2 + \sigma_b^2} \qquad (9\text{-}2)$$

But the best estimate for the standard deviation of a rate is the square root of the counting rate divided by the counting time ($\sqrt{r/t}$). Thus, $\sqrt{r_g/t_g}$ may be substituted for σ_g and $\sqrt{r_b/t_b}$ may be substituted for σ_b in Equation 9-2 to yield

$$\sigma_s = \sqrt{\frac{r_g}{t_g} + \frac{r_b}{t_b}} \qquad (9\text{-}3)$$

As an example of the effect of background error on the standard deviation of the net sample count rate, suppose that a sample is assayed for 40 min and 10,000 counts collected. The background is measured for 10 min and a total of 1000 counts registered. Thus, the gross sample count rate is 250 cpm, the background is 100 cpm, and the net sample activity is found to be 150 cpm. Ignoring the contribution of background error and calculating the standard deviation as the square root of the gross sample counts, the result could be reported as 150 ± 2.5 cpm. Using Equation

9-3, which takes background error into account, the results would be as follows:

$$\sigma_s = \sqrt{\frac{250}{40} + \frac{100}{10}} = 4.0$$

Thus, the more accurate expression of the counting data would be 150 ± 4.0 cpm. Such error differences assume great importance in certain types of radiotracer experiments and cannot be taken lightly.

3. Requirements of Counting Time for Sample and Background

As indicated previously, in a sample having a counting rate sufficiently high in comparison to the background counting rate, one can readily collect enough counts to insure an acceptable relative standard deviation of the counting operation without worrying about the contribution of the background to the over-all counting process. Such is not the case when one encounters a sample with a low counting rate. If the counting rate of the sample is only fourfold that of the background, it is necessary to count the sample and the background over defined durations of time so that the relative standard deviation of each of the two counting operations is of comparable magnitude. To this end, the ratio of background counting time (t_b) to gross sample counting time (t_g) is related to the ratio of the counting rates of the background (R_b) and the sample (R_g) as follows:

$$\frac{t_g}{t_b} = \sqrt{\frac{R_g}{R_b}} \tag{9-4}$$

Obviously, when the ratio of R_g/R_b approaches unity, in order to realize a respectable relative standard deviation of the net sample counting rate, one must count the sample as well as the background over a long period of time. The requirements of counting time for various ratios of R_g/R_b are given in Table 9-2. To avoid lengthy counting operations, it is, of course, essential to design a radiotracer experiment in such a way that the counting rate of the final counting sample is considerably higher, preferably tenfold or more, than that of the background radiation. By the same token, it is important to avoid "technical" contamination in a radiotracer laboratory from the careless handling or avoidable spillage of small amounts of radioactive material. Although such technical contaminations do not constitute a health hazard, they will undoubtedly raise the background observable in radiation detectors, and hence, lengthen the required counting time.

Browning (1) used the foregoing relation as a base for charts determining optimum distribution of counting time. Freedman and Anderson (5)

TABLE 9-2

Counting times required for a given standard error of net activity with a background counting rate of 30 cpm [from Calvin, et al. (2, p. 288)]

Ratio of Sample Counting rate to Background Counting Rate (R_g/R_b)	Standard Error in Net Counting Rate (R_x)*							
	1%		2%		5%		10%	
	Background Counting Time [in min[†] (t_b)]	Sample Counting Time [in min (t_g)]	Background Counting Time [in min (t_b)]	Sample Counting Time [in min. (t_g)]	Background Counting Time [in min. (t_b)]	Sample Counting Time [in min (t_g)]	Background Counting Time [in min (t_b)]	Sample Counting Time [in min (t_g)]
1.1	68,300	71,100	17,100	18,000	2,730	2,870	683	717
1.2	17,500	19,100	4,360	4,780	698	764	175	191
1.4	4,550	5,380	1,140	1,350	182	215	46	54
1.7	1,570	2,050	393	513	63	82	16	21
2.0	804	1,140	201	284	32	46	8	11
2.5	383	606	96	152	15	24	4	6
3.0	228	395	57	99	9	16	2	4
3.5	153	286	38	72	6	11	2	3
4.0	111	222	28	56	4	8	1	2
5.0	68	151	17	38	3	6	1	2
6.0	46	113	12	28	2	5	1	1
7.0	34	89	8	22	1	4	1	1
8.0	26	74	7	18	1	3	1	1
9.0	21	62	5	16	1	3	1	1
10.0	17	54	4	14	1	2	1	1

*Net counting rate (R_x) = sample counting rate (R_g) − background counting rate (R_b).

[†] Short times are rounded off to nearest minute greater than zero.

and Hughes (9) discuss the problem of counting time in the assay of very low levels of activity.

4. Rejection of Abnormal Data

Thus far, error based on the randomness of radioactive decay has been the primary consideration. Other factors, such as variation in sample preparation procedures, errors in measuring quantities, contamination of the detector, or mislabeling and confusion of samples, also contribute to errors in radioactivity measurement data. As a result, when repeated assays of similar samples are made under seemingly identical circumstances, one occasionally finds that one measurement differs from the others by a large amount. Since the number of observations is usually limited, one abnormal value can introduce considerable error into the over-all average, which is used as the best estimate of the "true" value. Various criteria for rejecting such suspected data are in use (10, 18), but most investigators prefer *Chauvenet's criterion*; namely, an observation should be rejected if the probability of its occurrence is equal to, or less than, $\frac{1}{2}N$, where N represents the number of observations involved. This relation is more conveniently used in terms of the ratio of the deviation of the suspected value to the standard deviation of the series of observations $[(n - \bar{n})/\sigma]$. Table 9-3 lists values of $(n - \bar{n})/\sigma$ for various numbers of observations (N). If the calculated value of $(n - \bar{n})/\sigma$ for a suspected observation exceeds that given in Table 9-3 for the appropriate number of observations, the value is discarded.

For simplicity, some investigators reject suspected values which deviate from the mean of a series by more than 2σ or 3σ. The probabilities of

TABLE 9-3

Values for use with the Chauvenet criterion

Number of Observations (N)	Ratio of the Individual Deviation to the Standard Deviation $[(n - \bar{n})/\sigma]$	Number of Observations (N)	Ratio of the Individual Deviation to the Standard Deviation $[(n - \bar{n})/\sigma]$
2	1.15	15	2.13
3	1.38	20	2.24
4	1.54	25	2.35
5	1.65	30	2.40
6	1.73	35	2.45
7	1.80	40	2.50
8	1.86	50	2.58
9	1.91	75	2.71
10	1.96	100	2.81
12	2.04	200	3.02

the occurrence of such deviations are 4.5 per cent and 0.27 per cent, respectively.

B. CORRECTION FACTORS IN RADIOTRACER ASSAY

In ordinary radioactivity assay encountered in radiotracer experiments, the observed counting rate is not equal to the true disintegration rate of the sample, but is nevertheless related to it. A number of factors affect the relation between absolute disintegration rate and the observed counting rate. Some tend to increase the observed counting rate, but most tend to decrease it in relation to the disintegration rate. Of these factors, some are inherent in the detectors, others arise from the nature of the counting sample, and still others are related to the sample-to-detector arrangement. Of the many recognized factors, only a few are important in connection with radiotracer experimentation. Figure 9-2 illustrates those that are relatively more important in relation to an end-window G-M detector. The factors to be described in detail are largely of importance in relative beta measurements, but some apply equally to gamma assay. Even though only relative measurements are being made,

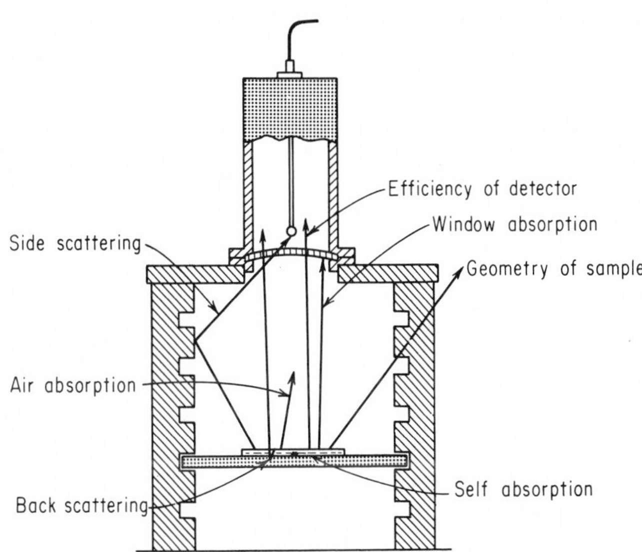

Figure 9-2. Factors in G-M radiotracer assay.

it is necessary to understand the origin and the effect of these factors and the corrections to be made for them.

1. Background

The background count rate registered on a radiation counter can come from such varied sources as cosmic radiation, natural radioactivity in the vicinity, artificial radioactivity (fallout), nearby X-ray generators, and thermal or other circuit noise. Several means are employed to reduce the background counting rate for various counter assemblies. Detector shielding with lead or iron is most widely utilized. In addition, coincidence circuitry and photomultiplier cooling in liquid scintillation counters, and anticoincidence circuitry in special low background G-M counters are exceptionally effective in reducing background count, in some cases to the level of 10 counts per hour (44). Regardless of such background reduction, the gross sample count rate (m_g) always includes some background count rate (m_b). The net observed counting rate (m_0) due to sample activity alone is thus,

$$m_0 = m_g - m_b \tag{9-5}$$

Scales (41) has discussed in detail the problem of determining background counts in liquid scintillation counting, where the complication of quenching also occurs.

By ignoring some minor factors, the net observed counting rate can now be related to the absolute disintegration rate (D) of a sample as follows:

$$m_0 = DE\ f_\tau f_b f_w f_s \tag{9-6}$$

where E represents the correction for geometry and detector efficiency, f_τ stands for the coincidence loss factor, f_b is the backscatter factor, f_w represents the factor for window and air absorption, and f_s stands for the self-absorption factor. In gamma ray measurements, the latter three factors may usually be ignored.

2. Geometry

Since sample radiation is emitted equally in all directions, the placement of the detector with respect to the sample is clearly a primary limiting factor on the percentage of disintegrations that will be detected. If Ω represents the solid angle subtended by the sensitive volume of the detector, then $\Omega/4\pi$ equals the fraction of the disintegrations that would be directed toward that sensitive volume. Figure 9-3 indicates this relationship and defines the terms of d, r, and α. The value of $\Omega/4\pi$ for an ideal point source may be calculated as follows:

$$\frac{\Omega}{4\pi} = \frac{1}{2}(1 - \cos\alpha) = \frac{1}{2}\left(1 - \frac{d}{\sqrt{d^2 + r^2}}\right) \tag{9-7}$$

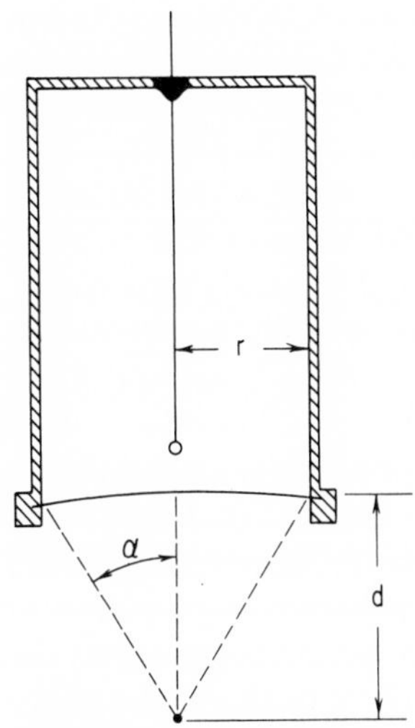

Figure 9-3. Geometry of an end-window G-M detector.

In practice a counting sample is spread over an often considerable area and is an extended source, rather than a point source. It is generally recognized that the size of the source should be as small as possible and should by no means approach the size of the detector window.

Since it is extremely difficult to calculate accurately the solid angle for extended sources, for comparative measurements it is strongly recommended that counting samples be prepared of uniform size and distribution and that they be placed at a reproducibly identical distance from the detector. A sample holding rack with several shelves usually provides for this latter feature. Where desired, the relative values of $\Omega/4\pi$ (shelf ratios) for the various shelf positions of a sample holder can be determined as indicated in Experiment I, Section B-5.

The value of Ω for G-M and proportional end-window detectors is inherently less than 2π, and frequently less than 1π (27). For G-M and proportional windowless detectors, where the sample is introduced into the detector, the solid angle approximates 2π. In counting with liquid scintillation detectors and internal-sample ion chambers, the geometry involved approaches 4π. An arrangement in which two windowless G-M detectors are placed face to face and the sample suspended in the center (a "4π counter") is widely used to standardize beta sources. A common method for greatly increasing the geometrical efficiency of NaI (Tl) crystal scintillation detectors is the employment of "well" crystals, where the counting sample (usually liquid in a vial) can be inserted deep into the crystal. In this case, sample volume is limited, since geometrical efficiency decreases sharply as the sample volume reaches and exceeds the well capacity (22, 31, 47).

3. Detector Efficiency

The factor E in Equation 9-6 is made up of the geometry factor $\Omega/4\pi$ and the intrinsic efficiency factor (f_e) of the given detector for the radiation from a specific nuclide. Factor f_e represents the fraction of radiation within the sensitive volume of a detector that is actually detected. For G-M detectors the values of f_e are 100 per cent, about 96 per cent, and 1 per cent for alpha, beta, and gamma radiation, respectively. With a NaI(Tl) crystal scintillation detector, the gamma detection efficiency varies from 10–60 per cent depending on the photon energy. Excessively high counting rates can, however, lead to a subsequent temporary decline in efficiency due to photomultiplier fatigue (39). Alpha and beta particles would not normally penetrate to the sensitive crystal, but even so would be very poorly detected. In an ion chamber, alpha and low-energy beta particles (^{14}C, ^{35}S) would be nearly 100 per cent detected, if the chamber was sufficiently large. Detection efficiencies would decrease with increasing beta energy, and gamma rays would pass through virtually undetected. The value of f_e in liquid scintillation detectors is strongly dependent on beta particle energy, degree of quenching, nature of the solvent and fluor, concentration of fluor, and the like (see Chapter 6).

Not only do detectors show a different intrinsic efficiency for different nuclides, but the sensitivity of a specific detector to a given nuclide will vary over a period of time. This problem particularly plagues scintillation and proportional counters in which the detection efficiency is a function of detector potential. Even slight fluctuations in this potential can offset detection efficiency noticeably. For this reason, stability of the high-voltage supply for these counters is essential. In addition, G-M detectors may show a variation in radial response within the sensitive volume of the tube (21).

In organically quenched G-M detectors, failure of the quenching mechanism may occur with increasing age, resulting in multiple pulses for a single ionizing event. The factor f_m (for multiple-pulsing) must then be incorporated into factor E. Generally speaking, however, multiple pulses are not a significant factor in counting with G-M detectors. Similarly, electrons may be created in a photomultiplier tube without a photon interaction. Such a phenomenon may create a serious problem in γ-ray spectrometry.

In order to determine the absolute value of E, it would be necessary to calibrate the detector with a standard source of the same nuclide to be later assayed, making the measurements under physical conditions identical to those later to be used (29). In most radiotracer assays, however, only relative values of E need be known for the purpose of correcting counting rates for variation in efficiency with time. This is readily accomplished by making routine measurements of the activity of a standard source, such as $Ba^{14}CO_3$, $Na_2{}^{14}CO_3$, toluene-^3H, or U_3O_8. These and many other radionuclide standards can be obtained from the National Bureau of Standards or commercial sources. Any variation in the counting rate of this standardized source over a few days or weeks can be attributed to a change in detector efficiency and all sample counts correspondingly corrected.

4. Coincidence Loss

A radiation counting assembly requires a finite time to clear the pulse created by each radiation particle. During this period, other incident radiation is either not detected or not differentiated. The result of this failure to resolve two incident radiation particles that are closely spaced in time is coincidence loss. Note that disintegrations are not evenly spaced in time. The minimum time interval between which two events can be registered is termed the *resolving time* of the counter.

Coincidence loss has several sources in a counting assembly. Loss can occur due to the amplifier circuitry. Normally this is negligible, since the better-quality amplifiers have resolving times of 1–5μsec. In the economical "training" scalers, however, this may be as high as 250μsec. A more common source of coincidence loss is the mechanical register used to record counting events. These registers, being very slow devices, must be used with scaling circuits to avoid coincidence loss. It is desirable to use a high scaling factor to group a number of pulses prior to the mechanical registers (100, or 1000 with decade scalers; 128 or 256 with binary scalers), if fast counting is anticipated. Davidon (28) has prepared a nomogram for computing such register losses. Recently, it has become common to eliminate the mechanical register altogether and to substitute a series of scaling units employing cold cathode decade tubes or similar devices. To accommodate the very high counting rates attainable with scintillation and proportional detectors, it is necessary to employ an initial "hard valve" scaling unit, which is obtainable with a 1–5μsec resolving time.

For the *G-M counter*, the most important source of coincidence loss is the detector. The resolving time (τ) of G-M detectors is typically 100–200μsec, but may be as high as 1000μsec. This resolving time has two components: dead time and recovery time. As seen in Figure 9-4, for a brief interval following each ionizing event a G-M detector is insensitive or "dead." For a longer period of time, during which the tube is "recovering," it will respond to incident radiation with pulses of increasing size, up to its maximum. The total resolving time of the detector will be the dead time (τ_d) plus a portion of the recovery time (τ_r). The portion of the recovery time included will be dependent on the sensitivity setting of the associated scaler. Typically, the coincidence loss in a G-M detector begins to be significant over about 3000 cpm. Scintillation and proportional detectors, on the contrary, have such extremely short resolving times (see

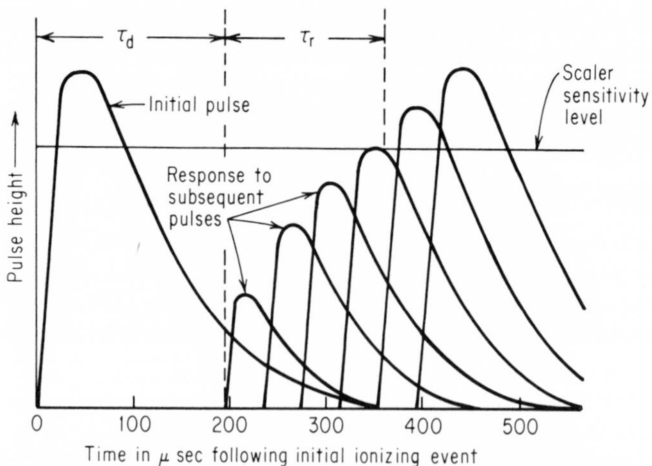

Figure 9-4. Resolving time of a G-M detector.

Table 6-1) that they are not the cause of significant coincidence loss except at counting rates of several hundred thousand counts per minute.

If the resolving time (τ) of a counting assembly is known, the correction for coincidence loss can be calculated. When τ is expressed in units of seconds, then a counting interval of τ sec (usually a small fraction of a second) is lost for each count registered. If m represents the observed counting rate per second, the total lost counting time is $m\tau$ sec for each second of counting time, and the net useful counting time per second is $1 - m\tau$ sec. Letting n represent the corrected counting rate per second, its value is found as

$$\frac{n}{m} = \frac{1}{1 - m\tau}, \quad \text{or} \quad n = \frac{m}{1 - m\tau} \tag{9-8}$$

As an example of the use of this equation for coincidence loss corrections, consider a situation where a counting rate of 6000 cpm (that is, 100 cps) was measured with a G-M counter whose resolving time was 200μsec. The corrected counting rate would be calculated as follows:

$$n = \frac{100 \text{ cps}}{1 - 100 \times 0.0002 \text{ sec}} = 102 \text{ cps}, \quad \text{or} \quad 6120 \text{ cpm}$$

By contrast where the same counting assembly observed a counting rate of 60,000 cpm, the corrected count rate would be

$$n = \frac{1000 \text{ cps}}{1 - 1000 \times 0.0002 \text{ sec}} = 1250 \text{ cps}, \quad \text{or} \quad 75{,}000 \text{ cpm}$$

The percentage coincidence losses in these two examples were 2 per cent and 25 per cent, respectively. Scott (43) has designed a useful slide rule for making rapid determinations of such coincidence loss corrections.

The resolving time of G-M detectors can be determined by several methods. An oscilloscope may be used to visualize the resolving time directly, essentially as in Figure 9-4. Another method involves making a consecutive series of measurements on a nuclide of short half-life, whose initial activity is such that considerable coincidence loss occurs in the detector. As decay occurs and the count rate decreases, correspondingly less coincidence loss occurs. The actual extent of loss can be determined graphically and the resolving time calculated from this (see Experiment V). As a variant of this method one may prepare a set of counting samples of proportionately increasing and known relative activities and determine the coincidence loss from the plot of apparent counting rate versus known activity (40).

The simplest means of determining detector resolving time is the paired-source method used in Experiment I, Section B-4. This involves comparing the sum of the measured activities of two individual sources (of approximately 7000–10,000 cpm each) with the activity of the two sources measured together. Clearly, the latter figure will be smaller because the relative coincidence loss is greater. Let n_1, n_2, $n_{1,2}$, and n_b represent the true counting rates (in cps) of source 1, source 2, both sources together, and background, respectively, and let m_1, m_2, and $m_{1,2}$ equal the corresponding observed counting rates. The background counting rate is represented by m_b. Then

$$n_1 + n_2 = n_{1,2} + n_b \tag{9-9}$$

Substituting values of n from Equation 9-8 would yield

$$\frac{m_1}{1 - m_1\tau} + \frac{m_2}{1 - m_2\tau} = \frac{m_{1,2}}{1 - m_{1,2}\tau} + \frac{m_b}{1 - m_b\tau} \tag{9-10}$$

This leads to a quadratic equation for τ. Normally a simplified approximation is used as follows:

$$\tau = \frac{m_1 + m_2 - m_{1,2} - m_b}{m_{1,2}^2 - m_1^2 - m_2^2} \text{ expressed in seconds.} \tag{9-11}$$

A source kit designed for this determination can be obtained from several manufacturers.

5. Backscattering

Radiation from a sample which is emitted in a direction away from the detector into the backing material and is subsequently scattered back toward the detector is said to be *backscattered.* The effect is consequently, to increase the apparent counting rate of the sample, above that anticipated for the given sample-to-detector geometry. Backscatter is primarily a phenomenon of 2π beta assay (26).

The backscatter factor (f_b) can be determined experimentally by first assaying a sample mounted on mylar film, and subsequently measuring the count rate with various thicknesses of backing material beneath it. It will be found that the observed counting rate increases directly with increased thickness of backing up to a "saturation" value (45). Theoretically, this saturation thickness would be at 0.5 of the beta particle range, but in practice it occurs at 0.2 of the range value. At saturation backing, the thickness is generally called the *saturation backscattering thickness* for a given beta emitter.

As Figure 9-5 shows, backscatter increases more rapidly with increasing backing thickness (d), the lower the beta energy and the higher the

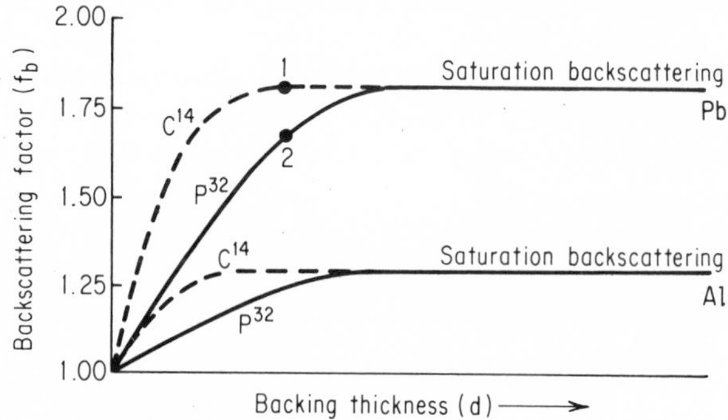

Figure 9-5. The effect of beta energy and backing thickness on backscatter.

atomic number of the backing material. But the ultimate backscatter value, f_b, attained (at saturation backscattering thickness) is independent of beta energy within a range between 0.3 Mev and 2.3 Mev for a given backing material. In addition, the value of the saturation backscattering thickness for a given beta energy is approximately the same for all backing materials.

The value of f_b at saturation backscattering thickness is directly related to the atomic number of the backing material as shown by Figure 9-6. This relationship can be used to advantage to increase the counting rate of weak samples. To this end it will be noted that lead and platinum sample planchets would give f_b values of about 1.80, compared to the value of about 1.30 for the commonly used aluminum planchets.

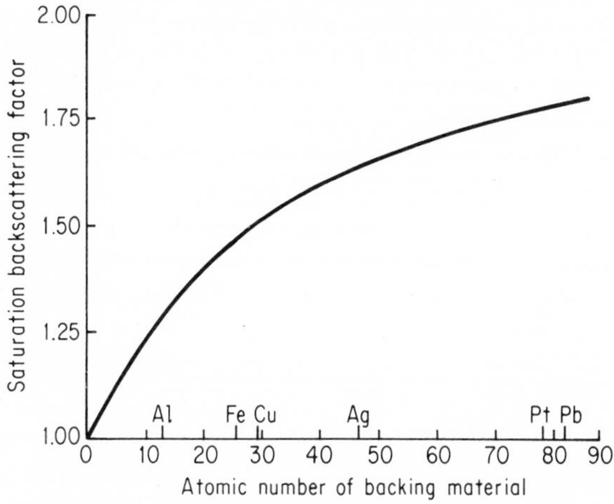

Figure 9-6. Saturation backscattering factor in relation to the atomic number of the backing material.

In practice, because of the variation of f_b with backing thickness up to the saturation value, it is necessary to use sample planchets of saturation backscattering thickness for the radiation being assayed. It is further advisable to employ planchets of the same material throughout a given series of experiments where comparisons will be made. Furthermore, a planchet designed to give saturation backscattering thickness for ^{14}C assay (point 1 on Figure 9-5), could be too thin for ^{32}P assay (point 2 on Figure 9-5), because only slight variation in thickness from planchet to planchet would produce a significant difference in counting rate observed. Thus, planchets must be selected with a view to the nuclides to be assayed in them.

A certain amount of *side scattering* of radiation into the detector may occur (see Figure 9-2). In beta assay, this can increase the observed counting rate noticeably if material of high atomic number is near the source or detector. Hence, sample holders are usually of lucite or other low Z material.

6. Absorption

An often considerable fraction of the radiation emitted in the direction of a detector may be absorbed before it reaches the sensitive volume of the detector. This absorption may occur in the sample itself (self-absorption), in the intervening air space, or in the window of the detector (G-M and proportional type). The latter two areas of absorption are included in the correction factor f_w; self-absorption, the more important consideration, is designed f_s.

a. Window and air absorption. Corrections for *window absorption* in the G-M detectors of earlier years with mica windows of over 2 mg/cm^2 thickness were often considerable. Figure 3-10 indicates the percentage transmission of beta particles of various E_{max} through different window thicknesses (25). With the more recent development of ultrathin aluminized mylar windows of about 0.15 mg/cm^2, window absorption becomes negligible for all nuclides but tritium. Since these mylar windows leak slightly, such detectors must be operated with a constant gas flow through the chamber. *Air absorption* of sample radiation is usually slight except for alpha and the very weakest beta particles.

Both components of f_w are normally determined together by means of an *absorption curve* prepared with various thicknesses of external aluminum absorbers. (The details of this technique are described in Experiment VI, Section A.) In brief, it consists of extrapolating the linear semilog plot of observed sample activity to zero thickness by accounting for air and window absorption and thus obtaining the corrected activity at zero total absorber. Figure 9-7 illustrates such an extrapolated curve.

b. Self-absorption. If radioactivity measurements are made on a series of beta-emitting samples, particularly soft beta emitters, of increasing thickness but of constant specific activity, the phenomenon of self-absorption can be readily demonstrated. Without self-absorption, one would expect that the count rate should increase linearly as the amount of

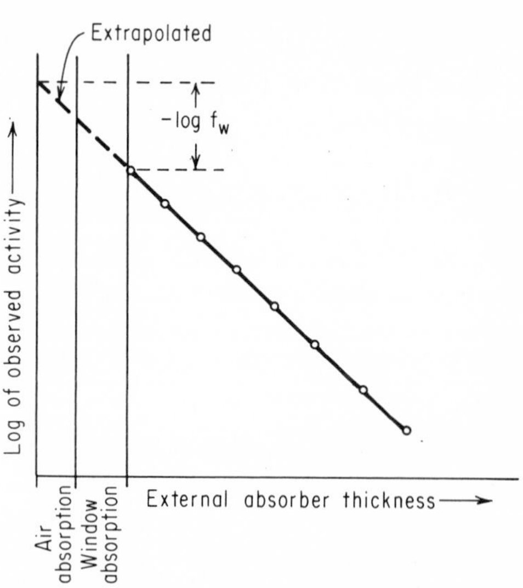

Figure 9-7. Correction for f_w by means of an extrapolated absorption curve.

sample is increased. In actuality, this is not so. Evidently with thick samples, beta particles from the lower layers are absorbed to some extent by the overlying sample material. Eventually, a thickness is reached where only the beta particles from the topmost layers are being measured. A plot of such counting data (Figure 9-8) shows that the observed activity curve bends away from the calculated activity curve (dotted line) and approaches a limiting value. This value is known as the *saturation* (or infin-

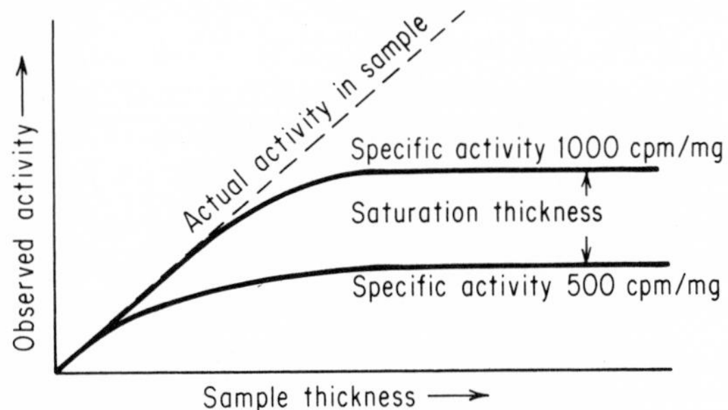

Figure 9-8. Self-absorption curve for samples of constant specific activity.

ite) *thickness*. As Figure 9-8 shows, for samples of two different specific activities, the observed activity at saturation thickness is directly proportional to the respective specific activities. The self-absorption curve can be theoretically calculated for a given radioisotope; however, since in reality the observed self-absorption curve also reflects backscattering and other factors related to the counting assembly, it is best to determine the curve experimentally for a given counting assembly.

Another version of the self-absorption curve (Figure 9-9) results if a constant total activity is maintained in a series of samples, each diluted

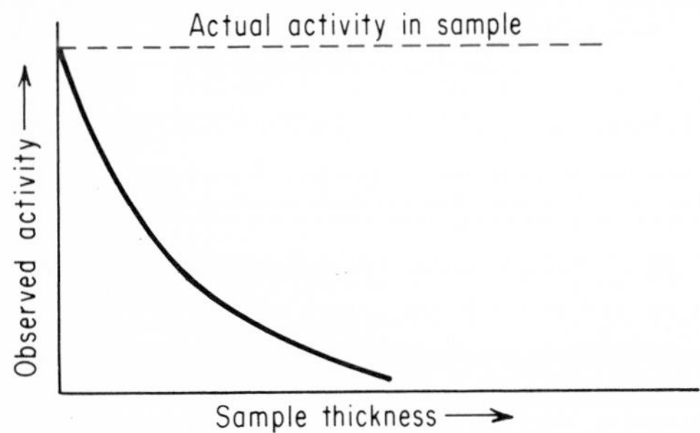

Figure 9-9. Self-absorption curve for samples of constant activity.

with increasing amounts of unlabeled material. Without interference from self-absorption, the observed activity should remain constant (dotted line). Instead, the observed counting rate decreases exponentially with increasing sample thickness. Since the specific activity in this series of counting samples decreases as the total amount of sample increases, the phenomenon of saturation thickness will not be realized.

Self-absorption correction is primarily a problem in the assay of low-energy beta emitters, such as ^{3}H, ^{14}C, ^{35}S, and ^{45}Ca (24, 30, 34–38, 42, 48–50). High-energy beta emitters suffer relatively little self-absorption with the usual sample thicknesses (less than 15 mg/cm^2). Alpha emitters, because of their typically short range, are almost always measured at saturation thickness, whereas gamma radiation is readily transmitted through the thickest assay sample with almost no absorption. In assaying liquid samples of beta emitters, it is advisable to adjust the sample thickness so that saturation thickness is exceeded. This principle applies to the use of dipping counters or counting liquid samples in cupped planchets.

The extent of self-absorption cannot be predicted on a theoretical basis because of the associated phenomena of self-scattering and backscattering. Therefore, it must be empirically determined. Several methods have been developed to *measure the effect of self-absorption* on counting rate when varying thicknesses are encountered. Some workers prepare all samples to a constant thickness. Although accurate for comparative purposes, this is an extremely tedious and impractical technique. Alternatively, direct plating of samples from solution may be used to produce samples of negligible thickness, so that the interference of self-absorption can be ignored. This requires preparing samples of less than 1 mg/cm^2 thickness for ^{14}C or ^{35}S. The accuracy of such measurements is inherently poor, since it is quite difficult to secure samples with a uniform thickness by the evaporation process. By contrast, if sufficient sample material is available, all samples can be prepared at or beyond saturation thickness. In this case the observed count rate will be directly proportional to the specific activity of the sample, regardless of the sample thickness. This method is quite satisfactory for comparative measurements, although it is often impossible to secure sufficient amounts of counting samples in radiotracer experiments.

The most commonly used method for the correction of the self-absorption effect among counting samples of varied thickness is that involving the use of a *transmission* or *self-absorption graph*. (This method is followed in Experiment VI, section C.) Briefly, this involves preparation and assay of a series of samples of constant specific activity, but varying thickness. A curve is prepared of the apparent specific activity of the samples plotted against the sample thickness in mg/cm^2 (or weight of sample, if a standardized size of planchet is to be used). This curve is extrapolated to zero sample thickness and the specific activity at that point is by definition the "true" specific activity of the samples, that is, specific activity unaffected by self-absorption. The extrapolation can be facilitated if one plots the data on semilog paper. A second curve is then prepared of percent specific activity (apparent specific activity/"true" specific activity, that is, percentage transmission) versus sample thickness, taking the true specific activity as the value corresponding to 100 per cent transmission, that is, no self-absorption. Correction factors can then be read from this curve for transmission at any sample thickness. Figure 9-10 shows a schematic version of such a curve.

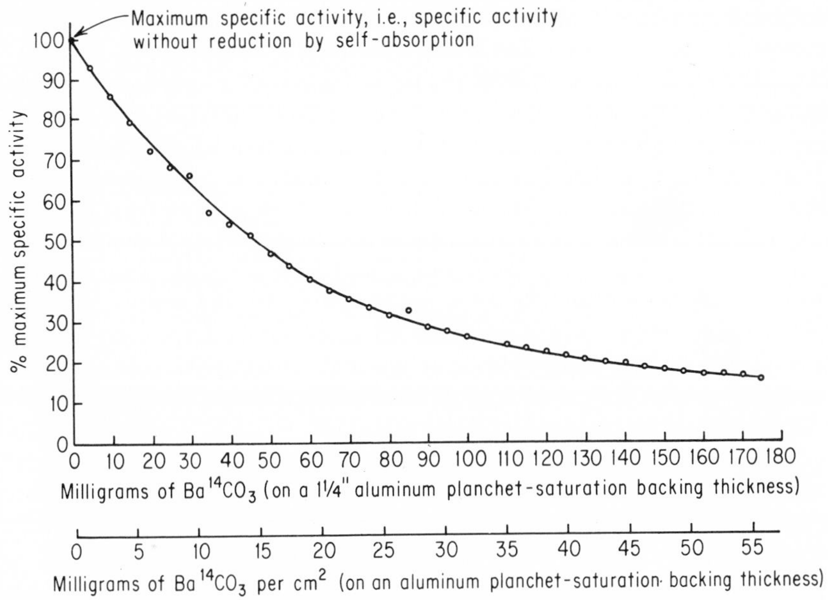

Figure 9-10. A typical self-absorption correction curve.

Experiment VI gives directions for preparing a correction curve for $Ba^{14}CO_3$ samples. The apparent counting rate divided by the percentage transmission corresponding to the sample thickness in question would then give counting rates corrected to zero thickness, or 100 per cent transmission of the counting sample. This treatment thus makes it possible to compare a series of counting samples of the same composition and varied thickness. A correction curve thus prepared is strictly applicable only to the counting assembly and the composition of sample used in its formation. Since the phenomenon of self-absorption is related directly to the atomic number of the constituent elements, as an approximation, the curve obtained with one type of sample may be applied to samples of other compositions. There exists no significant difference in the constituent elements with regard to atomic number. It is not, however, advisable to apply the curve with one type of counting assembly to samples counted with a different counting assembly.

C. SUMMARY

In making comparative measurements of beta sample activity with G-M counters, correction for all the factors in Equation 9-6, (except f_τ and f_s) and background can be avoided by keeping assay conditions constant. If sample counting rates are below 3000 cpm, and if the detector has a resolving time faster than 200μsec, f_τ may also be ignored. Correction for self-absorption is made by means of a correction curve (Figure 9-10). By contrast, when the activities of different samples of given gamma-emitting nuclides are being compared, all the factors in Equation 9-6 may be kept constant, thereby making it possible to cross-compare scintillation counting data directly, unless an exceedingly high count rate introduces some coincidence loss in the external scaler commonly used for such assays. In liquid scintillation counting, the value of factor E, that is, detector efficiency, and particularly the subfactor f_e, is of paramount importance as a result of variation in quenching effect. Other factors can be standardized or ignored. It must be stressed that such comparisons are possible only when assays have been carried out under conditions as nearly identical as possible.

Obviously, for absolute activity determinations each correction factor in Equation 9-6 must be individually evaluated as previously outlined. Zumwalt (51) has thoroughly described such absolute beta counting, using an end-window G-M detector.

BIBLIOGRAPHY

Statistical Considerations

1. Browning, W. E., Jr. 1951. Charts for determining optimum distribution of counting times. Nucleonics 9(3):63–67.

2. Calvin, Melvin, et al. 1949. Isotopic carbon. Techniques in its measurement and chemical manipulation. John Wiley & Sons, Inc., New York. 376 p.

3. Counting techniques, pt I. Dec. 2, 1957. Picker Scintillator (Picker X-Ray Corp.) 1(4):1–10.

4. Elmore, W. C. 1950. Statistics of counting. Nucleonics 6(1):26–34.

5. Freedman, Arthur J., and Ernest C. Anderson. 1952. Low-level counting techniques. Nucleonics 10(8)57–59.

6. Greenfield, M. A. and R. L. Koontz. 1960. A universal function for computing counting performance. Intern. J. Appl. Radiation Isotopes 8:205–210.

7. Herberg, R. J. 1961. Counting statistics for liquid scintillation counting. Anal. Chem. 33: 1308–1311.

8. Herberg, R. J. 1963. Statistical aspects of liquid scintillation counting by internal standard technique. Single Isotope. Anal. Chem. 35: 786–791.

9. Hughes, H. A. 1956. Reduction of counting time in low activity assays. Brit. J. Appl. Phys. 7: 415–416.

10. Is my nuclear instrumentation putting out valid data? Picker Scintillator (Picker X-Ray Corp.) 4(4):1–4. May 20, 1960.

11. Jaffey, Arthur H. 1960. Statistical tests for counting. Nucleonics 18(11):180–184.

12. Jarrett, Alan A. 1946. Statistical methods used in the measurement of radioactivity. Some useful graphs. U.S. Atomic Energy Commission. AECU-262. 63 p.

13. Kuyper, Adrian C. 1959. The statistics of radioactivity measurement. J. Chem. Ed. 36:128–132.

14. Miller, D. G., and M. B. Leboeuf. 1953. Effect of high beta backgrounds on precision alpha counting. Nucleonics 11(4):28–31.

15. Rainwater, L. J., and C. W. Wu. 1947. Applications of probability theory to nuclear particle detection. Nucleonics 1(2):60–69.

16. Schuler, Robert H. 1952. Short-lived radioactivity; correction for long counting periods. Nucleonics 10(11):96–97.

17. Tittle, C. W. 1962. How to apply statistics to nuclear measurements. Nuclear-Chicago Tech. Bull. No. 14. Des Plaines, Ill. 4 p.

18. When do you consider a nuclear measurement to be invalid? Picker Scintillator (Picker X-Ray Corp.) 5(2)1–2. Feb. 24, 1961.

19. Wilson, E. Bright, Jr. 1952. An introduction to scientific research. McGraw-Hill Book Company, New York. 375 p.

20. You can't beat statistics. Picker Scintillator (Picker X-Ray Corp.) 4(2):1–8. Dec. 29, 1959.

Correction Factors in Radiotracer Assay

21. Amith, Avraham, and W. Wayne Meinke. 1953. Radial response of typical end-window G-M tubes. Nucleonics 11(5):60–61.

22. Baskin, R., H. L. Demorest, and S. Sandhaus. 1954. Gamma counting efficiency of two well-type NaI crystals. Nucleonics 12(8):46–48.

23. Bayhurst, B. P., and R. J. Prestwood. 1959. A method for estimating beta-counting efficiencies. Nucleonics 17(3):82–85.

24. Beltz, Richard E. 1961. Self-absorption correction in the use of tritium-labeled substrates for enzyme assays. Anal. Biochem. 2:303–316.

25. Chang, Chia-Hua, and C. Sharp Cook. 1952. Relative transmission of beta particles through G-M counter windows. Nucleonics 10(4):24–27.

26. Christian, Darleane, Wayne W. Dunning, and Don S. Martin, Jr. 1952. Backscattering of beta rays in windowless G-M counters. Nucleonics 10(5):41–43.

27. Cook, G. B., J. F. Duncan, and M. A. Hewitt. 1951. Geometrical efficiency of end-window G-M counters. Nucleonics 8(1):24–27.

28. Davidon, William C. 1952. Nomogram for computing register losses. Nucleonics 10(12):76–77.

29. Gleason, G. I., J. D. Taylor, and D. L. Tabern. 1951. Absolute beta counting at defined geometries. Nucleonics 8(5):12–21.

30. Graf, Walter L., C. L. Comar, and Ira B. Whitney. 1951. Relative sensitivities of windowless and end-window counters. Nucleonics 9(4):22–27.

31. Gunnink, Ray, and A. W. Stoner. 1961. Photopeak counting efficiencies for 3 × 3 inch solid and well-type NaI scintillation crystals. Anal. Chem. 33:1311–1313.

32. Libby, W. F. 1947. Measurement of radioactive tracers. Anal. Chem. 19:2–6.

33. Loevinger, Robert, and Mones Berman. 1951. Efficiency criteria in radioactivity counting. Nucleonics 9(1):26–39.

34. Muramatsu, Masami, and Harris Busch. 1962. Self-absorption corrections for C^{14}-labeled protein. Anal. Biochem. 4:384–394.

35. Nervik, W. E., and P. C. Stevenson. 1952. Self-scattering and self-absorption of betas by moderately thick samples. Nucleonics 10(3):18–22.

36. Poddar, R. K. 1957. Quantitative measurement of S^{35} in biological samples. Nucleonics 15(1):82–83.

37. Pawsner, E. R. 1961. Self-absorption of carbon-14 samples on thin paper planchets. Intern. J. Appl. Radiation Isotopes 10:22–29.

38. Reid, Allen F., Adele S. Weil, and J. R. Dunning. 1947. Properties and measurement of carbon 14. Anal. Chem. 19:824–827.

39. Reid, J. F., W. E. Baker, and D. M. Compton. 1962. Low-counting-rate errors from photomultiplier fatigue. Nucleonics 20(3):80–82.

40. Rudstam, Sven Gösta. 1961. Measuring detector dead times accurately. Nucleonics 19(12):62–63.

41. Scales, B. 1963. Liquid scintillation counting: The determination of background counts of samples containing quenching substances. Anal. Biochem. 5:489–496.

42. Schweitzer, George K., and Bernard R. Stein. 1950. Measuring solid samples of low-energy beta emitter. Nucleonics 7(3):65–72.

43. Scott, James H. 1961. Slide rule for making dead-time correction. Nucleonics 19(9):90–92.

44. Softky, S. D., and R. E. Nather. 1957. Low-background counter for solid β-emitting samples. Nucleonics 15(5):90–93.

45. Tittle, C. W. 1961. How to compute absorption and backscattering of beta rays. Nuclear-Chicago Tech. Bull. No. 8. Des Plaines, Ill. 4 p.

46. Upson, U. L. 1953. Beta energy dependence in end-window G-M tubes. Nucleonics 11(12): 49–54.

47. Verheijke, M. L. 1962. Calculated efficiencies of a 3 × 3 in. NaI (Tl) well-type scintillation crystal. Intern. J. Appl. Radiation Isotopes 13:583–585.

48. Wick, Arne N., Harry N. Barnet, and Nancy Ackerman. 1949. Self-absorption curves of C^{14}-labeled barium carbonate, glucose, and fatty acids. Anal. Chem. 21: 1511–1513.

49. Yankwich, Peter E., Thomas H. Norris, and John Huston. 1947. Correcting for the absorption of weak beta-particles in thick samples. Anal. Chem. 19:439–441.

50. Yankwich, P. E., G. K. Rollefson, and T. H. Norris. 1946. Chemical forms assumed by C^{14} produced by neutron irradiation of nitrogeneous substances. J. Chem. Phys. 14:131–140.

51. Zumwalt, Lloyd R. 1950. Absolute beta counting using end-window Geiger-Mueller counters and experimental data on beta-particle scattering effects. U.S. Atomic Energy Commission. AECU-567. 76 p.

CHAPTER TEN

Design and Execution of Radiotracer Experiments

It would be most difficult to determine the magnitude of the contribution that radioactive tracer methodology has made to biological investigations. The use of radioactive isotopes allows the tracing of tagged molecules through biological processes in a manner hitherto impossible. This is the reason for the wide use of radiotracers in biochemical studies of intermediary metabolism and in physiological studies in general. Radiotracer methodology has certain inherent limitations and problems that must be understood and evaluated if it is to be used successfully. The bearing of these limitations on the proper design and execution of radiotracer experiments is examined in this chapter.

A. UNIQUE ADVANTAGES OF RADIOTRACER EXPERIMENTS

The *sensitivity of detection* using radiotracers far exceeds that with most other chemical or physical methods. This is equivalent to the magnification of biological processes to an extraordinary power to allow ready detection. For example, the specific activity of carrier-free tritium is approximately 50 curies/milliatom. This implies that a dilution factor of 10^{12} can be tolerated without jeopardizing the detection of tritium-labeled compounds. It is thus possible to detect the occurrence of metabolic substances which are normally present in tissues at such low concentrations as to defy the most sensitive chemical methods of identification. An example is the tracing of tritiated thymidine incorporation into nucleic acids in cell nuclei.

Perhaps the most outstanding advantage of the use of radioisotopes in biology is the opportunity afforded to *trace dynamic mechanisms* in organisms. Such biological phenomena as ion transport across cell membranes, turnover, intermediary metabolism, or translocation in plants could, before the advent of radiotracer methods, be approached only indirectly. Unfortunately, the very fact that radiotracer studies so commonly involve such dynamic conditions frequently renders the interpretation of experimental results most difficult.

The use of the *isotope effect* to study *rate-determining steps* in a sequence of biochemical reactions represents an additional, although less frequently employed, advantage of radiotracer methodology. The term *isotope effect* (to be discussed more fully later) refers to the influence upon a reaction rate due to the difference in the masses of isotopes. This effect may create significant problems in the use of radioisotopes as tracers but can, nevertheless, be used to advantage in a limited number of cases to understand the kinetics of certain chemical reactions.

Despite such advantages, radiotracers are often *indiscriminately used* in biological investigations. It should be emphasized that radiotracers are not magic tools that can be used to solve any problem. Rather, their use involves, *in addition to the knowledge of one's own field*, added complexity—radiation detection, safety precautions, and the like. Experimental design of a radiotracer experiment is often more complex than that of conventional tracer experiments. The problems of data analysis and data interpretation are inherently more difficult. In short, radiotracer methods should be employed only when their use can be fully justified.

The scope of radiotracer applications is so extensive that it is not feasible to attempt a detailed recital. Reynolds and Leddicotte (8), however, have prepared a comprehensive review of radiotracer uses in analytical chemistry. The current applications of ^{14}C and tritium in the biological sciences alone are so numerous as to merit annual (10) and monthly (14) bibliographies, respectively.

B. PRELIMINARY CONSIDERATIONS IN DESIGN OF RADIOTRACER EXPERIMENTS

1. Basic Assumptions Underlying the Validity of Radiotracer Experiments

Experiments with radiotracers will be valid and interpretations of results meaningful only insofar as careful consideration has been given to certain basic assumptions. These relate to the behavior and the nature of the radioisotope-labeled compound involved. It must be assumed that

a. *There is no significant isotope effect.* We have, stated, as a primary assumption in all radiotracer work, that a radioactive isotope behaves chemically in a fashion identical to the stable isotopes of the same element. This actually is not true. It is true, however, that in most cases the isotopic effect does not significantly jeopardize the utility of the radioisotope method. The isotope effect is derived from the difference in mass between isotopes of the same element. Since degree of chemical bond stability is directly related to the square root of the masses of the isotopes involved, it is apparent that an isotope effect will be of significance only for elements of low atomic weight.

The isotopes of hydrogen present the extreme case. Thus, ^{1}H, ^{2}H (D), and ^{3}H (T) could scarcely be expected to act as the same substances chemically, since the relative mass differences are so great. Hence, *tritium* cannot be uncritically employed as a tracer for hydrogen in regard to reaction rates, although, of course, this does not preclude its use to determine hydrogen location in an organism.

The so-called isotopic effect in reality should be considered from the standpoint of the two basic types: the *intramolecular* and the *intermolecular* isotopic effects. In regard to the first type, the decarboxylation of malonic acid-1-^{14}C ($HOO^{14}C—^{12}CH_2—^{12}COOH$) is a good example. Here the pyrolytic decarboxylation of malonic acid gives rise to CO_2 and acetic acid. Consequently, the reaction is concerned with the relative bond strength of $^{12}C—^{14}C$ and $^{12}C—^{12}C$. Since the former bond is relatively more stable (owing to the greater mass of the ^{14}C), one would expect that the CO_2 resulting from the reaction would be comparatively enriched in ^{12}C and that the acetic acid would be comparatively enriched in ^{14}C from the —COOH. Such is the case. Inasmuch as the competitive reactions occur within the same molecule, the isotopic effect will be observed even if the reaction goes to completion.

In the case of *intermolecular* isotope effect, the decarboxylation of benzoic acid-7-^{14}C can be cited as an example. Here, unless one is using carrier-free compounds, a rare case in radiotracer studies, one is in reality dealing with the decarboxylation of two compounds: $C_6H_5—^{14}COOH$ and $C_6H_5—^{12}COOH$. Since the $^{12}C—^{14}C$ bond is relatively more stable, one would expect that during the initial phase of the decarboxylation reaction there would be an enrichment of $^{12}CO_2$ as compared to the specific activity of the labeled carbon in the benzoic acid. As the reaction approaches completion, however, the reactant (benzoic acid) will be relatively enriched with the ^{14}C-labeled variety and, consequently, the decarboxylation product (CO_2) will have a specific activity higher than the labeled carbon of the original starting material. When the reaction is driven to completion, the over-all specific activity of CO_2 will naturally be the same as the labeled carbon atom in the benzoic acid, that is, no isotope effect can be observed. This is a very important concept since it indicates that the significance of isotope effect can be minimized or ignored in radiotracer studies if the intramolecular type of reaction is not involved.

A large volume of both theoretical and experimental literature concerning isotope effects exists: Eidinoff (9, p. 222–226) has discussed isotopic effect as it relates to C—H and C—T bonds. In his review, Yakushin (16) states that the replacement of ^{1}H by ^{2}H (deuterium) in a reactive bond usually results in a decrease in reaction velocity by a factor of 3–8, whereas a corresponding replacement of ^{1}H by ^{3}H (tritium) gives a decrease by a factor of 6–20. The temperature of the reaction and the specific character of the bonds involved are important factors in determining the exact magnitude of the isotope effect for a given reaction. The magnitude of the effect for the isotopes of carbon is much less than for hydrogen. The isotope effect in the decarboxylation of malonic acid-1-^{14}C has been determined experimentally and calculated theoretically as equal to approximately 4 per cent. Rabinowitz, et al (7) found that urea-^{12}C was hydrolyzed by urease at a rate about 10 per cent faster than urea-^{14}C. An excellent survey of the problem of biological fractionation of isotopic mixtures by Protista, higher plants, Mollusca, and vertebrates has been made by Bowen (1).

b. *There is no radiobiological damage to the experimental organism.* It is essential that radiation from the tracer dose used does not elicit a response from the experimental organism which would distort the experimental results. The amount of activity employed should be restricted to the minimum necessary to permit reasonable counting rates in the samples to be assayed (see further discussion in section 2c of this chapter). The possibility of excessive concentration of the tracer compound in certain tissues and the degree of radiosensitivity of these tissues must also be carefully considered, especially when alpha- or beta-emitting tracers are used. Fortunately the excellent sensitivity of most radioactivity assay methods minimizes the necessity of employing tracer doses of such a magnitude that any detectable radiation damage occurs. The possibilities of interference due to physiological response to radiation are further minimized because most studies are short-term and thus completed before any latent radiation effects appear.

c. *There is no deviation from the normal physiological state.* If, in order to administer the required tracer activity, the chemical level of the compound given to an organism greatly exceeds the normal physiological level, the experimental results are open to question. In other words, the specific activity of the tracer compound must be sufficiently high for the total chemical level administered to be within the physiological range. As an example, ^{36}Cl might be quite useful for biological investigation, but the maximum specific activity obtainable in the inorganic form is about $100\mu c/g$ Cl. This stands in contrast to specific activities of ^{14}C (as $Ba^{14}CO_3$) of up to 2.2 curies/g of carbon.

d. *The physical state of the radioisotope-labeled compound is identical to the unlabeled variety.* Some carrier-free tracers (usually cations) in solution behave like colloids rather than true solutions. The term *radiocolloid* has been applied to such substances. A radiocolloid behaves quite differently in biological systems than would the same element when present in the true solute form. Stokinger (12) has examined the problem of phagocytosis of radiocolloids in organisms and the consequent effect on their tissue distribution. Thus, an ill-defined physical state of the radiotracer compound leads to difficulty in interpreting its physiological and metabolic behavior.

e. *The chemical form of the radioisotope-labeled compound is identical to the unlabeled variety.* Anomalous experimental results have frequently been traceable to the chemical form of the administered radiotracer. Since reactor production of radioisotopes often results in side reactions, this is not surprising. In one case involving phosphate-^{32}P uptake in plants, the unexpected experimental results were explained by the fact that a large percentage of the tracer dose was actually in the form of phosphite-^{32}P.

The *radiochemical purity* of a compound cannot be assumed. The presence of other radioactive species in low chemical concentration, but high specific activity, is frequently encountered. This is particularly true in the labeling of compounds with ^{3}H by means of the Wilzbach direct exposure method (see Chapter 11). Thus, for example, direct hydrogenation of a double bond with ^{3}H during the Wilzbach operation may give rise to a small amount of impurity (saturated form of the compound in question) having a specific activity many times higher than the ^{3}H-labeled compound derived from the recoil-labeling operation. Cohn (2) has examined the sources, detection, and means of removal of such radioactive contaminants.

The problem of radiochemical purity with respect to the chemical state of aged tritium or ^{14}C-labeled compounds is still more acute. Because of the short range of the soft beta particles associated with these two isotopes, the sizable radiation dose delivered to such compounds by their own radiation leads to self-decomposition (*radiolysis*) and, hence, a variable concentration and number of products. This problem is more fully discussed by Lemmon (4) and Tolbert (9, p. 64–68; 13).

f. *Only the labeled atoms are traced.* Never assume that the appearance of the radioactive label in a given tissue indicates the presence of the administered compound. It is the labeled atoms that are being followed, not the intact compound. Not only may metabolic reactions involve the cleavage of the labeled atom from the original compound, but exchange reactions may also occur, removing any labile atom from the labeled compound. Such chemical exchanges particularly plague many experiments with tritium-labeled compounds. The extent of chemical exchange is strongly dependent on the molecular species involved, the position of the label in the molecule, and the environmental factors (such as the pH of a biological fluid).

2. Evaluation of the feasibility of radiotracer experiments

a. *Availability of the radiotracer.* A primary consideration is whether a radioisotope of the element to be traced is available with the proper characteristics (half-life, particle energy, and so on.) For example, although radioisotopes of oxygen and nitrogen would be highly desirable in biological investigations, the longest-lived radionuclides available of these elements have half-lives of 2 and 10 min, respectively. Clearly, such short half-lives severely limit the use of these isotopes for most tracer purposes. On the other hand, for several elements, a choice of usable radioisotopes may be available, such as ^{22}Na or ^{24}Na and ^{58}Co or ^{60}Co. Of equal importance is the available specific activity of a given radioisotope. There are radioisotopes, such as ^{36}Cl, which cannot readily be made with desirable specific activity.

A second consideration is whether the tagged compound desired is commercially available or can be readily synthesized. The number of labeled compounds available is large indeed, and most radiochemical suppliers will attempt custom syntheses of unstocked compounds. In some cases, however, it is not economically feasible or even possible to introduce a given radioactive atom into the molecular structure under consideration. Furthermore, the specific activity secured may be too low for the proposed experimental use of the tagged compound. This general problem will be considered in further detail in Chapter 11.

b. *Limits of detection.* The degree to which the administered tracer dose will be diluted by the biological system must be more carefully evaluated. Dilution must not be so great that the activity of the counting samples will be below the limits of detection. In situations where sample specific activity is unavoidably low, it will be necessary to consider the use of the most sensitive detecting system (see Table 6-1). Furthermore, the anticipated sample specific activity and means of detection will often dictate the choice of counting sample preparation. This choice will also be influenced by the number of counting samples to be prepared and the required precision of the experiment.

c. *Evaluation of hazard.* The first consideration is the possibility of harm to the experimenter himself or to his co-workers. In the great majority of radiotracer experiments, the hazard from direct external radiation does not pose a serious problem. The one exception is where high levels (millicuries) of gamma emitters are employed. For example, 10 mc of sodium-24 will deliver a dose of about 19 milliroentgens per hour (at 1 meter distance). The major item of concern in the use of alpha- or beta-emitting tracers is the possibility of ingestion of the labeled compounds, particularly those known to have a long turnover time in the human body. This problem is made acute where the sample is in the form of an aerosol or a dry powder at some stage of the experiment. (A more complete discussion of radiotracer hazards will be found in Chapter 12.)

Radiation damage to the biological system under study may occur at two levels: the physiological and the histological. In general, higher radiation doses are required to elicit the latter type of damage. Whenever it is suspected that radiation damage is influencing the physiological response of the organism, it is advisable to repeat the experiment with lower levels of radioactivity, while maintaining the same total chemical level of the administered compound. Biological effects of radiation from radiotracer doses have been reported to occur at the following dose levels: 0.045μc ^{131}I/g of body weight in mice, 0.8μc ^{32}P/g of body weight in mice, 47μc ^{24}Na/g body weight in mice and rats, 0.5 μc ^{89}Sr/g body weight in mice and rats, 0.05μc ^{32}P/ml of rearing solution for mosquito larvae, 2μc ^{32}P/liter of nutrient solution for barley plants.

Attention must also be given to the disposal of *radioactive wastes* resulting from the experiment, such as excreta, carcasses, or large volumes of solutions. The method of disposal possible will depend on the specific radioisotope present, its concentration and activity, and the nature of the waste. Disposal must conform to the Code of Federal Regulations, Title 10, Part 20. (Methods and principles of waste disposal are further discussed in Chapter 12.)

d. *Evaluation of proposed methodology and data analysis.* Experimental data are useless until they can be properly interpreted. This is particularly true in radiotracer experiments involving biological systems. Attention must first be given to a clear statement of the hypothesis to be tested. Next, the sampling process to be followed must be carefully evaluated. Only then can proper methods of data analysis be selected. For further discussion of this aspect of experimental design see Wilson's excellent general treatment (15).

The *precision* required in the proposed experiment must be clearly established. In radiotracer investigations, this is heavily influenced by the method of sample preparation and the assay technique employed. The inherent variability in organisms adds further complications where highly precise results are desired. If one is looking for only a small experimental difference, a high degree of precision is critical for the success of the investigation. Such a degree of precision is not always compatible with the nature of radiotracer methodology. (Chapter 9 considers the analysis of data in radioactivity measurements in greater detail.)

C. BASIC FEATURES OF EXPERIMENTAL DESIGN

1. The Nature of the Experiment

The use of radiotracers will not allow an investigator to approach an experimental problem with a lesser degree of preparation and forethought than is necessary in nontracer experiments. Rather, the tracer method requires that the investigator be even more familiar with the specific organism to be used and the general nature of the problem. In pursuing scientific studies, there is no substitute for a thorough knowledge of one's own field. Radiotracers must always be regarded as only a tool, not a panacea.

When radioisotopes are used in a dynamic biological system, one of the commonest difficulties is failure to recognize the *kinetic aspects* of the system. It is of prime importance to consider the possible pathways that a labeled compound may take in the experimental organism, based on what is already known about the kinetics of the system. One must ponder the effect of such factors as the existence of alternate pathways, the extent of dilution from endogenous sources, the possibility of the reentry of degraded products into the system, the degree of chemical exchange of the labeled atoms, and the general consideration of whether one is dealing with an open or closed system. Even if the kinetics of the system under consideration are not well known, the investigator must still be aware of their possible influence on his experimental results.

A recent outstanding volume by Sheppard (11) has discussed extensively what may be expected to occur in a kinetic system following the introduction of labeled material into a portion of it. The author mathematically analyzes multicompartmental systems, such as are presented in living organisms. There is a sizable literature on the experimental design necessary in radiotracer turnover measurement studies; one might cite the articles by Zilversmit and Shore (17), Lax and Wrenshall (3), Kamen (9, p. 210–216), and Jeffay (9, p. 217–221). Nevertheless, current understanding of the kinetics of biochemical processes is, by and large, limited to the simplest systems.

2. The Scale of Operation

A basic requirement in designing a radiotracer experiment is the calculation of the necessary quantity of labeled compound. In other words, will kilogram or milligram quantities be required? The factors affecting this calculation are discussed first; then specific examples will be cited. Putnam (6) has summarized some of these factors in a concise mathematical expression.

a. The labeled compound. If the labeled compound must be synthesized, the starting amount required to permit satisfactory physical or chemical manipulation and to give the desired yield must be determined. On the other hand, if the tagged compound is to be bought, one must consider cost. It is frequently necessary to redesign an entire experiment on the basis of the cost factor alone. For example, if one were using hydrocortisone-4-^{14}C (current commercial price \$36/mg), it would be unrealistic to design a single tracer experiment requiring gram amounts.

b. The biological system. The extent to which the labeled compound will be diluted in the experimental organism is a major consideration in determining the quantity to be administered. This *dilution* is primarily a function of the relative size of the biological system chosen. Clearly, a smaller quantity of tracer compound will be needed for a given purpose in a rat than in a dog, or in a seedling plant than in a mature tree. The use of microorganisms in radiotracer investigations offers the distinct advantage of requiring very small quantities of active material. This is most useful where the tracer compound used is available in quite limited amounts. When no reliable basis exists for calculating the extent of anticipated dilution, liberal estimates should be made to account for unexpectedly large dilution. In addition, the number of biological specimens necessary to achieve a given statistical validity must be determined in advance.

c. Purpose of the experiment. The purpose of the experiment will also be a determining factor in the calculation of the scale of operation. In some cases, as in assaying respired $^{14}CO_2$, the purpose will be merely to identify a labeled compound. In other investigations, the location of a labeled compound is sought, as in the use of tritiated thymidine to trace DNA localization in chromosomes. On the other hand, it may be desired to determine the labeling distribution pattern in a compound isolated from an organism metabolizing a specifically labeled substrate, as in a study of precursor-product relationships. Such investigations require not only isolation of the labeled compound, but further chemical processing in degradation studies. An example would be the identification of the labeling pattern in amino acids synthesized by microorganisms metabolizing ^{14}C-specifically labeled glucose. Where the labeled product is to be degraded to determine the pattern of labeling, the scale of operation must take into consideration the necessity of diluting the end product to a desired amount with carrier for degradation studies. Such an operation often involves the dilution of micrograms or milligrams of a compound to as much as the gram level; hence, the specific activity of the diluted sample goes below the limit of detection.

3. Detection Efficiency

A primary consideration as to the size of the initial tracer dose required is the detection efficiency of the counting system to be employed. This, along with the degree of counting precision desired, sets a minimum level on the required specific activity and total activity in counting samples. Furthermore, the detection efficiency of the various counting systems is dependent on the radioisotope being assayed. Thus, a much higher activity of the gamma emitter ^{131}I would be required if the detector were to be a G-M tube, than if a NaI (Tl) scintillation detector were used. (For discussion of the relative efficiencies of the various detection systems see Chapters 4–6. Other factors affecting counting efficiency, such as self-absorption, coincidence loss, and the like, were dealt with in Chapter 9.)

4. Specific Activity

Once the scale of operations for a given experiment is determined, one would know the exact amount, that is, the chemical amount in such units as milligrams, millimoles, and so on, of the labeled compound as needed for the experiment in question. The next question is, naturally, what is the desired specific activity of the labeled compound, and hence, the *total radioactivity* in the defined amount of the compound as determined by the scale of operation. The latter question can be answered only by evaluating the entire experimental procedure, particularly that portion relating to the radiation detection system and procedures for the preparation of the counting samples.

It is most convenient to determine the desired specific activity of the initial labeled compound by first calculating the desired specific activity of a *counting sample* one expects to secure in the experiment. Once the latter is determined, one can then consider the anticipated dilution factors involved in all steps of the experimental procedures, the anticipated loss of radioactivity due to biological operations, such as respiration and excretion, and any other pertinent factors to estimate the magnitude of the desired specific activity in the initial labeled compound. The most troublesome problem, in fact, is the dilution of labeled compounds by unlabeled compounds during a series of biological processes. In many cases, one can only make an educated guess in this regard. Hence a safety factor in the magnitude of two to ten fold is often incorporated into the experimental design to accommodate unexpected dilution factors.

5. Example of Experimental Design

As an *illustrative example*, one can consider the case of an experiment involving the study of the utilization of L-alanine-1-^{14}C by a microorganism such as *Azotobacter vinelandii.* The purpose of the experiment is to determine how much of the substrate activity is converted into respiratory CO_2. The experimental design follows:

a. *Scale of operation.* It has been previously concluded that the nonsterile incubation period for such radioisotope experiments should not exceed 5 hr to avoid contamination of the microbial culture. Results obtained in previous studies indicate that 10 mg (dry weight) of the microbial cells suspended in 10 ml of an aqueous incubation medium can utilize 10 mg of L-alanine in 4 hr. The amount of respiratory CO_2 given off by the microorganisms will be very small. This fact necessitates the addition of carrier carbonate ion to the CO_2-absorbing trap before sufficient amounts of barium carbonate can be isolated from the trap solution for radioactivity assay. Nevertheless, it is clear that in this particular experiment one would need 10 mg (or 0.11 millimole) of L-alanine-1-^{14}C, which in fact reflects directly the scale of operation.

b. *Specific activity requirement.* In this particular experiment a G-M detector assembly is to be used. The over-all detection efficiency of the counting assembly has been previously determined as 10 per cent. Counting will be carried out on duplicate samples of respiratory CO_2 in the nature of 100 mg of barium carbonate mounted on aluminum planchets. Inasmuch as 0.11 m mole of L-alanine is used as substrate, the maximum amount of respiratory CO_2 that can be collected in an absorption trap will be 0.33 m mole if the substrate L-alanine is completely converted to CO_2. In reality, the results of preliminary experiments reveal that the total amount of CO_2 produced in the entire experiment is only approximately 0.15 m mole. This fact implies that one has to add approximately 0.85 m mole of sodium carbonate to the CO_2-absorbing solution so that, upon addition of the $BaCl_2$-NH_4Cl precipitation solution, one can realize a yield of 200 mg of barium carbonate, which is just enough for the preparation of two counting samples.

The optimal radioactivity level of the counting sample is set as 1000 cpm (apparent counting rate). Such a counting rate will be fast enough for one to collect sufficient counts within a short length of time for good statistical precision, yet sufficiently slow to permit one to ignore the correction for coincidence loss. Since the transmission of ^{14}C beta particles in a 100-mg plate is approximately 25 per cent, it follows that the desired radioactivity in each plate is 1000 cpm/0.25 = 4000 cpm (counting rate corrected for self-absorption). The total radioactivity in 200 mg of barium carbonate (for both counting samples) is therefore 8000 cpm or 80,000 dpm (since the detection efficiency is 10 per cent in the present case).

In order to meet this requirement, one is faced with the question of how much of the substrate activity will be converted to respiratory CO_2.

This determination, however, is actually the purpose of the experiment, which clearly implies that the exact extent of conversion is unknown. It is entirely possible to make an educated guess at this point for the sake of the design of the experiment. Such a guess requires two separate considerations: First, the extent of oxidation of C-1 of L-alanine to CO_2 must be examined. From biochemical considerations this is likely to be extensive; consequently, an assumption that a minimum of 50 per cent conversion occurs is not too unrealistic.

Second, it is possible that the substrate L-alanine can be diluted by the unlabeled cellular compounds. The maximum dilution factor can be estimated if one considers that substrate L-alanine is in equilibrium with all carbonaceous compounds in the microorganism. The amount of the unlabeled compound can be crudely estimated as equivalent to 0.4 m mole of carbon. This value is derived from the consideration that the mean carbon content of biological samples is approximately 40 to 50 per cent. Since 10 mg (dry weight) of the microbial cells is involved in the experiment, the carbon content is therefore approximately 5 mg or 0.4 m mole. This sum in comparison to the carbon in the substrate L-alanine, that is, 0.11×3 (since L-alanine has three carbon atoms) $= 0.33$ m mole, constitutes a maximum dilution of approximately two-fold. On the other hand, the minimum dilution factor is naturally nil; that is, there exists no equilibrium between the substrate L-alanine and cellular compounds. On the basis of the foregoing, 25 per cent of the substrate activity will not appear in CO_2 samples as a result of equilibrium with the cellular compounds.

By taking into consideration the extent of conversion and the extent of dilution, one would then reach the estimation that (in order to realize 80,000 dpm in the CO_2 sample) the substrate L-alanine should contain approximately:

> $80{,}000 \times 2$ (factor to cover extent of conversion) $\times$ 1.25 (factor covering the possible equilibration of substrate with several compounds) $=$ 200,000 dpm, or

$$\frac{2 \times 10^5 \text{ dpm}}{2.2 \times 10^6 \text{ dpm}/\mu\text{c}} = 0.9\ \mu\text{c of L-alanine-1-}^{14}\text{C}$$

The foregoing example illustrates the primary pattern involved in the design of a radiotracer experiment. In this particular case the design is aimed at the radioactivity assay of the respiratory CO_2 sample. Obviously, if one desires to examine the incorporation of L-alanine into cellular constituents employing paper chromatography techniques, considerably more radioactivity must be contained in the substrate because the amount of cellular compound that can be separated on the paper chromatogram is necessarily small (10–50 μg for each compound), and the specific activity of each of the compounds must be sufficiently high (from 100 dpm/μg up) before a radioactivity assay can be conveniently made. It should also be emphasized that it may be further advisable to introduce a safety factor in an experimental design of this type so that unexpected dilution can be accommodated.

For actual examples of activity calculations in a variety of experimental situations, see the selected radiotracer experiments in Part Three. In the sections called "Experimental Design" the determination of the required activity and chemical level of the respective tracer doses has been carefully analyzed. Step-by-step calculations are indicated. Although the examples given by no means cover all cases, they do illustrate the general pattern of activity calculations.

The problem of *background* radiation must also be considered. Its effect on counting accuracy has been discussed in Chapter 9. Background radiation can be particularly troublesome in autoradiography, where it results in a fogging of the film. This necessitates having a significant amount of activity in the sample to be autoradiographed in order to give a good image in a reasonably short exposure time (see Chapter 7).

6. Anticipated Experimental Findings

Certain features of experimental design relate to the anticipated experimental results. If a time course is to be followed, one must decide in advance the number of samples to be collected and the collecting intervals to give the best kinetic information. With reference to procedures involving paper chromatography, one must know the optimal amount of sample that can be applied on the particular chromatograph paper to be used. It is of special importance to design the experiment so that the information derived can be interpreted meaningfully. To this end, it must be decided whether counting results will be expressed as percentage yield or specific activity (see Section E of this chapter).

Of equal importance is the *desired sensitivity* with respect to the projected findings. One can cite the following example to illustrate this point. Let us assume that one desires to study the conversion of glucose-2-^{14}C to lactic acid by a tissue culture. If the purpose of the experiment is to demonstrate the precise magnitude of such a conversion, even to the extent of only $\pm$ 1 per cent of the substrate glucose, then the experimental design must take this into consideration. This will probably call for the use of considerable amounts of radioactivity in the glucose. On the other hand, if one desires merely to determine that a conversion is extensive, the precision of the extent of conversion would not be critical. In other words, it is really immaterial whether the conversion is 81 per cent or 80 per cent. This fact makes it possible to design an experiment with much less radioactivity in the substrate glucose, since the sensitivity of the method need not be such as to differentiate one or a few percentage points of the substrate glucose conversion.

D. EXECUTION OF RADIOTRACER EXPERIMENTS

A major portion of this book has been concerned with aspects of executing radiotracer experiments (sample preparation, assay, and so on). A few specific points should be mentioned here. An initial step is determining the *radiochemical purity* of the labeled compound. Some degree of radiolysis in compounds labeled with ^{3}H, ^{14}C, or ^{35}S must be assumed if they have been stored for any length of time. Establishment of the purity, followed by the necessary purification operations if impurities are detected, is an essential step prior to carrying out the experiment.

Never assume that the employment of radiotracer methodology allows a decreased concern for accuracy in the routine procedures of *weighing and measuring*. On the contrary, errors in these activities will profoundly affect the significance of the most precise counting data. It is essential to build up the habit of proper laboratory techniques to reduce errors of this type to the minimum. It should be realized that the over-all accuracy of the experiment is determined by the precision associated with each step of the experimental operation, which includes physical manipulation, chemical measurement, and radioactivity measurement.

Good laboratory "housekeeping" is naturally important with regard to *safety* in the handling of radioisotopes. Careless technique rapidly results in a technically contaminated laboratory, if not one where an actual health hazard may exist. Note that technical contamination may render a laboratory unfit for sensitive radiotracer studies long before any health hazard develops.

E. DATA ANALYSIS

1. Expression of Results

One may express the results of radioactivity determinations in several ways. The most suitable form of expression is frequently determined by the nature of the specific experiment and the assay system employed. It is not practicable to use any standard form for all types of experiments. It is of utmost importance, however, that the results be presented unambiguously with sufficient information to permit comparisons. In expressing radioactivity data, since a "count" is a purely arbitrary unit, it is vital to state clearly the conditions under which the measurements were made and what, if any, corrections were applied to the observed count rates (that is, self-absorption corrections, net or gross counts, and so on). To this end, one expresses results in units of microcuries, millicuries, or similar expressions to facilitate cross-comparison of results. The results of radiotracer experiments are also commonly expressed as percentage yield, specific activity, and the like.

a. *Percentage yield.* The total radioactivity of the sample assayed can be expressed as a percentage of the labeled compound administered. This has the advantage of presenting a straightforward comparison and is especially useful in radiorespirometric studies.

b. *Specific activity.* The specific activity of a radioisotope sample is the amount of radioactivity per unit amount of material. Specific activity may be expressed in a wide variety of ways. The activity may be stated as count rate, disintegration rate, or in microcuries; the unit amount of material may be indicated as per gram, or per millimole of compound or element involved, or any other similar expression. The most convenient form for expressing specific activity of pure compounds is as microcuries per millimole (μc/mmole). To facilitate ready comparison of results, it is obvious that uniform expressions throughout a piece of work are of primary importance.

2. Interpretation of Results

The interpretation of the results of radiotracer experiments is subject to greater possibility of pitfalls than the actual conduct of the experimental procedures. Of course, this situation is not peculiar to tracer experiments, but the opportunities for misinterpretation are probably much greater in this type of investigation than in the traditional approaches. First and foremost, the investigator must take an *open-minded, unprejudiced approach* to the interpretation. An expert knowledge of the biological system under investigation is the best safeguard against unwarranted interpretations of tracer experiment results.

An important *historical case* involving a misinterpretation of valid radiotracer data concerns early studies of the tri-carboxylic acid (TCA) cycle mechanisms. It is generally recognized that the TCA cycle is one of the most important pathways for the biochemical oxidation of carbonaceous compounds to respiratory CO_2. Coupled with supplementary processes, such as CO_2 fixation or malate synthetase, the TCA cycle also functions as an important mechanism for the biosynthesis of the amino acids.

The reaction scheme for the TCA cycle is given in Figure 10-1. It is noted that citric acid is one of the essential intermediates in the cyclic mechanism. In the late 1930's, however, in experiments using labeled carbon dioxide along with unlabeled pyruvate administered to liver slices, it was found that the ^{14}C label was incorporated into the α-ketoglutarate, an intermediate in the TCA cycle. The incorporation is recognized as involving a CO_2 fixation process to give rise to oxaloacetate-4-^{14}C, that is,

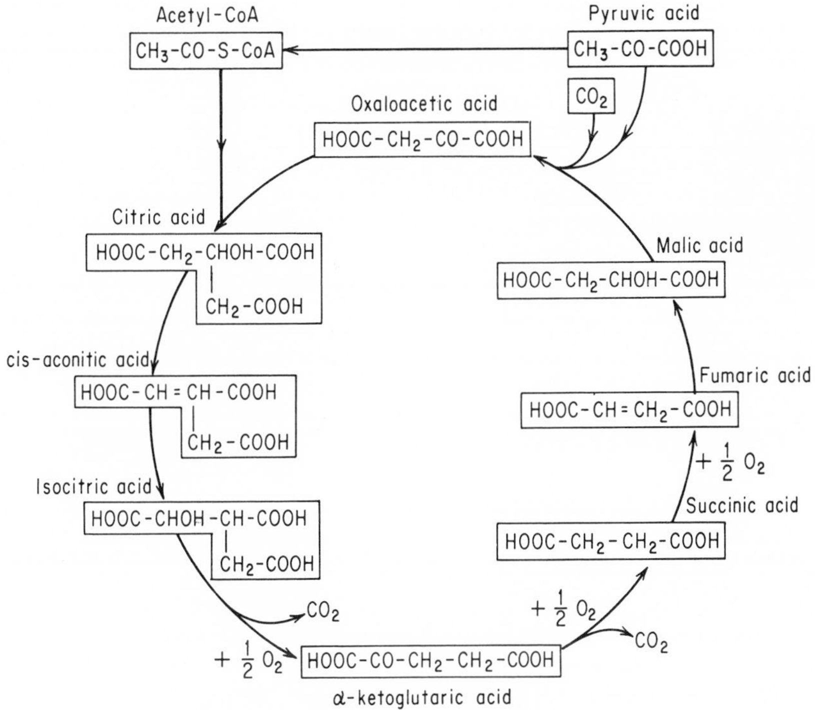

Figure 10-1. The tricarboxylic acid (TCA) cycle.

HOOC*—CH_2—CO—COOH. Conversion of the latter compound to α-ketoglutarate via a portion of the TCA cycle (Figure 10-1) will then give rise to labeling of α-ketoglutarate. On degradation of the latter compound, however, it was found that the labeling was confined to the α-carboxyl group (C-1 of α-ketoglutarate). Since citric acid appears to be a symmetrical compound, one would expect that the α-ketoglutarate derived from the citric acid would be labeled at both the C-1 and C-5 positions as shown here:

$$\underset{\text{(oxaloacetic acid-4-}^{14}\text{C)}}{\mathrm{HOOC^*{-}CH_2{-}CO{-}COOH}} + \underset{\text{(acetyl-CoA)}}{\mathrm{CH_3{-}CO{-}CoA}} \longrightarrow$$

$$\underset{\text{(citric acid-1-}^{14}\text{C)}}{\begin{array}{c} \mathrm{CH_2{-}COOH} \\ | \\ \mathrm{HO{-}C{-}COOH} \\ | \\ \mathrm{CH_2{-}C^*OOH} \end{array}} \longrightarrow \longrightarrow \longrightarrow \underset{\text{(}\alpha\text{-ketoglutaric acid-1,5-}^{14}\text{C)}}{\underset{(5)\quad\quad(4)\quad\quad(3)\quad\quad(2)\quad\quad(1)}{\mathrm{HOOC^*{-}CH_2{-}CH_2{-}CO{-}C^*OOH}}}$$

The observed discrepancy consequently led biochemists to believe that citric acid should not be considered a direct intermediate of the TCA cycle. Soon afterward, however, Ogston postulated that if the substrate is attached to the enzyme surface at three points which are catalytically different, it might pass through the stage of a symmetrical intermediate (citric acid) and then be converted to the unsymmetrical compound without randomization of the label. This attractive postulation was later confirmed experimentally by Potter and Heidelberger. This development accounted for biochemical texts of the late 1930's having citric acid in, out, and in again in the TCA cycle scheme. This occurred even though the radiotracer data were unchanged throughout the period. Besides its historical interest, the case offers a good illustrative example of the importance of proper interpretation of radiotracer findings.

Another common error of interpretation is failure to recognize that, in a radiotracer experiment, one is *following the label*, not the administered compound. If, for example, one detects ^{14}C in a biochemical compound isolated from a biological system metabolizing acetate-1-^{14}C, it simply means that there is incorporation of labeling in the biochemical compound. The incorporation mechanism could be direct in nature, but it could equally well be complex, involving many intermediate steps. Obviously one should not claim that the conversion of acetate to this compound has been realized, since such a statement implies the presence of a direct mechanism.

Equally confusing is the phenomenon of *randomization* encountered in metabolic studies with radiotracers. This problem is well illustrated in the following case of the biochemical production of fumaric acid:

$$\mathrm{C^*O_2} + \underset{\text{(pyruvic acid)}}{\mathrm{CH_3{-}CO{-}COOH}} \rightleftharpoons \underset{\text{(oxaloacetic acid-4-}^{14}\text{C)}}{\mathrm{HOOC^*{-}CH_2{-}CO{-}COOH}} \rightleftharpoons$$

$$\underset{\text{(l-malic acid-4-}^{14}\text{C)}}{\mathrm{HOOC^*{-}CH_2{-}CHOH{-}COOH}} \rightleftharpoons \underset{\text{(fumaric acid-4 or 1-}^{14}\text{C)}}{\begin{array}{c} \mathrm{HOOC^*{-}CH{=}CH{-}COOH} \\ \text{and} \\ \mathrm{HOOC{-}CH{=}CH{-}C^*OOH} \end{array}}$$

It will be seen that the fumaric acid is a symmetrical molecule. Consequently, in most textbooks the incorporation of the ^{14}C activity from CO_2 into fumaric acid is indicated as HOOC*—CH=CH—C*OOH. This designation implies that the labeling has been randomized to the two corresponding groups, so that each has one-half of the total radioactivity. It must, however, be recognized that, although the compound appears to be doubly labeled by such a designation, it is actually composed of a mixture of two singly labeled compounds.

Finally, one must be alert to possible *artifacts* derived from operations in radiotracer experiments. These may result from such causes as chemical or radiochemical contaminants in the original labeled compounds. In liquid scintillation counting, unreasonably high count rates may result from such phenomena as chemiluminescence (see p. 164) and, hence, be entirely unrelated to counting sample activity. Autoradiography is particularly prone to artifacts (see p. 147–148). Levi (5) has recently reported a unique artifact in the autoradiography of leaves of bean plants containing ^{32}P. He showed that the apparent accumulation of isotope in primary leaves oven-dried before exposure to X-ray films was not metabolic, but due to a drying gradient occurring within the leaves. This artifact disappeared when autoradiographs were made from leaves freeze-dried under vacuum. This illustrates the unexpected sources of artifacts.

In this chapter it has been possible only to highlight the basic features and problems of radiotracer experimental design. The task of applying these generalities to particular biological experiments must lie with the reader.

BIBLIOGRAPHY

1. Bowen, H. J. M. 1960. Biological fractionation of isotopes. Intern. J. Appl. Radiation Isotopes 7:261–272.
2. Cohn, Waldo E. 1948. Radioactive contaminants in tracers. Anal. Chem. 20:498–503.
3. Lax, Louis C., and Gerald A. Wrenshall. 1953. Measurement of turnover rates in systems of hydrodynamic pools out of dynamic equilibrium. Nucleonics 11(4):18–20.
4. Lemmon, Richard M. 1953. Radiation decomposition of carbon-14-labeled compounds. Nucleonics 11(10):44–45.
5. Levi, A. 1962. An artifact in plant autoradiography. Science 137: 343–344.
6. Putnam, J. L. 1962. An expression for source counting rate required in tracer experiments. Intern. J. Appl. Radiation Isotopes 13:99–100.
7. Rabinowitz, Joseph L., et al. 1956. Carbon isotope effects in enzyme systems. I. Biochemical studies with urease. Arch. Biochem. and Biophys. 63-437–445.
8. Reynolds, S. A., and G. W. Leddicotte. 1963. Radioactive tracers in analytical chemistry. Nucleonics 21(8):128–142.

9. Rothchild, Seymour (ed.). 1963. Advances in tracer methodology, vol. 1. Plenum Press, New York, 332 p.

10. Scharffenberg, R. S., and John K. Pollard. Carbon-14. 1963. A comprehensive annual bibliography of applications in chemistry, biology and medicine. vol. 1. January–December, 1962. Calbiochem, Los Angeles.

11. Sheppard, C. W. 1962. Basic principles of the tracer method. John Wiley & Sons, Inc., New York. 282 p.

12. Stokinger, Herbert E. 1953. Size of dose; its effect on distribution in the body. Nucleonics 11(4):24–27.

13. Tolbert, B. M. 1960. Self-destruction in radioactive compounds. Nucleonics 18(8):74–75.

14. Tritium. 1(1) et seq., 1963. (a monthly bibliographic newsletter by Calbiochem, Los Angeles).

15. Wilson, E. Bright, Jr. 1952. An introduction to scientific research. McGraw-Hill Book Company, New York. 375 p.

16. Yakushin, F. S. 1962. Application of the kinetic isotope effect of tritium to the investigation of the mechanism of hydrogen substitution and transfer reactions. Russ. Chem. Rev. (a translation) 31:123–131.

17. Zilversmit, D. B., and Moris L. Shore. 1952. A hydrodynamic model of isotope distribution in living organisms. Nucleonics 10(10):32–34.

CHAPTER ELEVEN

Availability of Radioisotope-Labeled Compounds

The investigator desiring to employ radiotracer methods in his own research is first faced with the practical problem of securing suitable radioisotope-labeled compounds. Most frequently this problem is resolved by buying labeled compounds from a commercial radiochemical supplier. In some cases, the desired tracer compound may not be commercially available and synthesis must be attempted. In either case, it is important to have some conception of the problems of primary radioisotope production and conversion of the primary product to an experimentally useful radiotracer compound. This chapter presents a brief survey of these steps, although these considerations are primarily in the province of the radiochemist. For an excellent, more detailed discussion, see the recent book by the staff of The Radiochemical Centre at Amersham, England (18).

A. PRIMARY PRODUCTION OF RADIOISOTOPES

1. Nuclear Reactor Production

The artificial production of radioisotopes has already been considered in some detail in Chapter 1 (p. 10–16). It will be recalled that the *nuclear reactor* is the most generally useful production source of artificial radioisotopes. The commonest production method utilizes the neutron irradiation in a reactor to bring about nuclear alteration in specific target atoms, for example (n, γ), (n, p), or (n, α) reactions. The problem of the (n, γ) process with regard to the specific activity of the product has already been discussed (p. 14). The advantage afforded by the *Szilard-Chalmers reaction* in allowing the attainment of high specific activities in the product of certain (n, γ) processes should again be mentioned. (This reaction is further described in Experiment V, where it is used in the production of radioactive ^{128}I from stable ^{127}I.)

Most of the fragments of uranium atoms which have undergone fission in the reactor are radioactive atoms ranging from atomic numbers 30 through 66. These *fission products* can be concentrated chemically to high specific activities, but since several isotopes of any one element are often produced, the isotopic purity will not necessarily be as high as that of radioisotopes produced by (n, p) and (n, α) processes.

In the United States the principal source of primary radioisotope material is from the reactors at the Oak Ridge National Laboratory of the U.S. Atomic Energy Commission. In England, the Radiochemical Centre at Amersham serves a similar function and in addition supplies a wide variety of labeled compounds. Commercial firms carry on some small-scale reactor production of specific isotopes.

The radioactive products of neutron irradiation or fission, as they come from the reactor, must be chemically processed. The processed isotopic materials are most generally sold as simple inorganic compounds or in elementary form. Table 11-1 lists all the radioisotopes currently available from the Oak Ridge National Laboratory, in order of increasing half-life. (Those with half-lives of less than 1 hr are omitted.) Data on the maximum specific activities available, type of radiation emitted, and production method are also noted. The wide variation in specific activities available from isotope to isotope has implications as to their suitability for radiotracer purposes. Further information on these primary radioisotopes can be found in the Oak Ridge National Laboratory (ORNL) Catalog of Radioisotopes (16). It should be mentioned that ORNL, as well as many commercial firms operating reactors, will perform service irradiation of materials on a custom basis.

2. Cyclotron Production

The cyclotron is a generally more versatile device for producing radioisotopes than the nuclear reactor because of the wider variety and energy of the accelerated nuclear particles it can employ. It has been previously pointed out that *deuterons* are the most useful charged particles for bringing about transmutation (p. 11), but, in addition, electrons, alpha particles, protons, or heavy ions may be used in the cyclotron. Operating costs for cyclotrons are so much greater than those for nuclear reactors, however, that the former are employed for radioisotope production only when they offer a significant advantage over reactors.

A major advantage of the cyclotron is that certain useful radioisotopes may be produced in it which are not produced in significant quantities in nuclear reactors. Some examples of isotopes in this category are ^{7}Be,

TABLE 11-1

Radioisotopes available from the Oak Ridge National Laboratory listed according to half-life

Half-life*	Radioisotopes	Maximum Specific Activity‡	Radiation†	Production Method§
12.47 *h*	Potassium-42	> 200 mc/g K	β,γ	(n,γ)
12.5 *h*	Iodine-130	≅ 40 c/g I	β,γ	(n,γ)
12.82 *h*	Copper-64	≅ 25 c/g Cu	EC, β^-, β^+, γ	(n,γ)
13.6 *h*	Palladium-109	≅ 2 c/g Pd	β,γ	(n,γ)
14.2 *h*	Gallium-72	≅ 2 c/g Ga	β,γ	(n,γ)
15.05 *h*	Sodium-24	≅ 10 c/g Na	β,γ	(n,γ)
19.0 *h*	Iridium-194	> 30 c/g Ir	β,γ	(n,γ)
19.2 *h*	Praseodymium-142	> 5 c/g Pr	β,γ	(n,γ)
24.0 *h*	Mercury-197m_2	≅ 500 mc/g Hg	EC, IT, γ	(n,γ)
24.0 *h*	Tungsten-187	≅ 10 c/g W	β,γ	(n,γ)
26.8 *h*	Arsenic-76	≅ 4 c/g As	β,γ	(n,γ)
35.55 *h*	Bromine-82	≅ 1 c/g Br	β,γ	(n,γ)
38.7 *h*	Arsenic-77	CF	β,γ	$(n,\gamma),\beta\rightarrow$
40.3 *h*	Lanthanum-140	≅ 5 c/g La	β,γ	(n,γ)
46.8 *h*	Samarium-153	≅ 20 c/g Sm	β,γ	(n,γ)
53.5 *h*	Cadmium-115	≅ 50 mc/g Cd	β,γ	(n,γ)
64.4 *h*	Yttrium-90	CF	β	Fission, $\beta\rightarrow$
64.8 *h*	Gold-198	≅ 25 c/g Au	β,γ	(n,γ)
65 *h*	Mercury-197	≅ 500 mc/g Hg	EC,γ	(n,γ)
66 *h*	Antimony-122	≅ 2 c/g Sb	β,γ	(n,γ)
67 *h*	Molybdenum-99	> 10 mc/g Mo	β,γ	(n,γ)
75.4 *h*	Gold-199	CF	β,γ	(n,γ), $\beta\rightarrow$
88.9 *h*	Rhenium-186	≅ 10 c/g Re	EC, β, γ	(n,γ)
4.53 *d*	Calcium-47	> 150 mc/g Ca	β,γ	(n,γ)
5.00 *d*	Bismuth-210	≅ 50 mc/g Bi	β	(n,γ)
5.27 *d*	Xenon-133	CF	β,γ	Fission
7.5 *d*	Silver-111	CF	β,γ	(n,γ), $\beta\rightarrow$
11.06 *d*	Neodymium-147	CF	β,γ	Fission
12.0 *d*	Barium-131	≅ 10 mc/g Ba	EC,γ	(n,γ)
12.8 *d*	Barium-140	CF	β,γ	Fission
13.7 *d*	Praseodymium-143	CF	β	Fission
14.3 *d*	Phosphorus-32	CF	β	(n,p)
16 *d*	Osmium-191	> 400 mc/g Os	β,γ	(n,γ)
18.68 *d*	Rubidium-86	≅ 1 c/g Rb	β,γ	(n,γ)
34.3 *d*	Argon-37	CF	EC	(n,α)
35 *d*	Niobium-95	CF	β,γ	Fission, $\beta\rightarrow$
39.7 *d*	Ruthenium-103	CF	β,γ	Fission
43 *d*	Cadmium-115m	≅ 100 mc/g Cd	β,γ	(n,γ)
44.3 *d*	Iron-59	≅ 10 c/g Fe	β,γ	(n,γ)
44.6 *d*	Hafnium-181	≅ 2 c/g Hf	β,γ	(n,γ)
45.4 *d*	Mercury-203	≅ 500 mc/g Hg	β,γ	(n,γ)
50 *d*	Indium-114m	≅ 1 c/g In	IT,γ	(n,γ)
50.5 *d*	Strontium-89	CF	β	Fission

(Continued)

TABLE 11-1 (continued)

Half-life*	Radioisotopes	Maximum Specific Activity‡	Radiation†	Production Method§
59.1 *d*	Yttrium-91	CF	β,γ	Fission
60.9 *d*	Antimony-124	≅ 2 c/g Sb	β,γ	(n,γ)
65 *d*	Zirconium-95	CF	β,γ	Fission
75.8 *d*	Tungsten-185	≅ 500 mc/g W	EC,β,γ	(n,γ)
84.2 *d*	Scandium-46	> 5 c/g Sc	β,γ	(n,γ)
89 *d*	Sulfur-35	CF	β	$(n,$p$)$
115.1 *d*	Tantalum-182	> 500 mc/g Ta	β,γ	(n,γ)
119 *d*	Tin-113	≅ 50 mc/g Sn	EC,γ	(n,γ)
119.9 *d*	Selenium-75	≅ 20 c/g Se	EC,γ	(n,γ)
129 *d*	Thulium-170	> 10 c/g Tm	β,γ	(n,γ)
165.1 *d*	Calcium-45	≅ 10 c/g Ca	β	(n,γ)
246.4 *d*	Zinc-65	≅ 500 mc/g Zn	EC, β^+, γ	(n,γ)
249 *d*	Silver-110m	≅ 1 c/g Ag	IT, β, γ	(n,γ)
285 *d*	Cerium-144	CF	β,γ	Fission
371 *d*	Ruthenium-106	CF	β	Fission
1.3 *y*	Cadmium-109	≅ 1 c/g Cd	EC,γ	(n,γ)
2.5 *y*	Promethium-147	CF	β,γ	Fission
2.78 *y*	Antimony-125	CF	β	(n,γ), $\beta\rightarrow$
3.57 *y*	Thallium-204	≅ 1 c/g Tl	EC, β	(n,γ)
5.24 *y*	Cobalt-60	≅ 25 c/g Co	β,γ	(n,γ)
10.27 *y*	Krypton-85	≅ 21 c/g Kr	β,γ	Fission
10.7 *y*	Barium-133	≅ 1 c/g Ba	EC,γ	(n,γ)
12.46 *y*	Hydrogen-3 (Tritium)	CF	β	(n,α)
12.7 *y*	Europium-152	> 250 mc/g Eu	EC, β, γ	(n,γ)
16 *y*	Europium-154	> 250 mc/g Eu	β,γ	(n,γ)
28 *y*	Strontium-90	CF	β	Fission
30 *y*	Cesium-137	CF	β	Fission
125 *y*	Nickel-63	≅ 5 c/g Ni	β	(n,γ)
5.57×10^3 *y*	Carbon-14	2 c/g C	β	(n,p)
2.12×10^5 *y*	Technetium-99	20 mc/g Tc	β	Fission
3.08×10^5 *y*	Chlorine-36	> 300 μc/g Cl	β	(n,γ)
1.56×10^7 *y*	Iodine-129	≅ 260 μc/g I	β,γ	Fission

**h* = hour; *d* = day; *y* = year. †EC = electron capture; IT = isomeric transition. ‡CF = carrier-free. §$\beta \rightarrow$ = beta decay.

^{22}Na, ^{26}Al, ^{48}V, ^{49}V, ^{54}Mn, and ^{74}As. In the case of ^{26}Al, ^{48}V, ^{49}V, and ^{54}Mn, these are the only isotopes of their elements suitable for use as radiotracers. An additional advantage is that, in many cases, radioisotopes may be produced with much *higher specific activities* (frequently carrier-free) in the cyclotron than in nuclear reactors. Certain radioisotopes cannot be produced free of other radioisotopes of the same element in a reactor without resorting to very expensive highly enriched target elements. By means of the cyclotron, however, it has been possible to prepare ^{55}Fe free of ^{59}Fe, and ^{85}Sr free of ^{89}Sr and ^{90}Sr.

B. CONVERSION OF PRIMARY RADIOISOTOPES TO LABELED COMPOUNDS

In certain experiments, the primary radioisotopes may be employed directly, but most frequently the investigator wants to secure a specific labeled compound for use in radiotracer experiments. A compound that is either randomly labeled or uniformly labeled (such as glucose-U-^{14}C) may suffice for the purpose of one particular experiment, whereas a specifically labeled compound (such as glucose-2-^{14}C) may be required in other investigations. Since the great preponderance of labeled compounds used in biological tracer studies are ^{14}C-tagged, the following discussion deals largely with carbon-14 labeling. Generally, atoms of the radioisotope (^{14}C) may be introduced into the molecules to be labeled by either chemical synthesis or biosynthesis. In the case of tritium, certain unique methods of labeling are also possible.

1. Chemical Synthesis

A carbon-14 label may be introduced into a wide variety of compounds by the standard synthetic procedures of organic chemistry. (The same generally applies to ^{32}P, ^{35}S, and ^{131}I labels.) In addition, some completely new methods have been devised in order to conserve the labeling radioisotope. When chemical synthesis is at all possible, it is usually *the method of choice*. Synthetic methods generally give the greatest control over yield, position of labeling, and purification of the product.

It is not feasible here to list all the possible syntheses that have been used. Figure 11-1, however, illustrates a few of the synthetic pathways that might be followed to produce certain biologically important compounds starting with $Ba^{14}CO_3$ via $K^{14}CN$. Calvin, et al. (2, p. 148–239), give a large portion of their book to a general survey of the synthetic routes used in producing ^{14}C-labeled compounds. Kamen (10, p. 311–332) has presented in tabular form an extensive list of specific syntheses for labeling with carbon-14. In addition, a more recent work by Murray and Williams (13) covers this field in an encyclopedic manner, although it does not treat biologically important compounds to any extent. Part 1 deals with carbon labeling, whereas Part 2 is concerned with halogen (I, Cl, Br), tritium, ^{32}P and ^{35}S compounds. Catch's recent book (3) is devoted entirely to ^{14}C compounds; the Radiochemical Manual (18) has separate chapters noting the general aspects of compounds labeled with ^{14}C, ^{3}H, ^{35}S, ^{32}P, ^{131}I, and ^{36}Cl, respectively.

Chemical synthesis of labeled compounds suffers from several *limitations* and problems. One limitation is the amount and cost of the isotopic

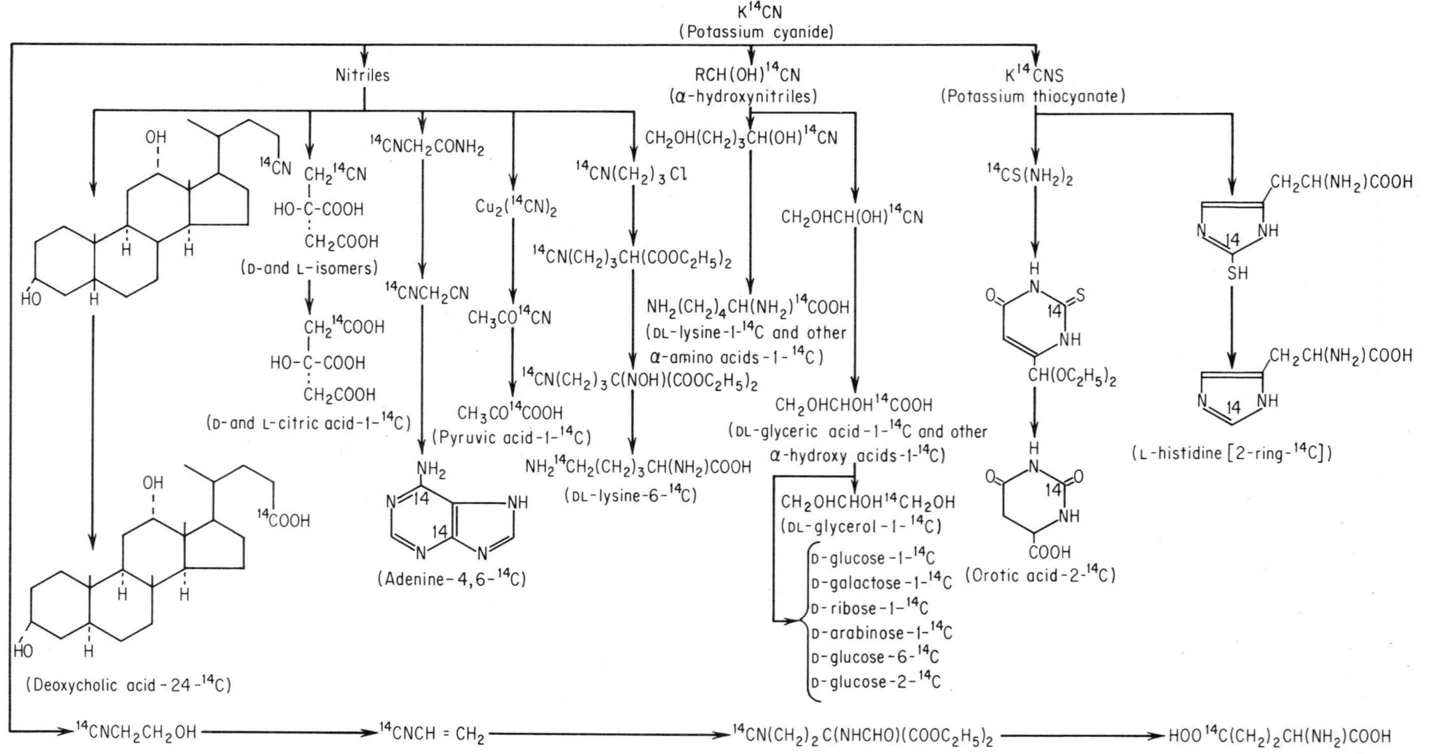

Figure 11-1. Synthetic pathways to some biologically important ^{14}C-labeled compounds via cyanide (by kind permission of the Radiochemical Centre, Amersham).

starting material available. This factor necessitates devising synthetic routes to the desired compounds in which the radioisotopic label can be introduced near the end of the sequence of reactions, so as to secure as high an over-all yield of labeled material as possible. Since the syntheses will normally be carried out on a micro or semimicro scale, losses due to transfer may be great and over-all yield consequently low. Often high-vacuum manifold systems are required for the transfer of liquid or gaseous compounds. At present, a great diversity of labeled compounds are available commercially as starting materials for syntheses. Still, it is necessary in planning a new synthetic route to consider its compatability with the specific starting material available.

Another disadvantage of chemical synthesis is that when it is used to produce certain biologically important compounds, such as amino acids, a racemic mixture of D- and L-isomers results. Since organisms, by and large, metabolize the L-form selectively, as in the case of amino acids, the use of such racemates in biological investigations is somewhat unphysiological and may lead to undesirable confusion. A method for the resolution of racemic mixtures is available. The method is rather tedious, however, and not well suited to small-scale operations.

Note that many compounds of biochemical importance cannot be synthesized in the laboratory by the classical methods of organic chemistry. Uniformly labeled L-amino acids are a good example. They are currently being prepared from hydrolysates of yeast cells grown on glucose-U-^{14}C as the carbon source. Nevertheless, it is generally recognized that chemical synthesis provides the most effective way to prepare specifically labeled compounds with the highest possible specific activity and purity and is capable of producing relatively large quantities of labeled compounds. Several commercial firms, such as New England Nuclear Corporation, offer custom synthesis service for desired labeled compounds that are not normally available.

2. Biosynthesis

Living organisms, or active enzyme systems, offer a biochemical means of synthesizing certain labeled compounds not obtainable by chemical synthesis. These include both the macromolecules (proteins, polysaccharides, nucleic acids, and so forth) and many simpler molecules (vitamins, hormones, amino acids, sugars). The successful employment of biosynthesis for production of a given labeled tracer compound is dependent on several factors. First, an organism must be selected that will synthesize and accumulate practical quantities of the desired compound. Culture conditions must be established to provide optimal yields of the highest specific activity. Last, and most important, procedures must be established for isolating and purifying the labeled compound, and determining the distribution pattern of the label, if a specific labeling is desired.

Photosynthetic methods offer the advantage of using the relatively cheap $^{14}CO_2$ (from $Ba^{14}CO_3$) as the starting material. Carbon-14-labeled starch, glucose, fructose, and sucrose can be isolated in good yields from green leaves or algal suspensions that have been exposed to a $^{14}CO_2$ atmosphere and illuminated for a prolonged period. Specific activities of up to 200 mc/mmole of glucose-U-^{14}C have recently been achieved in such biosyntheses. Similarly, green algae of the genus *Chlorella* can be used to produce ^{14}C-labeled amino acids.

Microorganisms, or the enzyme systems prepared therefrom, have been used to produce organic acids tagged with ^{14}C, either by direct synthesis or transformation of labeled substrates. Several species of microorganisms have been used to produce higher fatty acids by condensation. Calvin, et al. (2, p. 262–277), describe some of the specific biosyntheses that have been generally used.

The *distribution of label* resulting from biosynthesis of a given compound varies according to the conditions of the synthetic reaction. All the carbon atoms of a compound are not labeled with ^{14}C at the same rate. Under certain conditions, all the atoms in a given compound may be labeled, but not to the same extent. Such a compound is described as *generally*, *randomly*, or *totally labeled.* If the labeling is such that the specific activity of each carbon atom in the compound is essentially equal, the compound is *uniformly* or *evenly labeled*, such as glucose-U-^{14}C or glucose-E-^{14}C. Such uniform labeling can be realized only when the composition of the medium and the kinetics of the system involved are fully understood.

In general, biosynthetic procedures for preparing radioisotope-labeled compounds are likely to be laborious and are limited to small-scale operations. One often encounters purification problems when one attempts to isolate specific biological compounds from a number of other biological compounds in a typical biological system.

3. Tritium Labeling

Tritium-labeled compounds have been increasingly used in recent years (26), even though the mean energy of beta emission from ^{3}H is only about 5.5 kev. This increased attention is due largely to the development of improved methods of tritium labeling and the application of liquid scintillation counting to tritium assay. Since carrier-free tritium gas can be obtained, very high specific activities in ^{3}H-labeled tracer compounds are attainable. Commercially available compounds (such as thymidine, tryptophan, epinephrine, and so on) can be secured with specific activities of up to 13 curies/mmole when the label is tritium, whereas ^{14}C-labeled compounds are usually available only at specific activities of the order of mc/mmole. So important has tritium usage become that, in recent years, several symposia have dealt exclusively with the subject (8, 14, 15).

Compounds may be labeled with tritium by several methods (19). The classical *synthetic methods* utilizing labeled intermediates (as previously described) have the advantage of yielding products that have predictable specific activities, are specifically labeled, and have a minimum of tagged by-products. The disadvantages of synthesis are cost and the limitation on the variety of compounds that can be successfully labeled. Hence, many compounds are labeled by one of several unique methods.

a. ***By reduction of unsaturated precursors.*** The method of choice for labeling with tritium is the reduction of a suitable unsaturated precursor (containing a double bond, carbonyl group, and so forth) with carrier-free tritium gas. The major limitation of this method is the availability of a suitable unsaturated precursor of the desired compound. It is essential to carry out the reduction in a nonhydroxylic solvent (dioxane, ethyl acetate, and the like). Reductions carried out in alcohol or water will lead to almost complete exchange of the tritium gas with the solvent. Catalytic reduction may also be complicated by the occurrence of random catalytic exchange reactions, which obviously jeopardize the specific activity of labeling. Careful purification of the product is required, since competing reactions may also occur. The advantages of this method are the very high specific activities attainable, the purity of the product, and the known position of labeling.

b. ***By exchange reactions.*** Random tritium labeling may be secured by simple exchange methods, with or without catalytic action. For example, the simple exchange of tritiated water (^3H_2O) with the labile hydrogen of malonic acid, followed by decarboxylation, yields tritiated acetic acid. In catalyzed exchanges, either tritiated water or glacial acetic acid (CH_3COO^3H) is the usual medium and platinum black the commonly used catalyst. This method is suitable only for compounds which are stable in aqueous solution at temperatures up to 120°C. Garnett (7) has rather thoroughly reviewed catalytic tritium labeling.

Although high specific activities may be obtained by this method, much of the introduced tritium will be labile. Removal of this labile tritium and purification of the desired product is a troublesome necessity. One g of compound can be expected to be labeled with 40–400 mc of nonlabile tritium, if the exposure is carried out with 10 curies of tritium. In general, the labeled product is of higher purity and specific activity than that from the gas exposure method described, and complete purification is easier.

c. By gas exposure. In the mid-1950's Wolfgang and Rowland's (21, 32) work involving tritium-recoil labeling of organic compounds laid the foundation for a new method of ^{3}H-labeling. Wilzbach (30), in 1957, first described the simplified approach to random labeling with tritium that has come to be called the *Wilzbach gas-exposure method* and is largely responsible for the increased popularity of tritium as a tracer. In this method, the compound to be labeled is exposed to curie amounts of carrier-free tritium gas in a sealed reaction vessel for a period of a few days to several weeks. The energy released in the disintegration of the tritium and absorbed by the system provides the activation necessary to effect labeling. Wilzbach reported that specific activities of 1–125 mc/g of purified compound have been obtained (20, p. 4–11, 28–31).

Unfortunately, Wilzbach labeling is often accompanied by the formation of *tritiated by-products* of high specific activity. As in the case of exchange labeling (previously described) a considerable portion of the tritium in the labeled compound is often labile. Nystrom and Dutton (20, p. 18–27, 46–49) have shown that addition of tritium to unsaturated molecules accompanies the labeling process to a greater or lesser degree, depending on the nature of the double bond. This formation of labeled by-products is the major problem of the gas-exposure method, since the specific activity of the tritium addition product may be several orders of magnitude higher than the desired compound. Moreover, in a typical Wilzbach operation, although it is easy to remove contaminants with molecular weights different from that of the parent compound (such as those formed by fragmentation or polymerization), it is difficult to remove contaminants formed by hydrogenation, racemization, or isomerization. Thus, rigid purification procedures must be followed.

Modifications of the Wilzbach method have used external energy to accelerate the labeling process. Electric discharge through the reaction vessel has been widely employed (5, 9, 11, 28, 31). Microwaves (4), ultraviolet irradiation, and gamma irradiation have also been used. All these techniques increase the rate of incorporation and allow faster labeling with smaller amounts of tritium gas, but in many instances they lead to an increase in labeled degradation products. Mottlau (12) suggests that the addition of argon or helium gas to the reaction vessel atmosphere will reduce this competing decomposition.

The chief advantage of the gas-exposure method is that it permits the labeling of compounds of complex or even unknown structure which cannot be readily labeled in any other way (20, p. 32–41). As examples, insulin (27), digitoxin (23), and a variety of proteins (24) have been successfully tagged. At the end of their excellent review of the gas-exposure method Whisman and Eccleston (29), list preparative data on 138 different tritium-labeled compounds. The scanty information available on the yield of ^{3}H-labeled compounds by means of a Wilzbach operation does not yet permit one to predict the extent of tritiation for a given compound, particularly compounds having unusual structures. In general, because of the magnitude of the purification procedure required and the random nature of the labeling, it is suggested that all other synthetic routes be explored before the gas-exposure method is chosen.

4. Radiolysis of Labeled Compounds

In most situations, the biologist will prefer to secure labeled compounds from commercial sources, rather than attempt to synthesize them himself. The radiochemical purity of such purchased compounds cannot be assumed. Radiation-induced self-decomposition (*radiolysis*) can result in the formation of a variety of labeled degradation products, which must be removed before experimental use of the compounds. The extent of radiolysis depends on the nature of the labeled compound, the length of storage time, and the manner in which the compound is stored. Radiolysis is most significant with low-energy beta emitters (especially tritium), since the decay energy in this case is dissipated almost entirely within the compound itself.

Evans and Stanford (6) have made a most exhaustive study of radiolysis in a large number of tritium-labeled compounds stored under different conditions. Although knowledge in this field is still largely empirical, they were able to draw several general conclusions. Radiolysis is minimized by storage below room temperature (0°C is usually adequate). Storage in solution, rather than in the dry state definitely reduces radiolysis. Tritium-labeled compounds with specific activities below 500 mc/mmole stored in solution at 0°C suffer little serious decomposition in one year. At higher specific activities, the extent of radiolysis increases proportionately, but varies considerably, depending on the particular compound in question. These conclusions can be seen from the following general data for *tritium-labeled amino acids*:

Specific Activity (mc/mmole)	Storage State	Temperature (°C)	Maximum Decomposition per Year (per cent)
200	dry, solid	0, −40	5
200	aqueous solution	0, −40	5
500	aqueous solution	−40	10
2000	aqueous solution	room	30
5000	aqueous solution	0	30

Bayly and Weigel (1) have tabulated data on radiolysis in ^{14}C-labeled sucrose and glucose under various storage conditions. Tolbert (25) has also thoroughly examined the problem of radiolysis and listed recommended means of reducing its extent.

The most complete guide to commercially available labeled compounds is the *Isotope Index* (22). It lists hundreds of ^{14}C-tagged compounds, as well as those labeled with ^{131}I, ^{32}P, ^{35}S, and ^{3}H. In addition, consult the various radiochemical supply house catalogs for the most up-to-date information on compound availability. Reputable radiochemical suppliers will furnish chromatographic evidence of compound purity, but, nevertheless, establishment of the purity of the compound should be the initial step in any radiotracer experiment. This is particularly important when the compound has been stored for some time since purchase.

BIBLIOGRAPHY

1. Bayly, R. J., and H. Weigel. 1960. Self-decomposition of compounds labeled with radioactive isotopes. Nature 188:384–387.
2. Calvin, Melvin, et al. 1949. Isotopic carbon. Techniques in its measurement and chemical manipulation. John Wiley & Sons, Inc., New York. 376 p.
3. Catch, John R. Carbon-14 compounds. 1961. Butterworths, London. 128 p.
4. Chanem, N. A., and T. Westermark. 1962. Extensions of the techniques for the accelerated unspecific isotopic labeling of organic compounds. *In* Radioisotopes in the physical sciences and industry. vol. 3. International Atomic Energy Agency, Vienna. p. 43–67.
5. Dorfman, Leon M., and Kenneth E. Wilzbach. 1959. Tritium labeling of organic compounds by means of electric discharge. J. Phys. Chem. 63:799–801.
6. Evans, E. Anthony, and F. G. Stanford. 1963. Decomposition of tritium-labeled organic compounds. Nature 197:551–555.
7. Garnet, John L. 1962. Catalytic tritium labeling attractive for organics. Nucleonics 20 (12):86–91.
8. International Atomic Energy Agency. 1962. Proc. Symposium Detection Use Tritium Phys. Biol. Sci. vol. 2. Vienna, 1961. 438 p.
9. Jackson, Frank L., George W. Kittinger, and Frank P. Krause. 1960. Efficient tritium labeling with an electric discharge. Nucleonics 18(8):102–105.
10. Kamen, Martin D. Isotopic tracers in biology. 1957. An introduction to tracer methodology. 3rd ed. Academic Press, New York. 478 p.
11. Lemmon, Richard M., et al. 1959. Ionizing energy as an aid in exchange tritium labeling. Science 129:1740–1741.
12. Mottlau, A. Y. 1960. Effect of a noble gas on the labeling of n-hexane by exposure to tritium. J. Phys. Chem. 64:931–933.
13. Murray, Arthur, III, and D. Lloyd Williams. 1958. Organic syntheses with isotopes. Interscience, New York. 2096 p.
14. New England Nuclear Corp. 1958. Proc. Symposium on Tritium in Tracer Appl., New York, 1957. Boston. 40 p.
15. New England Nuclear Corp. 1959. Proc. Symposium on Advances in Tracer Appl. of Tritium, New York, 1958. Boston. 67 p.

16. Oak Ridge National Laboratory. 1963. Catalog: Radio and Stable Isotopes. 4th ed. Oak Ridge. 98 p.

17. Pearlman, William H. 1961. A method for labeling C_{21} and C_{19} steroid hormones with tritium at C-7: progesterone-7-^{3}H and 4-androstene-3, 17-dione-7-H. J. Biol. Chem. 236:700–704.

18. The Radiochemical Centre. 1963. The Radiochemical Manual. Part 2. Radioactive chemicals. Amersham. 77 p.

19. Rosenblum, Charles. 1959. The chemistry and application of tritium labeling. Nucleonics 17(12):80–83.

20. Rothchild, Seymour (ed.). 1963. Advances in tracer methodology. vol. 1. Plenum Press, New York. 332 p.

21. Rowland, F. S., and Richard Wolfgang. 1956. Tritium-recoil labeling of organic compounds. Nucleonics 14(8):58–61.

22. Sommerville, J. L. (ed.). 1962. The isotope index. vol. 6. Scientific Equipment Co., Indianapolis. 206 p.

23. Spratt, James L., George T. Okita, and E. M. Geiling. 1957. *In vivo* radiotracer stability of a tritium "self-radiation"-labeled compound. Intern. J. Appl. Radiation Isotopes 2:167–168.

24. Steinberg, D., et al. 1957. Preparation of tritiated proteins by the Wilzbach method. Science 126:447–448.

25. Tolbert, Bert M. 1963. Radiation self-decomposition of labeled compounds. *In* Advances in Tracer Methodology. vol. 1. Plenum Press, New York. p. 64–68.

26. Tritium tracing—a rediscovery. 1958. Nucleonics 16(3):62–67.

27. Von Holt, C., I. Voelker, and L. Von Holt. 1960. Markierung von Insulin mit Tritium. Biochim. Biophys. Acta 38:88–101.

28. Westermark, Torbjorn, Hans Linroth, and Bengt Enander. 1960. Isotope labeling by means of electrical gaseous discharges. Intern. J. Appl. Radiation Isotopes 7:331–334.

29. Whisman, Marvin L., and Barton H. Eccleston. 1962. Gas-exposure labeling of organics with tritium. Nucleonics 20(6):98–105.

30. Wilzbach, Kenneth E. 1957. Tritium-labeling by exposure of organic compounds to tritium gas. J. Am. Chem. Soc. 79:1013.

31. Wilzbach, K. E., and L. M. Dorfman. 1962. Labeling of organic compounds by electric discharge in tritium gas. *In* Radioisotopes in the physical sciences and industry. vol. 3. International Atomic Energy Agency, Vienna. p. 3–11.

32. Wolfgang, Richard, F. S. Rowland, and C. Nigel Turton. 1955. Production of radioactive organic compounds with recoil tritons. Science 121:715–717.

CHAPTER TWELVE

Safe Handling of Radioisotopes

The damaging effects of ionizing radiation on living organisms were recognized quite early and are somewhat better understood today (11). In certain situations (as in cancer therapy or radiation sterilization of food) these lethal effects are employed for man's benefit. The investigator using radioactive tracers is concerned with avoiding the potential biological effects of their radiations. In the United States, federal agencies, and more recently state agencies, have taken primary responsibility with regard to hazards arising from the use of radioisotopes. Carefully worded federal and state rules and regulations governing the use of radioisotopic materials are in force (16). The handbooks by Blatz (3) and Kinsman (9) give further useful reference material dealing with all aspects of radiation safety.

The problems involved in the safe handling of radioactive isotopes fall into three categories: (1) protection of personnel; (2) control of contamination; (3) disposal of radioactive wastes. At this point, it should be stressed that in the use of tracer amounts of all but the most hazardous radioisotopes the most pressing problem is the avoidance of *technical contamination* of the laboratory environment. Such contamination will usually cause technical difficulties, such as raising the background rate for a counting device, well before an actual health hazard exists (4). Hence, radiotracer users must constantly practice good housekeeping. Even though only tracer levels of activity are being used experimentally, however, higher levels of activity are commonly bought and must be handled initially. It should be emphasized that the purpose of all radiation safety procedures is to keep radiation exposure to a minimum. The permissible levels of radiation exposure that have been established (16, 23) are conservative, but still to some degree arbitrary.

A. THE STANDARD UNITS OF RADIATION EXPOSURE AND DOSE

In order to discuss radiation hazards adequately, it is necessary to consider the units used to denote the energy dissipation involved. Unlike a unit of radioactivity, the radiation dose is concerned only with the portion of energy associated with radiation that has been absorbed by the object in question. It is the absorbed energy that determines the biological effect of the radiation. In actuality, unequivocal statements of radiation dose must take into account the area of the irradiated object involved and the time factor, as well as the actual energy of the ionizing radiation that is dissipated in the object. Thus, dose rate and exposure time must be stated and the portion of the body affected defined (that is, whole body, hands only, and so on) before the extent of radiation exposure can be evaluated. Andrews (2) gives a good general survey of this whole topic of radiation biophysics. Rossi (12) discusses current recommendations of the International Commission on Radiological Units (ICRU) regarding radiation quantities and units.

1. The Roentgen

The most widely used unit of radiation exposure, the roentgen (named after the discoverer of X rays), is derived from consideration of the ionization in air produced by X radiation. The roentgen (abbreviated R) was officially defined by the International Radiological Congress at Chicago in 1937 as the quantity of gamma or X radiation such that the associated corpuscular emission per 1 cc of dry air at standard temperature and pressure produces, in air, ions carrying one electrostatic unit of electricity of either sign. When one converts this unit of electrical energy to the conventional energy unit (ergs) and expresses the energy dissipation in grams of air, one finds that the energy dissipated in the air is approximately 87.6 ergs for 1 hr of radiation. In health physics operations, the exposure is commonly expressed, taking into consideration the rate factor, in units of roentgens per hour (R/hr) or milliroentgens per hour (mR/hr). By definition, the roentgen is valid only for photon interaction with air and cannot be applied to particulate radiation or tissue absorption. Notice also, that, contrary to common misuse, the roentgen is a measure of energy dissipation in a given radiation exposure, not dose.

2. The rep

Inasmuch as the roentgen unit by definition is limited to the effects of X or gamma radiation, it was essential to develop another unit to describe the energy dissipation of other types of radiation in materials, particularly biological tissues. The unit *rep* (roentgen equivalent physical) was devised for such purposes. It is defined as the amount of energy derived from any ionizing radiation that is dissipated in 1 g of biological tissue and is equivalent to 93 ergs. This value is somewhat larger than 1 roentgen, that is, 87.6 ergs, a fact reflecting the difference in energy dissipation in tissue as compared to that in air. In practice, the rep did not prove to be a practical unit and it is now obsolete.

3. The Rad

From the biological standpoint, interest centers primarily on the energy of ionizing radiation absorbed by tissues rather than by air. Although the roentgen unit was in universal use by medical workers, some workers felt that convenience would be served by devising an arbitrary unit defined on the basis of energy dissipation in biological tissues. The International Commission on Radiological Units in 1953 proposed such a new unit and called it the *rad*. It was defined as 100 ergs of energy imparted by any ionizing radiation that is dissipated in 1 g of irradiated material and is therefore unrelated to the unit R. Since the absorption of radiation by various materials differs, one must state the nature of the irradiated material involved when using the rad unit. The rad is now the unit of choice when tissue irradiation is considered. It has generally replaced the rep for this purpose.

4. The RBE, rem, and LET

It is also known that radiation damage to biological tissue is dependent both on the type of tissue and on the type of ionizing radiation and the energy associated therewith. Consequently, all these factors must be considered before a given radiation exposure can be evaluated and correlated to another radiation exposure; hence, the term *relative biological effectiveness* (RBE) of the radiation absorbed must be considered. RBE values (in reality representing ratios) are stated as the ratio of the biological response derived (or damage inflicted) in the particular radiation exposure as compared to another radiation exposure. Generally the biological damage incurred by X rays, gamma rays, or beta particles is taken to be unity. On this basis, the following average RBE values may be cited: gamma rays, X rays, beta particles—RBE 1; thermal neutrons—RBE 2.5; fast neutrons, alpha particles, protons—RBE 10; heavy ions—RBE 20.

The RBE concept makes it possible to express the energy dissipation in a biological tissue system in a more meaningful unit. Such a unit is the *roentgen equivalent man* (or *mammal*), abbreviated *rem*. This unit reflects not only the amount of energy dissipated but also the amount of biological damage derived from such energy dissipation. It is defined as equal to the product of rep and RBE. Currently, statements of permissible exposure of humans to ionizing radiation are expressed in rem units.

The term RBE, although useful, does create a crucial problem in actually determining the values of RBE in precise experimental work. This is true, since biological damage from ionizing radiation is dependent on many other factors, including tissue pH, tissue temperature, oxygen content in tissue, and others. A more meaningful treatment of this subject is the consideration of the rate of energy transfer to the tissue as the ionizing radiation travels through the biological system. Such a concept is represented by the use of the unit, *linear energy transfer* (LET), which is in reality expressed in energy units or as kev/μ (micron) of path. When one expresses the energy dissipation in this unit, that is, in the linear energy transfer to water (kev/μ), one finds that the values range from 3.5 or less for X rays and electrons to well over 100 for heavy ionizing particles.

B. HAZARD FACTORS IN HANDLING RADIOISOTOPES

Many facets of radioactivity that relate to radiation safety have already been discussed in this book. Now we turn to the factors which make certain radioisotopes more hazardous than others. These include (1) half-life of the radioisotope; (2) energy and type of radiation; (3) biological half-life, or body turnover time; (4) selective deposition or localization in the body. The hazards from radioisotope use can be classified as internal or external, depending on the location of the activity with regard to the body. Taylor (14) has reviewed the development of radiation protection standards.

1. External Hazards

Radiation from external radioisotope sources poses the hazard of either whole body irradiation or local irradiation. Since the range of alpha and beta particles in air is relatively short, it is most unlikely that whole body irradiation could occur except from gamma or X rays. Local irradiation from an external beta source normally involves only the most superficial layers of skin (up to a few millimeters in thickness).

Current federal regulations (16, part 20.101) specify the *maximum permissible doses* to radiation workers as follows: whole body, head and trunk, active blood-forming organs, lens of eyes, or gonads—$1\frac{1}{4}$ rems in any 13 consecutive weeks; hands and forearms, or feet and ankles—$18\frac{3}{4}$

rems in any 13 consecutive weeks; skin of whole body—7½ rems in any 13 consecutive weeks. In addition, the accumulated radiation dose that the individual has received must be taken into consideration. It should be emphasized that the maximum permissible doses should not be casually accepted; it is advisable to strive for the lowest possible exposures at all times.

Roughly to determine the exposure from an external gamma-emitting isotope source, the following empirical equation may be used:

$$R = 6\ CE \tag{12-1}$$

In this equation, R = exposure rate in mR/hr at 1 ft, C = mc of activity, and E = total gamma energy per disintegration in Mev. The relationship stated holds fairly well for gamma energies from 0.3–3.0 Mev.

Another important factor affecting external exposure is the *inverse square law*, which states that the radiation intensity varies inversely as the square of the distance. Thus, an exposure rate of 100 mR/hr at 1 ft would be reduced to $100 \times 1^2/2^2 = 25$ mR/hr at 2 ft. The use of long-handled tongs and remote control pipetting devices often constitutes the only necessary precaution in handling small amounts of gamma emitters.

In most tracer investigations, the small amount of gamma activity used (less than 1 mc) precludes the possibility of serious external irradiation hazard. For example, it can be calculated that one would have to be exposed at a distance of 1 ft to a 100μc amount of ^{131}I for over 4500 hr to receive a 1 R exposure. To receive similar exposures from the same levels of ^{60}Co and ^{24}Na activities would require over 700 hr and nearly 400 hr, respectively.

Where higher activity levels of gamma emitting isotopes are being used, *shielding* may be required, in addition to maintaining reasonable distance from the source. Gamma shielding has been considered in Chapter 3 and we need not discuss the matter further at this point, except to stress again the value of using half-thickness calculations (Equation 3-15) in determining the required shielding to reduce gamma intensity by a given factor. Glass or Lucite barriers are usually adequate shielding when working with relatively high levels of energetic beta emitters.

2. Internal Hazards

Deposition of radioisotopes within the body as a result of ingestion, inhalation, or skin absorption poses an entirely different problem. In this case, isotopes whose radiations have very *short ranges* are the most hazardous, since they dissipate all their energy within a very restricted volume of tissue. Thus, alpha emitters and weak beta emitters present the greatest hazard, followed by energetic beta emitters and gamma emitters, respectively.

An added hazard from internal emitters exists where a given radioisotope is *selectively concentrated* in the body, rather than generally distributed, since it will produce a more intense local irradiation. Examples of this selective concentration are iodine in the thyroid gland, or Pu, Ra, Sr, P, or Ca in the bones. The radiation exposure from an internal radioactive source continues only as long as the isotope remains in the system. This is influenced by both the disintegration half-life of the particular radioisotope and its biological half-life; that is, the length of time until one-half of a given amount is excreted. Of course, the most serious internal hazard comes from ingestion of long-lived beta-emitting radioisotopes that are selectively concentrated and not readily excreted. Strontium-90 is a prime example.

Selected radioisotopes are grouped according to their relative radiotoxicity as internal emitters in Table 12-1 (17). The activity levels

TABLE 12-1

Relative internal hazard of selected radioisotopes

Hazard Class	Activity Levels		
	Low	Intermediate	High
Only slightly hazardous: ^{24}Na, ^{42}K, ^{64}Cu, ^{52}Mn ^{76}As, ^{77}As, ^{85}Kr, ^{197}Hg	$<$ 1 mc	1–10 mc	$>$ 10 mc
Moderately hazardous: ^{3}H, ^{14}C, ^{22}Na, ^{32}P, ^{35}S, ^{36}Cl, ^{54}Mn, ^{59}Fe, ^{60}Co, ^{89}Sr, ^{95}Nb, ^{103}Ru, ^{106}Ru, ^{127}Te, ^{129}Te, ^{131}I, ^{137}Cs, ^{140}Ba, ^{140}La, ^{141}Ce, ^{143}Pr, ^{147}Nd, ^{198}Au, ^{199}Au, ^{203}Hg, ^{205}Hg	$<$ 0.1 mc	0.1–1 mc	$>$ 1 mc
Very hazardous: ^{45}Ca, ^{55}Fe, ^{90}Sr, ^{91}Y, ^{95}Zr, ^{144}Ce, ^{147}Pm, ^{210}Bi	$<$ 0.01 mc	0.01–0.1 mc	$>$ 0.1 mc

regarded as low, intermediate, and high according to the degree of laboratory safety precautions required are also indicated. The activities stated are somewhat arbitrary and highly dependent on the nature of the experiment being performed and the chemical and physical form of the radioisotope.

Particular attention should be given to the relative health hazards from tritium and carbon-14, the most commonly used radiotracers in biology. Tolbert, et al. (15) and Skipper (13) have discussed the hazards involved in the use of carbon-14. The latter concluded that ^{14}C is relatively nonhazardous in tracer amounts in most experiments. Inhaled $^{14}CO_2$ and ingested $H^{14}CO_3^-$ are rapidly excreted; inhaled particulate $Ba^{14}CO_3$ undergoes 95 per cent turnover in about 2 hr. Thymidine-^{14}C has a long biological half-life, however, becoming incorporated into nucleic acids. Handloser (6, p. 201–202) has considered the health hazards in working with *tritium*. Tritium gas is less toxic than tritiated water. The latter is readily absorbed by the skin by a factor of 10^4 greater than tritium gas, thus requiring one to wear of gloves when handling it.

The *maximum permissible body burdens* and *maximum permissible concentrations* of radioisotopes in air and water for occupational exposure are clearly stated in federal regulations (16, 23). For example, the maximum permissible concentration of soluble ^{14}C in water is 0.02 $\mu c/ml$ and of soluble tritium-containing compounds in water is 0.1 $\mu c/ml$. Maximum permissible body burdens of the two isotopes are 400 μc and 2000 μc, respectively. By contrast, the maximum permissible body burden for a severely radiotoxic isotope, such as ^{90}Sr, is only 20μc, and that for ^{239}Pu is a mere 0.4 μc.

Possible hazard from the use of tracer quantities of radioactive isotopes is minimized by good laboratory housekeeping and adherence to simple laboratory precautions as embodied in the *radiation laboratory rules* set forth at the end of this chapter. It will be seen that the fundamental purpose of these safety rules is to prevent ingestion, inhalation, or other entrance of radioisotopes into the body and to reduce the amounts of external irradiation to permissible levels. In general, it is a good principle to treat all radioactive materials as if they were pathogenic bacteria, even though they are being handled by purely chemical techniques. Thus, the possibility of unnoticed contamination of the laboratory or one's person should always be considered. In many tracer experiments, however, chemical and fire hazards are far more significant than any hazard from the radiation involved.

C. RADIATION MONITORING INSTRUMENTATION

To determine the extent of possible radiation hazard and/or to detect contamination, one must use radiation monitoring instruments. Although the institutional radiation safety officer may conduct periodic radiation surveys in tracer laboratories, it is basically the responsibility of the individual isotope user to monitor his own laboratory for radiation hazards. In addition, where millicurie levels of gamma emitters are being used, each worker should have proper personnel monitoring equipment. Among the many references one might cite in the field of radiological monitoring, the National Bureau of Standards Handbook 51 (20) and Handloser's book (5) are perhaps the most suitable for radiotracer users.

1. Area Monitoring

Area monitoring of laboratory facilities is normally carried out by means of portable survey meters, although fixed monitors are used in certain cases. The commonest portable monitor is a battery-operated G-M counter (see Chapter 4) with a ratemeter. It is a very sensitive detector for relatively low levels of radiation, from either shielded isotopic sources or contamination. *G-M survey meters* are best used for the detection of radiation, not the measurement of radiation dose rate. If a G-M counter is calibrated for a particular gamma energy, however, it can be used to measure the dose rate associated with that gamma energy. In general, readings in counts per minute will be more meaningful than in mR/hr.

A second type of survey meter is a portable *ionization chamber* (see Chapter 4) utilizing a vacuum-tube electrometer. Ionization chamber survey meters are reliable, hold their calibration well, and are relatively energy-independent. Their major use is for measurement of gamma or X-ray dose rate at moderate to high radiation levels. They are commonly calibrated to read directly in mR/hr.

A variety of specialized area monitors are available. These include such instruments as portable scintillation counters, designed for gamma measurement, and air monitors (as for tritium) that pull a volume of air over an ion chamber by means of an air pump or fan. Recently revised permissible concentrations of tritium in air, make it necessary to recommend a sensitive electrometer, such as the vibrating-reed type, for tritium-monitoring devices.

2. Personnel Monitoring

Atomic Energy Commission regulations (16, part 20.202) require that those who enter areas where they are likely to receive a radiation exposure in excess of 25 per cent of the maximum permissible exposure must use appropriate personnel monitoring equipment. A variety of such equipment is commercially available. The *film badge* (8) is one of the most widely used personnel monitoring devices, since the developed film serves as a permanent record of the individual's cumulative exposure over a defined period and thus has some legal value. It usually consists of one or more film packets in a compact plastic or metal container and is worn on the clothing. Films with differential sensitivities to various radiation types are available. The major disadvantage of the film badge is the time lag between exposure and evaluation of the developed film. Films are changed and developed at regular intervals of 1 to 2 weeks. In no cases should the interval exceed a month. Film badges are not required in many radiotracer experiments because of the low activity levels in use or the character of the radiation exposure.

Pocket ionization chambers (about the size of a fountain pen) are designed to be worn by the individual. These give a rough estimate of the total exposure over the period from time of charging to time of reading. In the form of dosimeters (electroscopes) the accumulated exposures may be read directly by the wearer at any time; pocket ionization chambers of a condenser type require a separate reading instrument to determine the exposure.

D. DECONTAMINATION

The use of rubber or disposable polyethylene gloves and protective laboratory coats will usually eliminate the necessity for rigorous skin decontamination. If all handling of open radioisotopic sources is restricted to areas over trays (preferably polished heavy stainless steel) that are lined with absorbent paper, laboratory work surface contamination can be kept to a minimum. Accidental contamination, however, will occur on some occasions despite the strictest precautions. A regular habit of monitoring the hands and all working surfaces at the end of each working period must be established to detect contamination. Again, it should be recalled that the hazard from tracer doses of isotopic material is primarily technical contamination of the laboratory, rather than a threat to the health of the radioisotope user. National Bureau of Standards Handbook 48 (18) will serve as a source of information on the control and removal of radioactive contamination in laboratories. Only general decontamination principles are considered in this chapter.

Routine *hand washing* for 2–3 min with mild soap and lukewarm water should always follow any handling of isotopic material. After rinsing, the hands should be monitored. If the first washing has not reduced contamination to an acceptable level, a repeated washing, using a soft brush and heavy lather, may be required. Be careful not to scratch or abrade the skin with the brush.

Laboratory clothing should be routinely monitored when high levels of activity and/or more hazardous classes of isotopes are in use. Contaminated garments should be washed in the laboratory before being released. Rubber gloves are usually readily decontaminated by simple washing. Leather goods cannot readily be decontaminated.

Laboratory glassware and implements that have become contaminated must be thoroughly washed to eliminate both the radiation hazard and the possibility of cross-contamination of successive experiments. There is a considerable tendency for the adsorption of radioactive materials onto glass. To reduce this problem, never allow radioactive solutions to dry on glass surfaces. In case of unavoidable contamination of glassware, treatment with warm cleaning solution ($K_2Cr_2O_7$ and concentrated H_2SO_4) or with detergent in a sonic bath have proved to be practical procedures. Where the contamination is due to radiosulfate or radiophosphate, treatment with 6N HCl is preferable.

There is a considerable difference in the ease of decontamination of various *laboratory surface materials* (10). Wood, concrete, and soapstone are particularly difficult to decontaminate due to their high porosity. (This point is more thoroughly discussed in Chapter 13.) Polished stainless steel, vinyl floor coverings, and strippable plastic coatings are generally the materials of choice with regard to ease of decontamination.

The *routine cleaning* of a radiotracer laboratory must take into consideration the possibility of spreading contamination to other areas. Depending on the activity level and hazard rating of the isotopes used, it may be necessary to restrict the cleaning implements used to a single laboratory. Vacuum cleaners equipped with efficient filters have been found particularly useful (7).

E. DISPOSAL OF RADIOACTIVE WASTES

Laboratory use of radioisotopes inevitably results in radioactive wastes (that is, paper wipes, disposable implements, carcasses, excreta, and so forth) that must be disposed of without endangering the public. Possible routes of disposal are into sewers, by incineration, by venting directly into the atmosphere, by ground burial, or by disposal at sea. Hopefully, the means of disposal required will be reasonably convenient and economical.

Two general policies are usually followed in waste disposal: one seeks maximum dilution of the waste; the other obtains maximum concentration. Disposal by *dilution* usually involves release into the sewer, direct release into the air, or incineration of the wastes. Atomic Energy Commission regulations (16, part 20.303) restrict disposal via *sewage* to material that is readily soluble or dispersible in water and to activities below specified levels (for example 100 μc of ^{32}P per day). National Bureau of Standards Handbook 49 (19) discusses in detail such disposal of ^{32}P and ^{131}I wastes. For many radiotracer applications, this method offers both convenience and safety. There is always the possibility, however, that some aquatic organisms (see Experiment E) may reconcentrate these wastes to hazardous levels.

Direct release into the *air* via hood exhausts is feasible for $^{14}CO_2$ and other volatile or gaseous substances. But dilution by the air flow through the exhaust stack must be such that maximum permissible concentrations are not exceeded (for example, for ^{14}C this concentration is 1×10^{-6} μc/ml air). Specific approval by the AEC is now required to dispose of radioactive wastes by *incineration* (16, part 20.305), previous published statements notwithstanding.

Concentration and storage of radioactive wastes may be necessary for materials which cannot be disposed of by dilution. This method is more suitable for high levels of activity, such as reactor wastes (1). The storage may take the form of burial in the soil or in concrete-filled drums at sea. *Soil burial* is a particularly attractive method for disposing of carcasses and excreta contaminated with isotopes that are noncombustible (for example, iron, calcium, and so on). The quantity of wastes and conditions of burial have been clearly specified (16, part 20.304). In a sense, burial amounts to a type of dilution, since before the waste substances enter the biosphere affecting man they will hopefully have been diluted below the hazardous level.

The *physical half-life* of the isotopic material in the waste is an important factor in determining the most satisfactory method of disposal, especially for insoluble materials. For tracer levels of isotopes with half-lives of days to a few weeks, merely holding the wastes in storage will reduce the activity to tolerable levels. It can easily be calculated that after ten half-lives the original activity of a radioactive sample will be reduced by a factor of over 1000. Carcasses containing short-lived isotopic material can be either preserved in formalin or frozen for such a term of storage.

The biologist is perhaps most concerned with *^{14}C waste* disposal. Here, the long half-life precludes storage during decay. National Bureau of Standards Handbook 53 (21) describes various recommended methods of ^{14}C waste disposal. Isotopic dilution is a generally applied method that is often used for ^{14}C disposal. Carbon-14 may be disposed of in any manner, provided that it is intimately mixed with stable carbon in the same chemical form in a ratio that never exceeds 1 μc of ^{14}C for every 10 g of stable carbon. Bureau of Standards Handbook 65 (22) describes precautions in handling human bodies containing isotopes; the same principles apply to animal carcasses.

F. RADIOISOTOPE LABORATORY SAFETY RULES

One cannot give working rules to apply in all situations. As has been seen, the activity level and hazard class of the isotope being used will determine the degree of precaution required. The following list of regulations, however, is intended to minimize internal and external hazards, to prevent technical contamination of the laboratory, and specifically to comply with AEC rules (16).

(1) Eating, storing, or preparing *food*, smoking, or applying cosmetics is either forbidden or discouraged in any area where radioactive materials are stored or used.
(2) *Direct contact* with radioactive materials must be avoided by using protective laboratory coats, wearing rubber or disposable plastic gloves, and employing safety pipetters.
(3) All *spills* of radioactive material must be reported to the person in charge of radiation safety and decontaminated immediately.
(4) Complete *records* of receipts, transfers, and disposal of radioactive materials must be kept.
(5) A *film badge* should be worn whenever working with gamma emitters at levels exceeding 100 μc.
(6) Work should be carried out under a *hood* in all cases where radioactive material may be lost by volatilization, dispersion of dust, or by spraying or splattering. Wherever possible, work with closed containers.
(7) All radioactive samples should be properly *labeled* with the isotope and activity indicated, and covered.
(8) *Liquid wastes* should not be poured into the drain or contaminated apparatus washed in the sink unless the levels of activity entering the sewer system have been calculated as permissible (16, part 20.303).
(9) The disposal of *solid wastes* and contaminated articles (corks, paper wipes, and the like) should be into designated containers and, under no consideration, into ordinary trash receptacles.
(10) The disposal of *gaseous waste* through the hood can be carried out only after careful examination of the air dilution factor.
(11) The *storage* of all radioactive material must be in properly designated locations.
(12) At the close of a working period the laboratory work surfaces should be carefully *monitored.*
(13) Before leaving the laboratory after working with active materials, each person should *wash* his *hands* thoroughly and check them with a monitoring instrument.
(14) All *laboratory glassware* and equipment should be properly decontaminated after use before being returned to general usage.
(15) It is desirable to decontaminate one's hands and work surfaces completely, but the following arbitrary *surface contamination tolerances* (as measured by a G-M survey meter with a thin end-window) may be allowed after efforts at decontamination:

Hands	350 cpm
Working surface	250 cpm

The arbitrary nature of any such tolerances should be recognized, although, on the other hand, absolutely complete decontamination is not always feasible.

(16) Routine urine analyses should be carried out by means of liquid scintillation counting (3) whenever millicurie levels of carbon or tritium are handled.

BIBLIOGRAPHY

1. Amphlett, C. B. 1961. Treatment and disposal of radioactive wastes. Pergamon Press, New York. 289 p.
2. Andrews, Howard L. 1961. Radiation biophysics. Prentice-Hall, Inc. Englewood Cliffs, N.J. 328 p.
3. Blatz, Hanson (ed.). 1959. Radiation hygiene handbook. McGraw-Hill Book Company, New York. 926 p.
4. Catch, J. R. 1956. Radio-isotopes as tracers—the rational approach. Research 9:479–484.
5. Handloser, John S. 1959. Health physics instrumentation. Pergamon Press, New York. 182 p.
6. Handloser, John S. 1963. Tritium health physics considerations. *In* S. Rothchild's (ed.). Advances in tracer methodology. vol. 1. Plenum Press, New York. p. 201–202.
7. Holden, F. R., R. K. Skow, and J. Todd. 1953. Vacuum cleaner for radioactive decontamination. Nucleonics 11(2):67.
8. Jetter, Evelyn S., and Hanson Blatz. 1952. Film measurement of beta radiation dose. Nucleonics 10(10):43–45.
9. Kinsman, Simon (ed.). 1960. Radiological health handbook. Rev. ed. U.S. Public Health Service, Division of Radiological Health. Washington. 468 p.
10. Lane, W., et al. 1953. Contamination and decontamination of laboratory bench-top materials. Nucleonics 11(8):49.
11. National Academy of Sciences. 1956. The biological effects of atomic radiation. Summary reports. Washington. 108 p.
12. Rossi, Harold H. 1963. New ICRU recommendations on radiation quantities and units. Nucleonics 21(7):75–78.
13. Skipper, Howard E. 1952. The hazard involved in the use of carbon-14. Nucleonics 10(2):40–44.
14. Taylor, Lauriston. 1963. Radiation-protection standards. Nucleonics 21(3):58–60.
15. Tolbert, B. M., N. Garden, and P. T. Adams. 1953. Special equipment for C^{14} work. Nucleonics 11(3):56–58.
16. U.S. Code of Federal Regulations, Title 10—Atomic energy, Part 20—Standards for protection against radiation.
17. U.S. Dept. of Commerce, National Bureau of Standards. 1949. Safe handling of radioactive isotopes. Handbook no. 42. Washington. 30 p.

18. U.S. Dept. of Commerce, National Bureau of Standards. 1951. Control and removal of radioactive contamination in laboratories. Handbook no. 48. Washington. 24 p.

19. U.S. Dept. of Commerce, National Bureau of Standards. 1951. Recommendations for waste disposal of phosphorus-32 and iodine-131 for medical users. Handbook no. 49. Washington. 11 p.

20. U.S. Dept. of Commerce, National Bureau of Standards. 1952. Radiological monitoring methods and instruments. Handbook no. 51. Washington. 33 p.

21. U.S. Dept. of Commerce, National Bureau of Standards. 1953. Recommendations for the disposal of carbon-14 wastes. Handbook no. 53. Washington. 14 p.

22. U.S. Dept. of Commerce, National Bureau of Standards. 1958. Safe handling of bodies containing radioactive isotopes. Handbook no. 65. Washington. 20 p.

23. U.S. Dept. of Commerce, National Bureau of Standards. 1959. Maximum permissible body burdens and maximum permissible concentrations of radionuclides in air and water for occupational exposure. Handbook no. 69. Washington. 95 p.

CHAPTER THIRTEEN

Design Features of Radiotracer Laboratories

A beginning user of radioisotopes seldom needs to design special laboratory facilities for his purposes. He should, however, be aware of certain features unique to radiotracer laboratories. At some time in his career the experienced user of radioisotopes will almost certainly be called upon to collaborate either in planning new radiotracer facilities or in modifying existing space for radiotracer uses. This chapter is written with both these groups in mind, but is primarily intended as an example of desirable design features rather than a guide to actual planning.

A. THE NEED FOR SPECIALLY DESIGNED LABORATORIES

Recent advances in the use of radioisotopes as a research tool have considerably broadened the scope of the field and have created the need for specially designed laboratories to handle more hazardous operations. This is true because low-level experiments can be and are being carried out in conventional laboratories, but these laboratories are generally inadequate to accommodate operations involving higher levels of radioactivity. Notable examples of such operations are use of the Wilzbach method in preparing tritium-labeled compounds, which often involves the use of multiple curies of tritium gas; use of radioisotopes in studies with large animals, which often encounters problems in waste control; use of biosynthetic methods to prepare carbon-14 labeled compounds having a high specific activity, which may involve tens or hundreds of millicuries of carbon-14; and use of gamma emitters at the multiple-millicurie levels.

Laboratory facilities specially designed for these operations are generally expensive with respect both to construction and associated instrumentation. Consequently, it is often advisable to establish a coordinated laboratory in a scientific community to handle hazardous radioisotope experiments for all research workers in the area. Such a laboratory is designed to fulfill the following specific functions:

(1) Housing and managing special facilities for *handling radioisotopes* with respect to hazard control and waste disposal control. Facilities are designed to handle experiments involving "medium levels" of radioactivity (up to 10 millicuries of gamma or high-energy beta emitters and up to 100 mc of soft beta emitters) and "high levels" of radioactivity (up to 100 mc of gamma or high-energy beta emitters and up to 1 curie of ^{14}C and up to 100 curies of $^{3}H_2$.

(2) Housing and managing expensive *instruments* or equipment not readily available to individual research groups.

(3) Coordinated *storage of radioisotopes* and radioisotope-labeled compounds so that a continuous supply of short half-life radioisotopes can be maintained and a faster turnover of labeled compounds can be effected to avoid undue radiolysis.

(4) Provision of a *testing ground* with professional consultation to enable research workers to evaluate the feasibility of exploratory experiments.

B. THE PLANNING COMMITTEE

In designing such a laboratory, in addition to ordinary considerations necessary for the design of a science laboratory, attention is also directed to unique features derived from the type of the radioisotope experiments that are to be carried out in the facility. It is important that a planning committee be organized consisting of *scientists* in a broad spectrum of disciplines, each familiar with the use of radioisotopes. The *chairman* of such a committee, serving as its spokesman, should take the trouble to learn some basic concepts in architecture and construction engineering so that the committee's conclusions can be properly transmitted to the architect and the *administrative representative* of the scientific community. He can do this by reading key references in the literature; particularly useful are Ward's discussion (13) and a recent symposium report on construction of laboratory buildings (2).

The planning committee decides such matters as floor space required, orientation of varied functions, type of laboratories, special facilities and instruments to be housed, and the like. Those decisions in turn determine the *construction budget.* It should be recognized that the unit cost per square foot for a laboratory of this type is slightly higher than for an ordinary science building, particularly with respect to mechanical installation, because of the necessary elaborate ventilation, sewage systems, and radioisotope storage.

It is important that the *architect* assigned to the project have wide experience in designing science buildings. To insure that user, architect, and administration representative (for example, the institutional representative for construction) shall understand all aspects of the design task, these three men ought to visit a number of existing radioisotope laboratories in the country. Such a tour will enable the team to take advantage of the unique good features of existing installations and to avoid unnecessary and costly design mistakes.

C. BASIC DESIGN PREREQUISITES

Except for a few additional design features, the basic design prerequisites for a radioisotope laboratory are generally the same as those for conventional science buildings. The *building site* should not only fulfill the requirements prevailing in the scientific community, but should also take into consideration such problems as: (1) Hazard evaluation with respect to potential radioisotope contents in air and in sewage water; (2) soil loading requirement, which is of paramount importance to the construction of a hot cell and other heavy shieldings; (3) plans for future expansion; (4) operational costs; (5) nature of projected programs; thus, if a research reactor is to be added as an annex to the building in the future to fulfill such functions as radioisotope production, neutron activation analysis, and the like, it will be necessary to consult with the Atomic Energy Commission in the selection of a proper site; (6) relation to supporting facilities elsewhere in the scientific community. (The facilities in the radioisotope laboratory are likely to be specialized and the research capability of the workers in the building will be greatly enhanced if supporting facilities are in nearby areas.)

Due consideration should be given to selection of suitable *materials for construction*, bearing in mind the necessity for a fireproof structure, shielding problems, and surface contamination problems. In deciding the type of building, one must recognize such problems as (1) size limitations with respect to necessary clearance for equipment (lifting devices, shielding devices, instruments, and so on); (2) the movement of rack-mounted instruments and equipment inside the building; (3) the problems of radioisotope storage; (4) compliance with existing regulations and building codes.

D. SPECIFIC DESIGN FEATURES

A number of specific design concepts are unique to the design of a radioisotope laboratory. The remainder of this chapter discusses some of the important ones.

1. Floor Arrangement

The arrangement of individual laboratories should be based on the following considerations:

(1) *Segregation of areas* on the basis of prevailing radiation level. A logical arrangement calls for the zoning of offices, counting rooms, animal quarters, low-level laboratories, high-level laboratories, radioisotope storage, and radioactive waste disposal. For the convenience of the research workers, some of the laboratories can be used as combination offices and laboratories.

(2) *Utilities* to laboratories can be best accommodated by the insertion of a utility shaft between two rows of laboratories.

(3) *Space clearances* with respect to size of corridors, doors, and the like, for moving instruments and equipment.

(4) *Control of access* so that the building as a whole can be considered as a restricted area.

(5) Ample *space for storage* to facilitate the good housekeeping necessary in a radioisotope laboratory.

(6) *Segregated solvent storage* room to facilitate the control of fire hazards.

(7) Use of *airlock systems* to control air contamination. This is important in the event the ventilation system is rendered inoperative during a power failure.

2. Ventilation and Heating

The heating system for a radioisotope laboratory should be of a type that facilitates good housekeeping. The system is naturally related to the building's ventilation system. The most desirable design for the ventilation system in a radioisotope laboratory calls for the *unidirectional flow of air* from the office area to individual radioisotope laboratories, followed by exclusive exhaust via radiochemical hoods equipped with absolute filters. Recirculation of air can be permitted in the counting or instrument rooms provided that these rooms are pressurized against the corridors to prevent contamination from the atmosphere in the corridor. Air supply to individual laboratories is best provided from the corridor via louvered doors or louvered walls.

Preferably, no more than two rooms should be serviced by one exhaust blower so that ventilation control can be maintained in event of localized mechanical failures. Housing the *exhaust system*, including filter assembly for the hoods, in the utility shaft offers the advantages of simplicity of duct design and of accessibility to the filters and exhaust system for routine maintenance. Stainless steel is the preferred material for construction of ducts, but other materials, such as Fiberglas, are equally good. In a typical laboratory, having a total floor space of 400 sq ft and equipped with two hoods, the total air displacement in the room should exceed 1300 cu ft per minute to provide adequate rates of air change in the room. Several portable duct connections should be provided in each room to permit the connection of such devices as glove boxes, respiration chambers, and the like, to the exhaust.

3. Electrical Utilities

The basic requirements of electrical utilities in a radioisotope laboratory are similar to those for ordinary chemistry or physics laboratories. Attention, however, should be given to several requirements peculiar to radioisotope laboratories. The extensive instrumentation in handling and measurement of radioisotopes calls for an ample supply of 120-volt a-c outlets. This can be provided by wall outlets and particularly outlets attached to drop-down cords from the ceiling to allow maximum flexibility. The provision of 3-phase 240-volt power outlets is equally important in accommodating heavy equipment.

In a typical instrument room or counting room, it is highly advisable to equip the power supply with a voltage stabilizer and to isolate individual circuits so that cross interference of electronic instruments can be avoided. Provision in the nature of blank conduits should be made to accommodate present and future radiation monitoring devices. An intercommunications system actuated by voice or foot control is of some importance in the high-level laboratories.

Lighting should be selected with regard to ease of housekeeping and the undesirable interference of fluorescent light with liquid scintillation counting. Battery-powered emergency lights are necessary provisions for inside rooms that rely extensively on artificial lighting. Fire detection systems should be installed in each of the laboratories with signals transmitted directly to the fire station so that extensive fire damage can be avoided. The solvent storage room should, of course, be equipped with an automatic fire extinguishing system. Whenever possible, extra blank conduits should be provided, particularly in the shielded area, to permit ready accommodation of future projects.

4. Sewage disposal

Several important factors must be considered in designing the sewage system in a radioisotope laboratory. It is advisable to *segregate sewage systems* under the categories of storm water, toilet disposal, low-level radioactive waste, and high-level radioactive waste. Whenever possible, it is preferable to dispose of liquid radioactive waste of higher levels in isolated containers. The high-level sewage disposal system is installed primarily to handle area contamination that cannot be readily controlled. This includes accidental spills and, more importantly, radioisotope studies with large animals.

A *retention system* (one or more tanks of 5000-gal capacity) may be installed to permit temporary holding of radioactive waste in the high-level sewage system. Contents in the retention tank can be either transferred to a waste liquid transporting truck for permanent disposal, or allowed to decay in the case of short half-life isotopes.

The *low-level sewage disposal system* is designed to accommodate laboratory waste water from low-level radioisotope laboratories. Since the waste is discharged directly into the public sewage, an upper limit of radioactivity that can be disposed in each laboratory over a given period should be defined. To insure absolute control of hazards, it is advisable to install a liquid monitoring system at the downstream end of the low-level sewage line; provisions should be made to connect the low-level sewage line to the retention tank in event of a major accidental spill. Most of the commercially available liquid monitors are capable of detecting gamma or high-energy beta emitters. It may be desirable to install a liquid scintillation monitor in case tritium is used extensively in the laboratory.

Glass appears to be the most desirable material for *sewage piping* because it is resistant to chemicals and makes stoppage in drains visible. It is important that the sewage line in the laboratory and in the utility shaft should be exposed as much as possible to facilitate repair and replacement. The main sewage line should be routed to the outside of the building as directly as possible to minimize length of concealed sections of the line.

Floor drains should be limited as much as possible. They should be installed only in the areas where complete washdown of rooms is essential to the operations. Even then, it may be desirable to cap floor drains to minimize cross-contamination of rooms.

Master traps can be used to accommodate a number of sinks and floor drains. Such an arrangement avoids the lodging of radioactive materials in individual sink drains and prevents cross-contamination of areas through an untrapped draining system.

5. Radioactive Waste Disposal

The basic principles underlying disposal of radioactive waste call for isolation or dilution; hence a *waste disposal* room should be established as a separate unit in a radioisotope laboratory. The room should be designed to store high levels of solid or liquid radioactive waste before its transfer to a permanent disposal site. It may also be desirable to install a commercial-scale garbage disposal unit so that low-level solid wastes can be pulverized and disposed of via the sewage system. It is also important to have ample cold storage facilities to store radioactive biological specimens, such as animal carcasses. Adequate lifting devices should be provided in this room to permit ready transfer of shielded waste to the exterior of the building. Incineration of low-level waste containing ^{14}C or ^{3}H is a convenient means of disposal, although the operation is best carried out in remote areas.

6. Laboratory Fixtures

The arrangement of laboratory fixtures in a radioisotope laboratory should take into consideration ventilation requirements, accessibility of utilities, and flexibility of room usage. Standardization of fixture arrangement in a modular sense is highly advisable with respect to both program accommodations and economy in cost.

Figure 13-1 gives a typical arrangement in a *modular radioisotope laboratory* for low-level studies; Figure 13-2 shows an isometric view of one-half of the modular laboratory. Two radiochemical hoods, 10 in.

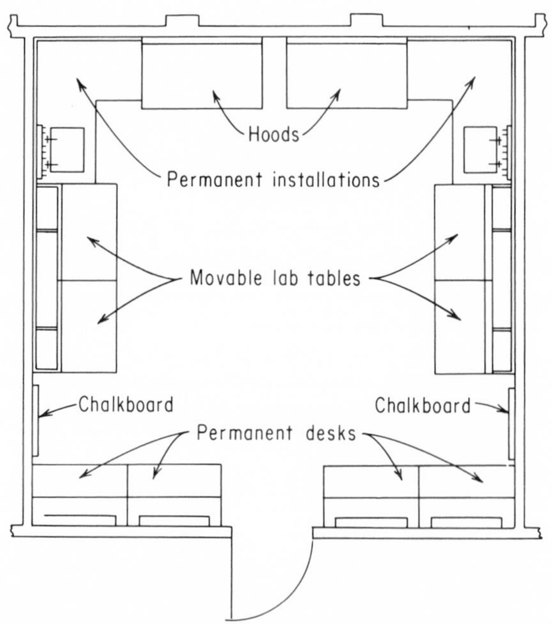

Figure 13-1. Floor plan for typical modular radioisotope laboratory for low-level studies.

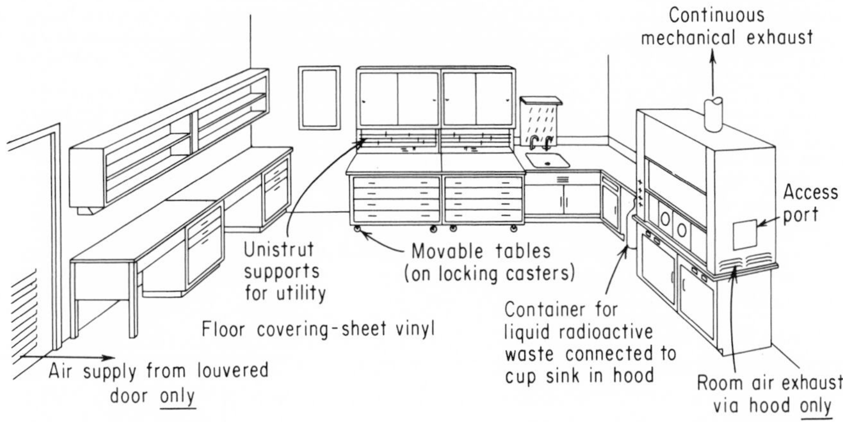

Figure 13-2. Isometric view of typical modular radioisotope laboratory for low level studies.

apart, are housed along the middle section of the wall next to the utility shaft. This location provides for the best air flow pattern. The ventilation system for this room should be so designed that the air supply is provided from a louvered door and the exhaust routed exclusively by way of the hoods. Permanent benches with a sink are located alongside each of the hoods. Utilities to the permanent benches can readily be provided from the utility shaft. The utilities to accommodate other portions of the room are available, exposed on unistrut supports attached to walls and floor. Such an arrangement makes available all utility outlets, including cup sinks, on the utility shelf attached to the wall. Equally important, utility accommodations of this type permit the use of movable benches.

In the arrangement depicted (Figure 13-1), four 4-ft *movable benches* are provided in the room. Each of these benches is equipped with an electric strip outlet underneath the edge of the bench top. The strip can be connected to either the wall outlet or the ceiling drop-cord outlets. Maximum flexibility in room usage is offered by this arrangement, since in a radioisotope laboratory it is often desirable to have ample space next to a laboratory bench to accommodate gas tanks, rack-mounted instruments, and portable vacuum benches. The movable benches can be used as single or double wall benches or as island benches.

Four *desks* are located on the side of the laboratory next to the corridor. Each is equipped with electric strip outlets so that it can be connected to a permanent outlet. The desk is designed to be used, as either an office desk or an instrument table.

Because steel is easily decontaminated, it is the preferred *material for construction* of laboratory benches or instrument desks. Extensive tests on many types of available materials have led to the designation of stainless steel as the best bench top material because it has excellent resistance to chemical agents and can easily be decontaminated in the event of minor spills. The laboratory floor should be covered with sheet vinyl to facilitate decontamination operations.

One or more laboratories should be designed to accommodate radioisotope work at higher levels. This is particularly important if one desires to carry out Wilzbach operations for labeling compounds with tritium. It is preferred that the *high-level laboratory* be segregated from low-level rooms by means of an air lock system to permit better control of air contamination. In addition to regular radiochemical hoods, the high-level laboratory should be equipped with a walk-in hood large enough to accommodate a portable vacuum bench and pertinent laboratory equipment. Air movement in this laboratory should be approximately 3000 cu ft per min, and all exhausts must pass through absolute filters. It is desirable to extend the exhaust stack from the high-level laboratory at least 10 ft above any nearby buildings. This will provide adequate air dilution in the event of an accident involving the release of curie amounts of tritium gas or other radioactive compounds that cannot be removed by the filter. It is important to provide this laboratory with an intercommunications system so that good contact with other personnel in the area can be readily maintained.

7. Radiochemical Hoods

The plan of the modular laboratory (Figure 13-2) shows a typical radiochemical hood which can be used for low- or high-level radiochemical work. The hood must be designed as a constant-flow type, since ventilation of the room relies exclusively on the continuous hood exhaust. When the front opening of the hood is closed, the bypass sash should automatically open to allow the passage of a constant amount of air through the hood. The hood is constructed of steel with the inside wall lined with transite and the bench tops covered with stainless steel. Coating the transite walls with strippable paint permits ready decontamination from time to time. Controls of all utility outlets in the hood are mounted on one side of the front frame with piping exposed. This facilitates repair and replacement of the utility system. A radiochemical hood of this type has the following unique features:

(1) The front window can be readily replaced with a panel equipped to accommodate a pair of *gloves*. This is essential if one desires to have absolute prevention of air contamination through back flow of the hood atmosphere, in more hazardous operations.

(2) The hood is equipped with *two cup sinks*: one is of the ordinary laboratory type, the other, mounted flush with the bench top, is specially

designed to permit the transfer of liquid radioactive waste directly into a carboy stored underneath the adjacent bench.

(3) A small *access port* on one side of the hood wall (see Figure 13-2) to permit direct transfer of solid radioactive waste into a storage container housed in the space between the two adjacent hoods (Figure 13-1).

The *air movement* through the depicted radiochemical hood is 125 linear ft per min across each front foot. Since the hood is 5 ft long, the total air flow through the hood is approximately 625 cu ft per min. The absolute filter for each of the hoods is housed in the utility shaft with the blower housed in the mechanical space in the ceiling of the shaft immediately before the exhaust stack.

It should be emphasized that this chapter represents merely an attempt to bring out important elements in the design of a radioisotope laboratory. No universal recommendations are intended, since it is impossible to set forth criteria to suit individual tastes and individual purposes.

BIBLIOGRAPHY

1. Branson, Byron M., et al. 1959. Assembly and operation of a low-level counting facility. J. Am. Water Works Assoc. 51:438–448.

2. Design and construction of laboratory buildings. 1962. Anal. Chem. 34(10):25A–46A.

3. Design and construction of radiochemical laboratories. 1951. A selected list of unclassified references. U.S. Atomic Energy Commission. TID-3013. 5 p.

4. Garden, Nelson B. 1949. Semihot laboratories. Ind. Eng. Chem. 41:237–238.

5. Grinberg, B., and Y. LeGallic. 1961. Caractéristiques fondamentales d'un laboratoire de mesure de très faibles activités. Intern. J. Appl. Radiation Isotopes 12:104–117.

6. Levy, Henri A. 1949. Remodeling a laboratory for radiochemical instruction or research. Ind. Eng. Chem. 41:248–250.

7. Mackintosh, A. D. 1949. The architectural approach to radiochemical laboratory design. U.S. Atomic Energy Commission. AECU-210; ORNL-335. 31 p.

8. Norris, William P. 1949. Radiobiochemical laboratories. Ind. Eng. Chem. 41:231–232.

9. Rice, C. N. 1949. Laboratory for preparation and use of radioactive organic compounds. Ind. Eng. Chem. 41:244–248.

10. Swartout, J. A. 1949. Research with low levels of radioactivity. Ind. Eng. Chem. 41:233–236.

11. Tompkins, Paul C. 1949. A radioisotope building. Ind. Eng. Chem. 41:239–244.

12. Tompkins, Paul C., and Henri A. Levy. 1949. Impact of radioactivity on chemical laboratory techniques and design. Ind. Eng. Chem. 41:228–231.

13. Ward, Donald R. 1962. Low level radioisotope laboratories. *In* Laboratory planning for chemistry and chemical engineering. Reinhold, New York. p. 156–170.

14. Webster, S. H., E. J. Liljegren, and C. C. Powell. 1952. Hood for radioactivity work. Nucleonics 10(4):65–67.

PART TWO

Basic Experiments in the Measurement of Radioactivity

Operation and Characteristics of a Geiger-Mueller Counter

Chapter 4 presented a detailed discussion on the nature and construction of Geiger-Mueller (G-M) detectors. There we saw that they are ionization chambers operated at a potential high enough to give the maximum usable gas amplification for an ionizing event within them. G-M tubes are perhaps the most widely used detectors for radioactivity determinations because of their simplicity and utility. The following experiment is designed to serve as an introduction to some of the component functions and operating characteristics of an entire G-M counting assembly.

A. COMPONENT FUNCTIONS OF A GEIGER-MUELLER COUNTER ASSEMBLY

1. Power Supply

This unit provides the necessary d-c potential across the electrodes of the G-M detector so that gas amplification through secondary ionization can be facilitated and the electrons formed therefrom can be readily collected on the anode. The voltage provided ranges from 500–5000 volts with different models, but 1500 volts is normally sufficient to operate most G-M detectors. A high degree of stability in the power supply is not necessary for G-M detectors, since minor voltage fluctuations do not bring about serious changes in the count rate observed within the operating plateau. A high-voltage transformer, a rectifier, and a voltage regulator comprise this component.

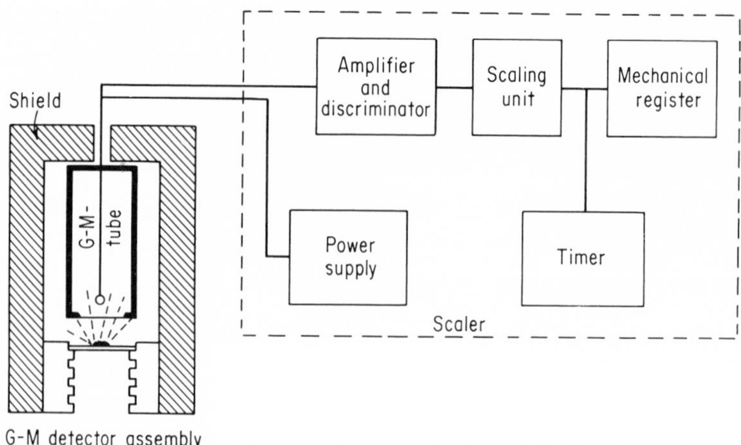

Figure I-1. Block diagram of a Geiger-Mueller counter assembly.

2. G-M Detector Assembly

The term *detector* is used to designate the G-M tube; *counter* applies to the entire counting assembly. The detector itself is usually surrounded by a lead shield to reduce interference derived from background radiation. In order to maintain a defined sample-to-detector geometry, a rigid sample-holding device, with several shelves, is included in the assembly.

3. Amplifier and Discriminator

Since the pulses from the G-M detector are of moderate size (several volts), extensive amplification is not required. Consequently, a more important function of the *amplifier* is shaping the pulses into a form more suitable for actuating the counting device. There is no need for a high degree of linearity in the amplifier used in a G-M counting assembly, since preservation of relative pulse height is not necessary. Pulses of all sizes from the G-M detector after amplification are passed to the *discriminator*, or trigger circuit. The discriminator has two functions: (1) it establishes a pulse-height threshold, permitting discrimination against noise pulses; (2) it produces a standardized pulse to actuate the scaling unit. Amplifier and trigger circuits in past years have commonly utilized vacuum tubes, which increased the bulk of these components. Recent use of transistorized circuits has allowed a very great reduction in component volume.

4. Scaling Unit

With a moderate amount of radioactivity in a given sample, the pulse rate from a G-M detector will be too high to be handled by an ordinary mechanical register. Consequently, scaling stages are interposed to group the pulses before actuation of the mechanical register. Scaling can be done by means of scale-of-2 (binary) or scale-of-10 (decade) circuits, which are commonly used in multiples. As an example, two decade scales in a series would feed only 1 pulse to the register for each 100 incoming pulses to the scaler. In this case, the true number of pulses detected would be found by multiplying the register reading by 100 and adding the interpolation indicated by the scaler lights. Most recent scalers eliminate the use of a register by employing scaling units based on cold cathode decades. These incorporate a scale-of-10 in one tube and can be used in multiples of five or six for direct reading of the total count from a sample. Since the resolving time of the G-M detector is rather long, a rapidly responding ("fast") scaler is less essential with it than with proportional and scintillation detectors.

5. Mechanical Register

As previously indicated, the mechanical register displays some multiple of the pulse count—usually 64×, 256×, 100×, or 1000×. If an improper scaling factor is used, this unit can be overwhelmed when the pulse rate is high, resulting in a significant loss of counting events. Many commercially available G-M counters include a presetting arrangement, by which the counting process will be terminated when a preset count is reached. With this arrangement, the standard deviation of all counting operations associated with a given experiment can be readily defined.

6. Timer

The accurate timing of counting duration is essential in ascertaining a given counting rate. Most commonly, these timing units are operated by a synchronous motor drive directly controlled by the frequency of the alternating current. More elaborate models also include a presetting device, whereby the counting process can be stopped after a predetermined time. This can also be accomplished by using a cheap external timer.

7. G-M Counting Assembly

In the commercially available instruments, power supply, amplifier, discriminator, scaling units, register, and often the timer are commonly grouped together in a single housing, for which the extended term *scaler* is used. This term is not to be confused with the scaling circuits alone, which are only a part of the scaler. The scaler, used in conjunction with a G-M detector in a lead shield and sample support, constitutes a G-M counting assembly, or simply a G-M counter.

B. OPERATION OF A GEIGER-MUELLER COUNTER

1. General Instructions

Although certain fundamental steps apply to the operation of all G-M counters, each model has distinctive individual features. Consequently, before operating a given counter, read through the manual of instructions furnished by the manufacturer.

It will be recalled that G-M tubes can be permanently damaged by the use of excessive d-c potentials (see Chapter 4). *Always* be certain that the high-voltage control is turned off, or as far down as possible, *before* turning on the scaler. This is one of the necessary precautions to be observed when operating the G-M counter.

The *sample holder* under the G-M tube usually has several shelf positions on which the radioactive samples may be placed for counting. These shelf positions, therefore, define the geometry of sample-to-detector, which is essential in obtaining reproducible and comparable results. Be careful to avoid contact between the counting sample and the detector window, both because the window may become contaminated in this way, and because the thin windows are extremely fragile.

2. G-M Plateau and Operating Potential

In order to determine the effect of applied potential on the behavior of a G-M detector, insert a prepared radioactive sample (for example, ^{14}C or Radium DEF) into a defined geometrical position in the sample support. A few minutes after the counter circuits have been turned on, move the "count" switch to "on" and slowly increase the potential in the detector by adjusting the high-voltage control. When the potential reaches a certain level, pulses from the detector begin to be registered in the scaling circuits. Record this potential as the "starting potential" and collect 3000 and 5000 counts at this setting, noting the counting time. Repeat this procedure at successive 50-volt intervals. The count rate will rise rapidly, then level off when the G-M plateau is reached. The plateau should extend approximately 300 volts followed by a sharp rise. Do not attempt to observe this rise since, at that stage, continuous discharge occurs (see Chapter 4) and the G-M detector can be permanently damaged.

Prepare a table indicating (1) potential applied to tube, (2) total number of counts, (3) counting time, (4) computed counts per minute (cpm). From this information plot a graph with counts per minute as the ordinate and detector voltage as abscissa (see Chapter 4). The optimal operating voltage is usually chosen as 75–100 volts above the beginning, or threshold, of the plateau. Continued use of higher potentials may shorten the detector tube life somewhat. An operating voltage for each G-M tube is generally recommended by the manufacturer. (How does your determined value compare with the manufacturer's?) As G-M tubes age the plateau becomes altered. Hence the slope of the plateau should be checked at regular intervals by a new determination of the plateau. When the slope of the plateau varies more than 20 per cent over a 100-volt span, the detector should be replaced.

3. Background

The background radiation level should now be determined with the G-M tube at the correct operating voltage. Use a counting duration of at least 10 min. It should be realized that the standard deviation for a count rate determination decreases with the number of counts accumulated (see Chapter 9). With low background counting rates, it is not feasible, during the limited laboratory period, to collect sufficient counts so that the relative standard deviation of the background matches that associated with the counting of a radioactive sample. In true determinations, however, the counting time of the background must be determined on the same statistical basis as that used for the sample.

Much of the background radiation comes inescapably from natural radioactive materials and cosmic ray effects, but radioactive contamination of the laboratory or inadvertent placement of radioactive samples in the vicinity of the counter can and should be scupulously avoided.

Make background determinations each time a group of radioactive samples is to be counted, or at least daily. The background count rate must then be subtracted from each sample count rate to arrive at the count rate due to the sample alone. If an unusually high background is encountered on some occasion, its cause should be sought immediately.

4. Counter Resolving Time—Coincidence Loss

In Chapter 4 it was indicated that, following an ionization ıncident in a G-M detector, an avalanche of electrons rushes to the anode wire. This initiates a negative pulse in the scaler circuit. The movement of positive ions to the cathode wall is much slower. During the brief interval while these events are occurring, the detector is either unresponsive (dead time) or too weakly responsive to produce a pulse exceeding the discriminator threshold (recovery time). This total interval during which succeeding ionization events are not registered is known as the *resolving time* of the detector. At higher count rates, this factor may lead to an observed count rate considerably less than the true rate. The difference between these two values is the *coincidence loss.*

The resolving time of a G-M detector can be observed directly by means of an oscilloscope. It can also be determined by means of the *paired source method.* To this end, cut a flat metal planchet into two equal halves. Number them at the outer edge #1 and #2 respectively (see Figure I-2). Toward the center of each, place roughly equal amounts of a suitable radioactive sample. Aqueous solutions of $NaH_2{}^{32}PO_4$ or $^{60}CoCl_2$, or powdered U_3O_8 are suggested. Each should give a count rate of 7000 to 10,000 cpm on the top shelf of the sample support.

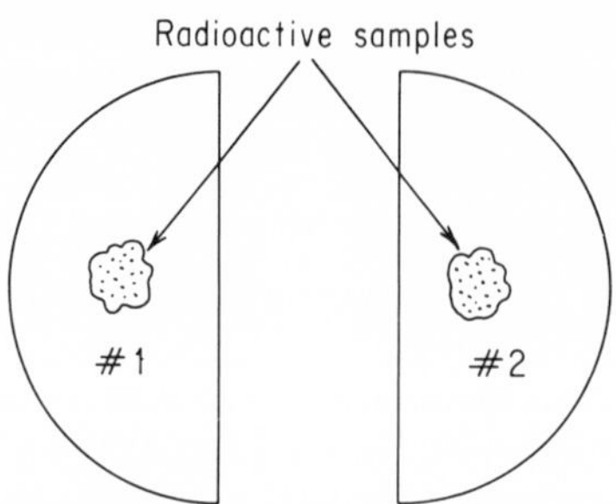

Figure I-2. Paired sources for resolving time determination.

Insert the two sources into the appropriate shelf of the sample support without any overlapping of the two halves. Now count the two samples ($m_{1,2}$) for 1 min, and record the result. Carefully remove sample #2 without disturbing #1. Count sample #1 (m_1) for 1 min and record count rate. Replace sample #2 (m_2) in its original position and remove sample #1. Again determine the count rate for 1 min. Finally, remove both samples from the vicinity of the counter and count the background (m_b) for at least 10 min. Repeat each counting three times. Reduce all the averaged data to counts per minute and subtract the background from the sample count rates. Calculate the approximate resolving time (τ) by means of the following equation (see Chapter 9 for derivation):

$$\tau = \frac{m_1 + m_2 - m_{1,2} - m_b}{m_{1,2}^2 - m_1^2 - m_2^2} \tag{I-1}$$

Since the count rate was expressed in minutes, the value of τ derived will be in minutes and will be quite small. This value is more commonly given in microseconds (μsec) for comparison of the resolving times of different detectors.

The true count rate of a sample may be determined, when the resolving time is known, by the equation:

$$n = \frac{m}{1 - m\tau} \tag{I-2}$$

where n = true count rate/min, m = observed count rate/min, and τ = resolving time in minutes. A curve can be constructed for various n/m ratios with a given counter. Coincidence loss with G-M detectors begins to be significant over 3000 cpm and becomes considerable at count rates approaching 10,000 cpm. Hence, sample counting rates should be kept below 3000 cpm to avoid the necessity of corrections for coincidence loss.

If the count rate is too high on the top shelf of the sample support, the counting rate can be reduced by moving the sample to a lower shelf position. Needless to say, such action drastically alters the sample-to-detector geometry.

5. Shelf Ratio and Geometry

A radioactive sample can be centered under the G-M tube window by correct positioning on the sample support. Its distance from the detector window will vary, however, depending on which shelf is used. Two or more such shelf positions are normally available in the sample holder. Any comparison of count rates for samples counted on different shelves must take into account the inverse square relation between count rate and distance from the detector referred to under "Counter Resolving Time." For the purpose of such comparisons it is valuable to find the ratio of count rates for the various shelves (shelf ratio). Comparisons can be made only between samples of the same isotope and under the same sample conditions.

Using the radioactive sample from Section 2, determine the net count rate on each of the shelves provided in the sample holder. Then arbitrarily assign the top shelf position a value of 1.0 and calculate the shelf ratios for the other shelves by dividing the top shelf count rate into every other value successively. This shelf ratio will then indicate clearly the fraction of counts observed on the given shelf compared to what would be observed on the top shelf position. Note that these values apply only to the isotope and detector employed. A detector with a thicker window would, of course, transmit less radiation. Likewise, an isotope emitting lower energy radiation would suffer greater air absorption.

SUMMARY

In this experiment several important operational characteristics of the G-M counter have been examined. To operate the counter correctly, the position of the G-M plateau with respect to voltage applied to the detector tube must first be found. The background radiation level should always be determined and subtracted from the gross sample count rate. The relatively long resolving time of the G-M counter necessitates keeping count rates fairly low and/or making corrections for coincidence loss. If shelf ratios are calculated, count rates for samples of the same type counted on different shelf positions may be compared.

Operation and Characteristics of a Proportional Counter

Various types of proportional detectors were discussed in Chapter 4. It will be recalled that they too are ionization-type detectors that are operated within a potential range where moderate gas amplification occurs. A distinctive feature of this level of gas amplification is that proportionality is maintained between the size of the output pulse from the detector and the magnitude of the initial ionization within it. The following experiment is designed to serve as an introduction to some of the component functions and operating characteristics of an entire proportional counter assembly.

A. FUNCTIONS OF THE COMPONENTS OF A PROPORTIONAL COUNTING ASSEMBLY

1. Power Supply

The d-c potential needed across the proportional chamber electrodes to facilitate gas amplification varies widely with the type of chamber and the composition and pressure of the counter atmosphere. Normally a power supply that can be regulated up to at least 2500 volts is adequate, but in some counting assemblies 5000 volts may be required. The voltage output must be reasonably stable for proportional counting, since the gas amplification factor is heavily dependent on the potential gradient across the electrodes within the chamber. G-M counters require a stability of power supply of only about $\pm$ 1 per cent, but the proportional counter requires better than $\pm$ 0.1 per cent.

2. Proportional Detector Assembly

Proportional detectors may take various forms. Since this type of detector is generally used for the detection of alpha particles, one finds they are commonly of the windowless flow chamber variety. To avoid surface charge of the sample, some manufacturers recommend thin-window varieties with window thickness as low as 0.15 mg/cm^2. The following discussion pertains particularly to the windowless type of detector.

In the windowless flow counter, the radioactive sample is placed inside the counting chamber and exposed to the counting atmosphere directly, without a window barrier intervening. The counting gas mixture, usually methane or an argon-methane mixture (90–10 $^v/_v$), passes through the

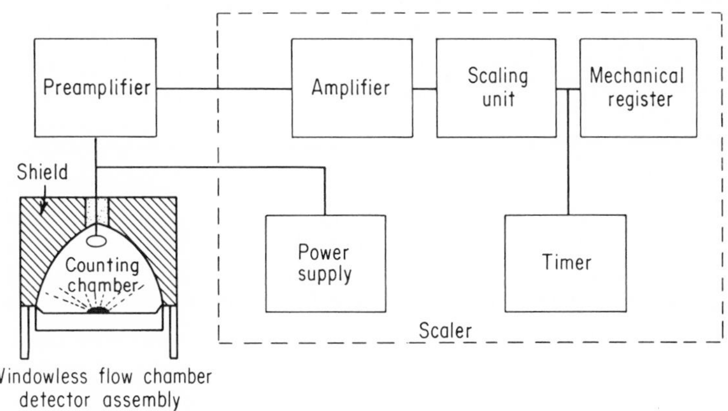

Figure II-1. Block diagram of a proportional counter assembly.

chamber continuously during the counting operation. When a new sample is inserted, air that has been unavoidably introduced must be "purged" from the chamber atmosphere by a brief increase in the flow rate of the counting gas.

The counting chamber is commonly hemispherical in shape with a thin anode loop suspended from the top. The chamber wall serves as the cathode. The sample-holding planchet itself acts as the lower side of the chamber. The planchet is introduced and held firmly in place by means of a movable piston to give a defined geometrical relationship of sample-to-chamber. The geometry of sample-to-chamber is close to a solid angle of 2π, which provides good detection efficiency. Lead shielding is normally used to reduce the interference of background radiation.

3. Preamplifier

The output signal from a proportional detector will seldom exceed 50 mv. Thus, in situations where the pulses from the detector must pass to the scaler through cables of even a few feet in length, a preamplifier is necessary. This is not usually the case where the detector is an integral part of the scaler itself.

4. Amplifier

Since the gas amplification factor is considerably lower in the proportional region than that in the Geiger region, a high gain amplifier is usually required. This amplifier must be highly stable. In addition, the pulse sizes initiated by different ionizing particles vary considerably. Consequently this component must be able to amplify a wide range of pulses linearly without distortion. By contrast, all pulses from the G-M detector tube are of nearly equal size, so that amplifier linearity is not so crucial there.

5. Scaling Unit

What has been previously said concerning scaling units in G-M counters applies here as well. Whereas the dead time of a G-M detector is relatively long (up to several hundred microseconds), the proportional detector generally has a very short dead time (as low as a few microseconds). Consequently, a compatibly fast scaling unit is essential in order to take advantage of this feature.

6. Mechanical Register and Timer

These are usually no different from the same components described for G-M counters in Experiment I.

B. OPERATION OF THE PROPORTIONAL COUNTING ASSEMBLY

Always read the instruction manual furnished with a particular counting assembly thoroughly before attempting to operate the counter. For the windowless flow counter, it is especially important to become familiar with the technique of introducing a sample into the counting chamber and controlling the gas flow.

1. Proportional Plateaus and Optimal Operating Potentials

Make sure that the high-voltage control is turned as low as possible. Then turn the instrument "on" and wait a few minutes before proceeding. The input sensitivity, if adjustable, is usually set quite low (at about 1 mv). This is in marked contrast to the sensitivity normally used with G-M counters (0.25 volt).

Insert into the counting chamber a prepared sample which emits both alpha and beta particles. Often these are furnished with the instrument. Otherwise a thorium or a uranium salt, or a radium DEF preparation is suggested for this purpose.

Purge the counting chamber with the counting gas for about 1–2 min. Then reduce the gas flow to the continuous rate specified by the manufacturer, usually one bubble per second through the bubbler.

Now slowly raise the potential across the detector electrodes to the point where pulses begin to be registered (about 700 volts), and collect at least 3000 to 5000 counts at this potential setting. If counting does not begin at about the voltage specified, the chamber may have been incompletely purged. Repeat this procedure at 50-volt intervals up to the point at which the count rate begins an abrupt rise from the second (beta) plateau (usually about 2000 volts).

Record the results in tabular form and plot a graph of applied potential versus computed counts per minute (cpm). This should result in a curve with two plateaus. The plateau at lower potential (*alpha plateau*) reflects the counting rate of the alpha components of the sample; that at the higher potential (*beta plateau*) includes both the alpha and beta counting rates. [See Chapter 4 (p. 80–81) for details on this relationship.]

The optimum operating voltages are usually determined as the centers of the respective plateaus. Determine and record this point for each plateau. Routine checks of this value should be made with a suitable standard from time to time.

2. Differential Counting of Alpha versus Beta Particles

Note that for mixed alpha-beta samples the pulses resulting from beta particles cannot be directly counted apart from those resulting from the alpha component. The count rate at the alpha plateau can, however, be subtracted from the rate on the beta plateau to find approximately the net beta count rate if desired. In addition, where the beta particle energy is sufficiently high, a thin absorber placed over the sample allows nearly all the beta particles to pass through, while completely absorbing the alpha radiation. Alpha particles, on the contrary, can be counted in the presence of beta emission (and gamma, too), by operating the detector at the alpha plateau. This feature is one of the great advantages of the proportional counter over the G-M counter. (See the discussion of gas amplification in Chapter 4 for further explanation.)

3. Counter Resolving Time

Paired radioactive samples, such as those used to determine counter resolving time with the G-M counter but with count rates of 50,000 to 100,000 cpm each, should now be used for the same purpose with the proportional counter. Operating on the beta plateau, follow the instructions given for the determination of resolving time with the G-M counter. Record data and calculate resolving time (τ) using Equation I-1. (How do the resolving times of G-M and proportional counters compare?)

4. Background

An important additional feature of the proportional counter is the magnitude of the *background radiation level.* On the alpha plateau the background may be as low as 1 cpm, and comes almost entirely from chamber contamination or natural radioactivity in the detector materials. (Why?) On the beta plateau, the background may be about 50 cpm, and is mainly from external sources, as with the G-M counter. Determine the background rate for a reasonable period of time (at least 10 min) on each plateau and compare the results. With a windowless detector there is a great hazard of contaminating the counting chamber itself by fine dust or vapors from radioactive samples. Whether a windowless counter is of the proportional or the G-M type, it is important to check the background level frequently. Decontamination of the counting chamber will be necessary if the background level is permanently elevated.

C. SUMMARY

Three salient operating characteristics of the proportional counter have been explored in this experiment. The double plateau (alpha and beta) allows the discrimination of particle type with a mixed alpha-beta emitting sample. The much shorter resolving time makes it possible to accommodate high counting rates (up to 100,000 cpm) without significant coincidence loss. Finally, the very low background radiation level on the alpha plateau makes possible the counting of very low-activity alpha samples.

EXPERIMENT III

Operation and Characteristics of a Solid (External-Sample) Scintillation Counter

The detection of an external source of radiation by means of a scintillation crystal coupled to a photomultiplier tube has been described in Chapter 5. This method of detection differs sharply from that of the ionization-type detectors (G-M, proportional, and the like). It depends on the interaction of radiation with a crystal fluor to emit a number of photons proportional to the radiation energy dissipated. These photons are converted to photoelectrons by the photocathode of the adjacent photomultiplier, and the photoelectrons are then greatly amplified through a dynode chain to produce a pulse. As with the other counting assemblies, a scaler is attached to record the detector pulses. A wide variety of solid scintillation counting assemblies is at present commercially available. The experiment that follows will introduce the reader to a typical counting assembly.

A. FUNCTIONS OF THE COMPONENTS OF A SOLID SCINTILLATION COUNTER ASSEMBLY

1. Power Supply

The d-c potential supplied to the scintillation detector plays a different role than it does in G-M and proportional detectors. Here it is used to impress a stepwise increase of potential on the successive dynodes of the photomultiplier. Because this potential gradient in the photomultiplier so

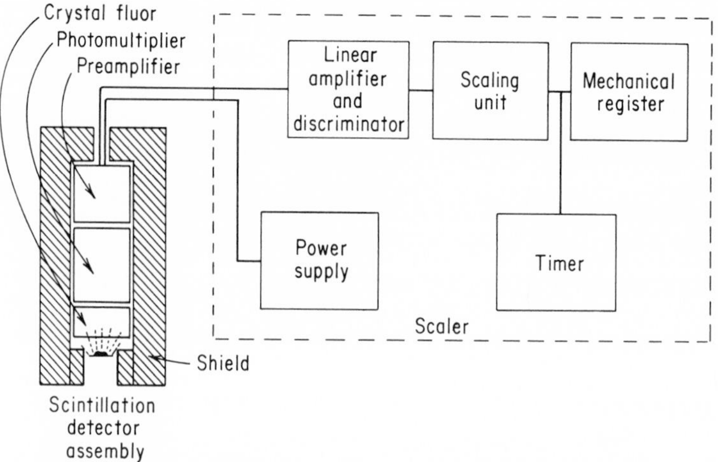

Figure III-1. Block diagram of an external-sample scintillation counter assembly.

directly affects the degree of amplification occurring, it is essential that the power supply be both highly stable and well regulated. This point is particularly crucial if pulse height analysis is to be attempted, in which case drift of less than 0.1 per cent per day is desirable. It is usually sufficient to employ a power supply with an output potential adjustable up to 3000 volts to operate most photomultipliers.

2. Scintillation Detector Assembly

The lead shielding and sample support used are normally similar to those found in G-M detector assemblies. Owing to the greater efficiency of the scintillation process for detecting gamma rays, and thus also the cosmic ray background radiation, lead shielding is more essential here.

The detector itself is usually a *solid crystal fluor*, most commonly of sodium iodide (thallium activated), 1 in. to 3 in. in thickness, encased in a light-tight jacket. In it, some of the energy dissipated by traversing radiation is transformed into photons of visible light. The photons pass through the rear transparent window of the crystal housing and the optical coupling layer into the photomultiplier tube. This tube contains a photocathode surface where the impinging photons cause photoelectrons to be ejected. In turn, these photoelectrons are electrostatically attracted through the series of dynodes and multiplied by secondary electron emission at each successive dynode in the photomultiplier, so that a sharp pulse results at the collecting anode of the tube. The scintillation crystal and photomultiplier tube must be sealed in a light-tight case and the tube further needs to be surrounded by a shield of Mu metal to avoid disturbance by external magnetic fields. (Consult Chapter 5 for further details of the scintillation process.)

For improved detection efficiency, a well scintillation crystal (usually 3 in. in thickness) may be employed (see p. 97). *Well detectors*, as they are called, are particularly suited for assay of liquid samples containing gamma emitters. (Experiments C and D, Part Three, illustrate such a use.) Scintillation well detectors are also available commercially with automatic sample-changing equipment.

A *preamplifier* (of the "cathode follower type") is commonly attached directly to the photomultiplier tube base. This serves the dual purpose of "shaping" pulses and amplifying them sufficiently to reach the scaler through the connecting cable. The gain setting of this preamplifier is adjustable in some models.

3. Linear Amplifier and Discriminators

These two components are optional. They are necessary when pulse height analysis is being carried out with the scintillation counter. The output pulse from the preamplifier is otherwise sufficient to actuate the scaler directly. The amplifier must be linear, in that it preserves the original relative pulse heights although amplifying them. Furthermore, the amplifier must be capable of handling a wide range of pulse heights. All these requisites, coupled with a necessarily high degree of stability, make this a component to be selected with care.

Discriminator circuits are used to reject certain pulse heights coming from the preamplifier. In *integral discrimination* all pulse heights below a selected level ("low gate") are rejected and only those above the discriminator setting pass on to the scaler. This allows low photomultiplier "noise" pulses to be rejected in favor of the larger pulse heights resulting from sample radiation. This discriminator level may be varied as the occasion demands.

In *differential discrimination* a *pulse height analyzer* is required. This component consists of two variable discriminators which pass on to the scaler only those pulses whose heights lie between their settings. This interval between the upper and lower discriminators is called the *window*, or *gate*. With the window-width (channel) kept constant while the two discriminators move across the voltage range of pulses from the preamplifier, the shape of the spectrum can be determined. A characteristic spectrum is a distinctive property of each specific radioisotope and is useful for identifying it in mixed samples. An additional advantage of using differential discrimination is that the window may be set to "straddle" the photopeak in the sample gamma spectrum (see Figure 5-2), thus greatly improving the sample-to-background counting rate.

Spectrum determination of this type is known as *scintillation spectrometry*. Gamma ray spectrometry using a NaI(Tl) crystal is the most widespread application, but spectra can be roughly determined for many beta emitters using organic scintillation crystals, such as anthracene. Gamma ray spectrometers find widespread use in clinical studies, such as those involving ^{131}I uptake by the thyroid gland. For more rapid determination of the spectrum without manually adjusting the two discriminators over its extent, *multichannel analyzers* are available. These essentially sort out and record the pulses of varying heights into a series of channels simultaneously. (For more detailed discussion, see the pertinent references at the end of Chapter 5.)

4. Scaling Unit, Mechanical Register, and Timer

These components are no different from those described for G-M and proportional counters and are commonly grouped together with the power supply as a *scaler*. Note that, as in the case of the proportional counter, a high scaling factor is necessary to take advantage of the very short resolving time of the scintillation detector.

B. OPERATION OF A SOLID (EXTERNAL-SAMPLE) SCINTILLATION COUNTING ASSEMBLY

1. General Instructions

Here again, as with the other counting assemblies previously described, it is important to become familiar with the manufacturer's specific operating instructions before attempting to use the counter.

Be particularly careful in handling the scintillation crystal and photomultiplier tube, if these are not already mounted in a fixed position. Both are extremely fragile and quite costly to replace. Photomultiplier tubes with focusing-type dynodes can be damaged by even moderate jarring. The photocathode in the photomultiplier is extremely light-sensitive and must never be exposed to normal room light with high potential applied to the tube or irreparable damage will occur. In addition, excessive d-c potentials applied to the tube can also produce permanent damage.

2. Scintillation Plateau Curves and Operating Voltages

Selecting optimal operating conditions for the scintillation counter is more complex than for the G-M counter. Unlike the situation with G-M counters, as the potential applied to the photomultiplier tube is increased, the background and "noise" count rates increase sharply. At very high potentials, they may even exceed the sample count rate. Furthermore, adjustments of the amplifier gain setting will lead to considerable alteration in the plateau characteristics of a counter. These characteristics also vary with different radioisotopes. Thus, there is not a "best" operating potential for all applications of the scintillation counter.

If a pulse discriminator is available with the detector assembly, the setting of the discriminator (windows or gates) introduces another consideration. Since gamma emission is discrete in energy levels, it is possible to set the window or gate at the site of the peak of the gamma spectrum (differential counting). Such action will result in good detection efficiency of the gamma rays, while enjoying low background counting rates (see p. 95). The site of the window setting is naturally dependent on the nature of the gamma emitter and can be determined by crude scanning of the entire gamma spectrum. On the other hand, it is also possible to leave the gate open (integral counting), that is, cover nearly the entire pulse range, so long as the low-level discriminator is set to prevent undesirable noise pulses being recorded. This simplified procedure is particularly suitable for counting samples with a reasonably high counting rate.

With the high-voltage control in the "off" position, and the window settings wide open, turn the power switch on and allow approximately 10 min for the circuits to come to stability before proceeding. Insert a suitable gamma-emitting sample (^{137}Cs or ^{60}Co) into a fixed geometrical position in the sample support and do not move it during the operations that follow. Set the amplifier at a low gain position (this corresponds to high "attenuation" for some models). Turn the high-voltage and scaler count switches to "on" and raise the potential slowly until the scaler begins to record pulses. Collect a minimum of 3000 counts and record count rate and photomultiplier potential. Successively, at 50-volt increments, make such count rate determinations and record the data. The counting rate will rise rapidly and then level off somewhat on a "plateau." Discontinue counting when a second rapid increase in counting rate is observed. In no case should the potential be advanced beyond the limit specified by the photomultiplier tube manufacturer.

Now plot the data obtained on graph paper, using photomultiplier potential as the abscissa and computed counts per minute as the ordinate. Label this curve "low gain." A suitable *operating potential* for this gain setting can be chosen as the center of the flattest portion of the plateau.

Now remove the radioactive sample from the counter and determine the background radiation rate at three points: the starting potential, the selected operating potential, and near the upper end of the plateau. Collect 3000 counts or count for a minimum of 10 min at each voltage setting. Enter this information on the foregoing graph. The resulting background curve will be only a rough approximation of what would appear if more points were plotted. It does, however, illustrate the rapid rise in background count rate with increasing photomultiplier potential. The high level of background detected at the operating potential stands out as one of the drawbacks of the inorganic crystal scintillation counter.

A more refined method of determining optimum operating potential is to find the point where the value for S^2/B is greatest. Here S represents the net sample count rate and B the corresponding background count rate. In this case, a more complete background curve should be plotted. (See Chapter 5 for details on this and the nature of the scintillation detector background.)

The procedure just described for plateau determination, selection of operating potential, and three-point background counting should be repeated for a medium and a high-gain setting (or, alternatively, medium and low "attenuation") of the amplifier, using the same sample and geometry. The three curves now obtained should be carefully compared to note the effect of gain setting on starting potential, background count rate, and on plateau length and slope. With due consideration for these factors, select an *optimal gain setting* and *operating potential* to be used in the remainder of the experiment. Of course, this strictly applies only to the isotope used here and will vary somewhat for other gamma-emitters. Similar procedures can be used to determine the optimal gain setting and the operating potential when the discriminator setting is narrowed to cover the emission peak of a given gamma emitter.

3. Beta Detection Efficiency of External Scintillation Counters

Scintillation crystals (commonly anthracene) are available for beta counting. Here, however, the beta efficiency of the NaI(Tl) crystal, the standard choice for gamma counting, will be examined for academic comparison. Use a high gain setting on the amplifier. (Why?) Place a suitable sample of a pure beta-emitting isotope (^{210}Bi, ^{32}P, or the like), having an E_{max} over 1 Mev in the sample support and collect 3000–5000 counts. Next, place the same sample in approximately the same geometrical relationship to a G-M detector, but introduce an intervening aluminum absorber (about $\frac{1}{16}$ in thick), and similarly determine the count rate. (The absorber is to compensate for the scintillation crystal housing.) (How do the two count rates compare? What would you conclude about the relative beta counting efficiency of a G-M counter and a scintillation counter with a NaI(Tl) crystal?)

4. Detection Efficiency of the Scintillation Counter for Different Gamma Energies

Secure three calibrated sources whose gamma energies differ markedly from one another. Using the optimal operating gain and voltage selected in Section 2, determine the net count rate of each. From the calibration data furnished for the sources and the net count rates, calculate the *relative detection efficiency* of this scintillation counter for each of these sources. (Is the counter equally efficient in detecting the various gamma energies?) It should be realized that this efficiency factor holds true only under the conditions employed.

5. Gamma Detection Efficiency of the G-M Counter

Select one of the calibrated sources used in Section 4 and present it to a G-M detector, maintaining a sample-to-detector geometry as close as possible to that used with the scintillation detector. If the G-M tube is not equipped with a beta shield, some type of metal absorber sufficient to keep sample beta radiation from entering the detector should be interposed. Determine the net gamma counting rate for the sample and, as in Section 4, calculate the relative detection efficiency of the counter for gamma rays. A rough comparison of the gamma efficiency of the two counters can be obtained by examining this value and the value calculated in Section 4 for the same source. (How many times more efficient for gamma rays of this energy is the scintillation counter than the G-M counter?)

6. Resolving Time

Carefully prepare a solution of a suitable gamma-emitting isotope (in the form of a nonvolatile compound) so that 0.1 ml gives about 10,000 dpm. Pipette 0.1 ml into a glass or stainless steel cupped planchet. Dry this sample under a heat lamp and determine the count rate with the scintillation counter. Add another 0.1 ml sample of the radioactive solution, dry, and re-count with the same geometry. Repeat this operation until the counting rate reaches a minimum of 50,000 cpm. Plot the resulting data as dpm versus cpm. (From the slope of the curve, what can be inferred about the resolving time of the scintillation counter? With the counting rates used here, how would a similar curve for a G-M counter appear?)

C. SUMMARY

The operating characteristics of the external scintillation counter examined in this experiment are quite in contrast to those of the G-M counter. First, the plateau length, slope, and potential vary with amplifier gain and gamma energy of the sample. One must select an optimal operating potential with these variables in mind. Secondly, the much higher background count rate of the scintillation counter and the tendency for this background level to rise sharply with increasing photomultiplier potential somewhat offsets the value of its greater gamma ray detection efficiency. Thirdly, although the G-M counter is quite highly efficient for detecting beta particles, it has a rather low gamma efficiency. With the external scintillation counter, the reverse is the case. In addition, the gamma efficiency of the external scintillation counter is somewhat dependent on the energy of the gamma radiation. Lastly, the extremely short resolving time of the scintillation counter allows very high counting rates with minimal coincidence loss.

EXPERIMENT IV

Operation and Characteristics of a Liquid (Internal-Sample) Scintillation Counter

The detection of radioactivity in an internal radioactive sample by means of a fluor solution and adjacent photomultiplier was described in Chapter 6. This method of detection differs from external-sample scintillation detection primarily in the intimate contact of the sample and the scintillation medium, and in the consequent energy transfer process. Energy is transferred from the ionizing particle to the solvent molecules and thence to the primary solute (a fluor) which emits some of the energy as light. A secondary solute (wave shifter) may be required to convert this light to photons of longer wavelength to match the spectral response of the photocathode better. Any process which reduces the efficiency of this energy transfer is termed *quenching*. The wide variation in quenching activity of the components of the sample-fluor solution, makes it necessary to evaluate the extent of quenching in almost all samples counted.

The most widespread use of liquid scintillation counters is to assay low-energy beta emitters. Since the resulting pulse height from such low-energy particles does not greatly exceed the size of thermal noise pulses originating in the photomultiplier, it is necessary to minimize thermal noise and preamplifier noise. This is normally accomplished by using two photomultipliers connected by coincidence circuitry and operating the entire detector in a shielded housing. The use of a pulse height analyzer with variable discriminator settings is also nearly universal in such counting assemblies. The following description pertains particularly to the Tri-Carb Liquid Scintillation Spectrometer Model 314 EX series (Packard Instrument Co., Inc., La Grange, Illinois), one of the most widely used internal-sample scintillation counters currently available. In addition to the features previously described, this counter is equipped with two independent pulse height counting channels, each with its own scaler. Other suitable counting assemblies, such as the Packard Company's Model 3000 and 4000 series and those manufactured by Nuclear-Chicago Corp. will have only slightly different features (see Figures 6-3 and 6-4). This experiment can be performed with equal facility on any of these counting assemblies.

A. COMPONENT FUNCTIONS OF A LIQUID (INTERNAL-SAMPLE) SCINTILLATION COUNTING ASSEMBLY

1. Power Supply

This component is essentially the same as that described for the external-sample scintillation counter in Experiment III. Perhaps the only significant difference is that it supplies a d-c potential to two photomultipliers instead of one.

2. Scintillation Detector Assembly

The entire detector assembly is normally enclosed in a heavy lead shield and operated in a freezer chest. These two features reduce external background radiation and photomultiplier noise levels, respectively. Models equipped with automatic sample changers have a turntable and elevator component mounted over the detector. This allows sample vials to be automatically inserted into, and removed from, the sample chamber without light leakage to the photomultipliers.

The detector itself includes a pair of photomultipliers which view the sample vial from opposite sides. One photomultiplier, the "analyzer," passes its pulses into the two counting channels (see Figure IV-1). The other photomultiplier, the "monitor," is used only to operate the coincidence circuitry. The sample vial contains the radioactive sample material, a solvent, and fluor solutes. Energy dissipated in the solution by ionizing particles emitted from the sample is converted to photons which pass to the photomultipliers and give rise to output pulses. A preamplifier attached to each photomultiplier base provides initial amplification of these pulses.

3. Linear Amplifiers

Signals from the analyzer tube pass to the channel I and channel II amplifiers; signals from the monitor tube reach the monitor amplifier.

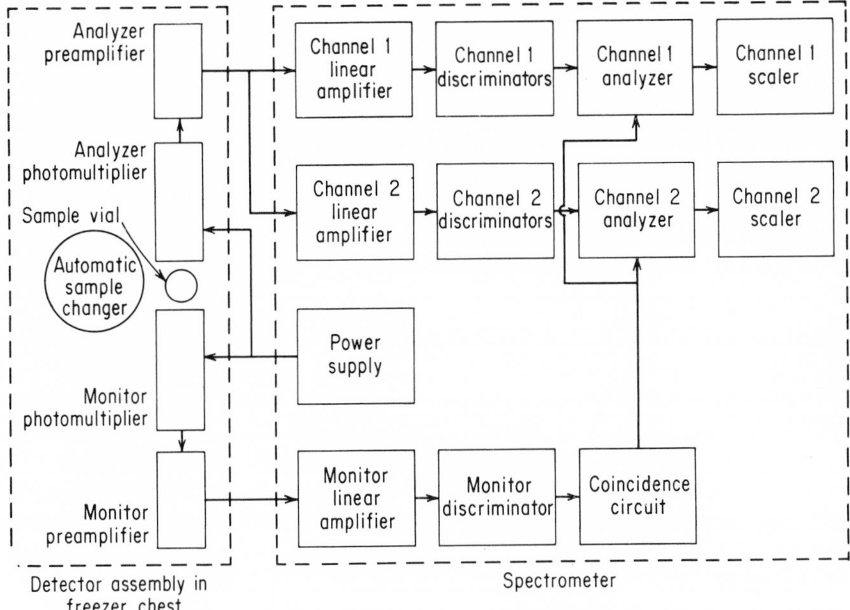

Figure IV-1. Block diagram of a typical (internal sample) scintillation counting assembly.

These amplifiers must provide linear amplification and must possess good overload characteristics to amplify small pulses faithfully in the presence of large pulses. In addition, the stability of the amplifiers is critical, since any amplifier drift will result in unreliable counting results. The gain of these three amplifiers is individually adjustable to allow optimal settings in either counting channel when two different isotopes are being assayed simultaneously.

4. Discriminators, Analyzers, and Coincidence Circuit

Five discriminators (*gates*) are used in this counter—two for each of the counting channels and one for the monitor channel. The two variable discriminators in each counting channel pass on to the analyzer only those pulses whose heights lie between their settings. This voltage interval between the upper and lower discriminators is called the *window*. The windows in the two channels may be overlapping, adjacent, or disjunctive, since they may be set independently of one another. The discriminator in the monitor channel rejects all pulses below a given level. Usually these pulses are a result of thermionic or preamplifier noise.

If an output pulse from the monitor amplifier exceeds the voltage setting of the monitor discriminator, a signal passes into the coincidence circuit which serves to open a pathway through the two counting channel analyzers for a given duration (~ 5 mμ sec). If during this period a pulse passes through Channel I which exceeds the lower discriminator setting, but is smaller than the upper discriminator setting, it can pass on through the analyzer and be registered on the Channel I scaler. Similarly, pulses in the Channel II window could pass to the Channel II scaler. Thus, detection requires a minimum of two photons to be emitted by the fluor within the counter resolving time. This fact is of primary importance in avoiding self-detection of the photon process, such as chemiluminescence or externally induced fluorescence.

On the other hand, if a thermal noise pulse were to originate in the analyzer photomultiplier without the monitor channel being actuated, the signal would be blocked at the analyzers for lack of a signal from the coincidence circuit. Only when a thermal noise pulse originates simultaneously in each photomultiplier within the resolving time of the circuits can such a spurious noise count reach the scalers. Since thermal noise is random and the counter resolving time is of the order of 10^{-7} sec, the number of such counts is negligible.

5. Scalers

These components are similar to those previously described for other counting assemblies. Owing to the very short resolving time of the liquid scintillation detector, the register is entirely based on "glow" tubes, rather than including a mechanical register. A high-speed electronic timer with provision for presetting the counting time is commonly included.

Automatic scintillation counters are used where large numbers of samples must be assayed routinely. These counter assemblies include a console unit to control the automatic sample changer, interrogate the scalers and timer at the end of each sample assay, and actuate the associated digital printer. This latter component prints out the scaler and timer readings for each sample counted to provide a permanent record. These components and the scalers, analyzers, coincidence circuit, discriminators, amplifiers, and the power supply are commonly housed together in a single chassis and termed the *spectrometer*.

B. OPERATION OF A LIQUID (INTERNAL-SAMPLE) SCINTILLATION SPECTROMETER

1. General Instructions

This counter assembly is considerably more complex and expensive than those operated in the past three experiments. Therefore, it is even more essential to become thoroughly familiar with the manufacturer's specific operating instructions before attempting to use the counter. Since there are a number of adjustable controls on this spectrometer (gain on each amplifier, photomultiplier high voltage, discriminator settings, counting mode selectors, and so on), and since the counting results are meaningful only when these control settings are stated, it is of the utmost importance to record each control setting at the time each assay is made.

2. Beta Pulse Spectrometry

Pulse spectra of beta-emitting nuclides of three different energy levels will be determined for comparison. ^{3}H (E_{max} 0.018 Mev), ^{14}C (E_{max} 0.157 Mev), and ^{36}Cl (E_{max} 0.714 Mev) are suggested as covering a suitable energy span. Four individual samples of equal volume should be prepared as follows:

(1) The scintillation solution is made up with toluene as the solvent, PPO (4 g/liter) as the primary fluor, and POPOP (0.05 g/liter) as the secondary fluor.

(2) Each sample vial should be filled with an equal measured volume (usually 15 ml) of the scintillation solution. One vial will have no radioactive sample and will be used in making background determinations.

(3) A trace amount (less than 1 mg) of benzoic acid-7-^{14}C (approximately 0.03 μc of radioactivity), benzoic acid-^{3}H (approximately 0.1 μc), and α-benzene hexachloride-^{36}Cl (about 0.02 μc) should be weighed out and added to the three remaining vials, respectively. Inasmuch as benzoic acid is a quenching agent, the quantity used should be carefully controlled. Labeled toluene or naphthalene-^{14}C are commonly used as standards for counter calibration, but the measurement of a defined volume of such a compound as liquid toluene often introduces undesirable errors.

The spectra of each of these four samples should now be determined at several different photomultiplier potential settings. This can be done at a given voltage setting ("tap") by maintaining a constant window-width of fifty divisions in one of the counting channels and making successive activity determinations from 50–1000 divisions across the pulse height scale. (Why is a measurement not made with the window setting of 0–50 divisions?) A family of spectra for each sample should be plotted from the data thus secured (see Figure 6-9).

3. Selection of Optimal Counter Settings

From the data of the previous section the optimal window and photomultiplier high-voltage settings should now be selected. The optimal settings (the "balance point") for each isotope will be those that give a maximal value for the expression efficiency^2/background. This implies that background determinations should be made for different settings. Alternatively, the "balance point" setting can be determined empirically from data as shown in Figure 6-10. The approximate counting efficiency for any photomultiplier potential and window-width can be estimated from the area included under the curve at those settings. The area under the background curve for the same settings must also be considered. The optimal counter settings will not be the same for each of the three isotopes.

Note that although a wider window setting results in an increased counting efficiency in most cases, it may also lead to a much greater increase in background count rate. In addition, the curves show that increased photomultiplier high voltage spreads the spectrum across the pulse height scale, whereas decreased high voltage compresses it at the lower energy ranges. Although it will not be necessary to prepare a family of curves as in Figure 6-10 to determine the optimal counter settings in this experiment, it may be necessary to do so in order to achieve greater precision in certain experiments. Note that, under balance point conditions, the pulse spectra are very vulnerable to the effect of quenching. Use care in calibrating the counter efficiency under the chosen balance point conditions for each type of sample preparation process. In counting situations where a large number of samples of similar composition have a respectable radioactivity (a few hundred cpm over background), it would be well to consider the feasibility of "flat spectrum" counting. (For a more detailed consideration of this concept, see pp. 127–129).

4. Determinations of Efficiency at Optimal Counter Settings

The counting efficiency at the optimal counter settings (balance point) should now be determined for each of the three isotopes used in Section 2. This will be done by the *internal standardization* or "spiking" method (see pp. 131–132). Each sample is first assayed at the previously determined optimal counter setting. Then, precisely measured amounts of calibrated standard source compounds should be added to each sample vial and the vials recounted.

It is suggested that toluene-^{14}C, naphthalene-^{14}C, toluene-^{3}H, naphthalene-^{3}H, and α-benzene hexachloride-^{36}Cl be used as the internal standards. The amount of radioacitivity in each of the internal standards should be chosen so that it is approximately of the the same order of magnitude as that in the counting samples to be calibrated. The pipetting of the labeled toluene, although difficult, must be done with the utmost precision. From the counting data thus derived, the counting efficiencies are calculated according to Equation 6-1. (What relationship, if any, exists between the E_{max} of the three isotopes and their counting efficiencies? How do the counting efficiencies of the original ^{14}C- and ^{3}H-labeled benzoic acid samples compare with the counting efficiences of the ^{14}C- and ^{3}H-labeled toluene "spikes"? Does this indicate any quenching effect by the benzoic acid?)

5. The Determination of Counting Efficiency by the Channels Ratio Method

As indicated in Chapter 6, there are several ways to apply the channels ratio method to establish the counting efficiency for a given counting sample. Such information is obviously necessary in cross-comparing the counting results of samples having different compositions, particularly with respect to the concentration of quenching agents.

The following procedure allows the construction of a working graph to correlate channels ratio with detection efficiencies for a given liquid scintillation counter. Such a graph can, therefore, in turn be used to ascertain the counting efficiency of any given sample, once the channels ratio relative to the counting data is known. The term *channels ratio* in this case is defined as the ratio of

$$\frac{\text{counts observed in window between gate 1 and gate 2 (channel 1)}}{\text{counts observed in window between gate 3 and gate 4 (channel 2)}}$$

The relative settings of the respective gates (or discriminators) are shown in Figure IV-2.

(1) Prepare a series of counting samples with compositions as prescribed in the following table:

Sample No.	Toluene containing PPO (6 g/l) and POPOP (0.05 g/l)	Toluene (ml)	20% Chloroform in Toluene (ml)
1	9 ml	5.0	0.0
2	9	4.5	0.5
3	9	4.0	1.0
4	9	3.5	1.5
5	9	3.0	2.0
6	9	2.5	2.5
7	9	2.0	3.0
8	9	1.5	3.5
9	9	1.0	4.0
10	9	0.5	4.5
11	9	0.0	5.0

To each of the samples add 1.00 ml of fluor solution (toluene containing PPO 6 g/liter and POPOP 0.05 g/liter) containing 0.001 μc of naphthalene-^{14}C.

(2) Place sample 1 in the liquid scintillation counter and carry out a spectrum determination in the same manner as described under Section 2. This step can be ignored if the beta spectrum of a counting sample of this type is available.

(3) Choose the high-voltage setting such that the beta spectrum of counting sample 1 is similar to that shown in Figure IV-2. Set the pulse discriminators G_1, G_2, G_3, and G_4 at the respective positions shown in Figure IV-2. Test the adequacy of these settings by counting the sample and computing the channels ratio:

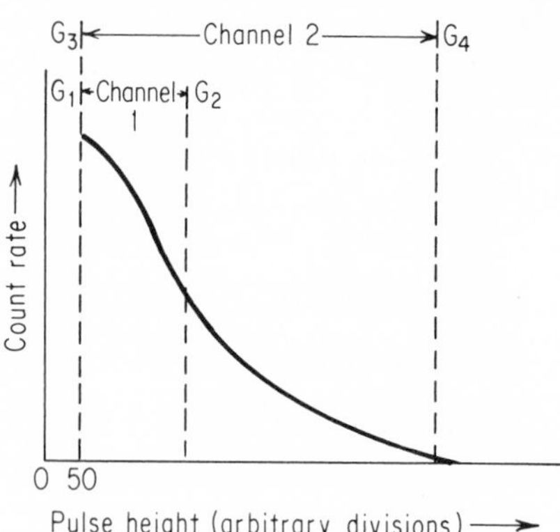

Figure IV-2. Discriminator settings for counting efficiency determination by the channels ratio method.

$$\frac{G_1 - G_2\,(\text{channel 1})}{G_3 - G_4\,(\text{channel 2})}$$

The magnitude of the ratio should approach 0.3.

(4) Count all the samples under the specified settings twice, as well as a blank vial to ascertain the background counting rate. The counting time of each sample should be that giving the counting result a relative standard deviation no greater than 1 per cent (see Chapter 9).

(5) Calculate the channels ratio as in (3) for each of the samples, using net counting rates.

(6) Calculate the counting efficiency for each of the samples and express the results on a percentage basis. For the calculations, make use of the net counting rates observed for each of the samples and the fact that 0.001 μc of radioactivity was originally added to each counting sample.

(7) Plot counting efficiency versus channels ratio for all the counting samples. The plot so constructed should be similar to that given in Figure IV-3.

Once the channels ratio-counting efficiency relationship is known, it is possible to use this plot to read off counting efficiency, for a given counting sample, from the observed channels ratio. Note that this arrangement does not apply to counting samples suffering from extensive color quenching.

Similar curves can be constructed for other radioisotopes or for

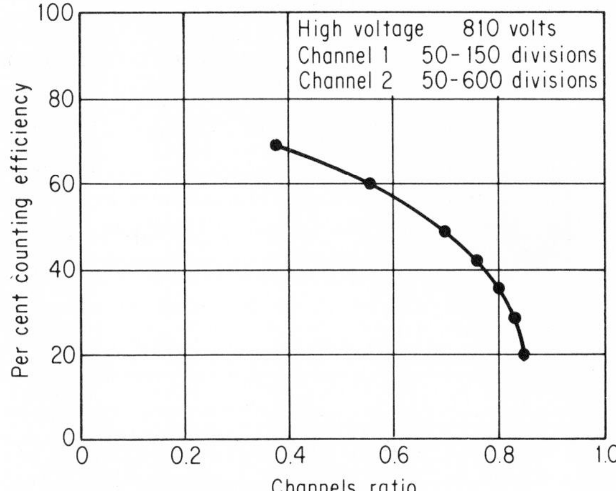

Figure IV-3. Counting efficiency-channels ratio curve derived using chloroform as a quenching agent with ^{14}C-labeled sample.

other sample preparation procedures drastically different from those just described. Notable examples are the counting of paper chromatograms immersed in fluor solutions and thixotropic gel preparations.

6. The Effect of a Quenching Agent

First count each of the foregoing samples under balance point conditions and "flat spectrum" conditions (a window of 100–1000 divisions and the photomultiplier potential set such that the respective beta spectra will be essentially flat—tap 7 for the ^{14}C sample). Then add to each of the counting samples 0.1 ml of chloroform (a potent quenching agent) and recount each at the balance point and under flat spectrum conditions. Add two additional 0.1 ml amounts of chloroform and count the samples after each addition under the two types of counter settings specified. From the data, plot curves of counting rate versus chloroform concentration (from 0–0.3 ml) for each of the isotopes at the two counting modes. (What can be concluded from these curves as to the relative quenching effect under balance point as compared to flat spectrum conditions? What relationship, if any, exists between the extent of quenching and the E_{max} of the three isotopes?)

It may be desirable to determine the beta spectrum of a quenched ^{14}C sample under balance point conditions. The quenched spectrum is then compared with the unquenched sample, that is, before the addition of chloroform.

7. Preparation of Gel Counting Samples

Homogenized tissues, water solutions, and solid organic and inorganic salts have been counted as gel samples (see pp. 171–172). For this experiment it is suggested that a 0.5 ml aqueous solution of an available water soluble organic compound, such as glucose-U-^{14}C be utilized. (Why would toluene-^{14}C not be satisfactory?) The activity level should be about 0.01–0.02 μc. The required quantity of gel is prepared by adding sufficient Thixcin (Baker Castor Oil Co.) to a toluene solution containing PPO (4 g/liter) and POPOP (100 mg/liter) to produce a concentration of 25 g/liter. Mix the resultant gel for about 10 min in a blender. The labeled sample should be added (using a large-bore syringe) to a measured amount of gel (usually 15 ml) in a counting vial and thoroughly mixed by shaking. The balance point settings for this counting sample and the pulse spectra at medium and high photomultiplier potential settings should then be determined. Flat spectrum counting is particularly suitable for gel samples. (How do the pulse spectra of this gel sample compare with the pulse spectra of the ^{14}C-labeled scintillation solution determined in Section 2?)

C. SUMMARY

The effect of photomultiplier potential and window-width on the counting efficiency of the liquid scintillation counter must be considered in determining the optimal counter settings. Counting efficiency is also clearly related to the beta energy of the isotope in the sample. Quenching agents in only low concentrations may drastically reduce counting efficiency. The extent of this decrease in counting efficiency may be determined by internal standardization or the channels ratio method, and minimized by use of flat spectrum counting.

The Nature of Radioactive Decay

For those radioisotopes having a decay rate of the magnitude of hours or a few days, the half-life can be readily determined as a laboratory experiment. Repeated activity determinations may be made and the data plotted against time. The half-life is readily found from the graph as the time required for the initial count rate to decrease by a factor of two. In this experiment two such half-life determinations are to be made. One is on the fission-produced nuclide ^{131}I and the other on the very short-lived isotope ^{128}I. The latter will be produced for this purpose by the Szilard-Chalmers reaction using a neutron source or training reactor.

A. DETERMINATION OF THE HALF-LIFE OF ^{131}I FROM A DECAY CURVE

From a stock solution of Na^{131}I transfer by pipette about 0.005 μc of ^{131}I activity to a planchet. Dry this sample slowly, using a heat lamp. Avoid excess heating. If a G-M counter is to be used for assay, it is necessary to place the planchet on the shelf of the sample holder which allows an initial count rate of less than 3000 cpm. (Why?) This will not be necessary if a NaI(T1) crystal scintillation detector is used.

Determine the net count rate of the ^{131}I sample, collecting a minimum of 10,000 counts, and record the exact time of the counting. Determine the background counting rate under counting conditions. The counting rate for background determination should be defined to match the standard deviation of the counting rate associated with the sample. Repeat this procedure daily, if at all possible, over a period of 7–10 days. A minimum of five such determinations must be made. It is essential that the same counter and geometry be used for every determination. If time allows, a long-lived reference source should be counted just after each sample assay. In this way, any variation in counter efficiency will be recognized and the sample count rates can be adjusted accordingly.

Plot the data of the net counting rate (on the logarithmic scale) against time elapsed from the first measurement on semilogarithmic graph paper with the initial count taken as time zero. A straight line should be realized through the points, and the negative slope of the line should be equal to $\lambda/2.303$. The half-life can then be readily calculated from the decay constant (λ). A precisely determined half-life of ^{131}I is 8.066 $\pm$ 0.016 days. (How closely does your graphically determined value come to this?) For a more detailed discussion of half-life and radioactive decay, see Chapter 2. In place of ^{131}I, one might use other readily available nuclides with half-lives of a few days, such as ^{198}Au (2.697 days) or ^{32}P (14.22 days).

B. PREPARATION OF ^{128}I BY THE SZILARD-CHALMERS REACTION AND DETERMINATION OF HALF-LIFE

1. Preparation of ^{128}I

The unfortunate consequence of the (n, γ) process of radioisotope formation is that the product atoms are isotopes of the precursor atoms and thus not chemically separable from them. In 1932, L. Szilard and T. A. Chalmers demonstrated that after neutron irradiation of ethyl iodide, most of the ^{128}I formed could be readily extracted with water. This was evidence that the iodine-carbon bond was ruptured as a result of the ^{127}I (n, γ) ^{128}I reaction. This alteration of the chemical form of a compound upon activation, allowing subsequent chemical separation of the product has come to be known as the *Szilard-Chalmers process*. The largest amount of work in the field of Szilard-Chalmers separations has been done on organic halides. In this experiment the original work of Szilard and Chalmers with ethyl iodide will be followed.

Three basic conditions must be met to make a Szilard-Chalmers separation possible: (1) Following its formation by neutron absorption, the radioactive atom must emit a gamma ray and recoil with sufficient energy to break the bond between it and the parent molecule; (2) it must neither recombine with its parent molecule nor rapidly exchange with inactive atoms of other target molecules; (3) a chemical method of separating the target compound and the radioactive material in its new chemical form must be available. Since recoil energy may reach several hundred electron volts, and most chemical bond energies are in the range of 1–5 ev per molecule, there will be more than enough recoil energy to break the C—^{128}I bond. Recombination or exchange of the "hot" atoms with inactive atoms of other target molecules is prevented by the addition of a small amount (but large in comparison to the amount of ^{128}I present) of inert I_2 carrier. The aqueous extraction of the ^{128}I is greatly enhanced by the addition of iodide ion (as KI).

The following procedures are designed for use where a nuclear reactor with a neutron flux of about 10^6 neutrons/cm^2/sec is obtainable (such as the AGN 201 model). Adaptations for use with a Ra-Be neutron source can be readily made. Pour a suitable amount (about 5 ml) of ethyl iodide into a polyethylene vial and place the capped vial in the sample holding rod. Then insert the rod so that the vial is in the center of the neutron flux (the "glory hole"). If neutron irradiation is carried out for 25 min (one half-life), the anticipated ^{128}I activity will be sufficient for ten experiments of the present type. At the end of this irradiation period, the rod should be withdrawn and the vial removed with tongs and carried to the laboratory.

The vial should be placed behind shielding material (^{128}I emits beta particles with a 2.12 Mev E_{max}, as well as assorted gamma rays) and the cap removed. Transfer 0.5 ml of the ethyl iodide by pipette to a clear polyethylene vial with an attached cap. Using a clean pipette, add exactly 1 ml of a solution containing 10 mg KI per milliliter distilled water to the sample. Cap the sample vial, and, using tongs, shake the two phases for about 30 sec. After the layers separate, carefully open the vial. By means of a micropipette, transfer 0.2 ml–0.5 ml of the upper aqueous phase to a stainless steel cup planchet. Evaporate the sample to dryness under a heat lamp and cover the dried deposit with mylar film or cellulose tape.

2. Determination of the Half-Life of ^{128}I

The assay of sample activity using a G-M counter should begin immediately. Record the time that counting starts. The background count rate should have been previously determined. Count the sample for 1 min and repeat the counting at 10-min intervals over a period of 2 hr. The time of each 1-min count should be recorded as the mid-point of each determination. For the determination of half-lives with known statistical accuracy, see the General Bibliography (7). Owing to the short half-life of ^{128}I, the counting rate will drop off appreciably over the total assay period with a resulting decrease in statistical accuracy. The counting data should be plotted against time on semi-log graph paper. Time zero is taken as the time of the initial sample counting. Graphically determine the half-life of ^{128}I from the observed values. If the initial counting rate is high, a straight-line relationship would not be realized in the beginning phase of the counting. The slope of the straight line should therefore be determined from the counting data obtained in a later phase of the counting process; that is, after the activity of the sample has decreased to a rate not high enough to cause coincidence loss in the detector.

3. Determination of G-M Counter Coincidence Loss Using ^{128}I

If time permits, the coincidence loss of the counter can be determined by the employment of a larger ^{128}I sample, such that the initial count rate is over 30,000 cpm. Assay of this activity level with a G-M counter will result in an observed count rate considerably less than the "true" count rate, owing to coincidence loss. With subsequent decline in activity, the degree of coincidence loss will decrease until eventually a true exponential decay curve will be observed. Extrapolation of the linear portion of the curve back to time zero will give the "true" initial count rate. The difference between this and the observed initial count rate represents directly the reduction of counting rate due to coincidence loss in the detector.

Interaction of Radiation with Matter

Some aspects of the interaction of the various types of radiation with matter were discussed in Chapter 3. This experiment deals with two aspects of interaction as they relate to radiotracer assay. One is the external absorption of beta and gamma radiation in aluminum and lead, respectively, and the second is self-absorption in counting samples of weak beta emitters.

A. EXTERNAL BETA ABSORPTION

1. Theory

A standard method in the characterization of beta radiation is the preparation of absorption (transmission) curves (see Figure 3-9). This is typically done by inserting a series of aluminum absorbers between a pure beta-emitting source and a detector up to thicknesses exceeding the beta particle range, and observing the counting rate for each thickness of absorber. The logarithm of the observed activity is then plotted against absorber thickness. In general, such absorption curves are not highly precise, but a rough value of the range and E_{max} of the beta particles involved can be derived from them.

In order to ascertain the E_{max} of a beta-emitter from an absorption curve it is necessary first to determine the range accurately. Range determination from an absorption curve is attended with considerable uncertainty. Although the curve will appear nearly exponential over much of its length, it commonly deviates from linearity at both ends. The production of bremsstrahlung (see p. 48) largely accounts for a flattening of the curve near the limit of range. In addition, the shape of the absorption curve varies somewhat with the geometry of the arrangement in which it is measured, because of the contribution of scattering effects.

A rough, though inaccurate, estimate of range can be made by simply extrapolating the linear portion of the absorption curve to the abscissa. In some cases the curve will be found to turn downward from the linear portion and to intersect the abscissa vertically at a point which may be taken as the visual range. (It should, of course, be remembered that the abscissa intercept does not have the same meaning on a semilog plot as on a linear plot.) Beta range may be alternatively determined more precisely, but with a greater expenditure of time, by methods such as the Feather analysis (see Chapter 3, references 3 and 7). Absorption methods for the precise determination of beta range have been superceded by the employment of the beta-ray spectrometer with which direct beta energy measurements may be made.

The E_{max} of a beta-emitter can be calculated from the measured range by the empirical relation developed by Glendenin, as follows:

$$\text{(VI-1)} \qquad E_{max}(\text{Mev}) = 1.85 \text{ range (g/cm}^2) + 0.245$$

This equation is reasonably valid for ranges greater than 300 mg/cm^2.

2. Procedure

A counting source of a pure beta emitter of reasonably high energy, preferably ^{32}P, should be prepared by evaporation on a planchet. It should be of sufficient activity to show 5000–10,000 cpm when placed on a lower shelf of the sample holder. A thin end-window G-M detector of known window thickness should be mounted in a fixed relation to the sample. Neither detector nor sample should be moved during the experiment. A set of calibrated aluminum absorbers will be required.

The optimal arrangement is to place the absorbers as near the detector window as possible, and the source somewhat farther away. The sample counting rate should now be determined with no absorber, and then with absorbers of increasing thickness until the counting rate is decreased to background or becomes constant. It will not be practical in the limited time available during a laboratory period to maintain a constant statistical accuracy in counting. Normally, longer counting times would be required with the thicker absorbers in place. The length of each activity determination can be determined, then, by the time available, not statistical considerations.

The observed sample activity must be corrected for background and coincidence loss (see Experiment I). Plot the corrected counting rate (on log scale) against absorber thickness on semilog graph paper with the appropriate number of cycles. In locating the origin allow room for extrapolation of the curve to the left. In order to extrapolate activity to zero absorber, the contribution of air and detector window absorption must be considered (see Figure 9-7). The distance between source and detector window should be measured. Air density may be taken as 1.2 mg/cm^2. The thickness of the G-M tube end-window will be found in the information supplied by the manufacturer.

From the extrapolated absorption curve estimate the range of ^{32}P beta particles in aluminum. Find the E_{max} for this emitter by Glendenin's equation (VI-1). (How do these experimental values compare to the recognized values for ^{32}P of a 790 mg/cm^2 range in aluminum and an E_{max} of 1.71 Mev? Why might the experimental values differ considerably from the accepted values? What bearing does this aspect of beta particle range have on the problem of shielding high levels of beta activity?)

B. EXTERNAL GAMMA ABSORPTION

1. Theory

Gamma ray absorption was fully discussed in Chapter 3, and it is suggested that the reader familiarize himself with that discussion before proceeding with this experiment. It will be recalled that the interaction of gamma photons with matter is markedly different from that of charged particles. Gamma rays (as well as X rays) show a characteristic exponential absorption and have no well-defined range.

In this experiment, a gamma absorption curve in lead will be prepared. From this plot, the *mass absorption coefficient* and *mass half-thickness* (the absorber thickness that reduces the incident gamma intensity by a factor of two) can be readily determined (see Equation 3-11). Also, from the experimentally determined value of $d_{1/2}$, the approximate gamma energy can be found using Figure 3-18.

2. Procedure

The only difference here, as compared to the previous absorption experiment with a beta emitter, is the placement of the detector, absorbers, and the counting sample. The geometry of the counting arrangement is particularly critical for gamma detection, since the photons are so readily scattered. Ideally the gamma rays should be collimated by placing the prepared source at the bottom of a lead well whose opening faces the detector. The source and the detector should be separated by as great a distance as the sample activity will allow, but at least 2 in. The lead absorbers will be inserted midway between the two. It is necessary to place an aluminum absorber of about 1 g/cm^2 close to the detector to absorb any secondary electrons ejected from the lead absorbers.

Suitable counting sources are those which emit gamma rays of a single energy (^{137}Cs) or of very similar energies (^{60}Co). A set of calibrated lead absorbers with thicknesses up to 25 g/cm^2 will be needed. The detector may be either a G-M tube or, better, a NaI(Tl) crystal scintillation detector. The required activity of the counting source will depend on the detector type employed.

Counting rate determinations for the various absorber thicknesses should be made as previously described. Then plot the net counting rate (log scale) on semilog graph paper against lead absorber thickness. (Is the resulting curve linear?) From the most linear portion of the curve determine the mass half-thickness and the mass absorption coefficient, and estimate the gamma energy as just described. (How do these experimental values compare with corresponding published values for the nuclide used?)

C. SELF-ABSORPTION IN A WEAK BETA-EMITTING SAMPLE

1. Theory

The effect of self-absorption on sample radiation was discussed in Chapter 9. Self-absorption is primarily a problem in the assay of low-energy beta emitters, where variations in sample weight and specific activity exist. This effect will be examined in this experiment as it concerns samples of $Ba^{14}CO_3$ of the same specific activity, but differing thickness. One of the commonest methods of compensating for differences in self-absorption from sample to sample is the use of a *self-absorption correction curve*. Such a correction curve can be readily prepared from the experimental data. It should be understood that a separate curve must be prepared for each nuclide and each form of counting sample assayed, and that a curve is valid only for the counting assembly and geometry used in its preparation. For uniformity in the mounting of the solid counting samples to be used, the method of slurry centrifugation will be employed here (see Chapter 8).

The observed specific activity of a $Ba^{14}CO_3$ sample will approach the actual specific activity in only the thinnest of samples. But there is considerable difficulty in securing uniformity in such very thin samples. A more precise means of determining actual specific activity (zero self-absorption) is to plot the apparent specific activities (cpm/mg) of a series of $Ba^{14}CO_3$ samples of different thickness against sample thickness and extrapolate the curve to zero thickness. A semilog plot facilitates the extrapolation considerably. Using this value of the actual specific activity as 100 per cent, a second plot is made of the percentage relative specific activity (apparent specific activity $\times$ 100/actual specific activity) against sample thickness (mg/cm^2). This plot, representing a beta transmission graph, serves as a correction curve for the effect of self-absorption in thick $Ba^{14}CO_3$ samples. The apparent sample specific activity for any thickness can then be graphically converted to the actual specific activity, that is, specific activity corrected for self-absorption; thus enabling one to compare the radioactivity of a number of samples.

When counting sample thickness becomes greater than the range of the beta particles it emits, only the radiation from the upper layer will be detected. Addition of more of the same sample will not affect the count rate. Such a sample is said to have reached *saturation thickness*, or is "infinitely" thick. Under these conditions, the counting rate of the sample will be directly proportional to the specific activity of the sample, not to the total amount of activity in the sample. Many workers prefer to count infinitely thick samples, if sufficient amounts of sample are available and, thus to avoid self-absorption corrections. Any samples in an experimental series that are thinner than the saturation thickness are then corrected to that thickness graphically for the sake of comparison.

2. Procedure

Prepare a stock solution of $Na_2{}^{14}CO_3$ (100 ml) containing 5 mmole Na_2CO_3 with a specific activity of about 9000 cpm/mmole. Dispense the stock solution into 10 Erlenmeyer flasks in the following amounts: 30, 20, 10, 8, 7, 6, 5, 4, 3, and 2 ml. Warm these flasks on a water bath to 70°C and then add to each 2 ml of the precipitation mixture (1 N NH_4Cl and 1 N $BaCl_2$). Stopper and gently agitate the flasks.

After cooling, transfer the contents of each flask quantitatively to polyethylene centrifuge tubes, using water to effect the transfer. Centrifuge the samples in a clinical centrifuge for 4 min at full speed. The resultant supernatant may then be decanted into a radioactive waste can. Add about 10 ml of 70 per cent alcohol to the residue in each tube, stopper the tubes with rubber stoppers, and shake violently to resuspend the $BaCO_3$. Transfer the alcohol suspension quickly to the special stainless steel centrifuge tubes (supplier is Atomic Products) equipped with preweighed aluminum planchets as false bottoms. Rinse any residual $BaCO_3$ from the plastic tubes with alcohol. The stainless steel tubes are balanced with respect to weight and immediately centrifuged at full speed for 6 min.

After centrifugation, remove the tubes and decant the supernatant alcohol immediately. Keep the centrifuge tubes in an upright position and remove the O-ring, which is holding the aluminum planchet as the false bottom. The aluminum planchet can then be detached from the centrifuge tube and dried *slowly* under a heat lamp. The counting samples so prepared should be stored in covered Petri dishes to minimize loss of radioactivity by way of exchange reactions involving CO_2 in the atmosphere, particularly under conditions of high humidity. All apparatus involved in the sample preparation procedure should be decontaminated by means of rinsing successively in 0.5 N HCl and water in the hood.

Weigh each planchet and calculate net sample weight. Each sample should be counted twice to a standard deviation of less than 1 per cent with a G-M tube or proportional detector. From the area of the planchets calculate the thickness of each sample in mg/cm^2. Now plot the net counting rate for each sample against the respective sample thickness. Compare the resultant curve with Figure 9-8. (Does it appear that any of the samples have a thickness greater than the saturation thickness?)

In order to prepare the self-absorption correction (transmission) curve, calculate the apparent specific activities for $Ba^{14}CO_3$ on each planchet (cpm/mg). Plot the respective apparent specific activities (on log scale) against sample thickness on semilog graph paper. Extrapolate this curve to zero thickness and consider the value as the actual specific activity. Now, using the value of the actual specific activity as 100 per cent, plot the percentage relative specific activity observed at each sample thickness against thickness. (Can the saturation thickness value be determined from this plot?) This plot should be preserved for possible later use in assay of $Ba^{14}CO_3$ samples with the same counting assembly and geometry.

Statistical Considerations in the Measurement of Radioactivity

This experiment is designed to illustrate the statistical considerations discussed in Chapter 9. It is suggested that that chapter be consulted in connection with the calculations at the end of the experiment.

A. THE NORMAL DISTRIBUTION OF COUNTING RESULTS AND ERROR PROBABILITY

Place a suitable radioactive source in a fixed relation to a radiation detector so that a counting rate about 500 cpm is obtained. G-M, proportional or external scintillation counters, are equally suitable for this purpose. Make a series of at least 20 consecutive observations (more would be preferable, if time permits) of 1-min duration each. The source should not be disturbed during these measurements.

Record the total number of counts (n) collected in each observation without making any correction for background or coincidence loss. These results will then be used to compute the standard deviation by calculating in order the following values:

(1) The mean total count ($\bar{n}$), that is, the sum of all the counts divided by the number of observations (N)
(2) The algebraic deviation (Δ) of each observation from this mean count ($\Delta = n - \bar{n}$)

(3) The square of the deviations of each observation (Δ^2)
(4) The sum of the squares of the deviations ($\Sigma \Delta^2$)
(5) The standard deviation (σ), that is, the root mean square deviation

$$\sigma = \left(\sqrt{\frac{\Sigma \Delta^2}{N}} \right)$$

(6) The algebraic sum of the deviations ($\Sigma \Delta$), which should be very nearly equal to zero
(7) The approximate standard deviation, that is, the root mean ($\sigma = \sqrt{\bar{n}}$)
(8) The percentage standard deviation (relative σ), that is, the reciprocal of the root mean (relative $\sigma = 1/\sqrt{\bar{n}}$)

Examine the observations for closeness of fit to a normal distribution as follows:

(1) Compare the approximate σ as calculated in (7) to the precise value of σ (from 5). They should be very nearly equal.
(2) Determine the number of observations showing deviations greater than 1 σ (using the exact σ value). This should occur in approximately one-third (31.7 per cent) of the observations.
(3) Similarly determine the number of observations showing deviations greater than 2 σ. This should occur in about one observation in 20 (4.6 per cent).

Precise agreement to the foregoing values is not to be expected, because of the relatively small number of observations.

B. REJECTION OF OBVIOUSLY ERRONEOUS DATA

Considering the data in Part 1, determine whether any of the activity measurements deviate so greatly that they cannot be accounted for by the mere randomness of radioactive decay. These may be discarded according to the following criteria:

(1) The observation differs from the mean by more than 2 σ.
(2) The observation differs from the mean by more than 3 σ.
(3) The ratio of the deviation to the standard deviation exceeds the appropriate value in Table 9-3 (Chauvenet's criterion).

(Explain how an observation might be rejected on the basis of one of the foregoing criteria, but not on others. Which of these criteria is the most lenient, that is, would tend to include observations with the greatest deviations?)

PART THREE

Illustrative Radiotracer Experiments

Incorporation of $^{14}CO_2$ into Amino Acids in Yeast

This experiment has been selected to illustrate the utilization of ^{14}C as a tracer in microbial metabolism. Specifically, it involves tracing the fate of $^{14}CO_2$ in amino acid metabolism in yeast cells. The $^{14}CO_2$ is administered in the gaseous state in a closed system, although it could as well be supplied as $H^{14}CO_3^-$ in solution in the culture medium. The amino acids in a hydrolysate of the yeast cells are separated by paper chromatography and the ^{14}C label detected by autoradiography or a paper chromatogram scanning counter. The pattern of amino acid labeling can serve as a clue to the mechanism and role played by CO_2 in the metabolism of microorganisms. Under the experimental conditions specified, the results will be largely qualitative, rather than quantitative.

The experimental procedure has been covered in an especially detailed fashion, so that the reader can carry out this type of experiment with ease. The materials and reagents needed are neither excessively costly nor uncommon, so that the experiment can be carried out in almost any biological or chemical laboratory. The step-by-step calculation of the amount of ^{14}C needed illustrates the type of experimental design required in radiotracer experiments.

A. SURVEY OF THE PROBLEM

It is well known that many species of microorganisms produce CO_2 from carbonaceous substrates as a result of their metabolic processes. It is also known that autotrophic microorganisms can utilize CO_2 as their carbon source. In addition, *CO_2 fixation* is carried on by many microorganisms in biosynthetic functions. This process has been studied in only a moderate number of species (3).

Such CO_2 incorporation can be readily followed if the carbon used is radioactive ^{14}C. The ^{14}C-labeled metabolic products can then be separated and identified by use of the techniques of paper chromatography and autoradiography. It is the appearance of ^{14}C *labeled amino acids* that will be followed in this experiment. Of course, other labeled products are also formed. This experiment demonstrates how such techniques can be applied to the study of a specific organism—*Saccharomyces cerevisiae* (baker's yeast). Davis, et al. (2), and Stoppani, et al. (5), have previously traced CO_2 incorporation into amino acids in yeast.

Briefly, the experiment consists of the following major activities: (1) Exposure of a known amount of yeast cells to $^{14}CO_2$ generated in the reaction vessel; (2) removal of residual $^{14}CO_2$, followed by separation and hydrolysis of the yeast cells; (3) development of one-dimensional paper chromatograms from measured aliquots of the yeast hydrolystate and amino acid reference standards; (4) detection and estimation of labeled compounds on the chromatograms by autoradiography or a scanning counter; (5) determination of the pattern of amino acid labeling as well as the relative quantities of ^{14}C incorporated into the various amino acids by comparison of the chromatograms and autoradiograms.

B. EXPERIMENTAL DESIGN

In the calculation of the amount of radioactive material to be used in this experiment certain *assumptions* must be made. These may be subject to some error and for this reason are conservative. The assumptions are in accord with experimental results (2,5).

Since the goal of the experiment is to determine ^{14}C labeling of various amino acids by autoradiography, the amount of ^{14}C to be used is based on the assumed amount fixed in a specific amino acid. *Aspartic acid* has been chosen for the following calculation (see Chapter 10 for the rationale behind this method of calculation).

1. Specific Activity Requirement

(1) The optimal amount of a substance on a chromatogram spot is usually estimated to be 10 μg.

(2) To produce a good image on X-ray film in a reasonable time (about a week), a 1 sq cm spot on the chromatogram should show about 100 cpm when assayed with a thin end-window G-M detector placed directly over the spot.

(3) Assuming that the detection efficiency of the G-M counter is 10 per cent and that the amino acid distributed in the paper chromatogram is

essentially in the nature of a sample having a saturation thickness, that is, approximately 25 per cent transmission, it follows that:

$$\frac{100\ \text{cpm/cm}^2}{0.10\ \text{(detection efficiency)} \times 0.25\ \text{(transmission correction)}}$$

$$= 4000\ \text{dpm/cm}^2\ \text{spot.}$$

(4) Since each spot is to contain about 10 μg of aspartic acid, this amounts to a *specific activity* of

$$\frac{4000\ \text{dpm/cm}^2\ \text{spot}}{10\ \mu\text{g/cm}^2\ \text{spot}} = 400\ \text{dpm}/\mu\text{g aspartic acid}$$

2. Scale of Operations

(1) The optimal amount of yeast cells to be used in this experiment is chosen as 20 mg in dry weight.
(2) If one assumes that all carbonaceous compounds in these yeast cells will have the same specific activity as derived from the incorporated $^{14}CO_2$, it follows that:

$$400\ \text{dpm}/\mu\text{g (desired specific activity)} \times 2 \times 10^4\ \mu\text{g}$$

$$\text{(total weight of carbonaceous compounds in questions)} =$$

$$8 \times 10^6\ \text{dpm total activity in yeast cells.}$$

(3) On the basis of general information with regard to CO_2 fixation processes, however, it is more likely that only a portion of the carbonaceous compounds in the yeast cells will be labeled from the incorporated $^{14}CO_2$ over the few hours of the experiment's duration. As a crude estimation, one can assume that only 10 per cent of the cellular compounds will be preferentially labeled from the $^{14}CO_2$. This particular consideration consequently reduces the foregoing calculated total activity in the cells to 8×10^5 dpm.
(4) It is also realized that only a small portion of the administered ^{14}C will be fixed by the yeast cells at all. The results obtained from preliminary experimentation indicate that the amount of $^{14}CO_2$ fixed is likely to be of the magnitude of 1 per cent of the amount of total activity administered. This fact implies that one should use

$$\frac{8 \times 10^5\ \text{dpm}}{0.01\ \text{(fraction of activity fixed)}} = 8 \times 10^7\ \text{dpm}\ ^{14}CO_2$$

for this particular experiment, which is equivalent to 36 μc of $^{14}CO_2$.
(5) Naturally, the next question is how many milligrams of $Ba^{14}CO_3$ are required for this experiment. The question cannot be answered unless one knows the specific activity of the $Ba^{14}CO_3$ available from the pro-

duction source, such as the Oak Ridge National Laboratory. Let us assume that the $Ba^{14}CO_3$ on hand has an *isotope content* of 40.0 per cent, that is in the barium carbonate sample, 40.0 per cent is $Ba^{14}CO_3$, the rest being $Ba^{12}CO_3$ and $Ba^{13}CO_3$. The specific activity, expressed as millicuries per millimole, can then be readily calculated. For 1 mole of barium carbonate containing 40.0 per cent $Ba^{14}CO_3$, the disintegration rate should be

$$-\frac{dN}{dt} = \lambda N_0, \text{ or}$$

$$\frac{0.693}{5570\,(\text{yr}) \times 365\,(\text{da}) \times 24\,(\text{hr}) \times 60\,(\text{min}) \times 60\,(\text{sec})}$$

$$\times\ 0.4\,(\text{isotope content}) \times 6.02 \times 10^{23}\,(\text{Avogadro's No.})$$

$$= 9.51 \times 10^{11}\ \text{dps}, \quad \text{or} \quad 25.7\ \text{curies}$$

The specific activity is therefore 25.7 mc/m mole or 0.130 mc/mg of $Ba^{14}CO_3$. Consequently, for the 36 μc of ^{14}C radioactivity required in this experiment, one would need:

$$\frac{36\ \mu\text{c}\ ^{14}\text{C}}{130\ \mu\text{c/mg Ba}^{14}\text{CO}_3} = 0.27\ \text{mg Ba}^{14}\text{CO}_3\ (40.0\ \text{per cent isotope content})$$

C. MATERIALS AND EQUIPMENT REQUIRED

This listing includes only special equipment and reagents used in the experiment and is not complete. Items are listed in order of usage.

(1) Reaction vessel: As illustrated in Figure A-1, this consists of a side flask (25 ml Erlenmeyer) and a test tube (about 10 ml) joined to a main flask (125 ml Erlenmeyer). Each of the openings should be provided with a tight-fitting serum cap. Although this piece must be custom-made, it can be utilized in a wide variety of radiotracer experiments involving $^{14}CO_2$. Much more elaborate vessels could, of course, be employed for this purpose.

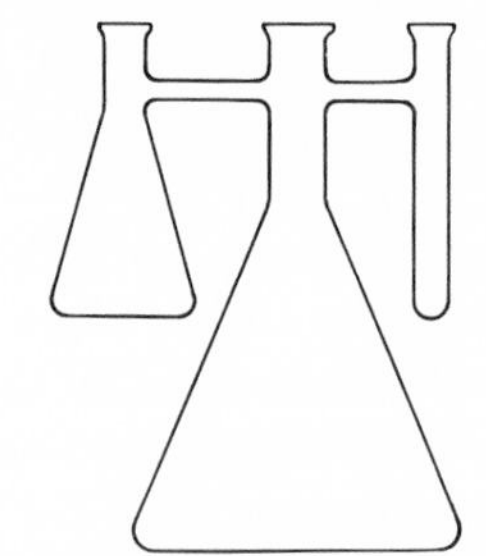

Figure A-1. $^{14}CO_2$ reaction vessel.

(2) Glucose-salts medium:

$(NH_4)_2HPO_4$	0.2 g	Yeast extract	0.05 g
KH_2PO_4	0.2 g	Glucose	2.0 g
$MgSO_4 \cdot 7H_2O$	0.01 g		

Dissolve in 100 ml water and sterilize by means of an autoclave, if not to be used immediately.

(3) 36 μc $Ba^{14}CO_3$ (specific activity 400 dpm/μg), or amount calculated for each individual situation.

(4) Perchloric acid ($HClO_4$)—40 per cent solution.

(5) Oxygen-gas torch and accessories for sealing pyrex hydrolysis tubes. [For these tubes, the round-bottomed drying ampoules made by Kontes Glass Company (Vineland, N.J.) are recommended.]

(6) Chromatographic equipment: jars, racks, troughs, papers, and so on.

(7) *Amino acid chromatography standard solution*: dissolve the following amounts of the amino acids specified in 100 ml of 10 per cent isopropyl alcohol. These amounts will provide 0.10 μg of α-amino nitrogen per 2.5 μl of solution (4). Store this solution in a refrigerator.

Aspartic acid	38 mg	Glutamic acid	42 mg
Lysine	42 mg	Arginine	49 mg
Serine	30 mg	Glycine	21 mg
Histidine	44 mg	Threonine	34 mg
Alanine	25 mg	Proline	33 mg
Tyrosine	52 mg	Valine	33 mg
Methionine	43 mg	Leucine	37 mg
Phenylalanine	47 mg		

(8) *Chromatographic solvent* (4): Prepare by thoroughly shaking together 120 ml of secondary-butanol (peroxide-free) and 40 ml of fresh 3 per cent NH_4OH. The solvent is then ready for use or may be stored in a refrigerator.

(9) *Ninhydrin solution*: Prepare by adding 0.625 g of ninhydrin (triketohydrindene hydrate) and 2.5 ml of glacial acetic acid to acetone and make up to 250 ml with additional acetone. Store in darkness.

(10) Geiger-Mueller counting assembly with a thin-end window detector (less than 2 mg/cm^2) mounted in a probe.

(11) Dark room facilities.

(12) X-ray fixer, rapid X-ray developer, No-Screen medical X-ray film (14 in. × 17 in.), and X-ray exposure holder (14 in. × 17 in.).

D. EXPERIMENTAL PROCEDURE

1. The $^{14}CO_2$ Incorporation Reaction

The steps in preparing the reaction vessel are as follows: Pipette 25 ml of the glucose-salts medium into the center flask of the reaction vessel (see Note 1). Next, add 20 mg of commercial dry yeast to the center flask (see Note 2). Add 36 μc of $Ba^{14}CO_3$ (wetted to avoid subsequent blowing) to the side tube. Immediately apply serum caps to all three openings.

Apply a vacuum in the reaction vessel by evacuating air through a hypodermic needle inserted through the middle serum cap. A water aspirator pump is sufficient for this task. Then inject about 1 ml of 40 per cent perchloric acid (see Notes 3 and 4) with a syringe into the side tube to liberate $^{14}CO_2$ (see Note 5). In order to sweep the $^{14}CO_2$ into the main flask, quickly introduce a flow of air by inserting a long hypodermic needle deep into the side tube, but not touching the liquid. Then remove this needle immediately.

Place the reaction vessel on a shaker table for 1 hr at about 30°C to allow the *fixation reaction* to proceed adequately. A longer time can be used with a consequently greater amount of $^{14}CO_2$ incorporation. Remove the reaction vessel from the shaker and inject about 10 ml of 6N NaOH through the serum cap into the empty side flask to react with and trap the excess $^{14}CO_2$. Inject about 10 ml of 6N HCl through the serum cap into the center flask to drive off the dissolved $^{14}CO_2$ and inactivate the cells. Replace the reaction vessel on the shaker table for about 10 min to assure complete $^{14}CO_2$ trapping.

The solution in the *side tube* may be pipetted out and discarded into the drain. It should not be radioactive, but to check on the completeness of the $^{14}CO_2$ generation from the original $Ba^{14}CO_3$, a planchet could be prepared for G-M assay.

The solution in the *side flask* contains the unreacted ^{14}C trapped as $NaH^{14}CO_3$. This should be carefully pipetted out and may be saved for other experiments. Wash out the side flask with two or three small amounts of distilled water and add these washings to the preceding solution for storage. If desired, an aliquot of this solution could be placed in a planchet and assayed to determine roughly the percentage recovery.

2. Preparation of the Protein Hydrolysate

Carefully pipette out the *yeast suspension* from the center flask of the reaction vessel and transfer it to a centrifuge tube. Centrifuge the yeast suspension at 2000 to 3000 rpm for 15–20 min. Decant the supernatant into a marked container and store in a refrigerator under cover for further examination, if such an action is needed later. In radiotracer experiments it is desirable to save all fractions involving separation procedures. This provides an opportunity to remedy mistakes and allows for unforeseeable developments.

Add about 1 ml of 12N HCl to the tube of centrifuged cells and then transfer this suspension quantitatively to a small pyrex hydrolysis tube (about 15 ml). Working over a tray, seal the open end of the tube in the flame of an oxygen-gas torch. Inspect the closure carefully to insure that no small openings remain. Allow the tube to cool before proceeding. It is wise to practice sealing a test tube of water before attempting the operation with the radioactive sample.

To prevent any possible loss of radioactive material due to leakage during *hydrolysis*, place the sealed tube in a larger test tube with the sealed end down. Place this, in turn, in a small Erlenmeyer flask and cover the top of the assembly with a small beaker. Autoclave this assembly at 15 psi for 6–8 hr to completely hydrolyze the cellular proteins to amino acids.

3. Separation of the Amino Acids by Paper Chromatography

a. *Separating the amino acids.* After the hydrolysis tube has cooled to room temperature, it should be cautiously opened under a hood. This is done by making a file scratch around the neck of the tube and then touching a red-hot glass rod to the scratch. A certain amount of black *humin* (a side product of the hydrolysis operation) will be seen in the tube, but it can be ignored.

The hydrolysate in the tube is next evaporated to dryness on a steam bath to remove HCl and water. Repeat this step at least twice. Alternatively, one can use a simplified procedure which involves placing the hydrolysis tube in a vacuum dessicator containing fresh P_2O_5 in the bottom and a beaker of concentrated NaOH. The dessicator is slowly evacuated to prevent splashing and is allowed to stand overnight. Whichever procedure is followed, the final dry residue should be redissolved in *exactly* 100 μl of water.

b. *Developing the chromatograms.* Prepare three sheets of Whatman No. 1 chromatographic paper of 6 × 22 in. in size with coarse serrations at one end of each (see Note 6). At the other end draw a line with a pencil across the paper 3 in. from the end. The spots should be made along these pencil lines (see Note 7). Mark these sheets A, B, and C, respectively.

On *sheet A* with a micropipette place four spots of the hydrolysate solution in respective amounts of 2.5, 5.0, 7.5, and 10.0 μl (4). Add no more than 2.5 μl at a time on a spot. Allow this amount to dry, then respot. Space the four spots equally along the pencil line at the upper end of the sheet and make a notation nearby in pencil of the nature and amount of the spot. This sheet will be used later for the autoradiographic detection of the labeled amino acids and will not be treated with ninhydrin.

On *sheet B* likewise place two spots of the hydrolysate solution in amounts of 2.5 and 5.0 μl and two spots of amino acid standard solution (item 7, section C) in the same amounts. On *sheet C*, apply spots as previously, but use 7.5 and 10.0 μl amounts of both sample and standard solutions. Thus, on the second and third sheets a direct comparison of the standard and sample amino acids in various amounts can be made later.

Place the three sheets on racks in a chamber prepared for descending chromatography. After closing the chamber, allow it to equilibrate with the dish of solvent at the bottom for 1–2 hr. At that time fill the solvent trough through the hole in the top of the chamber with the secondary-butanol/ammonia solvent (item 8, section C).

The *amino acids* which move most rapidly down the paper (leucine and phenylalanine) travel only about one-half to one-third the speed of the solvent front. Since the solvent front reaches the bottom of the paper in about 24 hr, it will take 48–72 hr to secure maximum separation of the amino acid mixture. The desirable time for the development of the paper chromatograms can be determined by placing a drop of phenol red alongside the hydrolysate spot. This dye stuff moves with this particular solvent at approximately the same rate as the fastest-moving amino acid.

Dry all three sheets in a hood. When dry, spray the whole of chromatogram sheets B and C with *ninhydrin* solution and again hang them up to dry. Save sheet A intact for subsequent autoradiography or scanning counting (see Note 8). Since ninhydrin decarboxylates the amino acids, some $^{14}CO_2$ will be released. Thus, these steps should be performed under a hood. The two dried chromatograms are then placed in a warm oven for about 30 min to intensify the colors.

Examination will reveal which one of the sample and standard amino acids increments used is optimal. By comparison of the colored spots on the sample and standard chromatograms, the *amino acid composition* of the yeast hydrolysate may be roughly determined. Of course, not all the amino acids separated from the hydrolysate are radioactively labeled (see Note 9).

The *linear arrangement of amino acid spots* in order of increasing movement (commonly called Rf values) on the standard chromatogram is given by Roland and Gross (4) as follows: aspartic acid—glutamic acid-cystine (unresolved), lysine, arginine, glycine-serine (unresolved), histidine-threonine (unresolved), alanine, proline (reacts with ninhydrin to give a yellow spot—easily overlooked), tyrosine, valine, methionine, isoleucine, leucine, phenylalanine. In general, the spots will be equally spaced, except for gaps occurring between alanine and proline, and between methionine and isoleucine.

4. Detection of the Labeled Amino Acids by Autoradiography

For an adequate exposure, a chromatogram spot and the film should remain in contact long enough for approximately 10^7 beta particles per square centimeter to be absorbed by the emulsion. This *exposure time* can be only roughly calculated. Using a thin end-window G-M detector, locate the radioactive spots on chromatogram A and select one of moderate activity. From the determined count rate of this spot, the area of the detector window (see Note 10), and the known ^{14}C detection efficiency of the G-M detector under similar conditions, calculate the exposure time required to produce an adequate image on the film. Since the various spots on the chromatogram will vary considerably in the amount of ^{14}C they contain, this calculated exposure time will represent a compromise value.

Using a rubber stamp and radioactive ink (that is, a few drops of sodium acetate—^{14}C solution on an ink pad in a self-contained box to control contamination) mark the chromatogram at three points to allow subsequent alignment of it with the developed autoradiogram. Working in a darkroom, place a 7 in. × 17 in. sheet of *X-ray film* in an X-ray film holder. Arrange chromatogram sheet A on it and attach it to the film at both ends with small pieces of cellulose tape. Close the holder and store in darkness for the required exposure time, either weighted or clamped tight.

At the end of the calculated exposure time remove the film, working under a red safe light. The film should then be *developed* in X-ray developer, washed briefly, fixed in X-ray fixer and finally washed in water for at least 20 min. Follow the directions on developer and fixer containers for time and solution temperature to be used, or use your own judgment of these parameters based on personal experience.

The optimal chromatogram of the amino acid standards and that of the hydrolysate sample should now be placed alongside the autoradiograms for comparison. The relative amount of radioactive ^{14}C in each spot on the autoradiogram can be determined by comparing the degree of blackening produced on the film. By comparison with the chromatogram of amino acid standards, the identity of the radioactive spots can be determined (see Note 11). Make a *table* of the amino acids detected on the chromatograms of the yeast hydrolysate and the degree, if any, of ^{14}C incorporation found in them, as judged from the autoradiograms. [For further information on the mechanism of CO_2 incorporation by yeasts see the articles by Davis, et al. (2), and Stoppani, et al. (5).]

E. EXPERIMENTAL NOTES

(1) Aseptic technique need not be rigorously followed here owing to the short growth time and the large number of cells introduced initially. Of course, the glucose-salts medium must be autoclaved, if prepared well in advance. Dried yeast cells are used here primarily because the experiment is intended as a course project to be performed in an instructional laboratory.

(2) Many other microorganisms could just as well have been used (3). It should be repeated that the basic techniques are applicable to such further study with little or no modification. If culture suspensions are utilized, appropriate calibration must be available to allow calculation of the dry weight of the cell sample.

(3) Why was perchloric acid used here, rather than some more common acid, such as HCl?

(4) An interesting variation could be followed here by flushing the reaction vessel with N_2 to determine CO_2 fixation under anaerobic conditions.

(5) If the medium is sufficiently acidic, a solution of $NaH^{14}CO_3$ could simply be added to it directly. The exposure of the yeast cells to gaseous $^{14}CO_2$ generated in a closed system is followed in this experiment, since this method is of more general application. It can also be employed with animal or plant tissues, where use of HCO_3^- solutions would not be possible.

(6) If available, the pinking shears used by seamstresses are useful for this purpose when many chromatograms must be prepared.

(7) Handle the chromatogram sheets as little as possible and then by the edges. Otherwise the later development of the chromatogram will bring out a blur of fingerprints. It is preferable to wash the hands thoroughly with soap before this part of the experiment.

(8) Why was the chromatogram to be used in autoradiography not treated with ninhydrin? It may be so treated, if desired, after the autoradiogram has been prepared.

(9) If one desires to preserve the ninhydrin-reacted spots, it is suggested that the chromatograms be stored in a desiccator in a nitrogen atmosphere in the dark.

(10) It is often convenient to prepare a lead shield with a 1 cm sq opening to fit over the end-window of the G-M detector. In this way the count rate from weak beta-emitters, such as ^{14}C, can be determined directly in cpm/cm^2. (Why would such a technique not be acceptable for use with ^{131}I-labeled chromatogram spots?)

(11) If a G-M chromatogram scanner attached to a chart recorder is available, its record of the radioactive pattern along the chromatogram sheet would offer a valuable comparison to the autoradiogram.

BIBLIOGRAPHY

1. Block, Richard J., Emmett L. Durrum, and Gunter Zweig. 1958. A manual of paper chromatography and paper electrophoresis. 2nd ed. Academic Press, New York. 710 p.

2. Davis, J. Wendell, et al. 1956. Carbon dioxide fixation and biosynthesis of amino acids in yeast. Biochim. Biophys. Acta 21:101–105.

3. Lynch, Victoria H., and Melvin Calvin. 1952. CO_2 fixation by microorganisms. J. Bacteriol. 63:525–531.

4. Roland, J. F., Jr., and A. M. Gross. 1954. Quantitative determination of amino acids using monodimensional paper chromatography. Anal. Chem. 26:502–505.

5. Stoppani, A. O. M., et al. 1958. Assimilation of carbon dioxide by yeasts. Biochem. J. 70:438–455.

A Time Course Study of $^{14}CO_2$ *Production from Rats Metabolizing Glucose-*^{14}C *Substrate*

A most important branch of radiotracer methodology concerns kinetic studies of respiratory metabolism. The term *radiorespirometry* has been given to this type of investigation. The present experiment illustrates one type of radiorespirometric study involving an ion chamber coupled with a vibrating-reed electrometer as the detection instrument. With this instrument, one can make a continuous measurement of the $^{14}CO_2$ respired by a rat previously administered specifically or uniformly labeled glucose. By means of an infrared analyzer in the flow system, the total CO_2 respired can also be continuously monitored. From these two concurrent measurements, specific activity can be readily calculated.

Detailed information is given on the assembly and operation of a flow system incorporating the foregoing two measuring instruments. Factors to be considered in the experimental design that are peculiar to flow measurements are discussed at length. In addition, a series of research applications for such a measuring system are described and representative references cited.

A. SURVEY OF THE PROBLEM

The rate of catabolism in rats of a labeled substrate can be followed by detecting the respiratory evolution of $^{14}CO_2$. Various methods of detection have been utilized, most of which depend on sweeping the expired CO_2 out of a respiratory chamber containing the rat and trapping it in a basic solution. The absorption trap is changed at intervals and counting samples (in the form of $BaCO_3$) prepared from the solution are obtained. Sample activity may then be assayed by means of a G-M counter, a proportional counter, or by a liquid scintillation counter if the respiratory CO_2 was trapped in an organic trapping agent. The chief drawback of these methods is the extensive time involved in sample preparation and counting, and even then only cumulative interval samples are obtained.

By contrast, the method employed in this experiment allows continuous and instantaneous measurements of both $^{14}CO_2$ and total CO_2 to be made over an extended period of time. The need for subsequent sample preparation and assay is entirely eliminated. The instrumentation required is relatively expensive to acquire, but this is compensated by the saving in research manpower and the availability of a better kinetic picture of rapid metabolic processes.

The *vibrating-reed electrometer* is particularly useful because of its extraordinary range of sensitivity (see Chapter 4). Since it is an integrating instrument, rather than a pulse counter, it is well adapted to continous gas flow measurements. As the respired $^{14}CO_2$ from the animal passes through the ion chamber connected to the electrometer, an *ion current* is produced which is exactly proportional to the instantaneous activity of the air sample. This ion current may be measured by two different methods: (1) the rate of charge of a calibrated capacitor, (2) the equilibrium voltage developed across a calibrated resistor. For flow measurements, the second method is preferable (see p. 73). In this case, the voltage (in millivolts) produced by the ion current is displayed on a meter. Simple calculations allow conversion of the meter reading directly to radioactivity (in microcuries). These instantaneous voltage measurements may be manually recorded at frequent intervals, continuously recorded on a strip chart, or converted to digital form by a suitable analog-to-digital integrating system.

If only $^{14}CO_2$ measurements were made, variations in the respiratory rate of the rat (as from physical activity) would cause artifactual peaks in the activity pattern. This being the case, it is necessary to determine total CO_2 respired and calculate the *specific activity* of the air flow being monitored. An infrared CO_2 analyzer is well suited for this purpose. It operates on the principle that CO_2 readily absorbs certain infrared wave lengths, whereas other components of the air do not. The extent of infrared absorption by the respired air passing through the sample cell is a direct measure of its CO_2 content. Since this instrument is not commonly found in biological laboratories, an alternative method of determining total CO_2 is also described.

It is suggested that the rats to be used in each experiment be fasted for 24 hr, after which the labeled glucose is administered by stomach tube.

The animal's respiratory CO_2 is measured over a 6–8 hr period and then it is again allowed access to food for two days. A 48-hr fasting is next imposed and subsequently a new dose of labeled glucose administered, followed by another 6–8 hr measurement period. Thus, the effect of length of fasting on the respiratory CO_2 pattern can be elucidated, with each rat serving as its own control. The number of rats to be used will depend upon the available time.

The research possibilities of this method are numerous. It offers an opportunity to investigate metabolic pathway participation when ^{14}C specifically labeled substrates are administered (1–2; 4–8). Domingues, et al (1) strongly emphasize the value of this respirometric method in evaluating the metabolic effects of various toxic substances. The method is not limited to rats, but could potentially be used with a wide variety of organisms. Tolbert, et al (7) and LeRoy, et al (2) have even adapted the apparatus for human subjects.

B. EXPERIMENTAL DESIGN

In determining the amount of activity to use in an experiment of this type, the many variables introduced because of the *dynamic* nature of the system must be considered. The following parameters deserve particular attention: air flow rate, size of ion chamber, response time of both electrometer and CO_2 analyzer, and rate of CO_2 evolution by the animal. In the present experiment, the response time of the CO_2 analyzer is so short with respect to that of the electrometer that it may be ignored. Likewise, the rate of CO_2 output by the rat will be quite small compared to the air flow rate through the system.

For optimal operating conditions, the electrometer response time, the ion chamber size, and the air flow rate must be in balance. The time in seconds for 63 per cent response of the electrometer is equal to the value of the input resistance (in ohms) times the capacitance (in farads) of the electrometer head. Since the higher the resistance used, the greater the electrometer sensitivity, a lower level of activity to be detected will, of necessity, result in a longer response time. Again, the air flow rate must not be such that the ion chamber is emptied at a rate exceeding the response time of the electrometer. Of course, the larger the ion chamber size, the greater the amount of $^{14}CO_2$ activity in it to be detected. It is equally true that ^{14}C detection efficiency is relatively better with larger sizes of ion chambers. When the size is reduced below 114 ml, ^{14}C detection efficiency is known to be reduced drastically. As chamber size increases, however, a given air flow rate will result in successively longer emptying times. These factors have been taken into consideration in the following calculations, but must be individually evaluated for systems other than that specified later. Tolbert, et al. (6) have discussed these features at great length.

(1) If an ion chamber of 1-liter volume is used with a constant air flow rate of about 333 ml/min, the ion chamber will then contain at any given instant the amount of $^{14}CO_2$ exhaled by the rat during a 3-min period.

(2) If the respiratory activity of the rat is to be followed for 8 hr (480 min), at any given instant the ion chamber would contain $\frac{3}{480} = \frac{1}{160}$ of the total respiratory output for the experimental period. This, of course, assumes constant mixing and emptying factors for both animal chamber and ion chamber.

(3) If, on the basis of electrometer sensitivity and response time considerations, it is desired to detect an average of 10 mμc of $^{14}CO_2$ in the ion chamber at any given time, then a cumulative total of

$$10 \text{ m}\mu\text{c } ^{14}CO_2 \text{ average per 3-min interval} \times 160 \text{ such intervals} = 1.6\ \mu\text{c } ^{14}CO_2$$

would need to be detected.

(4) If it is assumed that approximately 25 per cent of the intubated glucose ^{14}C activity will be cumulatively recovered over the 8-hr course of the experiment [in accord with Wang, et al. (8)], then the required initial dose of glucose ^{14}C would be

$$\frac{1.6\ \mu\text{c detected}}{0.25 \text{ recovery}} = 6.4\ \mu\text{c required}$$

Such calculations do not take into account the fluctuation of $^{14}CO_2$ activity in the expired air over the course of the experiment, but are based on an average activity measurement. The foregoing method is satisfactory, however, because of the electrometer's extraordinary range of sensitivity. The assumptions are also in line with the authors' own experimental results.

Wang, et al (8) found a surprising relation between substrate level of glucose used and respiratory $^{14}CO_2$ pattern. Not only was the time of the activity peak affected, but even the extent of cumulative $^{14}CO_2$ recovery. It is suggested, therefore, that the amount of "cold" substrate prescribed in this experiment be precisely followed. The glucose ^{14}C activity just calculated (1–2 mg in weight) should be added to 1500 mg of unlabeled glucose for optimal results. This amount is recommended to minimize the dilution effect derived from the presence of unlabeled endogenous glucose in a rat. Endogenous glucose, or its close derivative, is estimated to be approximately 300–500 mg for a rat weighing 300 g. The substrate administration procedure given here is in contrast to the intravenous procedure employed by other workers. With intravenous procedures, one can introduce only milligram quantities of labeled glucose into the rat, which will be diluted by a much larger amount of endogenous glucose. Such dilution introduces serious complications in the interpretation of $^{14}CO_2$ data obtained in an experiment of the present type.

C. MATERIALS AND EQUIPMENT REQUIRED

The measuring instruments required for this experiment are quite costly and may not be found in many biological laboratories; hence, an alternative experimental method is also described. In either case, the supplementary components needed are normally readily available, but will need to be assembled into the flow system to be specificed.

(1) Vibrating-reed electrometer (such as the Cary Electrometer model 31, manufactured by the Applied Physics Corporation, or the Dynacon, manufactured by the Nuclear Chicago Corp.) equipped with a 1-liter flow-type ion chamber. If a smaller ion chamber is used, the amount of activity required will be affected.

(2) (Optional) Harmonically-filtered voltage-regulating transformer for use with the electrometer when measuring very small ion currents.

(3) Infrared CO_2 analyzer (such as that made by the Mines Safety Appliance Company or the Beckman Instrument Company) fitted to measure CO_2 ranges from 0–1 per cent and 0–5 per cent.

(4) Tank of 0.5 per cent $^{14}CO_2$ in air (having a specific activity of 10 mμc/liter) for standardizing the electrometer and the CO_2 analyzer.

(5) Pair of strip chart recorders to make a permanent and continuous record of electrometer and CO_2 measurements during the course of the individual experiments.

(6) Male white rats of about 350 g.

(7) Calculated activity of glucose-^{14}C.

(8) Flow system: Figure B-1 illustrates the suggested arrangement of apparatus for this experiment. Of course, other variations and refinements are possible. The following items are needed for the flow system in addition to those previously listed:

   (a) Flow meter—covering the range of air flows to be used.

   (b) Animal chamber: A Roth metabolism cage (3) (from Delmar Scientific Laboratories, Maywood, Ill.) is desirable but a desiccator jar (2–6-liter capacity) with a hole in the lid to accommodate a large rubber stopper is also quite suitable. Seal the lid on with stopcock grease to prevent leakage of air.

   (c) Drying tube—of sufficient size to hold about ½ lb. of drying agent ($CaCl_2$, Drierite, or the like).

   (d) Demountable ball and socket joint, or three-way stopcock—mounted between the electrometer and the CO_2 analyzer to allow

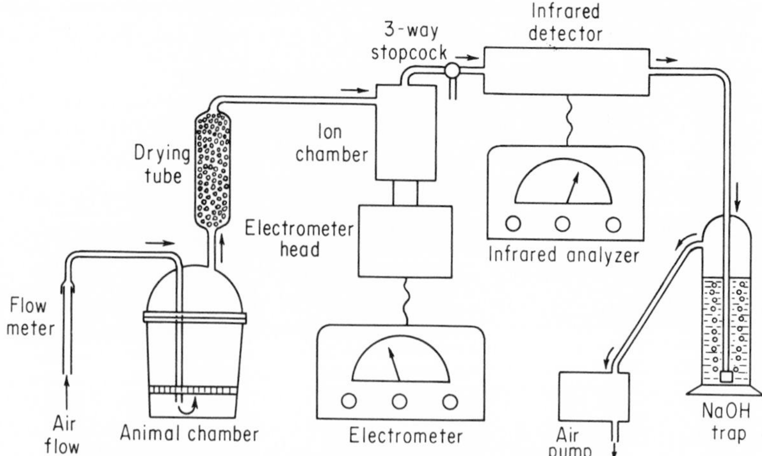

Figure B-1. Schematic diagram of continuous $^{14}CO_2/CO_2$ analyzer system.

introduction of standardizing gas to the latter without flushing the entire system.

(e) Gas washing bottle with fritted disk—for trapping the CO_2 in NaOH at the end of the flow system. If the alternative experimental procedure is followed, a trap that can be drained periodically must be used. The assembly for metabolic studies of this type manufactured by Delmar Scientific Laboratories is quite adequate for this type of experiment.

(f) Vacuum pump—equipped with a valve to regulate air flow.

D. EXPERIMENTAL PROCEDURES

1. Preparation of Animals and Apparatus

Assemble the flow system as illustrated in Figure B-1; test it for constancy of air flow and freedom from leakage. These two features are essential for the success of the experiment, and no effort should be spared in achieving them.

One should become thoroughly familiar with the operation of the measuring instruments to be used. In this regard, consult in detail the instruction manuals provided by the manufacturers. In the case of the electrometer, this would include determining the background current in the absence of an ion chamber, and subsequently with the chamber mounted in place and a normal air flow passing through it. Practice setting the zero point and standardizing the infrared analyzer with gas of known CO_2 concentration.

As the initial step in each experiment, measure the ion chamber background current (see Note 1) and adjust the electrometer zero point for the sensitivity range that will cover the anticipated activity levels to be encountered. The infrared analyzer should likewise be zeroed and standardized. In the case of both instruments, these settings vary somewhat with time. Thus, they must be determined anew for each experiment.

The rat to be used in each measurement period should be fasted for either 24 or 48 hr before administration of the glucose-^{14}C to reduce the size of the endogenous carbohydrate pool (see p. 325). It should be weighed just before intubation.

Prepare the glucose dose by mixing the calculated amount of glucose-^{14}C with 1500 mg of unlabeled glucose and dissolving this in sufficient water to yield a 50 per cent solution (w/v). Administer this solution to the rat by means of a syringe and stomach tube (1.14 mm I.D. polyethylene tubing on an 18-gauge Luer stub adapter), taking care to rinse any residue from the tubing into the stomach with a small quantity of water. Place the rat in the animal chamber immediately and start the flow of air through the system.

2. The Measurement Period

Throughout the entire 6–8 hr period of the experiment the air flow must be maintained at a constant rate. This rate will have been previously chosen, based on considerations discussed earlier.

Particularly in the early period of the experiment, it is necessary to observe the electrometer meter reading carefully so as to adjust the sensitivity range as the ion current increases to a maximum value. The CO_2 analyzer does not require such careful attention, since total CO_2 concentration should remain at a rather constant value throughout the experiment (see Note 2).

The meter readings on both measuring instruments may be recorded as frequently as the observer desires. Regular intervals of 10–15 min should be often enough. If chart recorders are available, even less attention to recording data is required. The simplicity of such a measurement system compared to other methods involving extensive sample preparation is evident (see Note 3).

At the end of the measurement period remove the animal from the flow system and return it to its cage. It will be necessary to place this cage under a fume hood or in a room equipped with an exhaust vent for at least 24 hr to prevent $^{14}CO_2$ contamination of the laboratory by the expired air.

Maintain an air flow through the system until the electrometer reading returns to the initial background level, in order to reduce the possibility of residual contamination of the apparatus.

3. Calculation and Evaluation of Data

The recorded electrometer meter readings (in millivolts) should be converted to $^{14}CO_2$ activity in millimicrocuries as follows:

$$\text{(B-1)} \qquad I \text{ in amperes} = \frac{E \text{ in volts (meter reading)}}{R \text{ in ohms (input resistance used)}}$$

$$\text{(B-2)} \qquad \text{Activity in microcuries} = \frac{I \text{ in amperes}}{\text{ion chamber constant in amperes}/\mu c}$$

Convert activity in microcuries to millimicrocuries. The ion chamber constant in amperes/μc can be readily determined by the use of the calibration gas mixture ($^{14}CO_2$ in air).

The recorded CO_2 analyzer meter readings should now be converted to mmole CO_2. Using the manufacturer's calibration curve, determine per cent of CO_2 in the air stream from the meter deflection.

$$\text{(B-3)} \qquad \text{Ion chamber volume in milliliters} \times \text{percentage } CO_2 = \text{milliliters } CO_2 \text{ in ion chamber}$$

$$\text{(B-4)} \qquad \frac{\text{ml } CO_2 \text{ in ion chamber}}{22.4 \text{ ml/mmole } CO_2} = \text{mmole } CO_2 \text{ in ion chamber}$$

From the preceding data, calculate specific activity as mμc $^{14}CO_2$/mmole CO_2 for each instantaneous measurement (see Note 4) and plot against time.

Note time and height of the specific activity peak for each curve. (Do secondary peaks occur? After the major peak, does specific activity decline steadily or does the curve flatten out to relatively constant specific activity during the latter portion of the measurement period?)

In comparing the curves for 24-hr fasted and 48-hr fasted rats, do any significant differences appear? (How might these be interpreted? If two or more rats have been used, how do their respiratory CO_2 patterns compare under the same fasting conditions?

From the activity data just calculated, prepare a curve of cumulative $^{14}CO_2$ recovery over the course of the experiment. (Do the cumulative recoveries at the end of the individual experiments differ for the various rats and conditions used?)

The data derived from this experiment can serve as a basis for further investigations of the effects of various chemical agents or physiological stresses on carbohydrate metabolism (1–2, 4–8).

E. EXPERIMENTAL NOTES

(1) With the activity level suggested for this experiment, the background ion current should be so small by comparison as to be ignored. If it does appear to be considerable at any time, institute decontamination of the ion chamber.

(2) Owing to the volume of air in the flow system and to mixing factors, an initial period of several min may be required before a constant CO_2 concentration is attained. Thus, measurements of CO_2 concentration in the air flow before this time will be lower than normal.

(3) In the absence of one or both of the measuring instruments, an alternative procedure may be employed. If an electrometer alone is available, the total expired CO_2 may be determined by draining and replacing the solution in the NaOH trap at brief intervals. (A pair of traps equipped with a stopcock to direct air flow into either trap alternately is advisable.) The absorbed CO_2 may then be precipitated from the solution as $BaCO_3$ by adding a mixture of 1 N NH_4Cl and 1 N $BaCl_2$. The function of the NH_4Cl is to reduce the alkalinity derived from the unaffected sodium hydroxide in the trap solution. Such a treatment is necessary if one desires to mount the $BaCO_3$ sample for assay of radioactivity. From the weight of this $BaCO_3$, the total CO_2 recovered during the sample interval may be calculated.

If neither an electrometer or a CO_2 analyzer is available, kinetic studies may still be carried out, although at the cost of considerably more time and effort. The NaOH trap is periodically drained as just described, but only an aliquot of the solution is used. Planchets are prepared of the precipitated $BaCO_3$ and a G-M counter is employed for activity assay. Again, from the weight of the $BaCO_3$ aliquot, the total CO_2 collected during the sample interval can be calculated. The cumbersome nature of such a method contrasts sharply with the directness and relative simplicity of the electrometer—CO_2 analyzer system.

(4) Even this calculation of specific activity can be done instrumentally if a ratio analyzer and recorder are employed (1–2,4, 6–7).

BIBLIOGRAPHY

1. Domingues, F. J., et al. 1959. An instrument and technique for the continuous measurement of respiratory CO_2 patterns in metabolic tracer studies. Intern. J Appl. Radiation Isotopes 7:77–86.

2. Le Roy, George V., et al. 1960. Continuous measurement of specific activity of $C^{14}O_2$ in expired air. Intern. J. Appl. Radiation Isotopes 7:273–286.

3. Roth, Lloyd J., et al. 1948. Studies on the metabolism of radioactive nicotinic acid and nicotinamide in mice. J. Biol. Chem. 176:249–257.

4. Tolbert, B. M., J. H. Lawrence, and M. Calvin. 1956. Respiratory carbon-14 patterns and physiological state. *In* Proc. Intern. Conf. Peaceful Uses of Atomic Energy, Geneva, 1955. vol. 12. United Nations, New York. p. 281–285.

5. Tolbert, B. M., et al. 1956. Effect of coenzyme A on the metabolic oxidation of labeled fatty acids: Rate studies, instrumentation and liver fractionation. Arch. Biochem. Biophys. 60:301–319.

6. Tolbert, B. M., Martha Kirk, and E. M. Baker. 1956. Continuous $C^{14}O_2$ and CO_2 excretion studies in experimental animals. Am. J. Physiol. 185:269–274.

7. Tolbert, Bert M., Martha Kirk, and Frank Upham. 1959. Carbon-14 respiration pattern analyzer for clinical studies. Rev. Sci. Instruments 30:116–120.

8. Wang, Chih H., et al. 1962. Catabolism of glucose and gluconate in intact rats. Proc. Soc. Exp. Biol. Med. 111:93–97.

The Effect of X Irradiation on Bone Marrow Activity in Rats as Measured by Iron-59 Incorporation into Erythrocytes

The following experiment is included to exemplify a specific use of ^{59}Fe as a tracer in the study of erythropoiesis. It involves tracing the fate of ^{59}Fe ions in the white rat as they are utilized in hemoglobin synthesis. The actual incorporation of the ^{59}Fe occurs in the erythroid bone marrow; the extent of the incorporation is ascertained from the degree of ^{59}Fe labeling later found in the circulating erythrocytes after their release into the peripheral bloodstream. Since the radionuclide used emits energetic gamma photons, the blood cell samples are readily assayed for radioactivity by means of a well-type NaI(T1) crystal scintillation detector.

Specifically, the experiment is designed to illustrate the use of a radiotracer to investigate a phase of *radiation biology*. Do not confuse the field of radiation biology, which concerns the effects of radiation on living organisms, with the employment of radiotracers. The two disciplines are distinct in both purpose and methodology. In this particular experiment, ^{59}Fe incorporation is used strictly as a means to secure information on the damaging effect of X-irradiation on erythropoiesis.

A. SURVEY OF THE PROBLEM

The marked radiosensitivity of the *hematopoietic organs* has been recognized for nearly sixty years. Penetrating radiation produces well-defined changes in both the circulating blood and the blood forming organs. The changes observed in the circulating blood, however, appear to be due primarily to radiation effects on the hematopoietic tissues. The major areas of hematopoiesis are the spleen, lymphatic tissue, thymus gland, and bone marrow. This experiment is concerned primarily with radiation effects on the latter tissue.

The bulk of earlier information concerning the effect of radiation on bone marrow was obtained by direct cytological examination of the tissue following irradiation. After large doses (several hundred roentgens) of whole body X-irradiation, a cessation of mitotic activity and a degeneration of hematopoietic cells is seen within less than an hour. On the other hand, mature erythrocytes in the circulating blood seemed relatively resistant to the same radiation dose. Since these mature red cells have a rather long life span (about 120 days) little change in the red blood cell count of the circulating blood would be noted immediately, even though all bone marrow production was completely stopped. Hence, the use of tracer doses of ^{59}Fe is a valuable method for following red cell production after irradiation. The earliest such work was done by Hennessy and Huff (6) at the University of California. Application of the ^{59}Fe technique became more feasible with the development of the NaI(Tl) crystal scintillation detector. Thereafter, the original technique was improved and applied to a variety of related radiobiological problems. The list of references at the end of the experiment includes most of these significant applications and can serve as a point of departure for further research adaptations.

This technique is effective because the incorporation of iron into the *hemoglobin* molecules of red blood cells takes place almost entirely in the bone marrow. Only a small amount of additional iron is taken up by the red cells once they have been liberated into the peripheral blood (8). Thus, the extent to which an injected dose of ^{59}Fe appears later in the circulating red blood cells is a direct indication of mitotic activity in the bone marrow. The method is both more sensitive and simpler than the use of cytological examination to determine the depression of erythropoiesis in marrow tissue. As an indication of the sensitivity of the method, Hennessy and Huff (6) found a detectable depression of ^{59}Fe uptake with X ray doses even as low as 5–25 roentgens.

The technique is well adapted for following a *time course* of erythropoiesis in irradiated animals. This experiment represents an abbreviated time course more suitable for class use. In this way, the sharp initial depression of bone marrow activity immediately following nonlethal doses of X-irradiation can be seen, as well as the rapidity of return to normal activity. Figure C-1, modified from the data of Hennessy and Okunewick (7), illustrates such a time course for rats given 100 roentgens of X-irradiation.

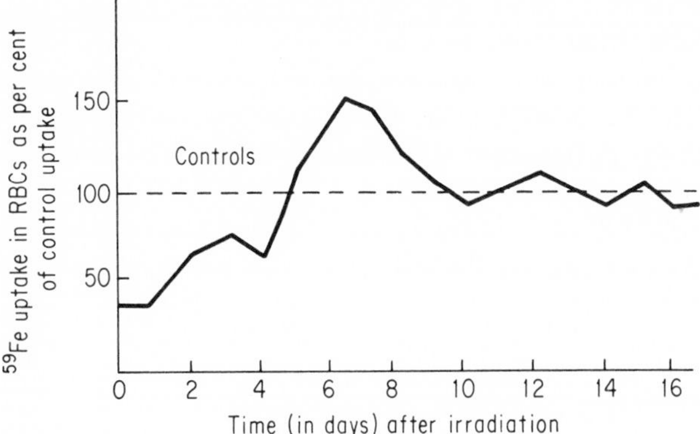

Figure C-1. ^{59}Fe uptake in rats following 100 Roentgens of x-irradiation.

The *time lag* between the incorporation of the ^{59}Fe into developing red cells in the bone marrow and the appearance of these cells in the circulating blood makes it necessary to wait for a predetermined interval after injection of the radioiron before removing blood samples. Investigators in the field have commonly used a 24-hr interval. Note that the degree of ^{59}Fe labeling found in the red cell samples is more nearly a measure of bone marrow activity soon after the original injection, rather than at the time of removing the sample.

One of the striking features brought out by this tracer method is the very clear relation between *irradiation dose and percentage uptake* of administered ^{59}Fe. This relation is an inverse one. The greater the irradiation dose given, the smaller the ^{59}Fe uptake into the red cells. This effect was demonstrated in the original work by Hennessy and Huff (6) and has been repeatedly confirmed since then. Their data are summarized in Figure C-2. On the basis of this relationship, Mirand, et al. (9) have suggested that uptake of ^{59}Fe would be useful as an indication of the degree of recovery occurring in an individual in the early post irradiation period before normal clinical tests could be applied.

In this experiment, the effects of only two irradiation doses on white rats will be followed over a period of one week. This arrangement is purely for convenience and economy in class use. It would be of interest to follow the effects of several different dosages over a longer time period.

Just after the initial irradiation of the experimental animals, one-third of the rats are injected intraperitoneally with appropriate tracer doses of ^{59}Fe. *Twenty-four hours* later these animals are sacrificed and a blood sample removed for separation of the red blood cells by centrifugation. The radioactivity in an aliquot of these washed cells is then determined by means of well-type NaI(Tl) scintillation detector. Appropriate calculations of the percentage of injected ^{59}Fe incorporated into the circulating red blood cells are then made.

At *three days* post irradiation, another one-third of the rats will be injected with ^{59}Fe, and likewise, blood samples taken 24 hr later. Finally on the *sixth day* of the experiment the last third of the animals are injected and their blood sampled 24 hr later. A graphic record can then be plotted reflecting erythropoiesis in the controls and in the two irradiated groups over the seven-day period studied.

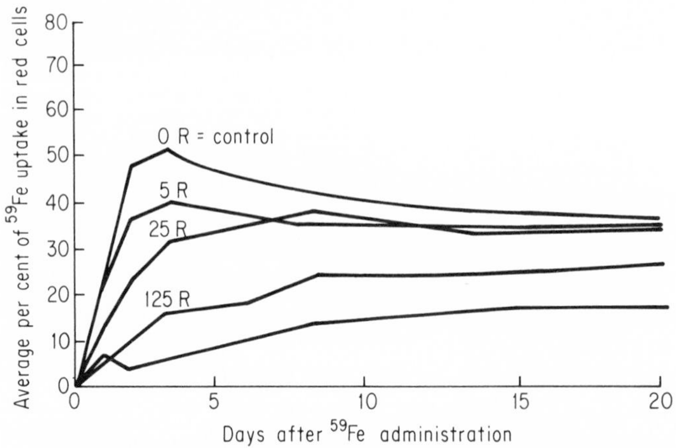

Figure C-2. Iron uptake in red cells of rats following exposure to varying dosages of total body x-irradiation.

The radioiron tracer technique has been employed as a measure of the effectiveness of *radiation protective agents* and therapy. It seems admirably suited for this purpose owing to its sensitivity and relation to dose received. Bose (3) has used it to determine the protective effect of cyanide on lethally irradiated rats. Mirand, et al. (9) have employed it to measure the therapeutic effect of various types of bone marrow transplants. This type of application of the technique offers broad potential for further research.

B. EXPERIMENTAL DESIGN

Two basic problems must be faced in designing this experiment: (1) how much radioactivity should be injected so as to get a readily measurable amount of activity in the red cell sample? Some factors to be considered are the amount of dilution occurring, the extent of iron incorporation into red blood cells, and the well capacity and efficiency of the scintillation detector. (2) What is the specific activity of the ^{59}Fe used?

The total amount of iron injected must not be so high as to create an unphysiological situation. These two issues will be taken up separately.

First, the *amount of activity* required must be calculated. Since the animals given the greatest dose of radiation (the 300-R group) will be expected to show the lowest iron uptake, the activity required for them will be calculated. This will then be a more than adequate amount of activity for the other two groups.

(1) Since rats average about 5 ml blood per 100 g body weight, if 200-g animals are used, they can be expected to have a total blood volume of around 10 ml.
(2) If a scintillation detector is used with a well volume of 1 ml, then the activity in one-tenth of the total blood volume could be determined in a single sample.
(3) Red blood cells normally comprise nearly 50 per cent (hematocrit value) of the blood volume of the rat. The 1-ml blood sample used could then be expected to have about 0.5 ml of red cells, or one-tenth of the total red cell mass.
(4) Under the conditions of this experiment, not less than 5 per cent of the intraperitoneally injected ^{59}Fe can be expected to be incorporated into the circulating red blood cells. Thus, the 0.5 ml of red cells in the counting sample would contain $0.1 \times 0.05 = 0.005$ of the dose of ^{59}Fe administered.
(5) With a scintillation well crystal having a detection efficiency of about 20 per cent for the 1.1 and 1.3 Mev gamma rays emitted by ^{59}Fe, only $0.005 \times 0.2 = 0.001$ of the ^{59}Fe activity would be detected by the scintillation counter in the 1-ml blood cell sample.
(6) If a minimum sample count rate of at least 4000 cpm is desired, then the activity injected must be $4000/0.001 = 4.0 \times 10^6$ dpm. This value is equivalent to just under 2 μc per animal. Should the experimental conditions differ from those indicated, appropriate adjustments following the outline foregoing would still allow a calculation of the amount of activity needed.

The second problem deals with *specific activity* of the ^{59}Fe used, that is, the ratio between the activity of the radioiron and the total amount of iron (all isotopes) in the sample. In this particular experiment, this poses no great problem. A specific activity of over 10 μc $^{59}Fe/\mu g$ Fe is readily obtainable. The calculated 2-μc activity could thus be secured in less than 0.2 μg of total iron. This amount is truly a tracer dose and is well within the normal range of physiological fluctuation of this animal.

C. MATERIALS AND EQUIPMENT REQUIRED

(1) X-ray unit—preferably one capable of 200–250 KVP output
(2) X-ray calibration instruments

(3) Well scintillation counting assembly, with supply of counting tubes to fit the well
(4) White rats—eighteen, preferably about 200 g and all of one sex
(5) 36 μc $^{59}FeCl_3$ in citrate buffer and sterile saline—available from most radiopharmaceutical suppliers
(6) Compartmentalized rat irradiation chambers—made of lucite, wood, or wire mesh
(7) Disposable syringes (1 ml and 5 ml) and disposable hypodermic needles (20 gauge and 26 gauge)
(8) Hematocrit capillary tubes (75 mm)
(9) Six cages capable of holding four rats each

D. EXPERIMENTAL PROCEDURES

1. Organization and Initial Irradiation

The 18 rats to be used in the experiment should be divided into *groups* of six each. The six control rats will be sham irradiated; the other two groups are to be given 100 and 300 roentgens whole body X-irradiation, respectively.

Immediately after irradiation two animals from each of the three dosage groups will be injected with radioiron. Twenty-four hours later, blood samples will be taken from these animals and the extent of radioactive labeling of their red blood cells determined. The irradiated animals in this set will be expected to show the greatest depression of iron uptake.

At *three days post irradiation* two more animals from each dosage group will be injected and likewise their blood sampled 24 hr later. Some recovery of bone marrow activity may be seen in the 100-R group by this time.

Finally, at *six days post irradiation*, the remaining animals will be injected and sampled after a 24-hr interval. The 100-R group should have recovered to normal or even above normal iron uptake, whereas the 300-R animals may still show bone marrow depression.

The *X-ray generator* should be calibrated with respect to dose delivery before the irradiation to insure reproducible results. Special attention should be paid to equalization of dose over the size of field to be irradiated. It is preferable to irradiate the two groups in a compartmentalized chamber that can hold all six animals of the group at one time.

Since the following instructions apply to all dosage groups during the course of the experiment, they are not repeated, although there are three different radioiron injections and blood sampling sequences according to the foregoing schedule.

2. Radioiron Injection

Calculate the *amount of* ^{59}Fe to be used according to the outline described in the preceding section on experimental design. Evaluate such factors as weight of the rats, detection efficiency of the scintillation crystal, and size of the scintillation detector well.

The *total volume* injected into each animal should not exceed 0.5 ml. It should be procured or made up in a sterile saline solution.

In injecting, take proper precaution to maintain *sterile conditions*. One syringe may be used for each set of injections if the needles are changed between animals.

Using a 26-gauge needle with a 1-ml syringe, make an *intraperitoneal injection* into each of the six rats in the series. Take care to avoid damage to the internal organs or injection into the intestines.

Danger of spillage requires that one take the *precaution* of wearing rubber gloves and working over a stainless steel tray. When the injections are completed, monitor gloves and working area and decontaminate if necessary. Dispose of syringes and needles immediately in the radioactive waste container.

Place the two injected rats from each dosage group in *separate cages* from their uninjected mates to avoid any radioactive cross contamination. These three cages should be arranged so that the animals' feces and urine fall through wire mesh onto shavings and paper. Since some of the radioactive iron may be excreted during the experiment, these wastes should be regarded as contaminated. The cages themselves will need monitoring and possibly decontaminating at the end of the experiment.

An accurately measured aliquot of the solution used for injection must be saved for later use as a *relative standard.* A 1 per cent aliquot is quite sufficient for this purpose. Place it in a tube of the same size to be used for the blood-counting sample and dilute it to the same volume as the scintillation well capacity.

3. Removal of Blood Samples

Twenty-four hours after the radioiron injection, *weigh* the rats and record the weights. Each rat in turn should then be moderately *anesthetized* (see Note 1) and prepared for dissection. The dissector should wear protective gloves and work over a tray which can be readily decontaminated.

Open the abdomen of each rat, taking care to avoid excessive blood loss, and pull the intestinal mass and fascia aside to expose the dorsal aorta. Now, using a 20-gauge needle with a 5-ml syringe previously treated with an anticoagulant (see Note 2), slowly withdraw as much *blood* as possible from the dorsal aorta. Take care in this operation to maintain the tip of the needle within the lumen of the aorta. If the needle slips out, a jet of blood will immediately issue from the opening, and the sample will be lost. After the sample has been drawn, agitate the syringe to insure good mixing of the anticoagulant.

The blood sample can now be dispensed directly from the syringe to a test tube. A *hematocrit* capillary is next filled from this tube and sealed at one end. Following this, a 1-ml blood sample is pipetted into a *counting vial* which will fit the scintillation detector well. Flush the pipette with saline solution, and add the washings to the blood sample in the vial. To avoid confusion, label each tube carefully. The blood sample vials and hematocrit capillary should now be *centrifuged* at 2000–2500 rpm for 3 min to separate the cells and plasma.

During this time, open the chest cavity of each rat to insure its death before disposing of the animal in the special "radioactive carcass" container. Regard as contaminated all dissecting implements, cotton swabs, and syringes and treat them appropriately.

After centrifuging is complete, the *hematocrit* (the volume percentage of red blood cells in a whole blood sample) can be determined. If a hematocrit reading device is not available, one can make the determination by simple measurement using a millimeter scale.

Very carefully pipette off the clear plasma layer from the *centrifuged sample* in the counting vial, avoiding any disturbance of the packed cells at the bottom of the vial. This step and the next are necessary to remove any traces of plasma which still contain some of the injected ^{59}Fe.

Add about 2 ml of saline solution (0.9 per cent) to the cells and centrifuge as before. Again pipette off the clear washing solution, leaving the packed red cells ready for counting. Dispose of the plasma and this wash solution in the "radioactive liquid waste" container.

4. Sample Counting and Calculations

Place the vial of *washed red cells* in the well of the shielded scintillation detector and record at least 10,000 counts on the scaler register. With all gamma-emitting sources well removed from the detector, determine the *background* radiation level for a minimum period of 10 min. A longer time period would, of course, be more desirable. From these two values and the calculated volume of red cells in the counting sample (hematocrit times milliliters of blood used), calculate the net counts per minute per milliliter of red cells.

The activity of the aliquot of ^{59}Fe prepared previously as a *relative standard* is now likewise counted in the well detector. Knowing what fraction this aliquot represents of the ^{59}Fe dose injected into the rats, the net counts per minute of the entire dose can be calculated. By determining the activity of such a relative standard at the same time that each of the sets of the red cell samples is counted, corrections for radioactive decay and changes in instrument sensitivity are avoided.

The calculation of the percentage uptake of the ^{59}Fe dose into the red blood cells can now be made by the following formula:

$$\text{(C-1)} \qquad \text{Percentage } ^{59}\text{Fe uptake in RBCs} = \frac{\text{animal weight in grams}}{100}$$

$$\times\ 5\ \times\ \text{hematocrit}\ \times\ \frac{\text{cpm/ml RBC sample}}{\text{Total cpm } ^{59}\text{Fe injected}}\ \times\ 100$$

The first two terms are based on the factor of about 5 ml blood per 100 g body weight in rats and, thus, yield total blood volume. Multiplying by the hematocrit gives the total red blood cell (RBC) volume.

Follow the foregoing procedure at each of the three times that blood samples are taken. Keep the same *relative standard* throughout the course of the experiment and count it with each of the three groups of samples.

When all data have been obtained and calculations made, prepare a *graph* plotting percentage of ^{59}Fe uptake in red blood cells against time for each of the dosage groups (see Figure C-2). For this purpose consider the time of uptake as 12 hr after the ^{59}Fe injection. Put all three curves on one graph for comparison. (What basic relations are found between X-irradiation dose and bone marrow activity as measured by ^{59}Fe uptake? What changes in percentage of uptake in the irradiated groups are found over the period of the experiment?)

When all experimental work is completed, rinse the red cell samples into the "radioactive liquid waste" container. Since the relative standard is readily soluble, it can be rinsed down the drain with a large amount of water. Place the tubes used in the container for contaminated glassware.

E. EXPERIMENTAL NOTES

(1) *Etherization* of the rats can be accomplished by placing a pad of cotton sprinkled with ether in a large jar. The cotton is covered with a paper towel, the rat placed in the jar, and the jar covered. Take special precuation to avoid over etherization. It is necessary that the animal's heart remain beating during blood sampling, so that blood is continually pumped through the aorta. Do not wait for complete collapse in the anesthesia chamber. Further etherization, if necessary, can be done during dissection by placing the rat's noze in a crucible containing a cotton pad moistened with ether. *Caution*: ether fumes are ex-explosive. Use a well-ventilated room and ban open flames during the work.

(2) *Anticoagulants* may be prepared as follows: Oxalate—pipette 0.1 ml of a 10 per cent potassium oxalate solution into the syringe to be used for blood sampling. Rotate the syringe so that the solution covers the inner surface with a film. Place this in a hot oven to dry as a film. Heparin—follow a similar preparation process, but use a solution containing 0.2 mg Heparin for every 1.0 ml of blood to be collected. EDTA—similarly use a 5 per cent solution of sodium EDTA.

BIBLIOGRAPHY

1. Baxter, C. F., et al. 1955. Anaemia and erythropoiesis in the irradiated rat: An experimental study with particular reference to techniques involving radiocactive iron. Brit. J. Hematol. 1:86–103.
2. Belcher, E. H., I. G. F. Gilbert, and L. F. Lamerton. 1954. Experimental studies with radioactive iron. Brit. J. Radiol. 27:387–392.
3. Bose, A. 1959. Modification of ^{59}Fe uptake in the circulating blood of lethally irradiated rats protected with cyanide. Intern. J. Radiation Biol. 4:383–386.
4. Furth, Jacob, et al. 1951. The effect of x-irradiation on erythrogenesis, plasma and cell volumes. S. Med. J. 44:85–92.
5. Girvin, Eb C., and John K. Hampton, Jr. 1959. Effect of whole body x-irradiation on plasma iron turnover in rats. Proc. Soc. Exp. Biol. Med. 100: 481–483.
6. Hennessy, Thomas G., and Rex L. Huff. 1950. Depression of tracer ion uptake curve in rat erythrocytes following total body x-irradiation. Proc. Soc. Exp. Biol. Med. 73:436–439.
7. Hennessy, Thomas G., and James P. Okunewick. 1956. Radioiron study of erythropoiesis after x-irradiation. U.S. Atomic Energy Commission. UCLA-383. (Microcard.) 10 p.
8. Lamerton, L. F., and E. H. Belcher. 1957. Effect of whole-body irradiation and various drugs on erythropoietic functions in the rat. Studies with radioactive iron. *In* Advances in radiobiology: Proc. Fifth Intern. Conf. Radiobiol., Stockholm, 1955. Oliver and Boyd, Edinburgh. p. 321–332.
9. Mirand, E. A., J. G. Hoffman, and T. C. Prentice. 1960. Erythropoietic recovery measured by Fe^{59} uptake in irradiated mice protected with bone marrow. Proc. Soc. Exp. Biol. Med. 104:457–461.

An Investigation of Sodium Ion Regulation in Crayfish Using Sodium-22

One of the most valuable contributions of radiotracer methodology to biological science has been to make possible the tracing of ionic movement across semipermeable membranes under physiological conditions. This has been applied not only to simple physical diffusion studies, but also to situations where active ion transport seems to occur. The present experiment illustrates such a study on a freshwater crustacean, the crayfish. The radioisotope ^{22}Na is used to follow sodium uptake by these animals over a two-day period under three quite different osmotic environments. The experiment involves activity determination by means of a well-type scintillation detector and shows the value of such a detector for direct assay of liquid samples.

A detailed description of the experimental procedure is given. The needed materials, except for the scintillation counting assembly, are commonly found in an animal physiology laboratory or otherwise readily available. Variations in the experimental procedures and potential research applications of this type of study are indicated. A representative list of references in this field is appended.

A. SURVEY OF THE PROBLEM

Crayfish have long been recognized as osmotically unique crustaceans. They are able to maintain a high level of hypertonicity in their body fluids although living in fresh water. This *osmoregulatory ability* is such that they can adjust to a wide range of salinities with little variation in internal osmotic concentration. A prominent feature of this ability is their ionic regulation of sodium. Blood sodium concentrations of 200 mmole/liter are not uncommon in these animals, although the water bathing them may have a sodium concentration of only 0.4–2.0 mmole/liter. This situation clearly indicates one or more sites for active transport of sodium on the animal's external surface. Bryan (1) has identified certain cells in the gill tissues as the most important of these sites. Since some body sodium is constantly being lost by diffusion in the normal freshwater environment, active uptake must operate more or less continually to maintain a constant internal sodium concentration.

In order to investigate the extent and rate of this active sodium uptake, ionic ^{22}Na will be employed as a radiotracer. The *rate of ^{22}Na uptake* from a freshwater medium will be followed in three groups of crayfish. One group will be *normal* animals. Their ^{22}Na uptake will reflect the rate of active uptake necessary to replace diffusional loss of sodium. A second group of animals will be greatly *depleted* in body sodium by prior perfusion with distilled water for several days. Sodium-22 uptake in this group should be much more rapid, since the animals are replacing prior depletion of sodium as well as correcting for continual loss by diffusion. Still a third group of crayfish will be *NaCl-loaded* by prior exposure to a hypertonic salt solution for several days. This latter group will be expected to show a net outflux of sodium ions into the dilute fresh water until the normal blood sodium concentration is attained. Thus, ^{22}Na uptake by the animals of this group should be very slight. The appearance of any ^{22}Na in the blood of these crayfish illustrates the dynamic nature of ion movements through semipermeable membranes.

In ion uptake studies of this sort, a variety of *sampling techniques* have been employed. Bryan (1) used a clamp to hold the crayfish being sampled just at the water surface. He then withdrew successive blood samples of only a few microliters from the same animal through a needle hole in its dorsal surface. In this present experiment, a larger blood volume is desired and this results in the death of the animal sampled. Shaw (8) employed a circulating water arrangement that allowed a continuous determination of activity in the external medium. Interval water sampling, as prescribed for this experiment, should provide sufficient data to plot an adequate disappearance curve.

The investigation of sodium regulation in aquatic animals, especially marine forms, by means of radioisotopes of sodium, has been pursued by only a comparatively few research workers. The investigations of Fretter (5) and Green, et al. (6) represent typical studies on organisms other than crayfish. In addition, regulation of other commonly present ions has been but little explored. Bryan (4), using the radioisotope ^{137}Cs, has further investigated cesium uptake in crabs. Chlorine-36, ^{45}Ca, and ^{28}Mg have also been utilized in similar studies. Thus, the technique presented in this experiment has potential for broad application in studies of ionic regulation in aquatic animals.

B. EXPERIMENTAL DESIGN

In calculating the amount of radioactive material to be used in this experiment, the major concern is to have sufficient activity in the water samples so that excessively long counting times will not be necessary. The assumptions on which these calculations are based are in line with the references cited. The specific activity of the ^{22}Na poses no problem, since the sodium concentration found in fresh water is normally in the range of 0.4–2.0 mmole/liter. Sodium-22 is usually produced by the reaction ^{24}Mg (d, α)^{22}Na, and it is thus carrier-free. Even a much reduced specific activity would not result in a significant addition of sodium ions in the experimental solutions.

The amount of ^{22}Na activity required per liter of solution can be determined as follows:

(1) If it is assumed that the background counting rate is about 100 cpm and that, for reasonably short counting times, the final 5-ml water samples should show a net count rate at least ten times the background, then a final water activity of 1000 cpm/5 ml is required.

(2) Assuming that, under the varied conditions of the experiment, the uptake of sodium by the crayfish will deplete the solutions by a factor of ten on the average, an initial water activity of 10,000 cpm/5 ml will be needed.

(3) If the over-all detection efficiency for the 1.28 Mev gamma rays from ^{22}Na is about 25 per cent in the scintillation counter used (see Note 1), the foregoing counting rate is equivalent to 40,000 dpm/5 ml of solution.

(4) The activity to be introduced into each container at the outset of the experiment would then be

$$\frac{4 \times 10^4 \text{ dpm}}{5 \text{ ml sample}} \times 10^3 \text{ ml solution} = 8 \times 10^6 \text{ dpm}$$

or just over 3.6 μc. To allow for a margin of error, it is suggested that approximately 4 μc of ^{22}Na be used.

C. MATERIALS AND EQUIPMENT REQUIRED

The following list is not exhaustive. Only those items are listed which might not be commonly found in a physiology laboratory.

(1) Crayfish: 15 active animals of the same species are required. Crayfish between 10 and 20 g are desirable. It is preferable that all weights be as similar as possible to insure comparable blood volumes.
(2) Shielded, well-type (5-ml capacity) NaI(Tl) scintillation detector and counting assembly.
(3) A supply of counting vials to fit the scintillation detector well, preferably of a disposable type.
(4) An amount of ^{22}NaCl per container to be used as calculated according to the foregoing outline.
(5) Containers: Plastic canisters of about 1.5-liter capacity with tight-fitting lids will prove quite satisfactory. Two $\frac{3}{8}$ in holes can be drilled through the lids at opposite edges. One will admit the air line and the other will allow both air escape and water sampling. This arrangement prevents the radioactive solution from splashing out of the containers during aeration.
(6) Distilled water: The animals to be depleted of sodium will be perfused with distilled water for three days at a flow rate of about 1 liter per hour. This will require a total flow of about 75 liters. It is most desirable to have a distilled-water tap available. Otherwise, a gravity flow system from a large carboy may be arranged. It is quite important that the distilled water be cooled to room temperature before exposing the animals to it.
(7) Glass capillary tubes (3 in. lengths) and 5 per cent EDTA solution; these are used for drawing crayfish blood samples. Although EDTA is not a true anticoagulant for crayfish blood, it does slow coagulation sufficiently to allow the subsequent micropipetting to be done. Prepare the capillary tubes by filling them with the EDTA solution and then allowing the solution to dry to a film in them.

D. EXPERIMENTAL PROCEDURES

1. Initial Preparation of Apparatus and Animals

The 15 crayfish are divided into three equal groups. Each group of five animals is placed in a 2–3 liter container partially filled with filtered pond water. If that is not available, tap water that has been standing in an open vessel for several days may be substituted. The water in each container should be aerated continuously. It is advisable to observe the animals for a day or two under these circumstances to determine their degree of activity. Discard torpid, or obviously sick animals.

After the observation period, replace the solution in one container with distilled water. Now make an arrangement to circulate a flow of about 1 liter/hr of distilled water through this container. The flow rate must be carefully adjusted. This *perfusion with distilled water* will gradually deplete the sodium ion concentration in the crayfish. Continue it for three days. Longer perfusion times or higher flow rates may lead to death of the animals. Aeration is continued.

To the second container, 300 mmole NaCl is now added per liter of solution. This concentration is above the normal blood sodium level (about 200 mmole/liter) and will result in a gradual increase in blood sodium concentration (see Note 2). Presumably this increase occurs because the rate of sodium excretion cannot keep pace with the rate of inward diffusion from the *hypertonic medium.* This group of animals is left in this solution for three days under constant aeration.

The crayfish in the third group will serve as *controls* and will be left in the pond water under aeration while the other two groups are being treated as just described.

Fifteen containers with tight-fitting lids are now filled with 1 liter each of filtered pond water. Arrange *aeration* of the water, using a manifold system to distribute compressed air evenly to individual bubblers in each container. This system can be easily prepared from glass T- or Y-shaped connectors, rubber tubing, and air stones. A compressed air line or pump should prove adequate as an air supply. Make provision to maintain a reasonably *constant temperature.* This can be accomplished by placing the containers in a large tray through which cold water slowly circulates.

The calculated amount of ^{22}NaCl can now be added to each container and thoroughly mixed with the water. Each container must be marked to identify the animal it will hold. At the end of the three-day "conditioning" period, the crayfish may be transferred to their respective individual containers and ^{22}Na uptake initiated.

2. Sampling and Activity Determinations

The uptake of sodium by these crayfish will be followed over the next 48 hr. This is accomplished by determining the change in ^{22}Na activity in interval water samples (see Note 3) and in crayfish blood samples secured by successive sacrifice of the animals in each group. Details on sampling techniques are given later. The suggested *sampling schedule* is as follows: take water samples from all containers with animals at 0, 2, 4, 6, 8, 16, 24, 28, 32, 40, and 48 hr after introducing the crayfish. At 4, 8, 24, 32, and 48 hr, remove a blood sample from one animal in each of the three groups. This schedule is arranged for the experiment to be started in the morning so that the most rapid activity changes may be observed during the first 16 hr.

Remove 5-ml *water samples* from each container by pipette and place in marked counting vials according to the foregoing schedule. Each vial may then be capped and placed in the detector well directly for activity determination. This direct counting of liquid samples constitutes an important advantage of the well-type scintillation detector. After the counting operation, return the contents of the vials to the respective containers from which they came. Thus one avoids a loss of activity from the solution.

The quantity of blood removed and the manner in which it must be taken results in the death of the crayfish involved. Preparatory to drawing the *blood sample*, the animal is removed from its container with rubber gloves and compressed air is blown over its ventral side to dry off the region of puncture (see Note 4). The crayfish is held on its back and its legs bent dorsally along its sides. A prepared capillary tube is then thrust through the membranous joint at the basal segment of its pincer claw (cheliped) into the ventral sinus. The animal is turned so that droplets of clear blood fall from the end of the capillary tube onto a piece of Parafilm. It is particularly important to maintain the tip of the capillary tube in the sinus and not to probe into internal organs, such as the hepatopancreas. This would be evidenced by the appearance of yellow-orange colored tissue fragments in the blood (see Note 5).

When blood ceases to flow, the animal is laid aside and immediately a 125 μl sample of the blood (see Note 6) is drawn up into a micropipette using a safety pipetter. This sample is dispensed into a marked counting vial and two distilled water rinsings of the pipette are added to the sample. Since the crayfish blood will commence to coagulate in a very short time, despite the action of EDTA, these manipulations must be done as rapidly as possible. To maintain a comparable sample-to-detector geometry, add water to the blood sample in the counting vial to bring its volume up to that of the water samples, namely 5 ml. The crayfish is then weighed and placed in a 30 per cent solution of formalin to hasten death and prevent subsequent tissue decay.

In assaying the activity of each of the water and blood samples a total of 10,000 net counts should be collected on the scintillation counter register. Adjust the calculated net activity in counts per minutes of each sample to net cpm/ml of blood or water.

3. Evaluation of Results

From the counting data previously derived, two sets of *curves* can be drawn for each of the three groups of crayfish. One set is a plot of the activity per milliliter of water against time. This will show the extent of sodium disappearance from the water with increasing time. Since in the early hours of the experiment, up to five water samples will be taken from each group and considerable variation within a group may occur, average values should be plotted.

The second set of curves is a plot of ^{22}Na activity per milliliter of blood against time. Only one value per sampling interval will be available here, and because of individual variations in sodium uptake, these curves may be somewhat less than smooth.

In comparing the ^{22}Na disappearance curves for the three groups of crayfish, what are the significant differences between them? Do these results seem in harmony with what might be expected, based on the initial blood sodium concentrations in the three groups (see Note 7)? Likewise, what differences appear between the three curves of blood ^{22}Na activity with time? During which portion of the experimental period does ^{22}Na uptake proceed at the most rapid rate? Since the NaCl-loaded crayfish actually have a lower blood sodium concentration at the end of the experiment than at the start, what can be inferred from the appearance of ^{22}Na in their blood? Could this effect have been detected without the use of radiotracer sodium?

The half-life of ^{22}Na (2.6 yrs) makes decay corrections unnecessary for the activity determinations in this experiment. The length of the half-life does, however, complicate *waste disposal* procedures. The water solutions may be emptied into the drains, along with a large amount of tap water, since the isotope is in a soluble form and will be readily diluted, but this cannot be done with the blood samples and carcasses. These must first be ground in a garbage disposal before their disposal into sewage with a large amount of water.

E. EXPERIMENTAL NOTES

(1) Why is ^{22}Na much more suitable for this type of experiment than *^{24}Na*? This latter isotope emits both an energetic beta particle and two gamma photons per disintegration. Thus, ^{24}Na disintegration would presumably be more readily detected.

(2) A variation of this procedure would be to expose some crayfish to such a concentrated medium that had also been labeled with ^{22}Na. After their blood sodium concentration had been thus increased, they could be returned to normal fresh water. The outflow of sodium from the blood to the solution could be followed by detecting the rise in ^{22}Na activity in the previously unlabeled water. Bryan (3) has employed such a procedure in kinetic studies of sodium transport.

(3) A more sophisticated arrangement employs a *circulating water system*, in which the solution passes through a flow-type scintillation detector connected to a ratemeter (8). The change in activity with time can thus be graphically registered on a chart recorder responding to the ratemeter signal.

(4) To avoid being pinched by the claws (chelipeds) during handling of crayfish, it is advisable to slip short "gloves" of large-diameter rubber tubing over the pincers.

(5) If time allows, it will be worthwhile to *dissect* the animals and to remove samples of various organs for activity determinations. This will reveal the internal distribution and concentration (on a per gram wet weight basis) of sodium. It is suggested that samples be taken from the hepato-pancreas, muscle, exoskeleton, gills, gut, and excretory organ (4).

(6) A *blood sample volume* of 125 μl is chosen because this quantity can be dependably drawn from crayfish of the size range specified. If larger blood quantities are secured from some animals, these may be used as counting samples with a consequent reduction in the counting time required.

(7) Some difficulty exists in *interpreting* these ^{22}Na disappearance curves. Because of the relatively small water volume to which the animals are exposed here, the sodium concentration in the external medium will change during the course of the experiment in the case of the Na-depleted and the NaCl-loaded crayfish. This change would be negligible in the natural environment of a pond or stream. Shaw (7) attempted to correct for this by assaying the water for sodium by flame photometry at intervals and adjusting the sodium concentration accordingly.

BIBLIOGRAPHY

1. Bryan, G. W. 1960*a*. Sodium regulation in the crayfish *Astacus fluviatilis*. I. The normal animal. J. Exp. Biol. 37:83–99.

2. Bryan, G. W. 1960*b*. Sodium regulation in the crayfish *Astacus fluviatilis*. II. Experiments with sodium-depleted animals. J. Exp. Biol. 37:100–112.

3. Bryan, G. W. 1960*c*. Sodium regulation in the crayfish *Astacus fluviatilis*. III. Experiments with NaCl-loaded animals. J. Exp. Biol. 37:113–128.

4. Bryan, G. W. 1961. The accumulation of radioactive caesium in crabs. J. Mar. Biol. Assoc. U. K. 41:551–575.

5. Fretter, Vera. 1955. Uptake of radioactive sodium (^{24}Na) by *Nereis diversicolor* (Mueller) and *Perinereis cultrifera* (Grubs). J. Mar. Biol. Assoc. U. K. 34:151–160.

6. Green, James W., et al. 1959. The regulation of water and salt by the fiddler crabs, *Uca pugnax* and *Uca pugilator*. Biol. Bull. 116:76–87.

7. Shaw, J. 1959. The absorption of sodium ions by the crayfish *Astacus pallipes* Lereboullet. I. The effect of external and internal sodium concentrations. J. Exp. Biol. 36:126–144.

8. Shaw, J. 1960*a*. The absorption of sodium ions by the crayfish *Astacus pallipes* Lereboullet. II. The effect of the external anion. J. Exp. Biol. 37:534–547.

9. Shaw, J. 1960*b*. The absorption of sodium ions by the crayfish *Astacus pallipes* Lereboullet. III. The effect of other cations in the external solution. J. Exp. Biol. 37:548–556.

Determination of Coefficients of Zinc-65 Accumulation in Freshwater Plants

This experiment has been chosen to illustrate the use of the gamma-emitting isotope ^{65}Zn in following the accumulation of the trace element zinc by various aquatic plants and algae. The experimental procedure is described in detail. The experiment is designed so that the activity in the plant tissue and water samples will be detected by means of a NaI(Tl) scintillation detector mounted to accept cup planchets. Other than the scintillation counting assembly, all the materials required will be commonly found in a botanical laboratory. Potential research applications of this study are indicated and an extensive list of pertinent references is appended.

A. SURVEY OF THE PROBLEM

It has been known for some time that many aquatic plants are capable of accumulating certain trace elements in their tissues. These tissue concentrations of trace elements may greatly exceed those of the water in which the plants are growing. This is true although such accumulation may proceed to concentrations several orders of magnitude greater than required for normal metabolism. Algae, both marine and freshwater, have a particularly pronounced ability in this regard.

In the present experiment, this accumulative action will be quantitatively determined for the element zinc by the use of the radioisotope ^{65}Zn. A *coefficient of accumulation* based on the uptake of ^{65}Zn will be determined for several species of freshwater plants and algae. As defined by Gileva (4), this coefficient represents the ratio between the activity detected in 1 g of dry plant tissue and the activity in 1 ml of the water in which the plant has been immersed for a defined period of time under standard conditions. It has been found that the coefficients of accumulation vary widely for different species of aquatic plants, and for different isotopes (4, 8–9). Since it has been reported that ^{65}Zn uptake, in algae at least, is markedly affected by the degree of photosynthetic activity occurring (7), the variable of illumination versus darkness will be introduced into this experiment.

The major steps in the experiment are as follows:

(1) Selection and preparation of plant cultures and apparatus
(2) Exposure of various plants to a defined amount of ^{65}Zn activity in aqueous solution
(3) Preparation and counting of plant and water samples
(4) Calculation of coefficients of accumulation from counting data

Since it is desirable to have coefficients of accumulation that are comparable from species to species, the proper selection, culturing, and wet weighing of the plant and algae samples are of considerable importance.

The accumulative action of aquatic plants with regard to zinc has some practical consequence. Although a high concentration of stable zinc in such plants does not pose a biological hazard, the situation is altogether different when even low concentrations of radioactive ^{65}Zn are present in rivers and coastal waters. This ^{65}Zn will also be accumulated in the tissues of these organisms. Since algae and other water plants are the primary food source for aquatic animals, large amounts of ^{65}Zn may thus enter food chains that may end with man.

Extensive studies of this *environmental hazard* have been made along the Columbia River and the inshore waters of the Oregon and Washington coasts (2–3, 6, 10). Since 1944, the plutonium-producing reactors at Hanford, Washington, have added 8–55 curies of ^{65}Zn daily to the Columbia River in their cooling water effluent (10). The ecological impact of this activity on the aquatic plants and animals in the river has been under continuing study by biologists at the Hanford facility. The various environmental sampling techniques used by these workers and the particular problem of dissemination of this activity through food webs have been described (2–3, 6, 10). Davis, et al. (2) state: "Although its abundance in the organisms is less than phosphorus, sodium, or iron, the Zn^{65} was readily transferred through the food web and occurred in relatively large concentrations in almost all organisms sampled."

Since ^{65}Zn may be discharged in measurable concentrations by nuclear-powered ships as a corrosion product, contamination of harbor waters may be a serious problem of the near future. The study by Taylor (7) was part of a continuing investigation of the accumulative ability of marine algae for ^{65}Zn.

Gileva (4) has investigated the possibility of exploiting the action of algae as trace element "scavengers" for the purification of surface waters contaminated with radionuclides. Other Soviet investigators (8–9) have explored the action of the chelating agent EDTA to decrease uptake of ^{65}Zn and other radionuclides by aquatic plants, in order to minimize the problem of radioactive material entering natural food webs.

In most of the studies just cited, ^{65}Zn has not been employed as a *radiotracer*, but has been investigated from the standpoint of the hazard it poses in the environment. Knauss (5), however, used it and a number of other radioisotopes to study uptake of inorganic ions, *per se*. Thus, the procedures employed in this experiment have application both in radiotracer studies of stable isotope uptake, as well as in investigation of environmental contamination. Considerably more understanding of the ecological relationships involved is needed for the development of proper waste disposal practices in view of the increasing number of nuclear reactors in this country and abroad. Marine and freshwater biologists also will find trace element accumulation studies for various organisms important.

B. EXPERIMENTAL DESIGN

In calculating the amount of activity to be used in this experiment the available *specific activity* of ^{65}Zn must be taken into consideration. A high specific activity is especially important in this case, since a *trace element* is used. Plants generally require the element zinc in only trace amounts. A concentration of 0.02 ppm is commonly used for plant nutrient solutions. At concentrations approaching 60 ppm, zinc is toxic to most plants. The concentration of zinc found in natural surface waters varies with locale, whereas sea water normally contains about 0.01 ppm. The highest specific activity of ^{65}Zn readily obtainable is about 100 mc/g, or 1 μc/10 μg. Thus, for each 1 μc of ^{65}Zn activity used per liter of solution, 0.01 ppm of zinc will be added.

On the other hand, the *amount of activity* added to the culture solutions must be such that a detectable quantity remains in the water at the end of the experiment. This is necessary since the "coefficient of accumulation" to be calculated is based on the ratio of the activity in dry plant tissue to the activity in the final solution. It is important that both activity determinations be made to the same degree of statistical accuracy. If uptake of the ^{65}Zn by the plants depletes the solutions to a very low level of activity, the water samples may require an excessively long counting time for a given standard error (see Chapter 9).

An additional factor to be considered in the case of ^{65}Zn is the *decay scheme*. As seen in Figure E-1, 1.11-Mev gamma rays are emitted in only 49.3 per cent of the radioactive disintegrations. Since the detector to be employed is a metal-encased NaI(T1) scintillation crystal, only these gamma rays will be detected to any extent. The positrons and low-energy X rays resulting from electron capture will be almost completely absorbed in the crystal housing. Thus, only one-half of the disintegrations in the sample can be detected at best.

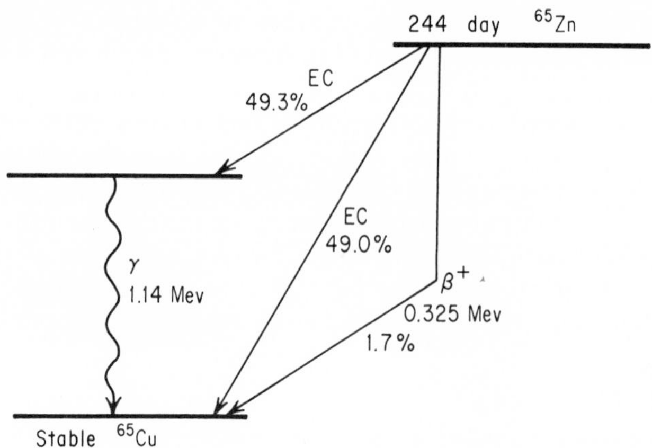

Figure E-1. Decay scheme of ^{65}Zn.

With the foregoing considerations in mind, the amount of activity needed in each 500 ml of solution can be determined as follows:

(1) If it is assumed that the background counting rate is about 100 cpm, and that, for reasonably short counting times, the final 2-ml water samples should show a counting rate five times the background level, a final water activity of 500 cpm/2 ml or 250 cpm/ml is required.
(2) If, under the conditions of the experiment, the plant uptake of isotope depletes the solutions by a factor of two on the average, the initial water activity would need to be approximately 500 cpm/ml.
(3) A detection efficiency of only 5 per cent could reasonably be assumed under the prescribed counting conditions (see Note 1). This would mean that an initial activity of 10,000 dpm/ml, or 5×10^6 dpm in the entire 500 ml of solution, would be required.
(4) Since only about 50 per cent of the disintegrations of ^{65}Zn yield detectable gamma radiation, on the basis of the foregoing decay scheme, a total nominal activity of $2(5 \times 10^6) = 1 \times 10^7$ dpm would be initially needed. This is equivalent to about 4.5 μc of ^{65}Zn.

(5) At the specific activity just stated, this level of activity would contribute 0.9 ppm of zinc. Although somewhat above normal surface water concentrations, this should not prove toxic to the plants used, nor is it an unrealistic level compared to concentrations found in rivers receiving reactor effluent.

C. MATERIALS AND EQUIPMENT REQUIRED

The following list is not exhaustive, but includes only the special materials or supplies needed for this experiment:

(1) An amount of $^{65}ZnCl_2$ of the indicated specific activity as calculated according to the preceding outline.

(2) Plant and algae cultures: It is suggested that a minimum of four different forms be used, including unicellular planktonic algae (*Chlorella*, *Chlamydomonas*, or *diatoms*), filamentous algae (*Spirogyra*, *Cladophora*, *Ulothrix*, and the like), floating aquatic plants (*Lemna*, *Salvinia*, *Azolla*, and so on), and rooted aquatic plants (*Elodea*, *Cabomba*, *Sagittaria*, and so forth). The specific forms chosen depend on local availability.

(3) Shielded NaI(Tl) scintillation detector and counting assembly.

(4) Supply of cupped metal planchets to fit sample support of detector.

(5) Growing containers: Plastic canisters (about 1-liter capacity) with tight-fitting lids are quite satisfactory. A hole can be drilled through the lid large enough to admit the air line and allow air to escape around it. This arrangement prevents the radioactive solution from splashing out of the container during aeration. Spray with black paint the outside of containers holding the plants to be kept in darkness during the experiment.

D. EXPERIMENTAL PROCEDURES

1. Initial Preparation of Apparatus and Cultures

For each plant or algal species to be used in the experiment prepare two *containers* as described in the preceding section. Place one container so that it receives continuous illumination, preferably fluorescent. Paint the other container black or cover it with an opaque material and place it in a dark cupboard or closet during the time of ^{65}Zn uptake. These containers must be thoroughly cleaned and rinsed before use, since algae especially are quite intolerant of chemical contamination.

Fill each container with 500 ml of filtered pond *water*. If that is not available, substitute tap water that has been allowed to stand in an open vessel for several days, to allow loss of added chlorine. It is important that all the water used be from the same source, and presumably of uniform mineral composition. Mark the water level on the outside of each container, so that any evaporative losses during the experimental period may be noted, and appropriate amounts of distilled water added.

Provision must be also made to maintain a reasonably uniform *temperature* in both experimental groups. This is readily accomplished by placing the containers in a large tray through which cold water is slowly circulated.

Aeration of the culture solutions must be arranged, using a manifold system to distribute compressed air evenly to individual bubblers in each container. Such a system can be readily prepared using T- or Y-shaped glass connectors, rubber tubing, and air stones. A compressed air line or pump should prove adequate as an air supply.

It is advisable to add the plants and algae to their respective containers several days before the introduction of the radioisotope. This procedure will allow the cultures to adjust to the new growing conditions before the experimental phase begins. During this period all containers should be illuminated and aerated.

Each plant and algal culture should be reasonably pure. Gross *contaminants* in the plant cultures can be removed with forceps. It may be necessary to rinse the algae with filtered pond water to remove some adhering microorganisms.

Before introducing the ^{65}Zn, determine the *wet weight* of the plant or algal material in each container. Use similar, but not identical, weights. Weights of 10 $\pm$ 1 g will prove optimal for the water volume and isotope activity specified. The plant material may be directly weighed after excess water has been blotted off with tissue paper. Algae, especially the unicellular forms, require filtration to collect the normally dispersed cells before wet weighing is feasible.

The calculated activity of $^{65}ZnCl_2$ solution can now be introduced into each container. Mix it thoroughly with the culture solution. Determine the pH of each culture solution at this time and adjust it to within the range pH 6–8, since zinc solubility is considerably decreased at higher pH levels.

2. Sample Preparation and Counting

Pipette 2-ml *water samples* from each container out into marked cup planchets as soon as thorough mixing of the activity has occurred. Then place the plant containers in their illuminated or darkened positions; maintain constant aeration. The water samples in the planchets may be slowly evaporated to dryness under an infrared heat lamp. The heat applied must not be so intense as to cause boiling, or loss of the sample will occur.

The activity in these initial water samples may now be determined by means of the *scintillation counter*. At least 10,000 counts should be collected from each sample and likewise for the background determination. Calculate and record results as net cpm/ml water. (How do these results compare with the amount of activity introduced into the solution?)

It has been found that the coefficients of accumulation stabilize rather quickly (4, 8–9). Under the conditions of this experiment, approximately four days should prove an adequate period for such *stabilization* (see Note 2). Inspect the cultures at least twice daily for regulation of the aerating system, possible addition of distilled water to maintain the original level, and temperature adjustment.

At the end of the experimental period, a *final* 2-ml *water sample* is removed from each container. These water samples are dried and counted as described before.

The plant material in each container is now harvested by filtration and rinsed with tap water on the filter. The active filtrate may be disposed of into the sink drain and flushed down with a large quantity of water. Place each plant sample in a marked, dry, preweighed Petri dish and dry for 48 hr in an oven at 70°C. After drying, the dishes are again weighed and the net dry weight of each sample calculated and recorded.

Now pulverize the *dried plant samples* or grind them to a coarse powder. At this point, observe particular caution to prevent spread of the powdered material. It is advisable to carry out this step in a draft free area. Next, marked, preweighed cup planchets are partially filled with this plant material. They are reweighed and the net dry sample weight calculated and recorded.

It is advisable at this point to cover the top of each *planchet* with a small piece of cellulose tape or thin plastic film (see Note 3). This will prevent loss of material and/or contamination of the scintillation detector. As an additional precaution, store the samples in covered Petri dishes.

The *activity* of each plant sample is now determined by means of the scintillation counter. Collect at least 10,000 counts for each sample and the background radiation. Calculate and record net counts per minute for each sample.

3. Calculations and Evaluation of Data

Using the plant sample weights and activity determinations, the net counts per minute/gram dry weight for each sample may now be calculated. This value divided by the net counts per minute/milliliter of final water samples yields the desired *coefficient of accumulation*. (How do these calculated coefficients of accumulation compare with the values cited in references 4, 8, and 9? How can any marked differences be explained? Is there a significant difference in the coefficients of accumulation in the continuously illuminated plants as compared to those maintained in darkness? What conclusion concerning zinc uptake could be drawn from this; see Note 4?)

From the activity of the initial water samples compared to the activity of the final water samples, calculate the *depletion factor* resulting from plant uptake of the ^{65}Zn (see Note 5). Based on the counting results from the initial water samples, how many net counts per minute were in each container at the start of the experiment? How do these values compare with the measured amount of activity introduced into each container?

Based on the counting results from the final water samples, how many net counts per minute were in the water of each container at the conclusion of the experiment? Can the difference in water activity between these values and those previously calculated be accounted for by the calculated activity in the total plant material in each container? If not, how might activity have been lost from these closed containers?

Similar experimental work can be done using a wide variety of radionuclides, such as ^{60}Co, ^{137}Cs, ^{59}Fe, ^{86}Rb, and so on (8). Data on isotope accumulation in marine algae are of particular importance, both from the standpoint of algal physiology and inshore contamination by nuclear vessels and coastal reactors. In following up the work cited in references 8 and 9, it would be valuable to investigate practical methods of decreasing trace element uptake by aquatic plants, for example, by use of chelating agents like EDTA.

E. EXPERIMENTAL NOTES

(1) A well-type scintillation detector, if available, could be used with an increase in detection efficiency and simplification of sample preparation.

(2) If time allowed, it would be of interest to investigate the extent of uptake with increasing time. Multiple containers of each species could be prepared and each sampled at a different time. In general, algae seem to reach their maximum uptake in a shorter time than higher aquatic plants (4, 8).

(3) What would be the effect on counting efficiency of covering a similar ^{14}C-containing sample in this way? Why can this be tolerated here?

(4) If time and facilities allowed, it would be of interest to set up plant cultures under graded levels of illumination. Then it could be determined whether zinc uptake is a direct function of degree of illumination, or if there is merely an illumination threshold.

(5) Why can decay of activity over the course of this experiment be ignored here and in subsequent calculations?

BIBLIOGRAPHY

1. Boroughs, Howard, Walter A. Chipman, and Theodore R. Rice. 1957. Laboratory experiments on the uptake, accumulation, and loss of radionuclides by marine organisms. *In* The effects of atomic radiation on oceanography and fisheries. Nat. Res. Council Publ. no. 551. Washington. p. 80–87.

2. Davis, J. J., et al. 1958. Radioactive materials in aquatic and terrestrial organisms exposed to reactor effluent water. *In* Proc. Second UN Intern. Conf. Peaceful Uses Atomic Energy, Geneva, 1958. vol. 18. UN, Geneva. p. 423–428.

3. Foster, R. F., and J. J. Davis. 1956. The accumulation of radioactive substances in aquatic forms. *In* Proc. Intern. Conf. Peaceful Uses Atomic Energy, Geneva, 1955. vol. 13. UN, New York. p. 364–367.

4. Gileva, E. A. 1960. Coefficients of radioisotope accumulation by fresh-water water plants. Trans. Biol. Sci. Sec., Doklady, Akad. Nauk SSSR 132:343–344.

5. Knauss, H. J., and J. W. Porter. 1954. The absorption of inorganic ions by *Chlorella pyrenoidosa*. Plant Physiol. 29:229–234.

6. Osterberg, Charles, L. D. Culm, and John V. Byrne. 1963. Gamma emitters in marine sediments near the Columbia River. Science 139:916–917.

7. Taylor, W. R. 1960. Some results of studies on the uptake of radioactive waste materials by marine and estuarine phytoplankton organisms using continuous culturing techniques. U.S. Atomic Energy Commission. TID-11783. (Microcard.) 64 p.

8. Timofeev-Resovskii, N. V., et al. 1960. Coefficients of accumulation of radioactive isotopes of sixteen different elements by freshwater organisms and the effect of EDTA on some of them. Trans. Biol. Sci. Sec., Doklady, Akad. Nauk SSSR 132:369–372.

9. Timofeeva-Resovskaya, E. A., and N. V. Timofeev-Resovskii. 1960. Effect of ethylenediaminetetraacetate (EDTA) on the coefficients of accumulation of different radioactive isotopes from an aqueous solution by freshwater plants. Trans. Biol. Sci. Sec., Doklady, Akad. Nauk SSSR 130:9–11.

10. Watson, D. G., J. J. Davis, and W. C. Hanson. 1961. Zinc-65 in marine organisms along the Oregon and Washington coasts. Science 133:1826–1828.

EXPERIMENT F

Determination of the Content of Aspartic Acid in Cheese by Means of the Isotope Dilution Method

The present experiment is designed to illustrate the value of the *isotope dilution method* as an analytical tool. The procedure described is relatively simple, but nevertheless covers the basic principles underlying the method and, at the same time, introduces the *Schöniger technique* for counting-sample preparation and radioactive assay by liquid scintillation counting.

A. SURVEY OF THE PROBLEM

The *amino acid composition* of a biological specimen is one of the fundamental pieces of information to be ascertained, particularly in the area of protein studies. Analytical methods in this regard have been undergoing dramatic improvement in recent years, particularly as a result of the employment of paper chromatography, ion-exchange resin chromatography, electrophoresis, and more recently, gas chromatography, as techniques for the separation of amino acids. After the isolation task, one can readily estimate the content of each of the amino acids by using colorimetric methods. Not to be underrated is the method classified as microbiological assay, which makes use of the specific response of certain microorganisms to certain amino acids.

To determine the content of a single amino acid in a mixture of amino acids, such as that encountered in a protein hydrolysate, it is feasible to apply the *isotope dilution method:* This method is advantageous because it requires the isolation in pure form of only a very small fraction of the amino acid in question from a mixture, but not the recovery of all the amino acid in question. One can use any of numerous chemical procedures for the isolation task so that a small fraction of amino acid can be obtained in pure form. For example, aspartic acid can be readily isolated from a protein hydrolysate as a copper salt in pure form, even though the procedure by no means yields a quantitative recovery.

The *principle* underlying the isotope dilution method is indeed very simple. In the present experiment, it is desired to determine quantitatively the amount of aspartic acid present in a hydrolysate of cheese. If the laboratory is not equipped with an expensive amino acid analyzer, it will be a very tedious task employing traditional methods, but the task can be much facilitated by use of the isotope dilution method. All that is required is to add a known amount of L-aspartic acid-U-^{14}C, having the proper specific activity, to the cheese hydrolysate, followed by a simple procedure to isolate a portion of the aspartic acid in the mixture, unlabeled as well as labeled varieties, as copper aspartate. Determination of the specific activity of the copper aspartate so obtained will reveal immediately the extent of dilution of the added ^{14}C-labeled aspartic acid. This information can then be utilized to calculate readily the amount of unlabeled aspartic acid originally present in the hydrolysate.

The *equation* derived for simple isotopic dilution analysis follows:

Let C_1 = amount of the labeled compound Z
S_1 = specific activity of the labeled compound Z
C_2 = amount of unlabeled compound Z present in the mixture to be analyzed
S_2 = specific activity of compound Z isolated from the mixture (after the addition of the labeled compound Z to the mixture to be analyzed).

C_2 is therefore the unknown quantity to be determined by the isotope dilution method. The total radioactivity, derived from the labeled compound Z, present in the mixture to be analyzed is naturally equal to $C_1 \times S_1$. The total amount of compound Z, labeled and unlabeled, present in the mixture to be analyzed is $C_1 + C_2$. Consequently, the specific activity of the diluted compound Z isolated from the mixture should be

(F-1) $$S_2 = \frac{C_1 \cdot S_1}{C_1 + C_2}$$

Solving for C_2, one finds that

(F-2) $$C_2 = \frac{C_1(S_1 - S_2)}{S_2}$$

A glance at the foregoing equation immediately indicates the *basic limitation* encountered in the use of the isotope dilution method. This limitation is derived from two basic factors: (1) the precision involved in the determination of the values S_1 and S_2, since the difference between S_1 and S_2 may be very small; (2) the relative magnitude of C_1 and C_2, which in reality also determines the magnitude of S_1 and S_2. Thus, if C_1 is tenfold greater than C_2, one would find that S_2 is approximately 90 per cent of the value of S_1, in magnitude. The difference between S_1 and S_2 will, therefore, be very small. In fact, this difference lies very close to the limit of practical precision in determining the values S_1 and S_2, which are usually in the neighborhood of 2 to 3 per cent. One can therefore conclude that, in order properly to apply the isotope dilution method to a given analytical task, one must first have a crude idea of the magnitude of C_2, the supposedly unknown value. Such information will then help one to decide on the proper magnitude of the value C_1. This requirement implies that, in the event the magnitude of C_1 is very small, say in microgram quantities, one is bound to encounter insuperable difficulties in attempting the isotope dilution method.

B. EXPERIMENTAL DESIGN

The present experiment is designed to estimate the amount of aspartic acid in typical protein hydrolysates. American cheese is chosen as a representative test sample. As indicated previously, it is important first to estimate the amount of amino acid in question that may be present in the test sample. In the case of aspartic acid, one finds the content in common protein ranges from 5 per cent to 15 per cent. Consequently, it can be assumed that the order of magnitude of aspartic acid content in cheese is in the neighborhood of 10 per cent on a dry weight basis. In designing such an isotope dilution experiment, it is preferable that the *specific activity* of the sample to be assayed be about 3000 cpm/mmole of carbon (apparent counting rate). If the efficiency of the detection assembly is 50 per cent (assuming that a liquid scintillation counter is used), the specific activity requirement can therefore be expressed as 6000 dpm/mmole of carbon, or 24,000 dpm/mmole of aspartic acid, since it is a four-carbon molecule.

The *scale of operation* for the present experiment is determined primarily by considering the optimal amount of protein that can be hydrolyzed and subjected to the direct isolation of aspartic acid. Following Chibnall's modification of the Ritthausen-Foreman method (1, p. 320) and noting that the present experiment does not involve the quantitative isolation of aspartic acid, 5 g of dry protein can be conveniently used. On this scale, the estimated amount of aspartic acid will be approximately 0.5 g. Since the amount of labeled aspartic acid should be of the same order of magnitude, it follows that 0.5 g of L-aspartic acid-U-^{14}C (prepared by biosynthetic methods and commercially available) is required for this experiment.

Since the labeled aspartic acid will suffer approximately a twofold dilution upon mixing with the aspartic acid in the protein hydrolysate, the required specific activity of the labeled aspartic acid will therefore be $2 \times 2.4 \times 10^4$ dpm/mmole aspartic acid. Since 500 mg of aspartic acid is equivalent to

$$\frac{500 \text{ mg}}{133 \text{ mg/mmole}} = 3.75 \text{ mmole of aspartic acid,}$$

it follows that the *total amount of radioactivity* required for this experiment is

$$4.8 \times 10^4 \text{ dpm/mmole compound} \times 3.75 \text{ mmole} = 1.8 \times 10^5 \text{ dpm,}$$

or about 0.08 μc

C. MATERIALS AND EQUIPMENT REQUIRED

The apparatus required for the experiment is basically ordinary laboratory glassware, except for the necessary apparatus for the Schöniger combustion operation. The latter is available commercially under the name of Thomas-Ogg Safety Oxygen Flask Ignitor Assembly, Model 11 (Arthur Thomas Company, Philadelphia). This assembly includes the Schöniger flask, a surrounding safety shield housing, and an infrared lamp and focusing device.

It is often desirable to have several flasks available where multiple combustions must be performed in a brief period of time. These can be easily constructed in the laboratory. Figure F-1 shows such a combustion flask made from a 1-liter filter flask. The side arm of the flask is closed with a serum cap through which an organic base solution can be injected following the combustion in order to absorb the CO_2 produced. A platinum wire inserted through the rubber stopper is attached to the platinum wire basket used to support the sample to be combusted (which is wrapped in black paper). For economy, a nichrome wire and basket may be substituted. Flushing with oxygen may be done through the serum-cap–topped glass tube inserted through the rubber stopper.

The instrument for the detection of radioactivity is the liquid scintillation counter of any commercial make. Chemicals required for this experiment include those commonly available in a chemical laboratory, such

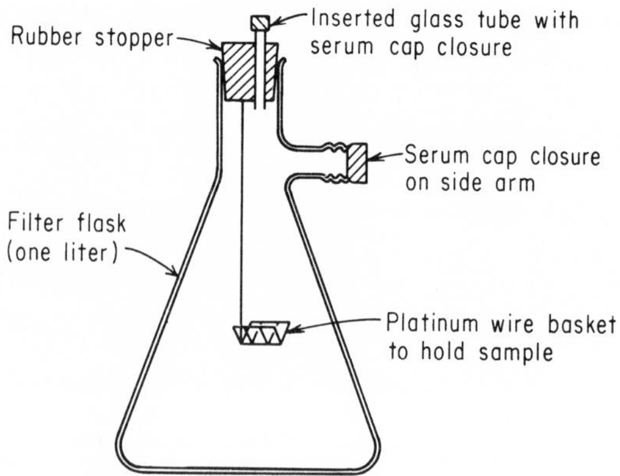

Figure F-1. Laboratory model of a Schöniger combustion flask.

as cupric carbonate, and chemicals for the preparation of liquid scintillation counting samples, such as *p*-terphenyl, POPOP, and toluene. In addition, the calculated amount of L-aspartic acid-U-^{14}C must be secured.

D. EXPERIMENTAL PROCEDURES

1. Hydrolysis of Protein and Separation of Aspartic Acid

Five grams (dry weight) of American cheese is mixed with 30 ml of 6N HCl and boiled under reflux conditions for 24 hr. The water and the HCl are then removed by repeated concentrations *in vacuo*. The residue so obtained is taken up in 50 ml of boiling water, and to this is added 500 mg of L-aspartic acid-U-^{14}C (with specific activity of approximately 4.8×10^4 dpm/mmole of compound, that is, total activity approximately 0.08 μc), and then an excess amount of $CuCO_3$ powder. An aliquot of L-aspartic acid-U-^{14}C (at least 15 mg) should be set aside for later use (Section 2). Upon digestion on a water bath for $\frac{1}{2}$ hr, the hot suspension is filtered and the precipitate washed thoroughly with hot water. The combined filtrate and washing are evaporated *in vacuo* to a final volume of approximately 20 ml. The solution is then placed in a refrigerator for two days; one will then find that the copper aspartate has crystallized out in blue crystals.

To improve the purity of the crude copper aspartate, the crystals may be *recrystallized* by dissolving them in a small amount of hot water, followed by chilling in a refrigerator. The pure copper aspartate crystals are then collected on a sintered glass filter, washed with ice-cold water, alcohol, and ether. The copper aspartate crystals so obtained have a molecular formula of $C_4H_5O_4NCu \cdot 2H_2O$ and are ready for the determination of their specific activity.

2. Sample Preparation by Schöniger Combustion and Liquid Scintillation Counting

To determine the specific activity of the labeled copper aspartate, a sample for liquid scintillation counting must be prepared. The *Schöniger combustion* technique offers a direct procedure in this case. A 15-mg portion of the copper aspartate crystals is weighed out carefully and transferred quantitatively onto a small piece of black paper (an ashless variety available through the Arthur Thomas Company). The weighed sample is carefully wrapped inside the black paper and the package is placed in the platinum basket of the ignition flask assembly (see Figure F-1). A stream of oxygen is now passed through the combustion flask to flush out most, if not all, of the air originally in the flask. The flask is then closed and placed within the safety shield (see Note 1). Combustion is accomplished by momentarily focusing a beam of infrared light, from the infrared lamp that is a component of the ignition assembly, onto the black package (2).

Upon completion of the combustion, introduce 2 ml of a 1:2 ethanol-ethanolamine solution into the combustion flask through the injection port. Allow the closed system to stand for a half hour to allow complete *absorption of the* CO_2 in the organic base solution. The flask contents are then transferred quantitatively with the aid of 2 ml more of the ethanol-ethanolamine solution to a 15-ml liquid scintillation counting vial. An additional amount of the ethanol-ethanolamine is subsequently introduced into the vial to give a total of 5 ml in the vial. To this add 10 ml of a scintillation solution containing *p*-terphenyl (3 g/liter) and POPOP (50 mg/liter). The vial is then closed, placed in a liquid scintillation counter, and kept in the dark for at least 30 min before counting (see Note 2).

Repeat the Schöniger combustion and sample recovery in ethanol-ethanolamine, using the 15-mg aliquot of the L-aspartic acid-U-^{14}C previously set aside (see Section 1).

Now count the two samples thus prepared with the counter controls set for *balance point counting* (see Experiment IV). The counting time should be sufficiently long so that at least 10,000 counts are collected. Upon completion of the counting operation, remove the vials from the counter and add to each 0.100 ml of toluene-7-^{14}C having a specific activity of 50,000 dpm/ml. Count the vials again at the same counter setting and with the same statistical accuracy. This *internal standardization* is necessary to determine the extent of quenching. Background determinations must also be made so that all counting rates can be reported in net counts per minute.

3. Calculations and Evaluation of Data

Using the net counting rates determined for each of the two samples before and after the addition of the internal standard, calculate the counting efficiency for each from Equation 6-1. From these counting efficiencies, convert the net cpm observed from each of the samples to disintegrations per minute. The specific activity of the respective samples, that is, the original L-aspartic acid-U-^{14}C and the copper aspartate-U-^{14}C, can then be determined from the known sample weights and the calculated disintegration per minute. Specific activity should be expressed as dpm/mmole of compound.

The specific activity results thus obtained can in turn be used to calculate the amount of aspartic acid originally present in the cheese hydrolysate, using Equation F-2. (What percentage of the cheese was aspartic acid? How does your result compare with published values ranging from 5 per cent to 15 per cent by weight?)

E. EXPERIMENTAL NOTES

(1) It is important that no trace of organic solvent remain in the combustion flask, lest a violent explosion occur. The safety shield is a precaution against such an event.

(2) Maintaining liquid scintillation counting samples in darkness for such a period is important in order to reduce fluorescence of the scintillation solution (see p. 164).

BIBLIOGRAPHY

1. Block, Richard J., and Diana Bolling. 1951. The amino acid composition of proteins and foods. C. C. Thomas, Springfield, Ill. 576 p.

2. Kelly, R. G., et al. 1961. Determination of C^{14} and H^3 in biological samples by Schöniger combustion and liquid scintillation techniques. Anal. Biochem. 2:267–273.

GENERAL BIBLIOGRAPHY

1. Aronoff, Sam. 1956. Techniques of radiobiochemistry. Iowa State College Press, Ames, Iowa. 228 p.
2. Bleuler, Ernst, and George J. Goldsmith. 1952. Experimental nucleonics. Holt, Rinehart & Winston, Inc., New York. 393 p.
3. Broda, Engelbert. 1960. Radioactive isotopes in biochemistry. Elsevier, Amsterdam. 376 p.
4. Brown, B. 1963. Experimental Nucleonics. Prentice-Hall, Inc., Englewood Cliffs, N.J. 245 p.
5. Chase, Grafton D., and Joseph L. Rabinowitz. 1962. Principles of radioisotope methodology. 2d ed. Burgess Publishing Co., Minneapolis. 372 p.
6. Comar, C. L. 1955. Radioisotopes in biology and agriculture. McGraw-Hill Book Company, New York. 481 p.
7. Cook, G. B., and J. F. Duncan. 1952. Modern radiochemical practice. Clarendon Press, Oxford. 407 p.
8. Faires, R. A., and B. H. Parks. 1960. Radioisotope laboratory techniques. 2d ed. George Newnes, Ltd., London. 244 p.
9. Francis, G. E., W. Mulligan, and A. Wormall. 1959. Isotopic tracers. 2nd ed. Essential Books, Fair Lawn, N.J. 524 p.
10. Glascock, Raymond. 1951. Labeled atoms. The use of radioactive and stable isotopes in biology and medicine. Sigma, London. 227 p.
11. Hevesy, George. 1948. Radioactive indicators—their applications in biochemistry, animal physiology, and pathology. John Wiley & Sons, Inc., New York. 556 p.
12. Kamen, Martin D. 1957. Isotopic tracers in biology, 3rd ed. Academic Press, Inc., New York. 478 p.
13. Overman, Ralph T., and Herbert M. Clark. 1960. Radioisotope techniques. McGraw-Hill Book Company, New York. 476 p.
14. Quimby, Edith H., and Sergei Feitelberg. 1963. Radioactive isotopes in

medicine and biology: basic physics and instrumentation. 2nd ed. Lea and Febiger, Philadelphia. 343 p.

15. Sacks, Jacob. 1953. Isotopic tracers in biochemistry and physiology. McGraw-Hill Book Company, New York. 383 p.
16. Sakami, Warwick (ed.). 1955. Handbook of isotope tracer methods. Western Reserve University, Dept. of Biochemistry. Cleveland. 188 p.
17. Schweitzer, Geo. K., and Ira B. Whitney. 1949. Radioactive tracer techniques. D. Van Nostrand Co., Inc., Princeton, N. J. 241 p.
18. Siri, William. 1949. Isotopic tracers and nuclear radiations with applications to biology and medicine. McGraw-Hill Book Company, New York. 653 p.
19. U.S. Dept. of Commerce, National Bureau of Standards. 1961. A manual of radioactivity procedures. Handbook no. 80. Washington. 159 p.

Problems

NUCLEAR REACTIONS (CHAPTER 1)

1. In the following incomplete nuclear reactions supply the missing items:

a. $^{27}Al\,(n, \alpha)$ ____	g. ____ $(n, p)\,^{27}Mg$
b. $^{23}Na\,(n,$ __ $)\,^{24}Na$	h. $^{32}S\,(n,$ __ $)\,^{32}P$
c. ____ $(n, p)\,^{14}C$	i. $^{35}Cl\,(n, p)$ ____
d. $^{12}C\,(n, 2n)$ ____	j. $^{6}Li\,($ __ $, \alpha)\,^{3}H$
e. $^{9}Be\,($ __ $, n)\,^{12}C$	k. $^{44}Ca\,($ __ $, \gamma)\,^{45}Ca$
f. $^{58}Fe\,(n, \gamma)$ ____	l. ____ $(n, \gamma)\,^{65}Zn$

RADIOACTIVE DECAY SCHEMES (CHAPTER 2)

2. From the following information construct a set of decay schemes:

PARENT NUCLIDE	DAUGHTER NUCLIDE	PARTICLE OR PHOTON EMISSION
a. 164 day ^{45}Ca	stable ^{45}Sc	β^-, 0.256 Mev, 100%
b. 18.66 day ^{86}Rb	stable ^{86}Sr	β_1^-, 0.698 Mev, 10%
		β_2^-, 1.776 Mev, 90%
		γ, 1.078 Mev
c. 2.696 day ^{198}Au	stable ^{198}Hg	β_1^-, 0.282 Mev, 1%
		β_2^-, 0.959 Mev, 99%
		β_3^-, 1.371 Mev, <1%
		γ_1, 0.4118 Mev
		γ_2, 0.676 Mev
		γ_3, 1.089 Mev
d. 3.03×10^5 yr ^{36}Cl	stable ^{36}A	β^-, 0.714 Mev, >98%
	stable ^{36}S	*EC*, (1.19 Mev), <2%

RADIOACTIVE DECAY RATES (CHAPTER 2)

3. In order to determine the decay constant (λ) and half-life ($t_{1/2}$) of an unknown radioisotope the following activity determinations were made:

TIME OF DETERMINATION (HR)	CORRECTED NET COUNT RATE (CPM)
0	8500
0.16	7050
0.30	6000
0.50	4756
0.65	3998
0.80	3370
1.06	2499
1.30	1880

a. Plot these results on both a linear and a semi-logarithmic basis (logarithm of count rate) as shown in Figures 2-9 and 2-10 (p. 26). As illustrated in Figure 2-12 (p. 30) determine the half-life in hours of this radioisotope by the graphic method.

Answer: ~0.6 hr.

b. Now, using the graphically determined half-life value ($t_{1/2}$) in hours, calculate the decay constant (λ) of this radioisotope from the equation:

$$\lambda = \frac{0.693}{t_{1/2}} \qquad \text{(Equation 2-11 rearranged)}$$

c. If your resulting value for λ equals or exceeds unity, there is clearly some grave error in the approach. Such a value would indicate complete decay of the radioisotope, an impossible situation in view of the decay kinetics. Convert your graphically determined half-life value to seconds and again calculate λ by the preceding equation. Is a more reasonable value obtained? From these calculations it should be clear that $t_{1/2}$ must be expressed in appropriately small units in order for λ to appear as a small fraction of unity. The reason for this situation is evident when one realizes that the decay equation is derived on the basis of integration of many infinitesimally small time intervals (see p. 29).

Answer: $\lambda = 0.00032/\text{sec}$

4. An investigator is using colloidal ^{198}Au, which has a half-life of 2.696 days. He has on hand a shipment assayed at 50 μc as of 12 noon Monday. He intends to use this radioactive substance on Thursday of the same week at 9 A.M. Determine the radioactivity level as of the time of use.

a. First, calculate the decay constant on an hourly basis as in the previous problem.

b. Next, use Equation 2-9 to calculate the fraction of activity remaining at the indicated time.

c. Finally, calculate the μc level of activity as of 9 A.M. Thursday.

Answer: $\sim 24\ \mu c$

5. An investigator has received a shipment labeled only "30% ^{14}C enriched $BaCO_3$—weight 2285 mg." He realizes that this designation means that 30% (by weight) of the material is $Ba^{14}CO_3$, the rest being $Ba^{12}CO_3$ and $Ba^{13}CO_3$. He desires to know how much radioactivity the shipment contains. In order to ascertain this information he proceeds as follows:

a. Since the decay constant (λ) is related to the half-life ($t_{1/2}$) as follows:

$$\lambda = \frac{0.693}{t_{1/2}}$$

it follows that if the half-life of ^{14}C (5568 yr) is expressed in seconds, then the λ value will indicate the fraction of ^{14}C atoms decaying per second.

b. There are 6.02×10^{23} atoms per mole (Avogadro's number). In the sample material in question only 30% of the carbon atoms are of the radioactive species ^{14}C. Thus,

$$(6.02 \times 10^{23})(0.3)(\lambda/\text{sec} \quad \text{for} \quad {}^{14}\text{C}) = \text{dis/sec/mole of carbon}$$

c. It is then a simple matter to calculate the number of moles of barium carbonate present in the 2285 mg sample and to determine the dis/sec (dps) from this quantity of material. This disintegration rate can then be readily converted to millicuries.

Answer: ~220 mc

6. Using the same general procedure followed in problem 5 calculate the specific activity of carrier-free ^{32}P in the form of Na_3PO_4. Express your result as mc/mg Na_3PO_4. Use a half-life value of 14.221 days for ^{32}P. It is understood that in a carrier-free compound all the atoms of the radioactive element in question are radioactive.

Answer: 5.55×10^4 mc/mg $Na_3{}^{32}PO_4$

7. In a synthetic reaction carrier-free tritium gas (T_2) is used to hydrogenate fumaric acid to succinic acid as follows:

$$\text{HOOC—}\overset{\text{H}}{\overset{|}{\text{C}}}\text{=}\overset{\text{H}}{\overset{|}{\text{C}}}\text{—COOH} + T_2 \xrightarrow{\text{catalyst}} \text{HOOC—}\underset{\text{T}}{\underset{|}{\overset{\text{H}}{\overset{|}{\text{C}}}}}\text{—}\underset{\text{T}}{\underset{|}{\overset{\text{H}}{\overset{|}{\text{C}}}}}\text{—COOH}$$

Using the same procedure as in problems 5 and 6 calculate the specific activity in mc/mg of the resulting succinic acid. Use a half-life value of 12.262 yr for tritium.

Answer: ~470 mc/mg succinic acid-T_2

RADIATION ABSORPTON RELATIONSHIPS (CHAPTER 3)

8. A β-, γ-sensitive G-M detector with a wall thickness of 30 mg/cm^2 is used for assay of an isotope emitting 1-Mev gamma rays. Ignoring air absorption, what fraction of gamma radiation of this energy would be transmitted through the detector wall? This wall is of aluminum, which has a mass absorption coefficient for 1-Mev gamma rays of 0.062 cm^2/g. (Use equation 3-10, p. 58.)

Answer: Virtually 100%

9. Could the same detector of problem 8 now be used to assay a ^{14}C-containing sample emitting β-particles with an R_{max} of about 28 mg/cm^2 in aluminum? Would any of these beta particles be expected to penetrate the aluminum wall of the detector?

Answer: No

10. An investigator has on hand a one curie source which emits 1.5-Mev gamma radiation. He desires to reduce the radiation level at the outside of his source shielding to the equivalent of that from a 5 μc source. He plans to use steel plates to shield the source which have a linear absorption coefficient (μ_l) of 0.4/cm for this gamma energy. How many inches of steel will be needed around his one curie source to attain the desired shielding?

The linear half-thickness ($x_{1/2}$) may be calculated from the linear absorption coefficient as follows:

$$x_{1/2} = \frac{0.693}{\mu_l}$$

Then determine the gamma attenuation factor desired and use this value in equation 3-15 to calculate the number of half-thicknesses required. From this value and linear half-thickness, the thickness of steel required can be readily found.

Answer: ~12.1 inches thickness

RELATIVE COUNTING WITH A G-M COUNTER (CHAPTERS 4 AND 9)

11. A $Ba^{14}CO_3$ *standard* with a known specific activity of 423 dpm/mg was assayed to a 1% standard deviation using a thin-window G-M detector. The sample was evenly spread over a 9.0 cm^2 aluminum planchet of sufficient thickness to give saturation backscattering. Sample thickness was 15.0 mg/cm^2. A net count rate of 1430 cpm was recorded. Next, a $Ba^{14}CO_3$ sample of *unknown* activity was prepared by the same procedure as the standard, mounted on an aluminum planchet of the same size and thickness and assayed using the same counting assembly to a 1% standard deviation. Sample thickness was 20.0

mg/cm^2. A net count rate of 1350 cpm was recorded from this sample. What was the total activity (in μc) of the unknown sample? In order to determine the activity of the unknown sample by comparing it to the activity of a known standard, the counting data must be comparable. This must involve a consideration of self-absorption (see Figure 9-10, p. 205) and any other factors that do not have constant values.

Answer: ~0.03 μc

12. An 18.0 mg sample of glucose-1-^{14}C is completely combusted to $^{14}CO_2$ and subsequently converted to $Ba^{14}CO_3$. This entire $Ba^{14}CO_3$ sample is then mounted on an aluminum planchet of the same size and thickness as that in problem 11 and assayed with the same counting assembly to a 1% standard deviation. A net count rate of 2540 cpm is recorded. Assuming a 100% conversion of the glucose to $Ba^{14}CO_3$, what is the specific activity in dpm/mmole of glucose? (Again, refer to the self-absorption curve on p. 205.)

Answer: ~924,000 dpm/mmole glucose

RELATIVE COUNTING WITH A SOLID SCINTILLATION COUNTER (CHAPTER 5)

13. The following counting data were recorded using a solid crystal NaI (Tl) scintillation counting assembly in the integral counting mode:

PHOTOMULTIPLIER POTENTIAL	GROSS SAMPLE CPM	BACKGROUND CPM
700 v	600	100
800	30,000	650
900	40,000	1800
1000	41,500	2400
1100	44,000	2800
1200	48,000	4000

Determine the optimal operating point on the basis of the equation S^2/B = maximum (see page 100), where S = net count rate, and B = background count rate. Subsequently, using the differential counting mode (limited window centered on the photopeak), a gross sample count rate of 6050 cpm was recorded with a background count rate of only 24 cpm. In this particular circumstance, which counting mode gives the most favorable sample-to-background ratio?

Answers: 800 v; differential mode

RELATIVE COUNTING WITH A LIQUID SCINTILLATION COUNTER (CHAPTERS 6 AND 8)

14. One ml of an aqueous solution containing 1 mg of glucose-U-^{14}C is assayed in a Thixcin gel preparation (p. 171) using a liquid scintillation spectrometer. At the balance point, a net count rate of 65,000 cpm was registered. The counter had previously been calibrated at the same balance point settings using two different standards as follows: 0.10 cc of $Na_2{}^{14}CO_3$ standardized at 4900 dpm gave a net count rate of 2200 cpm; 1.0 mg of toluene-^{14}C standardized at 3400 dpm gave a net count rate of 1870 cpm. Considering the nature of the sample, which one of the standards would be chosen for calibration purposes? Why? What was the activity of the glucose-U-^{14}C sample in microcuries?

Answer: ~0.066 μc

COUNTING STATISTICS (CHAPTER 9)

15. Six aliquots of a tritiated water sample were assayed using a liquid scintillation spectrometer. The following time intervals were required to accumulate a gross count of 10,000 counts for the six samples respectively: 36.30, 35.51, 36.24, 36.01, 36.98, and 37.40 min. Subsequently, 1900 background counts were registered in 15 min. Calculate the average net count rate of these six samples and, considering the contribution of background error (see pages 189–190), express the reliability of the net counting rate as $\pm$ so many cpm.

Answer: 148 $\pm$ 4 cpm

RADIATION SAFETY (CHAPTER 12)

16. Using equation 12-1 (p. 246) calculate the approximate gamma radiation exposure in mR/hr at 1 ft distance from an unshielded 50 mc ^{60}Co source. The decay scheme of ^{60}Co is shown in Figure 2-3 (p. 21). Follow the decay path through β_1.

Answer: ~750 mR/hr at 1 ft.

17. Iodine-129 emits one gamma ray of 0.039 Mev per disintegration. Using equation 12-1 and the inverse square relationship (p. 246), calculate the approximate gamma radiation exposure in mR/hr at 1 yd distance from an unshielded 4 curie ^{129}I point source.

Answer: ~104 mR/hr at 1 yd.

18. Absorbed doses from internal emitters pose a serious radiation hazard. Ignoring excretion and loss of activity by radioactive decay, the approximate absorbed dose for a tissue can be calculated in rads/day (D) as follows:

$$D = \frac{(3.7 \times 10^4 \text{ dps}/\mu\text{c})(\text{mean } \beta \text{ energy in ev})(1.60207 \times 10^{-12} \text{ ergs/ev}) \\ (\text{tissue conc. of isotope in } \mu\text{c/g})(86{,}400 \text{ sec/day})}{100 \text{ ergs/g/rad}}$$

(Attempt to think your way through the derivation of this equation for dose calculation.) Using this equation, calculate the respective doses to liver tissue in rads/day where the liver tissue concentration is maintained uniformly at 1 $\mu c/g$ of ^{32}P, ^{14}C, and ^{3}H, respectively. The results should show the relation of beta disintegration energy to internal dose.

Answers: ^{32}P ~36 rads/day, ^{14}C ~ 2.5 rads/day, ^{3}H ~ 0.3 rads/day

19. If no excretion or turnover occurred, what would be the approximate absorbed doses in the liver tissue of problem 18 two months later from these three radioisotopes, respectively? The results will reveal the relation of physical half-life to internal dose.

Answers: ^{32}P ~ 2 rads/day, ^{14}C ~ 2.5 rads/day, ^{3}H ~ 0.3 rads/day.

20. Assume that the turnover time (biological half-life) of ^{14}C is 8 days and that of ^{3}H is 57 days in the situation discussed in problem 18. What would be the approximate absorbed dose in rads/day to the liver tissue two months later from ^{14}C and ^{3}H, respectively? The decline in activity due to turnover can be treated mathematically in the same manner as physical decay. These results should illustrate the importance of biological half-life to internal dose.

Answers: ^{14}C ~0.014 rads/day, ^{3}H ~0.15 rads/day.

LABORATORY, SAFETY, AND EXPERIMENTAL DESIGN FACTORS (CHAPTERS 10, 12, AND 13)

21. You are interested in submitting a research proposal involving the use of of radioisotopes. It is necessary to describe the desired counting and monitoring instruments, sample preparation procedures, special laboratory facilities, safety features and procedures, waste disposal arrangements, etc. Select one or more of the following types of investigations to be described in this regard.

ACTIVITY LEVEL	ACTIVE COMPOUND	AREA OF INVESTIGATION
1 mc	Sodium carbonate-^{14}C	CO_2 incorporation in selected plants
5 mc	Sodium phosphate-^{32}P	Phosphate distribution in seedling apple trees
2 mc	Thymidine-^{3}H	DNA synthesis in rabbit liver
8 mc	Calcium chloride-^{45}Ca	Ion transport through gill tissue of fish
10 mc	Ferrous citrate-^{59}Fe	Iron metabolism in dairy cattle.

Index

Absolute counting, 65
Absorption, *see* types of radiation
Absorption coefficient
  linear (μ_l), 56–58
  mass (μ_m), 58–59, 62, 305–306
Abundance of stable isotopes, 7–8
Actinium series, 9
Alpha particles, 24, 37–43
  absorption, 40–43
  detection, 43, 80–81, 83, 109, 279–280
  emission, 24
  energy characteristics, 37–39
  energy dissipation, 39
  equivalent thickness, 43
  half-life and energy relationships, 38–39
  health hazard, 43, 246
  interaction with matter, 39–41, 68
  nature of, 24, 37
  range, 41–43
  range-energy relations, 41–42
  specific ionization, 40–41
Alpha plateau, 81, 279
Amplifier, 73–74, 100, 270, 278, 290–291
Ashing procedures for mineral elements, 155
Atomic number (Z value), 4
Atoms, 3–5
Autoradiography, 67–68, 144–151, 320–321
  artifacts in, 147–148, 227, 322
  cellular, 149–150
  detection of amino acids by, 320–321
  estimation of radioactivity by, 144–151
  gross specimens, 148–149
  specific techniques, 148–150

Background
  effect on counting time, 190–192
  error, 100, 126, 189–190, 194
  reduction of, 81, 83–84, 95, 136, 273, 280, 285
  sources of, 81, 194, 242, 273, 280
Backing thickness, 200–201
Backscattering, 160, 199–201
Barn, 13
Beta energy spectrometry, 45, 115–116, 293
Beta particles,
  detection of, 51–52, 70, 73–74, 80–81, 83–84, 107–109, 279–280, 286
  emission of, 20–22, 46–48
  energy characteristics, 44–48
  energy spectra of, 44–47
  Feather analysis, 50
  health hazard, 52, 246–248
  interaction with matter, 48–49
  maximum energy (E_{max}), 45–46
  mean energy (E_{mean}), 45–46
  nature of, 20–21, 44
  negatrons, 20, 44
  positrons, 21–22, 44
  range, 49–50
  relation to neutrino, 46–47
  self-absorption, 202–206, 306–308
  specific ionization, 48–49
  transmission curves for mica windows, 51
Beta plateau, 81, 279
Biological effects of radiation, *see* Radiation biology
Bragg scattering, 54
Bremsstrahlung, 48, 50

Calibration of detectors, 66, 196, 287, 330
Carrier free radioisotopes, 14, 35, 232
Cascade of gamma rays, 53
Channels ratio method in liquid scintillation counting, 132–134, 295–297
Chauvenet's criterion, 192, 310
Chemiluminescence, 164, 292
Chromatrogram scanning counter, 162–163, 322
Chromatography, *see* Paper chromatography
Cloud chamber, 40, 44, 48
Coincidence circuitry, 110, 114, 194, 292
Coincidence loss corrections, 197–199, 273–275
Combustion methods, 155–158, 363–365
Composite decay, 32–33
Compton effect, 55, 61–63
Compton smear, 93
Contamination hazards
  removal of, 250–251, 253–254
  technical, 190, 242
Counters, *see* Detectors
  comparison of, 136
Counting sample preparation, 152–185
  beta emitters, 153–185, 365
  centrifugation techniques, 161
  choice of sample form, 152–154
  conversion to suitable form, 154–158
    ashing methods, 155
    combustion methods, 155–158, 365
    miscellaneous methods, 158
  electroplating, 162
  gamma emitters, 159–162, 340, 347–348, 356
  gaseous form, 159, 166–170
  liquid, assay of, 159–160, 163–172
  liquid form, 159–160, 340, 347–348
  for liquid scintillation counting, 110–111, 163–172, 298, 363, 365
    composition of solutions, 165, 167–169
    direct solution, 164–165
    filter paper, 172
    fluorescence quenching problems, 111–112, 163, 165, 297
    gel, 171–172, 298
    indirect solution, 165–170
    for inorganic ions, 168–170
    particle suspension, 171
    Schöniger combustion, 157–158, 363–365
  solid form, 160–163, 356–357
Counting time, 190–192
Curie (unit), 34–36
Cyclotron, 10, 230–232

Dark current, *see* Thermal noise
Dating, age, 10, 83–84, 164–165
Dead time, *see* Resolving time
Decay constant, 25–31, 33, 299–300
  for selected radioisotopes, 27
Decay correction tables, 27
  for ^{32}P, 28
  for ^{131}I, 29
Decay scheme, 20–24, 354
Decay series, 9, 24
Decontamination, 250–251, 253–254, 263–264
Detectors
  continuous-flow, 73–74, 124–125, 324 ff

Detectors (cont.)
Electroscope, 72
gas flow, 80, 277
Geiger-Mueller
characteristics of 77–79, 84–85, 269–271
operation of 84–85, 272–275
types of 81–84
internal gas type, 80
ion chamber, 69–74, 324ff
large-volume scintillation, 123–124
liquid scintillation (internal-sample), 89, 104–143, 289–298
proportional, 76, 79–81
characteristics of 76, 80–81, 276–278
operation of 80–81, 278–280
selection of 136, 152–153
solid scintillation (external-sample) 67, 89–103, 281–288
well scintillation, 97, 159, 283, 337–338, 343, 347, 358
Deuterons, 11, 230
Deviation, standard, 188–192
Differential counting, 95, 283–284
Discriminator, pulse, 92–95, 110, 113–118, 126–129, 283, 291–295
Disintegration rate, *see* Decay rate
Distribution, Poisson, 187
Dosimeter, 72, 250
Double-labeled sample, 108, 116–117
Dynamic capacitor electrometer, *see* Vibrating-reed electrometer
Dynodes of photomultiplier, 90–92

Efficiency
of counting assemblies
electrometer-ion chamber, 73, 136
Geiger-Mueller, 136, 287
liquid scintillation, 109, 126–136, 294–297
proportional, 136
solid scintillation, 95, 98, 136
of detectors, 85, 96–97, 100–102, 111–112, 120–123, 195–197
Electromagnetic radiation, 8, 52–53
Electrometers
operating characteristics of, 72–74
vibrating-reed (dynamic capacitor) 73, 323–324
Electron capture (EC), 22–23
Electrons, 3
internal conversion, 23, 44
Electron volt, 4
Electroscopes, 72
Elements, 4
Emulsion, photographic
in autoradiography, 67–68, 144–150
Energy, *see* various types of radiation
Energy dissipation
excitation, 39, 88, 90–91, 106–107
ionization, 40–41, 68–69
Energy transfer
in liquid scintillation counting, 105–108
in solid scintillation counting, 90–92
"Energy Well" concept, 38–39
Equivalent thickness, 43, 49
Error probability
measure of, 188
Excitation, *see* Energy dissipation
Experimental design
basic features of, 217–222

Experimental design (cont.)
data analysis in, 223–227
evaulation of feasibility, 215–216
execution of, 223
preliminary considerations in, 211–215
External standard method in liquid scintillation counting, 134–135

Factors in relative counting, *see* Backscatter, Coincidence loss, Self-absorption
Fast neutron reactions, 12–13
Feather analysis, 50
Film badge, 144, 249–250, 253
Fission products, 14, 230–232
Fission reactions, 11–12
Fluorescence quenching, 111–112, 131–135, 163–165, 293–297
Fluors
energy transfer in, 88, 90–92, 105–108
liquid, 89, 96, 104–109, 121–125, 163–170, 290, 293–298
plastic, 89, 96–97, 125
solid crystal, 67, 89–92, 96–98, 282, 286
Four-π geometry, 104, 195

Gamma rays,
absorption
dependence on energy and density, 61–63
exponential nature of, 60–61
half-thickness ($x_{1/2}$, $d_{1/2}$), 59–63
linear coefficient (μ_l), 56–58
mass coefficient (μ_m), 58–59, 62
detection of, 63, 109, 286–287
electromagnetic nature of, 8, 52–53
energy characteristics, 53
health hazards of, 63, 245–246
interaction with matter, 54–56, 61–63
isomeric transition, 23, 53
secondary energy dissipation
Bragg scattering, 54
Compton effect, 55, 61–63, 93
Mössbauer effect, 54
nuclear transformation, 54
pair production, 55–56, 62–63
photoelectric effect, 55, 63
shielding, 60–61, 63, 246
spectrometry, 93–95, 283–284
Gas ionization mechanism, 67–86
Geiger-Mueller region, 77–79
ionization potential, 68
limited proportional region, 75–77
potential gradient, 69–71, 74–77
proportional region, 75–76
saturation current, 71
Townsend avalanche, 74
with gas amplification, 74–79
without gas amplification, 69–74
Geiger-Mueller counter assembly
components of, 84, 269–271
operation of, 272–275
Geiger-Mueller detectors, 77–79, 81–85
characteristics of, 77–79, 84–85
coincidence loss, 197–199, 273–274
quenching mechanisms, 77–79
types of, 81–84, 249
Geiger-Mueller region, 77–79
Gel sample in liquid scintillation counting, 171–172, 298

Half-life
  biological ($T_{1/2}$), 31, 247–248
  determination of, 30–31, 34, 299–302
  radioactive decay ($t_{1/2}$), 27–31, 34, 299–302, 349
  relation to decay constant, 29
  relation to radioactive emission mechanism,
    alpha decay, 38–39
    beta decay, 19, 48
Half-thickness ($x_{1/2}$ and $d_{1/2}$)
  relation to absorbtion coefficient, 59–60
  relation to shielding requirements, 60–61
Halogen quenching in G-M detectors, 78–79

Infinite thickness, 203–204, 307
Integral counting, 94–95, 283
Internal conversion, 23, 44
Internal health hazards, 43, 52, 63, 246–248
Internal standard method in liquid scintillation counting, 131–132, 294–295
Inverse square law, 246, 275
Ion chamber, 69–74, 249–250
Ionization, 40, 68–69
    gas, *see* Gas ionization
    specific, 40–41, 48–49
Ionization potential, 68
Ion pair formation, 40, 68–69
Isomeric transition (IT), 23, 53
Isotope dilution method, 360–362
Isotopes,
  defined, 5
  number of, 5
  stable, 6–8
    natural abundance of, 8
Isotopic effect, 211–213

K-capture, *see* Electron capture
Kilo electron volt (kev), 4

Labeled compounds, availability of, 215, 229–241
Laboratory, radioisotope, 256–265
Laboratory safety regulations, 252–254
Lauritsen electroscope, 72
Limited proportional region, 75–77
Linear absorption coefficient (μ_l), 56–58
Linear energy transfer (LET), 245
"Line of stability" (atom), 18–20
Liquid counting samples, 159–160, 340, 347–348
Liquid (internal-sample) scintillation counters,
  for age dating, 164–165
  beta particle spectrometry, 116–118, 125–131, 293, 298
  chemiluminescence, 164, 292
  components of,
    coincidence circuitry, 110, 114–117, 194, 292
    detector assembly, 119–123, 290
    linear amplifiers, 290–291
    logarithmic spectrum amplifier, 114–118
    power supply, 113, 290
    preamplifiers, 107, 110, 113–114, 290
    pulse discriminators, 110, 113–118, 126–129, 291–295
    pulse height analyzer, 113–117, 125–129, 132, 289, 291–295
    scaler, 292
    timer, 119, 292
  conversion of specimen to counting sample, 110–111, 155–158, 163–172

Liquid scintillation counters (cont.)
    Parr oxygen bomb combustion, 158
    Schöniger flask combustion, 157–158, 360, 363
    sealed tube combustion, 157
  counting sample types,
    accomodating aqueous solutions, 124, 166
    double radioisotope labeled, 108, 116–117
    filter paper, 170–172
    gases (absorbed), 121, 125, 166, 168–170
    gel, 170–172, 298
    metallic ions, 121, 168–170
    minimum quenching, 163–165
  detection of,
    alpha particles, 109
    beta particles, 107–109, 112, 116–118, 129–131, 289, 293–294
    gamma rays, 109, 123
    neutrinos, 124
    neutrons, 123–124
  detector assembly components,
    photomultipliers, 104–110, 119
    primary solutes, 106, 121–122, 165–169, 293
    primary solvents, 105–106, 120, 165–169, 293
    sample vials, 119
    secondary solutes (wave shifters), 106, 122–123, 165–170, 293
    secondary solvents, 120–121, 165–169
  determination of counting efficiency,
    by channels ratio (pulse height shift) method, 132–134, 295–297
    by dilution method, 132
    by external standard method, 134–135
    by internal standard method, 131–132, 294
  efficiency of, 109, 111–112, 114, 120–123, 126–136, 294–297
  energy transfer in, 105–108
  fluorescence quenching, 111–112, 120, 131–135, 163–165, 293–297
    chemical, 111–112, 163, 297
    color, 111–112, 163
    corrections for, 131–135, 294–297
    dilution, 111–112
    effect on counting, 111, 126–129, 293–294, 297
    optical, 112
    oxygen, 112
  fluors,
    characteristics and varieties of, 104–109, 121–125, 163–170, 290, 293–298
    energy transfer in, 105–108, 289
  four-π geometry of, 104
  operating characteristics of,
    balance point operation, 126–127, 294
    effect of photomultiplier potential, 126, 293–294
    effect of window setting, 126, 293–294
    flat spectrum operation, 127
    pulse summation, 129–131
  special detector types,
    continuous-flow, 124–125
    large volume, 123–124
    whole-body counter, 109, 123
  thermal noise problems, 92–93, 108–110, 289
    reduction of, 92–93, 109–110, 292
Logarithmic amplifier in liquid scintillation counter, 114–117
Low background counter, 83–84

Mass absorption coefficient (μ_m), 58–59, 62

Mass number (A value), 5
Maximum permissible body burden, 248
Maximum permissible concentration (MPC), 248, 251–252
Maximum permissible dose, 248
Mean life (T_a), 33
Mechanical register, 197, 271, 278, 284
Metastable nuclides, 23
Microcurie (μc), 34
Millicurie (mc), 34
Million electron volt (Mev), 4
Mössbauer effect, 54
Multichannel pulse analyzers, 95, 284

Naturally occurring radioisotopes, 9–10
Negatron (β^-) emission, 20–21
Negatrons (β^-), 44
Neutrino, 46–47, 124
Neutron activation analysis, 14–15
Neutron-capture cross section, 13
Neutron flux, 13, 15, 301
Neutron generators, 15–16
Neutrons,
  defined, 5
  reactions induced by, 12–14
Neutron source, 15
Nuclear emulsion, 147
Nuclear potential barrier, 38–39
Nuclear reactions, 10–16
Nuclear reactors, 11–15, 229–230, 301
Nuclear resonance scattering, 54
Nuclear stability, 18–19
Nucleons, 4
Nucleus of atom, 4–5
Nuclides, 5–16
  metastable, 23
  radioactive, *see* Radioisotopes
  stable, 6–7
  symbolic expression of, 5

Oak Ridge National Laboratory,
  radioisotopes available from, 11, 230–232
Operating potential for counters, 69–71, 81, 84, 99–100, 126–129, 272–273, 279, 284–286, 293–294
Oppenheimer-Phillips process, 11

Paired sources for determination of resolving time, 199, 274–275
Pair production, 55–56, 62–63
Paper chromatography, 319–320
  autoradiography of, 148, 320–321
Paralysis time, *see* Resolving time
Parr oxygen bomb, 158
Particle accelerators, 10–11, 230–232
Persulfate combustion method, 156–157
Phosphors, *see* Fluors
Photocoupling, 97, 119
Photoelectric effect, 55, 63
Photomultipliers,
  effect of potential applied to, 99–100, 126–129, 284–285, 293–294
  energy transfer in, 91
  nature of, 97–99, 282, 290
  thermal noise, 92–93, 109–110
Photons, 8, 52
Pipetting radioactive solutions, 154
Planchets for counting sample, 160–162, 199–201

Plateau
  for G-M detector, 84–85, 272–273
  for proportional detector, 81, 279–280
  for solid scintillation, 99–100, 285–286
Pocket dosimeter, 72, 250
Poisson distribution, 187–188
Positron, 44
  annihilation of, 44
  emission of, 21–22
Potential-drop method (electrometer), 73, 324
Power supply, 269, 276, 281–282, 290
Preamplifier
  in proportional counting assembly, 278
  in scintillation counting assembly, 99, 107, 110, 113–114, 283, 290
Primary solute in liquid scintillation counting, 106, 121–122, 165–169, 293
Primary solvent in liquid scintillation counting, 105–106, 120, 165–169, 293
Probability, error, *see* Error probability
Probable error, 188
Proportional counter assembly
  components of, 276–278
  operation of, 80, 278–280
Proportional detectors
  alpha plateau, 81, 279
  beta plateau, 81, 279
  characteristics of, 76, 80–81
  coincidence loss in, 76, 280
  types of, 79–80, 277
Proportional region, 75–76
Protons, 4
Pulse height analyzer, 95, 113–117, 283, 289
Purity, radiochemical, 214, 239–240

Quenching (fluorescence) in liquid scintillation counting,
  chemical, 111–112, 297
  color, 111–112
  corrections for, 131–135, 294–297
  dilution, 111–112
  effect on counting, 111, 126–129, 293–294, 297
  optical, 112
  oxygen, 112
Quenching mechanisms in G-M detectors, 77–79
  external, 78
  internal, 78–79, 82
    halogen, 78–79, 82
    organic, 78, 82
Q value, 20

Rad, 244
Radiation, *see* individual types of radioactive emission
Radiation biology, 333
Radiation dose
  units of effect consideration
    linear energy transfer (LET), 245
    relative biological effectiveness (RBE), 244
  units of exposure and dose
    roentgen (R), 243–244
    roentgen absorbed dose (rad), 244
    roentgen equivalent mammal (rem), 244–246
    roentgen equivalent physical (rep), 243–244
Radiation dosimetry, 65–66, 243–246
Radiation monitoring instruments, 248–250
Radioactive decay
  by alpha particle emission, 24
  average life (Ta), 33

Radioactive decay (cont.)
composite, 32–33
constant, 25–31, 33, 299–300
correction tables for, 27
^{32}P, 28
^{131}I, 29
by electron capture, 22–23
half-life ($t_{1/2}$), 27–31, 34, 299–302, 349
determination of, 30–31, 34, 299–302
by internal conversion, 23, 44
by isomeric transition, 23, 53
nature of, 18–36, 299–302
by negative beta (negatron) emission, 20–21
by positive beta (positron) emission, 21–22
rate of, 24–33
schemes, 20–24, 354
types of, 20–24
Radioactive wastes,
disposal of, 216, 251–252, 260–262
Radioactivity
absolute counting, 65
detection by,
autoradiography, 67–68, 144–151
gas ionization, 67–86
liquid (internal-sample) scintillation method, 104–143
solid (external-sample) scintillation method, 88–102
measurements of
analysis of data in, 186–209
general considerations, 65–68
radiation dose and, 65
statistical considerations, 187–193, 309–310
nature of, 3–4, 8
relative counting, 65–66
standard unit of, 34–35
Radioautography, *see* Autoradiography
Radiocarbon dating, 10, 83–84, 164–165
Radiochemical hoods, 264–265
Radiochromatograms, 147, 319–320
Radiochromatogram scanning counter, 162–163, 322
Radiocolloid, 214
Radioisotope labeled compounds
preparation by
biosynthesis, 235–236
chemical synthesis, 233–235
tritium exposure, 236–239
radiolysis of, 214, 239–240
Radioisotopes
artificially produced, 10–16, 229–232
by nuclear reactors, 11–15, 229–232
by other neutron sources, 15–16
by particle accelerators, 10–11, 230–232
availability of, 229–241
average life values for, 33
carrier-free, 14, 35, 232
decay constants for, 27–31, 33, 299–300
hazard factors in handling,
external 43, 52, 63, 245–246
internal, 43, 52, 63, 246–248
naturally occuring, 9–10
preparation of labeled compounds from, 233
safe handling of, 242–255
specific activity of, 14, 35–36, 215
Radiolysis of labeled compounds, 214, 239–240
Radionuclides, *see* Radioisotopes
Radiorespirometry, 323
Radiotracer experiments,
Radiotracer experiments (cont.)
anticipated findings, 222–223
basic assumptions, 211–215
data analysis, 223–227
expression of, 223–224
interpretation of, 224–227
design of, 36, 210–223
basic features of, 217–223
example of, 219–222
preliminary considerations in, 211–216
execution of, 223–227
feasibility of, 215–216
hazards, 215–216
isotope effects, 211–213
scale of operation, 217–218
specific activity requirement, 219
unique advantages of, 210–211
Radiotracer laboratories
design features of, 256–265
basic, 258
specific, 258–265
electrical utilities, 260
fixtures, 262–264
floor arrangement, 259
hazard evaluation, 258
heating, 259–260
radiochemical hoods, 264–265
sewage disposal, 260–261
ventilation, 259–260
waste disposal, 261–262
Range
of alpha particles, 41–43
of beta particles, 49–50
Range-energy relationships
for alpha particles, 41–42
for beta particles, 50
Rate-of-change method (electrometer), 73, 324
Recovery time, 197–198
Regulations, laboratory, 252–254
Relative biological effectiveness (RBE), 244–245
Relative counting, 65–66, 193, 206
Relative standard deviation, 188, 310
Resolution in autoradiography, 145–150
Resolving (coincidence, dead, paralysis) time
correction for loss of counts by, 197–199, 273
determination of, 197–199, 273–275, 280, 287
of various detectors, 76–77, 136, 197–198
Roentgen (R), 243–244
Roentgen absorbed dose (rad), 244
Roentgen equivalent mammal (rem) 244–246
Roentgen equivalent physical (rep), 243–244
Roth metabolism cage, 327

Sample geometry, 194–195, 275, 305
Sample mounting, 160–162
Saturation backscattering thickness, 199–201
Saturation current, 71
Saturation thickness in self-absorption, 203–205, 306–308
Scaler, 270–271, 278, 284, 292
Scattering, *see also* Backscattering, Self-scattering, Side scattering, 54–55
Schöniger combustion method, 157, 360, 363–365
Scintillation counters, *see* Liquid scintillation counters, Solid scintillation counters
Scintillation mechanism, 67, 88–89
Scintillators, *see* Fluors
Secondary solute in liquid scintillation counting, 106, 122–123, 165–170, 293

Secondary solvent in liquid scintillation counting, 120–121, 165–169
Self absorption, 160, 202–206, 306–308
Self scattering, 204
Sensitivity of detection methods, 14, 210
Shelf ratio, 275
Shielding
from beta particles, 52, 246
from gamma radiation, 60–63, 246
Side scattering, 201
Solid angle, 194–195
Solid (external-sample) scintillation counters,
components of,
detector assembly, 282–283
discriminators, 94–95, 283–284
linear amplifier, 283–284
mechanical register, 284
power supply, 281–282
preamplifier, 92, 99, 283
pulse height analyzer, 94–95, 282–285
scaler, 284
timer, 284
counting sample types,
liquid, 159–160, 340, 347–348
solid, 160, 351
detection efficiency,
for beta particles, 92, 97, 196, 286
for gamma rays, 63–64, 92, 95–97, 100–102, 159, 195–196, 286–287, 337, 345, 354
detector assembly components,
detector housing, 95–96, 282–283
fluor, 88–91, 96–97, 282
photocoupling, 97
photomultiplier, 88–93, 96–99, 282–283
energy transfer in, 67, 88–91, 98
fluors,
characteristics and varieties of, 88–90, 96
energy transfer in, 88–91, 96–97, 281
gamma ray spectrometry, 93–95, 283–285
operating characteristics,
differential counting mode, 95, 283–285
effect of photomultiplier potential, 99–100, 284–286
effect of preamplifier (or amplifier) gain, 100–101, 285–286
integral counting mode, 94–95, 283, 285
plateau, 99–100, 284–286
resolving time, 92, 287
sample preparation for, 159–160, 340, 347–348, 356–358
special detector types,
continuous flow, 349
well detector, 97, 159, 195, 283, 333, 337–338, 340, 343, 347–348, 358
thermal noise problems, 92–93, 99–100, 283–285
reduction of 92–93, 100
Solid sources, 160–162
Specific activity, 14, 35–36, 215
expression of results as, 224
Specific ionization
of alpha particles 40–41
of beta particles, 48–49
Spectra
of beta particles, 44–47
of gamma rays, 93–95, 283–284
Spectrometry
of beta particles
by magnetic spectrometer, 45
by liquid scintillation spectrometer, 113–118, 125–131, 293
of gamma rays, 93–95, 283–284
Stable isotopes, 6–8
Standard deviation, 188–192, 310
Standard source, 131, 196–197, 294
Starting potential of G-M detectors, 84, 272
Statistical consideration
background error, 189–190
error probability, 187–189
normal distribution curve, 187
rejection of abnormal data, 192–193, 310
relative standard deviation, 188, 310
requirements of counting time, 190–192
standard deviation, 188–192, 310
Straggling
of alpha particles, 41
of beta particles, 50
Stripping film, 147, 150
Synthesis of labeled compounds, 215, 233–239
Szilard-Chalmers process, 14, 229, 300–301

Thermal neutrons, 12–13
Thermal noise, 92–93, 100, 108–110, 283–285, 289–290
Thorium series, 9
Threshold
alpha, 81, 279–280
beta, 81, 279–280
Timer, 119, 271, 278, 284
Townsend avalanche, 74
Tritium and tritium labeled compounds, 10, 146, 154–155, 157–159, 165–167
health hazards from, 247–248
labeling methods, 236–239

Units
of radiation absorption, 56–60, 62, 305, 306
of radiation dose and exposure, 243–246
of radiation energy, 4
of radioactive decay rate, 25–31, 33–34, 247–248, 298–302, 349
of radioactivity, 34–36
Uranium-radium series, 9

Van Slyke-Folch combustion, 156
Vibrating-reed electrometers, 72–74, 323–324

Waste disposal of radioactive material, 216, 251–252, 260–262
Wave shifter, 106, 122–123, 165, 167–169
Well scintillation counter, 97, 159, 283, 337–338, 343, 347, 358
Wet ashing method, 155
Wilzbach gas-exposure, 238, 256
Windowless gas flow counter, 80, 82–83, 277
Window of pulse height analyzer, 95, 117, 125–129, 132, 283, 285, 291–295

X-ray film, 146–-47, 149, 321
X-rays
compared to gamma rays, 8, 52–54
emission in electron capture decay, 22–23, 37, 52–54, 146

Yield, expression of results as, 224

Z value, 4